THE SEARCH
FOR MIND

ABLEX SERIES
IN COMPUTATIONAL SCIENCE

Derek Partridge, University of Exeter
Series Editor

THE SEARCH FOR MIND

A NEW FOUNDATION FOR COGNITIVE SCIENCE

Sean Ó Nualláin

Dublin City University and
National Research Council of Canada

Ablex Publishing Corporation
Norwood, New Jersey

Printed in the United States of America

Library of Congress Cataloging-in-Publication Data
Ó Nualláin, Seán.
    The search for mind : a new foundation for cognitive science /
Seán Ó Nualláin.
        p.   cm. —(Ablex series in computational science)
    Includes bibliographical references and index.
    ISBN 1–56750–138–9. —ISBN 1–56750–139–7 (pbk.)
    1. Cognitive science.   2. Interdisciplinary approach to knowledge.
3. Philosophy of mind.   I. Title.   II. Series.
BF311.O58   1995
    153—dc20   95–787
                                                       CIP

TO THE MEMORY OF MY FRIEND JIM DELANEY

CONTENTS

INTRODUCTION

THE SEARCH FOR MIND

At the time of writing, Cognitive Science (CS) is academia's best shot at an integrated, multidisciplinary science of mind. If its ambitions could be even partially realized, the importance of such a science cannot be overstated. Our view of the mind not only shapes our view of ourselves; less obviously, it also shapes our view of that part of our experience we conceive of as dealing with the external world. As we learn about the structure of this aspect of experience, we find that the world presents itself to consciousness only after being mediated to lesser or (more often) greater extents by mental structures and processes. Consequently, truly to realize the ambitions of a science of mind does not solely involve learning about such issues as how we know, perceive, and solve problems; it involves finding out to what extent the world outside us is knowable by us, and indeed prescribing the limits of inquiry for disciplines like Physics which claim to afford knowledge of the external physical world.

Small wonder, then, that the stakes in this field should be so high. The contest has been so fierce, and the evidential standards assumed for science so restrictive, that there still remains a degree of skepticism abroad that academia can deliver a science of mind that does justice to the overwhelming bounty of human conscious experience while remaining constrained by the rather medieval intellectual ascesis of current Western Science. A cursory scan of the racks at any major magazine shop or bookstore will yield a vast harvest of titles (at least one of which will be the *Science of Mind*) that attempt to satisfy the human hunger for some degree of self-understanding through disciplines ranging from the wacky through that application of accumulated human wisdom we call common sense. That the higher insights of this residue are still outside our purview in academia is our loss.

The reasons for this intellectual bereavement rest in scientific method's insatiable drive for ever-harder—more externalized—evidence. The details of this issue as well as that of the rest of this section need not concern us here (I have dealt with them in

Ó Nualláin, 1994, 1995a). To return to the main theme, CS and the science of mind, we should note that CS is now being attacked with a great deal of justification precisely for its perceived inability to deal with experience itself as attempted in consciousness studies, (Ó Nualláin, 1995b) and the emotional and social factors that play a large part in the infrastructure of experience. The insight that originated CS and that comprised the greater part of its seed capital, often stated in oversimplified fashion as "the brain is a computer and mind is a set of programs run on this computer," precluded the acceptance of these factors. It is now clear that, its original momentum exhausted, there is a host of problems with the view of mind and its proper study given rise to by this insight.

In the wake of this debate, a second issue, that of the degree to which CS is an integrated subject, arises. One problem is the sheer range of disciplines included in CS; the subjects examined here—philosophy, psychology, linguistics, neuroscience, artificial intelligence, ethnoscience, ethology and consciousness studies—are each masterable only by a scholar of rare gifts. To complicate matters further, they each admit of numerous subdivisions, by no means exhaust the domain inhabited by researchers who consider themselves cognitive scientists and, finally, are extremely diverse. We need to see if there are any precedents. Biochemistry, says one account, existed as a subject in the 50s before it found a proper focus in the gene. A series of such "single focus" proposals has been made for CS by such workers as Fodor and Pylyshyn (Von Eckardt, 1993). In general, academic programs in CS have built themselves explicitly or implicitly on such proposals. However, the resulting structures are riddled by the tension that arises when CS strives for the "science of mind" mantle. An alternative view is that CS is yet another academic animal looking for an ecological niche. As it evolves, it usurps new areas of academic inquiry (like consciousness) and needs a single unifying principle no more than Physics does. At this stage in the development of their subject, the members of a Physics department lack a common language through which to communicate all their ongoing work. Why expect CS to be different? As we see below, this book attempts at least to arrest the momentum of the confusion of tongues. While its main business is the intuiting of a view of cognition compatible with the major findings from relevant disciplines, it also explores precisely how the information-processing tenet at the root of CS can be extended in a principled way to answer the current criticisms. With this extension also comes a recognition of CS's own true central role in a federation of mind sciences.

It is fair to say that CS is currently perceived, particularly by its critics, as dependent on a notion of mind as a set of programs. That this view is a simplification need not concern us here; the situation in all its real complexity is discussed at length throughout this book (particularly in Chapter 5) and in Ó Nualláin (1994, 1995a). We can learn much from the problems it poses.

For the moment, let's glance at a few of them. First of all, we don't seem to be able to write such programs ourselves outside a few carefully chosen applications, despite our best efforts (Chapter 5). Second, some programs that are being written on the basis of a theory of neural functioning have a structure that compromises the traditional dichotomization of program and computer architecture (Chapter 4). Third, the evidence that the mind is wholly material in the rather outdated sense that this word *material* is currently used is not quite as compelling as is occasionally claimed (Chapter 1)—to establish the validity of the computational metaphor any further requires that we establish materialism.

We might also ask whether the computationalist approach, taken to the point where it is used to constrain the data acceptable in CS, risks omitting much valid data about cognition. It may, for example, require that we jettison emotion and consciousness, which seems on common-sense grounds a bad move. It is argued in Chapters 2 and 8, respectively, that these factors must be included. In particular the section on role of affect in cognition shows how emotion can be regarded as rational and therefore as cohering to an expanded, more encompassing view of knowledge. A further question is whether a concept as minimalist as computation can bear the burden of knowing in all its forms.

Occasionally, diverging from conventional CS, we'll make reference as well to thinkers who have treated mind as something immanent in nature—as an ordering principle in nature (the Greek word *Nous* is used to capture this aspect of mind). The work of at least one of these thinkers, Gregory Bateson, has become relevant to AI, and we'll consider it in that context. In Part I, however, we're essentially reviewing the subdisciplines that comprise CS. No previous knowledge of any of these disciplines is assumed. The major findings of the area are introduced, often through outlining a brief history of the area, as well as those techniques without mastery of which no progress can be made in understanding further theoretical discussion. The path taken through each discipline is presuppositionless (we are analyzing each field on its own merits on these paths). The areas of contention, and the manner in which they relate to CS, emerge naturally. In such a vast field as CS, it is unwise to take the methodology of any single area, even if, as is the case of AI, it is the area that excited much of the current interest in CS, beyond its own domain.

THE FIELD OF COGNITIVE SCIENCE AS TREATED IN THIS BOOK

Cognitive Science, as noted, is a discipline with both theoretical and experimental components that, *inter alia,* deals with knowing. In doing so, it quite often finds itself walking in the footprints of long-dead philosophers, who were concerned with the theory of knowledge (epistemology). A lot of the considerable excitement in the area derives from its ability to experimentally test conjectures of these great minds, or on occasion to establish that these conjectures are too abstract to be so tested.

The disciplines that traditionally comprise the core of CS are AI, linguistics, philosophy (including philosophical epistemology and philosophy of mind), and cognitive psychology. The boundary disciplines are neuroscience, ethnoscience, and ethology. These latter three disciplines are, respectively, the study of the brain and central nervous system, the study of cognition in different cultures, and the study of animal and human behavior in natural environments. The first task of this book is to give a clear account of all these disciplines where they relate to cognition, with an indication of the direction of the most exciting current lines of research. A more detailed outline of the structure of these accounts is given below.

It is fair to say that CS is currently in ferment, with all the apparent chaos and promise that term connotes. On the one hand, the variety of disciplines that comprise CS are foci of intensive research effort. On the other, in the case of several of the disciplines the intensity of this research effort has had reverberations that threaten to undermine the methodological foundations of the discipline. The clearest example of this is AI.

It is worthwhile for a variety of reasons to immerse oneself in the philosophical antecedents of current CS. Even a cursory glance at the history of philosophy reveals some marvels as philosophers struggle conceptually with the notion of computation. The notion of an *Ars Magna,* a general computational device, goes back at least a millennium in European and Arabic thought, starting with the Spaniard Ramon Lull and extending through the experimental devices of Leibniz and Pascal before culminating in Turing's and Church's work.

In parallel with the struggle with the notion of computation was the struggle with the more general problem of knowledge. The lines of approach taken to this problem were extremely varied. The key to the myriad conceptions of knowledge that arose is consideration of the problem of the relation between mind and world. These conceptions, diverse and theoretical though they are, often find themselves incarnated in the design principles of AI systems. Moreover, speculations about the origins of knowledge often find themselves subject to experimental test in psychology. This multifaceted, sometimes implicit and sometimes explicit, relation that exists between philosophical epistemology and CS is a major theme of this book. In a limited sense, CS is and always has been epistemology; just to what extent this is the case is the focus here. We shall find that even the specifics of AI techniques were often foreshadowed in philosophy.

CS would be pointless were it not to lead to a theory of cognition. Ideally, this theory should have psychological and computational consequences. The former should possess *ecological validity;* that is, it should inform about real everyday life in a real environment. The latter should lead to recommendations both for implementations in AI systems and occasionally for the pointlessness of attempting such implementation. The book ends with such a theory of cognition.

CS has traditionally ignored emotion (which seemed irrelevant), and social factors in cognition, in the latter case on the basis that these factors must be in some sense processed, and could consequently be properly treated simply by complete explanation of the operations of the processor. It is hoped that by the end of this book the reader will be convinced of the necessity of granting autonomy to these factors.

History of Cognitive Science

To understand why these factors have been ignored, it is necessary to delve a little into the history of CS. There are many histories in this book, most of them brief, and this is to be one of the briefest: I am concerned only with outlining in the most general terms how CS has arrived at its present juncture. It will be reiterated time and again in the course of this book that in a "Science of Mind" sense CS has always existed: The criteria current in any culture for "science" may change greatly, but there always has been and always will be a "science" that deals with "mind." Two events stand out in the formation of modern CS. One is the Hixon symposium at Caltech in 1947 on "Cerebral Mechanisms in Behavior." The major significance of this symposium lay in the algorithmic analysis of complicated behavioral sequences by the neuroscientist Lashley. A major consequence of this was that the contemporary dominant paradigm of psychology (behaviorism; cf. Chap. 2); lost what would have seemed to be its most sure ally.

Models from formal logic were beginning to inform the neuroscience of such brilliant thinkers as Warren McCulloch (1965/1989) by the 1930s and he produced a model of neuronal function with this conceptual motivation. In the meantime, linguists were beginning to produce a formal theory of their area, culminating in the work of Chomsky (Chapter 3); phenomena in cognition were being subjected to informational analysis (Chapter 2); and the beginnings of AI, which we discuss in Chapter 5, were bearing fruit in abundance. By 1956, these strands were pulled together in a symposium on information theory at MIT. Cognitive Science effectively had arrived, and funding from the Sloan Foundation ensured its continuation.

The success of computing has ensured that computation is the dominant paradigm in CS. However, as we discuss in Chapter 5 in particular, computation is a minimalist concept and a great deal more infrastructure must be added to lay a possible foundation for the discipline. The resulting framework has yielded many interesting results like the work of Marr and Kosslyn (Gardner, 1985). However, attacks have recently been launched on this paradigm, *inter alia* by Searle (1992) chiefly on its ignoring of consciousness, by Edelman (1992) also on its ignoring biology and the assumptions it makes about the structure of the world and the consequent relation of the mind and world, finally, by the current author (Ó Nualláin, 1993) on various grounds, including its mistaken view of mind.

We review this material time and again in the course of this book. It is apposite to quote the director of the French national initiative in CS, André Halley, to close this section:

In the pages which follow, the picture of a fully mature science with its own methods, achievements and concepts will not be found . . . the objective and condition of existence of cognitive science requires that these diverse and insulated perspectives should open, exchange more methods and concepts, and develop a common language. (Translation by the present author) (1992, p. 1)

That neatly summarizes the goals of this book.

TOPICS TREATED

As may be expected, the first chapter deals mainly with philosophical epistemology. Equally inevitably, it abounds in "isms" like realism, historical nativism, and nominalism. These terms will recur in different contexts throughout the book, so a glossary is supplied at the start of the chapter. We will find that the arguments—presented in historical sequence—using these terms have enormous relevance to present day AI, in particular. Most importantly, it will become clear that the most pressing debate in AI—that concerning situated, embodied intelligence—was presaged in the debate surrounding the French philosopher called Maurice Merleau-Ponty. We then concern ourselves with the appropriate relation of the philosophy of mind to cognitive science. Finally, the epistemological stance taken in the book is detailed.

Chapter 2 deals with cognitive psychology. We first of all describe the different approaches to experimental psychology that have been attempted. We examine some of the valid results obtained from each of these approaches and begin to examine the concept of psychology as experimental epistemology. This done, we find that we cannot sensibly discuss knowledge without taking its development in the individual into account. This leads us naturally to the discipline of genetic epistemology, as pioneered by the Swiss Jean Piaget. As was the case with Merleau-Ponty, we find there is almost as much to learn from criticism of Piaget as there is from his brilliant restatement of the central question of knowledge: How does knowledge develop? A new theme emerges, *crescendo:* We need a central notion of equilibration—the paradoxical need for stability but at a level of increased mastery of the environment—in order to explain the process of cognitive development. It is found, moreover, that the epistemological stance of Chapter 1 is consistent with the lessons learned from both the strengths and the weaknesses of the work of Piaget and J. J. Gibson. The latter's work leads us to consider the troubled issue of the relation of perception to cognition.

There are still those who say that knowledge is essentially linguistic, that language is an innate capability, and that knowledge unfolds in accordance with a predetermined genetic instruction. In the third chapter, we shall analyze the attempts of linguists to characterize this innate capability, whether it is considered coextensive with thought or not. We will find that such attempts at a monolithic formalization all seem to fall short. Situated cognition in such nonsymbolic contexts as a robot's perception–action connection is easy to elucidate: One of the major tasks of the linguistics chapter is to consider the nature of symbolic situated cognition through analysis of the notion of context.

It certainly will be a long time before the neurological processes supporting linguistic activity in the biochemical process that structure the unfolding of our DNA's germ of language are isolated. Chapter 4 focuses on what actually is known about the brain in terms of its anatomy, localizations (and otherwise) of function, and transmission of nerve impulses, and how these facts were discovered. We find ourselves *en route* considering the burgeoning subdiscipline of connectionism as the *alter ego* of experimental neuroscience. One issue in particular haunts this chapter: What is the relation between neurophysiological and symbolic functioning? We discover that this question can be answered properly only by positing a hierarchy of other levels between the two. The raising of a second issue, that of how the brain adapts itself to the environment, results in the conclusion that a Darwinian struggle between neural groups takes place. We find in this a neural mechanism to implement *equilibration,* aka (also known as) "The Principle of Rationality."

People skeptical about AI are often criticized for being purely destructive—for not producing the ideas they feed on. How better to refute this than by using AI skeptics to introduce the main AI techniques! Some of these gentlemen (Husserl, Wittgenstein) were unfortunately not alive to disbelieve in AI when it came around, but they showed every sign of shaping to spoil the fun, in that they produced theories of mind resembling AI formalisms and then proceeded to refute them. We then get down to the serious business of considering the applications that AI actually has achieved. It is found that the most useful categorization of these applications is with respect to a subsymbolic/syntactic/semantic triad. *En route,* we discuss how AI has, sometimes harmfully, set the agenda for discussion of the foundations of CS. When we finally get down to discussing the current methodological debate in AI we find ourselves in a situation similar to the crises in philosophy and cognitive psychology that attracted our attention at the end of those chapters.

Ethnoscience and ethology occupy us briefly before we come to Part II. In ethnoscience, we find it established that classification is done opportunistically within certain general universal constraints by the human mind. Ethology leads us to a discussion of sociobiology, and *en passant* the nature of evolution itself.

In Part II, the main conclusions from Part I first are summarized. Then a set of attributes common to all symbolic functioning is proposed. It is seen to be valid for language and vision, and to gain in strength from brief consideration of music as a formal system. A summary of the ways in which these systems resemble each other is presented.

Finally, it will have become clear that we cannot discuss cognition without detailed reference to its development. We find that such development requires changes within both the subject and the subject's world that require us to introduce the concept of consciousness that mediates subject and object. Nor can we speak very long about this without reference to the individual in her social context. A final chapter then reviews all the themes that have emerged and synthesizes them in an overall theory of cognition and its development. It considers also what the future shape of CS is likely to be. "Cognition" itself was first used by Aristotle to set aside states of mind of which one could predicate "true" or "false"; I believe the viewpoint which emerges from this book to be consonant with this tradition.

USER'S GUIDE TO THIS BOOK

Having written about the structure of the book, I'd like to point out some aspects of its style. This does not claim to be the final word on any of these disciplines, or indeed anything but a readable introduction to each. As has been mentioned, the current controversies are allowed to enter naturally, and the point of view taken is then spelled out, when appropriate with supporting argument. On occasion, the reader is pointed to a reference that provides this argumentation, particularly if it is peripheral to the major concerns of the book.

CS is such a vast area that the most one can hope to do is to deliver an overall impression of where the area is at present, and where it might go. Moreover, each of the constituent disciplines, as I repeat throughout the book, strives for domination of the whole area. My own academic formation was in psychology and computer science. I worked in computational linguistics for the past decade. It is inevitable that this book will reflect my own experience, often in ways of which I am not wholly conscious.

Technical terms are introduced as gently as possible, either with a glossary or by giving a definition alongside the first occurrence of the term. Every book creates its own language and I shall have achieved much if by Chapter 9 you are speaking mine. The diagrams feature (among other characters, including a pint-swilling robot), a figure loosely based on the great Irish comic writer, Myles na gCopaleen (aka Brian Ó Nualláin, his real name, or Flann O'Brien, his more famous pseudonym). In his honor, the main position emerging from Chapter I is termed the *Mylesian position* and the overall view the *Nolanian position,* which is the English form of both our names. John Nolan and Sean Ó Nualláin have been the same person for some time. After a decade of teaching, I find that learning occurs best with an admixture of comic anarchy, which is why Myles was hired. Finally, I regret the fact that the gender of English pronouns is governed the way it is— don't be surprised if you find "he," "she," "his," and so on being used apparently at random! (And so also with endings of Latin adjectives, but here I plead guilty.)

A great deal of this material has been successfully presented to computer science, computational linguistics, cognitive science, and electronic engineering students, both undergraduate and postgraduate. Where a technical discussion is not necessary for understanding the subsequent argument, it's set off by a row of asterisks. I invite you to share the excitement of a discipline that will certainly fundamentally change how we think of ourselves and our relation to the world.

FURTHER READING

The Mind's New Science (Gardner, 1985) is an excellent historical introduction to each of the disciplines that comprise CS. At the time of writing, it is a little out of date. *The Computer and the Mind* (Johnson-Laird, 1988, 1993) is a more technical, computational introduction. The *Journal of the French National Research Center* produced a special issue in October 1992 featuring one-page summaries of the major research ongoing in France, which is often a great deal intellectually more open than that in the English-speaking world. Many more references will be given in this course of this text to books with strengths in particular areas of CS.

REFERENCES

Ó Nualláin, S. (1995a). Cognitive science and the search for mind. In Sean Ó Nualláin and Paul Mc Kevitt (Eds.), *Workshop on the Foundation of Cognitive Science.* AISB 1995 Conference, Sheffield, England.

Ó Nualláin, S. (1995b). Consciousness, selfhood and cognitive science. In Sean Ó Nualláin and Paul Mc Kevitt (Eds.), *Workshop on the Foundation of Cognitive Science.* AISB 1995 Conference, Sheffield, England.

ACKNOWLEDGMENTS

I have often thought that this section in a book was mainly an opportunity for academics to pretend they have friends. Whatever about that, I certainly feel a need to acknowledge the frequent gratuitous kindnesses that either helped speed up the writing or made what is inevitably a stressful period more bearable. I of course accept the usual responsibility for any errors that remain.

In Dublin, the most insightful comments on the basic epistemological ideas came from Brendan Purcell, whose enthusiasm was and is always infectious. Brendan and Andrew Way commented on Chapters 1 to 3. My undergraduate students at Dublin City University were always a challenge and a stimulant. Thanks to Faris Naji for the diagrams. On the nonacademic side, I wish particularly to thank Vincent Weldon, Barbara Lougheed, Connie Fennell and Katy Miller. In Canada, I wish to thank the staff of the Knowledge Systems Lab in the National Research Council; in particular, Martin Brooks, Anne Parent, Arnold Smith, and Peter Turney (alphabetical order!). The early reviewers of the book, many of whose comments appear with the advertising material, helped greatly. Thanks also to Noel Evans and to Julie Dennis and the Fineman family of Lake Tahoe.

However, I feel it dishonest not to include some anti-acknowledgments for those without whose interference the book would have been finished more quickly and pleasantly. To do otherwise would be to start a book that deals with the mind with a biased view of reality. Pride of place here goes to the Irish Gárdaí (rough translation: cops). This precedent-setting section should include at least one individual so Faris, take another bow. Were there such a thing as bad publicity, I would feel obliged to mention other institutions.

Finally, I am sure I have run many debts up of which I am not even aware: to you, my unknown benefactors, I offer my humble thanks.

October 5, 1994

· I ·

THE CONSTITUENT DISCIPLINES OF COGNITIVE SCIENCE

• *one* •

PHILOSOPHICAL
EPISTOMOLOGY

Empiricism states that all knowledge comes from the senses. Its opponents are rationalists and idealists.

Rationalism states that all knowledge comes from mental operations.

Idealism states that knowledge is essentially a trickle-down from a world of ideas.

Innatists believe that knowledge is genetically or otherwise inherited. Their natural enemies are empiricists.

Kantians believe that knowledge derives from sense data mediated through mental structures, which they call **categories.**

Conceptualists believe that concepts are naturally occurring aspects of reality.

Nominalism states the opposite; that is, that a concept is just a name.

Materialists hold that mental properties are in some way an aspect of matter. Their allies are **Reductionists,** who won't be happy until all mental activity can be reduced to description in purely physical terms.

There is also an **eliminativist** (another buzzword) tendency about these last three, who have as their common enemy:

Dualists, who hold that their is a spiritual principle at work in mind, together with the material processes, and

Holists, who claim that there are whole properties associated with any biological processes from the level of the cell upward, and who insist the same about mind.

Realists insist that knowledge is impressed in the mind directly by objective properties of the world. They hate Idealists.

Situatedness is the notion that all of cognition is profoundly affected by the physical and social situation in which it takes place. It is related to

Embodiment, the notion that cognition can only be considered with respect to the copresence of a body, and also to

Mundanity, the notion that mind, body, and world are different, but profoundly interrelated, and can best be considered together.

Existentialism is the school whose slogan is "existence precedes essence"—we should attend to the necessary facts surrounding our immediate existence before launching into theory.

Reductionism attempts to describe mental activity in observable neural events.

Eliminative materialists attempt to do away with all the common concepts of folk psychology like belief and desire, describing these entities purely in physical terms.

The **philosophy of mind** deals with the analysis of certain psychological constructs. These include propositional attitudes, which are terms which relate subjects to hypothetical objects—for example, "believe" in "X believes Y."

Functionalism is the doctrine that mental processes have "multiple realizability"—that it is irrelevant to their formal analysis whether they are run on my brain, your brain, a computer, or an assembly of tin cans. Functional equivalence thus falls under that category of equivalence analysis called

Token–token analysis, which is satisfied with a demonstration of equivalences under some system of identification or other. In contrast, type–type analysis insists on the more stringent requirement of physical identity.

Intentionality, as originally formulated by Fr. Brentano, points out as a crucial property of mental states the fact that they point to objects. It must be clearly distinguished from any of the connotations of its colloquial association with "will."

I refrain for now from attempting to define *Consciousness*
> *Being*
> *Knowledge*

The diagrams in Figure 1.1 all have a ring of beads representing disjoint sense data. A solid ring represents structured sense data. The inner space represents mental contents.

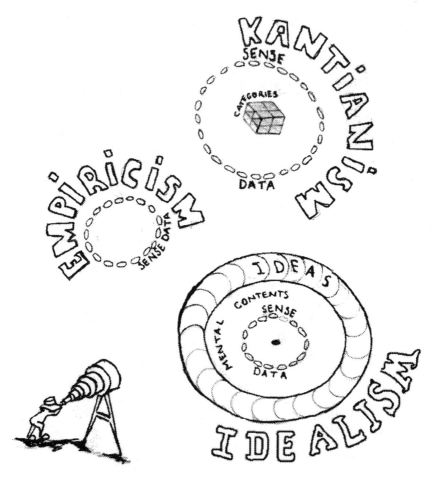

FIGURE 1-1.

Mind has not yet been defined: Where does it fit in these diagrams?

WHAT IS PHILOSOPHICAL EPISTEMOLOGY?

A short answer to this question is that philosophical epistemology is the theoretical approach to the study of knowledge. It can be distinguished, in these terms, from experimental epistemology, which features in the remainder of the disciplines within cognitive science.

Philosophy (literally, love of knowledge or wisdom) has recently had very bad press. As we shall see, it used to comprise disciplines like physics, chemistry, and mathematics, all of which in turn broke away from it. At present, it sometimes looks like the exclusive property of two wildly antagonistic camps. The first camp, the analytic school, seem to hope through the analysis of language to analyze philosophy right out of existence and themselves out of jobs. The continental school, on the other hand, is still concerned with the Big Questions like God and the Meaning of Existence. However, its members have a predilection for all-encompassing book titles like *Being and Nothingness*, which can't possibly live up to their advance publicity.

When psychology broke away from philosophy in the mid-19th century to set up shop as experimental epistemology, people began to ask whether philosophy might not eventually reduce to the null set. The consensus is now that it's best regarded as a method of rational inquiry that can do a useful task in making explicit some of the assumptions inherent in various aspects of structured human activity, or in general as rational inquiry in any field.

One such activity is science. One task of a philosophy of science is to compare the stated assumptions about the methodology of science with the reality. Moreover, it can prescribe on the basis of thorough analysis that which is likely to be a worthwhile area or method of investigation, and that which isn't. A vast such literature has grown up around cognitive science (mainly, in the philosophy of mind) and we analyze it at the end of this chapter.

However, we're going to find philosophy useful for other reasons as well. Up to Warren McCulloch's (1965/1989) early work, "*epistemology* meant quite simply philosophical epistemology. In other words, historically speaking, philosophy is *the* area in which the problem of knowledge has been discussed. Philosophers lacked the experimental tools featured in the other chapters of this book: They had to find some way of systematically appealing to experience.

It's fair to say that they didn't come to any lasting, comprehensive solution to the problem of knowledge. However, we can learn a lot from the clarity with which they discuss issues of perception and cognition. They did manage also to ask the right questions. Having taken a position—for example, empiricism—on those questions they often found themselves backed into a corner. It is when fighting their corners that they tend to be at their best—we'll see this in particular in Hume's response to Berkeley. One of the really important things about cognitive science is its ability, through the current availability of appropriate experimental evidence, to show how all these brilliant minds, though apparently greatly at odds, were in a sense correct.

The path this chapter takes is the following. First of all, we're going to briefly look at the history of Western philosophical epistemology. Second, we're going to regroup by considering at length the central problem treated (that is, the relation between mind and world). Third, we're going to examine the work of existentialist philosophers who had a view of this problem very similar to that emerging in AI. Finally, we're going to examine current controversies in the philosophy of mind that relate to cognitive science.

THE REDUCED HISTORY OF WESTERN PHILOSOPHY

THE CLASSICAL AGE

The Reduced Shakespeare Company performs the Complete Work in one thrilling evening, culminating in a 30-second Hamlet. The following pages are analogous. We'd better start, as we've a lot to get through.

To make things easier, we'll ignore Oriental as distinct from Occidental thought for the moment. The content of this section, then, is those schools of thought that originated in Greece around the seventh century B.C. and were preserved through the Dark Ages by the then-great civilization of Islam and by Irish monks before coming to a later flowering through the rediscovery by Europeans in Islamic Spain of their own cultural heritage.

The first stirring of philosophical thought around the seventh century B.C. in Greek culture consisted of an attempt to grasp a single underlying principle that could explain everything manifest. The earlier suggestions for such a principle (from Thales and his followers) were the basic elements as conceived of at the time (air, water, earth, and fire); the later suggestion of Herakleitos (or Heraclitus) was change, or fire alone. Let's note that no distinction was made between the material and the mental, or knowledge and being.

Later came the Pythagorean school, with the first attempt at an abstract description of reality independent of its felt existence. The kind of experience that fueled this work is epitomized by the laws of musical harmony. There is a detected harmonious relation between strings on an instrument with certain simple mathematical relationships to each other (if one string is precisely double the length of another, for instance, its pitch is an octave lower). The insight that we can home in on an aspect of reality by manipulation of abstract symbols in this manner is still an exhilarating one.

Let's call Pythagoras and his school the "Neats." The "Scruffs," or Sophists, were in the meantime teaching virtue, as they understood it. With Socrates, the hero of Plato's dialogues, the Neat–Scruffy division falls apart. To know Plato's world of ideas is to be virtuous. The good, the true, and the beautiful are one.

Plato's schema, depending on one's perspective, is one of the great intellectual constructs and/or one of the great pieces of self-delusion of all time. The world of appearances is flickering shadows on a cave wall. Reality is a set of other-worldly forms, which objects in this world can somehow participate in or reflect, and thus borrow some of their being. Let's note, parenthetically, that many contemporary mathematicians (Gödel, Penrose) still take these ideas seriously with respect to mathematical concepts; for example, what in this world is an infinite set?

It is said that everyone is drawn by temperament either to Plato or to his pupil Aristotle. One huge issue that puzzled Aristotle is this: how many forms are there? Is there a form for a CS text? We see this issue again in AI.

The materialist–dualist war (it has all the characteristics thereof) is essentially part of Plato's heritage. Recent pitched battles: Libet (1985) versus Flanagan (1992); and Eccles (1987) versus all comers. If you contrast a world of ideas with the actual world, the war is inevitable. Aristotle produced a framework in which this type of issue doesn't arise. Substance, he argued, is form plus matter. Consider a biological cell. There are material processes going on *by which* the cell is a cell (that is, by which it has its form as a cell). A statue is a more obvious example: The matter of the statue is that by which it has its form. Can we separate the material and mental in the brain in this way?

We'll consider this issue again presently. For the moment, let's note that Aristotle was an insatiable collector of facts about everything that came across his path. This insistence on observation continued in Greece to Almceon and his school, which by the fourth century BC had located thought in the brain and had at least a sketchy idea of neural functioning. Had a Hellenic Warren McCulloch connected this anatomical work with what was already known about electrochemical plating, we might have had some very precocious cognitive science.

Let's pause for breath for a moment. These themes have emerged:

1. The search for a single underlying explanatory principle for all that is.
2. The idea that abstract operations on symbols can inform about an external reality to which these symbols point. (If we incarnate these symbols in computer programs, we get what's called the Physical Symbols Systems Hypothesis, or PSSH.)
3. A notion that substance can be divided into form and matter.

Let's again note that philosophy was, up to this point, also the activities we call science, politics, and theology. It has lost a lot of capital since then.

Had Greek thought maintained this breathtaking rate of progress, there would be little for us to do. We haven't touched on the advances in logic, mathematics, and politics that occurred. However, as has been mentioned, the works of Plato and Aristotle were lost to the Western world during the Dark Ages. Before we fast-forward two millennia, let's note one speculation of St. Augustine, Bishop of Hippo in North Africa. Words name objects, and children learn language by correlating the word and its object. We're noting this point because it's (at best) incomplete, both as a theory of linguistics and as developmental psycholinguistics.

SCHOLASTICISM AND THE FIRST STIRRINGS OF MODERNITY

Thomas Aquinas.

The reduced history of philosophy would normally skip the 400 years between Aquinas and Déscartes. This is particularly the case because Aquinas is normally identified as the foremost defender of the Roman Catholic faith. In turn, this role may seem to involve aiding particularly nasty South American dictators while condemning the sexual act in all its manifestations.

In fact, Aquinas is relatively blameless on these points. He is important to cognitive science for two reasons. First, he provides the first great medieval treatment and development of classical philosophy. Second, he and his modern Thomist followers (e.g., Lonergan, 1958) have much to say on the act of understanding.

Thomas Aquinas joined the Dominicans against his father's wishes, and read Aristotle contrary to the stated wishes of his contemporary church. He seems to have suffered terribly from overweight: Eventually, a large piece had to be cut out of the table so he could sit at it!

Aquinas's first great contribution to philosophy is on ontology; that is, the problem of Being (what is), and what different types of beings there are. This problem manifests itself as the mind–body problem in CS. Aquinas's solution is worth looking at for this reason.

Aristotle had no distinct concept of existence to complement his notion of substance. Aquinas, in common with philosophers of his time, attributed different vital principles of existence to beings at different levels of evolution. For example, a tree had a vegetative soul. This is not the main thrust of his argument—however, let's note that these kinds of notions are re-entering biology under the heading of *entelechy*, and they cast welcome mud into the deceptively clear waters of the monism–dualism debate.

Aquinas asks us to look at a person or anything that exists. He distinguished the following:

1. That which is.
2. Its existence, which it possesses by virtue of an act of existence.
3. Its form, which it possesses by organizational patterns in its matter.

Thus we have a form–matter distinction as well as an issue of the potential for existence being fulfilled by an act of existence. Instead of the Cartesian mind–matter dualism we are going to confront later we now have a trio of substance, act, and potency.

Moreover, the notion of substance allows us to speak of the form, as distinct from the matter, of all biological entities, including mind. Much effort has been expended on attempting to show that either monism or dualism is correct (e.g., Libet, 1985 vs. Churchland, 1988): The position of this book is that the ontological issue is a great deal more complicated.

Thomism has much to say about understanding. For its followers, understanding is about more than mere cognition: It quickly, in turn, structures one's ethical concept, then one's concept of God. Thomism sharply distinguishes understanding, which has as its object an idea, from imagination, sensation, perception, and so on. It is from analysis of the act of understanding that the whole of Thomist philosophy gets its main thrust.

And so on to modern Thomists. The major figure is Bernard Lonergan (1958), who takes on board a great deal of modern mathematical science. He begins his major work, *Insight,* with an account of Archimedes in the bath. Let's examine this story.

King Hiero of Syracuse had a crown with much filigree work fashioned, and he doubted whether it was actually made of gold (as mentioned earlier, electroplating was already an established technique). To establish that it was, it would be necessary to find the precise volume of the crown with all its filigree, an unenviable task for Archimedes.

Disconsolate, he took a bath. As he stepped into the water, he noticed the water level rising. At that moment, he realized several different points:

1. The volume of water displaced was equal to the volume of his body.
2. Therefore, he now had a way of measuring the crown's volume.
3. He could remain on good terms with the king.

He simultaneously forgot several other things about social decorum and ran naked through the streets for a while before remembering them again. Before discussing Lonergan's analysis of the Eureka moment, I want to emphasize what Archimedes forgot, as well as the fact that the insight arose as a result of his experience of his body. Thomists, good Catholics as they are, sometimes tend to ignore the body.

Lonergan claims that insight supplies the key to cognition. He says that it has five characteristics:

1. It comes as a release to a period of inquiry.
2. It comes suddenly and unexpectedly.
3. It is largely a function of conditions both external and internal.
4. It has both abstract and concrete aspects.
5. It becomes part of the structure of one's mind.

The last point in particular is extremely important for CS. It's now accepted that we can't develop AI systems without a valid theory of cognition and that we can't discuss cognition except with respect to its development. What this analysis of insight informs us is that one central aspect of cognitive development is Eureka moments.

Understanding for the Thomists is mainly an unembodied act. That is where their system falls down for CS purposes. However, they certainly treat the ontological problem much better than Déscartes did, and the scope of their thought is impressively wide.

René Déscartes: The First Modern?

In 17th-century France, it was unusual to stay in bed until 11 a.m. in order to think. That being Déscartes's wont, he moved to Amsterdam, where, as he explained, people were too busy making money to notice a philosopher in their midst.

It is hard to overstate Déscartes's influence on the sciences of mind. He wrote also on physics and famously invented Cartesian coordinates and other mathematical techniques. At one point, he turned his attention to the "robots" in the Tuileries gardens, which operated by hydraulics—water directed through their limbs caused them to move. The human nerve passageways seemed similar—could it be that their functioning was identical?

In the meantime, Déscartes was also considering how to root a systematic philosophy. He could doubt everything, he decided, except his own existence. He could conclude the latter by the fact that he could think: *Cogito, ergo Sum.* Moreover, this "I" who thought had to be a thinking thing (*res cogitans*), as distinct from the rest of nature, which merely was extended in space (*res extensa*). *Res cogitans* interacted with the world through the pineal gland in the brain by releasing the watery humors in the nerves.

Thus, unlike Aquinas, Déscartes has a very sharp spirit–matter distinction, which lumps all aspects of mind under spirit. (Even today, the French *Esprit* confusingly connotes both mind and spirit, sometimes in technical CS texts). He then went on to ask how this soul could get to know about the external world. So far, we've got a theory of its action.

Its perception, Déscartes argued, was due to abstract represen-tations of the external world being served up by the senses. These could be just encodings, rather than strict models of the objects they represented. So far, if we substitute the central processing unit of a computer for the Cartesian soul, we have a precise anal-ogy to the AI metaphor.

The analogy cuts even deeper for the whole of the methodology of CS. That we could usefully discuss the models of objects without knowing anything about their essence is one consequence. To continue this point, we can exclude all external factors except as represented to ourselves, and by studying the action of our minds in this manner we can know all there is to know about the world. This tenet is called *methodological solipsism.*

These points have a familiar ring precisely because Déscartes's influence has been so massive. In fact, it is unlikely that the founders of AI were even aware of how profoundly they were influenced by them. In this light, we can look on AI as a working through of the Cartesian program in real, implemented computer systems. Looked at in this way, that program has been an interesting failure in ways that we consider in Chapter 5.

British Empiricism.

The Cartesian program forces one to focus on the soul (or homunculus) hovering around the pineal gland and obtaining knowledge through symbolic operation. This latter symbolic point makes Déscartes fit into the rationalist tradition. The British empiricist school is essentially a set of replies to Déscartes.

Hobbes was a contemporary of Déscartes, who became acquainted with his work during his several periods of political exile in France. Unlike Déscartes, he stressed the primacy of empirical data; that is, of sensations. How else could we obtain knowledge about things in the world? Moreover, concepts were not "naturally occurring kinds" but simply the result of the process of naming (this idea was called *nominalism*). There is a certain almost attractive bloody-mindedness about Hobbes: He seems also to have been an atheist, whose political views (in his classic *Leviathan*) allowed him to support any political system as long as it used force properly.

What we're concerned with here, however, is the epistemological correctness of Hobbes's work and its relation to CS. In the debate between rationalist Déscartes and empiricist Hobbes, we see prefigured a debate that currently rages in AI. It hinges on the question about to what extent we can or should try and express the content of the domain on which a computer system for AI is to work in terms of explicit symbols.

Hobbes's follower John Locke adds another plank to empiricism. He insisted that the child's mind at birth is a blank state (Latin: *tabula rasa*) on which the world impressed itself. The full British empiricist view of mind has one T-junction to navigate before coming to its conclusion in David Hume's work.

Though self-consciously Irish (he once replied to an English-man, "We Irish think otherwise"), George Berkeley has suffered the lot of any successful Gael in being adopted by the British. In between his educational work in the United States, which resulted in a university in his name, and his duties as the Bishop of Waterford, he somehow got the time to write his *Principles of Human Knowledge* and other philosophical works.

As we see later, it is by no means unusual for a philosophical viewpoint, followed consistently to its conclusion, to engender its antithesis as a logical consequence. Berkeley took the British empiricist critique of Déscartes on board and followed its line of argument to an unforeseen destination.

Consider a household chair. As we move around it, our perspec-tive continually changes and the image on our retinas alters corre-spondingly. How do we manage to identify it as the same object? AI vision work has demonstrated that it is excruciatingly difficult to continually update the image and compare it with a stored rep-resentation. (Note that this is one manifestation of the frame prob-lem.) Berkeley argued that because all that the empiricist view of mind allowed was sense data from the chair, we are compelled to appeal to a notion like the material substance of the chair. But where was this material substance, which was required by theo-ries such as Locke's? It was, according to Berkeley, a nonsensical idea.

Berkeley's statement of the frame problem is brilliant, and a paradigmatic example of what we can learn from philosophical epistemologists' acute analysis of perception. However, his solu-tions are not quite as good, and left him vulnerable to the attack of the Scot David Hume (another Brit, of course), which we note presently. Berkeley ended by appealing to notions like the soul to unify the various appearances of the chair, and to God to some-how keep in existence things that were not being perceived (*esse, sed non percipi*).

Hume, whose early career had a shaky start (involving, for example, using a pseudonym to give a rave review to one of his own books), eventually ended up working for the English embassy in Paris. Let's start with a thought experiment to give a flavor of Hume's system. OK, let's look within (introspect) for Berkeley's soul.

Two things will happen: If we divide ourselves into subject and object, and try to find the soul as an object, the regress is infinite. Alternatively, if we try and grasp the essence of the soul by subtracting all the mental contents that life impresses on us, we end up with the null set. Hume's conclusion was that Berkeley's soul did not and could not exist. (We review these arguments later in the discussion of Merleau-Ponty.)

Hume is a thoroughgoing empiricist, and now he's lost his soul. It is at this point that he introduces the main themes of what was to become the standard British empiricist view of mind. Mind, he insisted, was flux of ideas and sensations that succeeded each other in a manner outside our control. Empiricism, in its later formulation (Hume, 1888), stated that ideas followed in accordance with the laws of similarity (that is, they were alike), contiguity (they were first experienced together), or contrast.

We've now come to the culmination of the empiricist reply to Déscartes. As noted, the tension between rationalism and empiricism presages the central issue in current AI, the use of explicit symbols. Our view of mind has, it's fair to say, become somewhat simplified.

Immanuel Kant.

With Kant, we get the beginnings of a view of mind that is specific enough in its details to be computationally useful and that does justice to the wealth of philosophical debate in the context of which it was put forward. Kant has had more explicit influence on CS than any other philosopher: It is arguable, however, that the influence of Déscartes has been so all-pervading that most non-philosophers default to a Cartesian mindset.

Kant spent all his like around Königsberg, which was at that time in East Prussia. He ended his days as by far the most famous phenomenon in an undistinguished town. So regular did his days eventually become that the town's populace began to set their watches by him: Here comes Herr Kant—it must be 4:03 p.m.! It was still regular practice for philosophers to hold forth on various subjects. Consequently, Kant wrote on astronomy as well as epistemology and proposed correctly that galaxies were formed by gravitational attraction.

Kant's *Critique of Pure Reason* is perhaps the most important epistemological text since Aristotle. We need to consider what his intellectual motives were to consider his work properly.

Hume, we have seen, was a thoroughgoing empiricist. The shock that Hume's theory of mind still produces was, according to Kant himself, enough to wake him "from his dogmatic slumbers." Hume's mind is a wild succession of ideas and sensations replacing each other according to laws of association. Yet there is definite structure in how all we humans perceive the world and communicate to each other about it: We have concepts of number, self, causality, logic, and so on.

Let's look at a few of these concepts. Modus Ponens in Logic (the "positing" mode) has this structure.

If P then Q
P
Therefore Q

For example:

If it's May, the French Tennis Open must be on soon.
It's May.
Therefore The French Open will be on soon. Check your TV set.

Let's note that modus ponens doesn't allow us any choice about q once p is established. Analogously, we tend to infer that a causes b if event a always precedes event b: Thus, our notion of causality is similarly deeply entrenched. It might be hypothesized that knowledge of modus ponens is a generalization from experience. Kant countered that this wasn't enough—from experience, we might gather that q is *probably* true having established p, but not *necessarily* true. An analogous situation exists for causality, and much of arithmetic.

So where do we get these concepts if they can't be inferred from experience? Well, maybe they're purely internal structures in some kind of Cartesian homunculus. But if that's so, how is it that they are so effective when dealing with the world? (We'll come across these arguments again in the section on objectivity).

Kant's answer is that such notions as number, self (see Chapter 8), causality, and substance (about which Berkeley was so contemptuous) were not wholly inside the mind, or wholly abstractions from experience. He argued that there was a third force. This third force is the manner in which mind must necessarily structure its experience. These structures he called *categories* and they included such entities as modus ponens. This is Kant's conceptual Copernican revolution and it has consequences for the methodology we use for cognitive science. He argued that by a method called *transcendental deduction* we could arrive at conclusions concerning the nature of these categories. In the chapter on psychology, we'll note an experiment in which the concept of causality is shown to be built in as Kant pointed out. Not that Kant would have approved—he was notoriously antipsychology (as a science), stressing that it could never achieve quantification of its observations. Transcendental deduction can involve quite simply noting the performance of experimental subjects on a given task, tweaking the conditions of the task to try to isolate the category that we're looking for, and making the necessary deductions.

There is a final corner to be navigated in our account of Kant. The essence of categories is in fact more abstract than homely notions like number. In fact, *quantity*, comprising unity, plurality, and totality (Copleston, 1962), would be the category corresponding to number. On the one hand, then, we have these abstract categories, and on the other, we have sensory experiences like *yellow* and *loud*. Obviously, we need a connecting layer. This layer must comprise experience that is sufficiently sensory to allow ready connection with the world, and sufficiently abstract to allow relation to these fixed categories. Kant posited a notion of schemata very similar to Piaget's (see Chapter 2) to fit into this space. The schema for quantity—the link from quantity to sensory experience—is number. It is through number that quantity and world interact. Similarly, it is through the schema of permanence in time that the category incorporating causality comes into play.

We need not concern ourselves further with the labyrinthine world of Kantian metaphysics. The crucial point from Kant is that we now have the third force that we noted earlier—that is, a notion that there are systematic rules by which mind must structure its experience. We can attempt to isolate these rules by appropriate psychology experiments or we can try and build them into our AI programs. We are not even particularly concerned that we sometimes (if very rarely) have to abandon such notions as causality in quantum mechanics or Euclidean geometry in general relativity. These categories work for everyday experience.

Another useful path would seem to be to study how children develop these categories and schemata to their full adult maturity. If we can show that this development has many of the characteristics of biological adaptation, then we've really got something. Jean Piaget's work, which we discuss in the next chapter. attempts to do this.

We're beginning to talk biology, but we've forgotten the body. This is an omission we'll redress in the discussion of modern philosophy. For the moment, we're going to take a well-deserved breather. We need to review where we've been so far. Let's do this review in the context of a general discussion of how mind relates to the external world.

MIND AND WORLD, PART I: THE PROBLEM OF OBJECTIVITY

So far, we've had a package tour of the main philosophical schools. If this is Tuesday, it must be empiricism. Well, we liked some of those places, and we'd love to see them again.

If we start considering the problem of objectivity in the abstract—the extent to which we can have correct knowledge of the external world—we have the excuse we needed to revisit those cathedrals of thought.

We're working under a single premise: There is an "out there" (the world) and an "in here" (the mind). It's like fencing—he's got a sword, you've got a sword, and the only rule is that you win if you hit him better than he hits you. We're going to find reasons in a later section of this chapter for nuancing even this rule.

So, how does the in here (the mind) relate to the out there (the world)? There seems to be a choice to be made between two primary options: idealism (such as Platonism) and realism (for instance, ecological realism). The former school tells us that mind is informed by the action of ghostly external entities called *ideas*. The latter tells us that the external world fully forms our mental contents.

Given the rules of our game, we can't actually refute a determined idealist! He's going to argue that all his experience, including his experience of your arguments against him, is of (Platonic-type) ideas. We can force him to defend an apparently absurd position by asking him whether there is a Platonic idea corresponding to, for example, the middle of the NFL season, but we can't refute him.

Realists, on the contrary, say that all mental contents explicitly reflect something external. We've already noted Berkeley moving around a chair and getting different perspectives: For realists, all the perspectives are objective properties of the chair. They have problems with the fact that we can create images of impossible things like unicorns, but that doesn't overly concern a really determined realist. As in life, the hard-core realists are the really crazy ones.

Let's start focusing on the development of this knowledge. Rationalists insist that it's developed by some kind of structured mental operations; we've seen empiricists insisting that it's sense data. Moreover, we've also seen that these schools take opposing views on what concepts are. For conceptualist rationalists, concepts reflect some naturally occurring divisions of reality. For nominalist empiricists, on the other hand, concepts are just names.

These arguments rage through the centuries. They seem to lack any neat resolution. You're a rationalist? You've come to a new conclusion through reasoning? But what new empirical fact did you notice to provoke this new conclusion?

Until recently (e.g., Ayer, 1982) it was thought that perhaps philosophy might settle these issues (and others, like innatism versus empiricism) using its own techniques. It has long given up trying to produce a worldview by starting with isolated reflection and building up to an encompassing theory of Life, the Universe, and Everything. The chances are, however, that even its attempts to resolve issues like rationalism versus empiricism on its own are bound to be fruitless.

For a start, stating these schools of thought as antagonistic philosophical positions and trying to resolve them in some way may be a pointless exercise. We've seen that this kind of antagonism can yield breathtaking creativity like Berkeley's, but it's not going to give us the type of principles we need to engineer AI systems correctly.

Second, it's possible that these questions simply can't be answered on philosophical grounds alone: We also need to be able to experiment. This is the primary aim of cognitive science as experimental epistemology. We're going to see, for example, psychological evidence on the innatism issue in Chapter 2.

More interestingly, we're going to find that all these philosophical schools seem correct in their own ways. For example, we going to find that different AI systems working well on different tasks seem to be implicitly based on different philosophical schools.

Let's take the apparently simple task of trying to get a robot to move around a room, avoiding obstacles and picking up cans. The rationalist school would suggest that the way to do this is to:

1.   Internally represent the room explicitly.
2.   Update this model as changes occur.
3.   If asked to perform an action, refer to this model.

Unfortunately, this approach does not work. We discuss why in more detail in Chapter 5: For the moment, let's note that an empiricist, situated approach seems to work better. Contrariwise, empiricism has problems with explicitly symbolic behavior like mathematical reasoning, where rationalism shines. When it comes to infinite sets even idealism has its day.

One of the main themes of this book, as was noted in the introduction, is that these historically intractable problems can be greatly elucidated by cognitive science. Moreover, the apparently contrasting (dichotomous) schools are seen to reflect different maximally effective modes of cognition in different types of domains.

Where does this leave philosophy? It is best thought of in this context perhaps as the study of evidence, in the manner of a legal trial. New techniques like genetic fingerprinting may be developed, upsetting a previously apparently safe verdict, just as a psychological experiment may upset a previously sure "fact." However, philosophy has much to contribute both in the rigor of the argument it demands and in the imaginative scope of the philosophers who are still willing to go beyond science.

The genii of the imagination and rigor are in modern terms, respectively, the continental and analytic schools. Let's pay them a visit.

THE REDUCED HISTORY OF PHILOSOPHY, PART II: THE 20TH CENTURY

The Continental School

The title granted to mainland European thought in the English-speaking world is reminiscent of the famous English newspaper headline "Fog on Channel: Continent Isolated." The types of problems dealt with by philosophers such as Heidegger and Merleau-Ponty, whom we will consider as the best examples of Continental philosophy (qua epistemology) tended to be quite different from those dealt with in the Anglo-American world. In particular, the mainland Europeans insisted that there had to be more to philosophy than analysis of language, of whatever degree of precision. For them, philosophy was to consider essential issues of our existence as thinking beings in the world. Moreover, they refrained in their analysis from separating the *res cogitans* from the *res extensa*, mind from world. The primary experience was to be considered as Being-in-the-world, which Heidegger called *Dasein* (being there). The difference between Heidegger and Kant is possibly best reflected by their attitudes on proving the existence of the external world. For Kant, the scandal of philosophy is its inability to provide this proof; for Heidegger, it is that it should feel itself impelled to do so.

In a sense, these philosophers are heirs to Thales and his school in their concern with the general problem of being. Their refusal to adopt either monism or dualism is absolutely categorical: Man is a unity of both psyche and body. Heidegger was the first philosopher to truly emphasize a person's *mundanity,* that his or her existence can be considered only with respect to a changing, conditional world. Nor can we properly consider mental structures without respect to the context in which they are being used: The word Heidegger used for this is *thrownness.* This latter term has been imported into AI literature (particularly by Terry Winograd; see Chapter 5) as *situatedness.*

With Merleau-Ponty, we get an enormous emphasis on *embodiment*—the fact that human cognition relies heavily on the body. Whereas Heidegger has often been reproached both for—ahem— German chauvinistic sympathies and linguistic obscurity, Merleau-Ponty has managed to preserve much more of his reputation.

His working through of the embodiment precept is meticulous in its detail. He realizes that there is a great danger of falling into old habits of linguistic materialism and dualism and he steadfastly avoids them. Merleau-Ponty's work is the nearest approach we have to a coherent basis for a full analysis of situated, embodied cognition, so we'll study it in some detail. Yes, that is him as Michelangelo's Adam on the first page of this chapter!

MAURICE MERLEAU-PONTY. Let's start again with that crucial point about mundanity. Merleau-Ponty would stress that if we start by separating the knower from the known, there is no way of putting them back together again. There has to be some alternative form of description that can omit this distinction. Merleau-Ponty also wants to nuance that in here–out there (subject–object) distinction that we held onto throughout our discussion of objectivity. He argues that our experience of the body runs counter to this distinction. At times, there is no question that the body is subject: If I feel pain, this body is me. Let's call this *egocentric* cognition. However, if I am about to ascend in a lift that has a maximum capacity of 12 and there are already that number of people inside, the body is an object. In like fashion, we can call this *intersubjective* cognition.

Let's do a simple experiment: Grasp your left forearm with your right hand. Then direct your awareness to the sensation of pressure on your left forearm. The movement here is from feeling this forearm as an object to feeling it as a subject. As Figures 1.2 and

1.3 show, it's possible to tie yourself up in knots a little bit here!

Merleau-Ponty uses the term *the body-subject* to express the embodied experience of reality we all share. It is a little bit confusing, in that the body can also be object. We're a little closer to the reality of what he meant if we use the translation of the appropriate French term—*incarnated mind.*

A lot of Merleau-Ponty's work is a brilliantly detailed analysis of the flow of information between body-subject and world as we live. He argues that there is a dialectical relationship between the world and self as we impose richer and richer meanings on objects as our consciousness develops. Conversely, these objects are the necessary context for this development. He has set himself an enormously hard task, then—it's no less than the analysis of what our relationship with the world is like at the level beneath which we usually actually start to reflect on the world. He insists that this relationship is already full of meanings that we may not even be conscious of. Whether these meanings are genetically given is not the concern here.

What is genetically given, he insists, is a notion of three-dimensional space. (We'll note that J. J. Gibson's notion of *affordance* is very close to Merleau-Ponty here.) He argues this point against the theorists of this time who would have insisted that depth percep-

Merleau-Ponty discovers the Subject-Object ambivalence of the hand.

FIGURE 1-2

FIGURE 1-3

tion required touch and other physical experiences. Recent psychological experiments seem to vindicate him on this point (Streri & Lécuyer, 1992).

By a series of paradoxes, he argues also that we are plunged from the start into a world that involves the active existence of other people. He uses the existentialist distinction between *en-soi* (the being of objects) and *pour-soi* (the being of subjects) to build the crucial paradox. Other people must be both pour-soi and en-soi. If we deny the primary reality of the intersubjective world, we are faced with a vertiginous realization. Other people are en-soi for us, as our consciousness fills to encompass the world. Yet we must be objects for them, as their consciousness likewise swells. The solution, he argues, must be that the intersubjective world is primary in even the first act of consciousness.

A notion of Being involving 3-D space, objects with meanings attached, and the existence of others is therefore primary. It is now that we begin to notice a few problems with Merleau-Ponty's work. His analysis of the reality underlying perception is superb, but where do the symbols we use in, for example, language and math come in? For him, language also is an egocentric phenomenon (and it also comprises anything worth mentioning about thought). How can it relate to the intersubjective mode of the body-subject's existence? We'll find the perception–symbol problem coming up again in discussion of mobotics in Chapter 5. Piaget's work complements Merleau-Ponty's well with respect to the crucial problem of moving from egocentric to intersubjective modes of existence. In fact, both are also very compatible with the trend to root mind in biologically based interactions with an environment. Development of mind is describable through a process called *equilibration.* We examine this point at length in Chapter 2.

The themes of mundanity, embodiment, and thrownness introduced here are developed greatly in Chapter 5. These are indeed the new dogmas of AI. It has thus been of extreme importance to analyze the concepts of the first philosopher to work them through properly. Moreover, Merleau-Ponty in particular makes psychological statements that are scientific in essence—for instance, his hypothesis about 3-D vision. With him we've come to the point at which philosophy has become specific enough to be experimentally testable.

The Analytic School: The Campaign to Clean Up Philosophy.

It's possible, of course, that we've been wasting our time discussing the history of philosophy in the first place. The analytic school claims that a great deal of the apparent "problems" of philosophy are quite simply puzzles thrown up either by inadequate scientific knowledge or by abuse of language. Take the mind–body problem, which we discuss presently. It seems initially remarkable that one can internally formulate a desire like "I want to go to Portugal" and on this basis perform the requisite external, observable acts (buying a ticket, packing the bags . . .) that fulfill this desire.

However, this internal–external distinction could surrender to science. Let's imagine that our brain imaging techniques (cf. Chapter 4) became good enough to plot all firings of specific brain cells (neurons). We could, theoretically at least, establish characteristic patterns of firing that indicate a desire to go to warm climes, further specify those for Portugal, and so on. Now both the apparently internal desires and external acts are within the domain of the same kind of observational analysis.

In order to introduce the technique of linguistic analysis, I'm going to take what is in this chapter an unusual step: I'm going to quote somebody. Heidegger won the linguistic obscurity Olympics with statements like: "Nihilation is neither an annihilation of what is, nor does it spring from negation. . . . Nothing annihilates itself" (Passmore, 1966). The standard analytic's reply to this statement is that Heidegger has made the mistake of assuming that "nothing" is a name, that is, that it refers to something. In the most fundamental sense of this hackneyed phrase, Heidegger's statement is nonsense and means nothing. Similarly, terms like *being, consciousness,* and so on, must now be viewed with some suspicion.

The campaign to clean up philosophy had its initial meetings in post-World War I Vienna. It is reasonable to expect that all knowledge is going to be expressed in language. Consequently, the focus of the Vienna Circle was language and its abuses.

Though only a tangent to the circle, Ludwig Wittgenstein produced the fullest deconstruction of language. We discuss at length his role as an AI skeptic in Chapter 5. For the moment, it suffices to note that Wittgenstein's (1922) first project was to invent techniques to analyze the logical structure of language. He and others, including Schlick, Carnap, and Neurath, who attempted the same project, assumed that this analysis would bottom out on "atomic propositions," which referred to simple objects (*Tatsachen*) in the world (see Figures 1.4 and 1.5). The world could be described completely in terms of *Sachverhalten* (states of affairs), which ultimately were just regular combinations of *Tatsachen.*

It is a lovely story and, with the correct tune, would make a great ballad. Unfortunately, there are at least two major problems with it. The first is the nature of these atomic propositions. Associated with this first problem is the issue of analysis itself. Wittgenstein gives no fully worked-through example of a sentence being mapped to atomic propositions, nor does he give any examples of the second issue, the question of how to map these atomic propositions onto logical atoms. His original conjecture was that the atomic propositions and logical atoms were the same for everybody. However, the mapping from one to the other was done by an idiosyncratic "private language," unique to each person. The parallel with AI is so inviting that I'm going to pre-empt some of the discussion in Chapter 5 by accepting the invitation. We can usefully think of this private language as the instruction set of a computer. Two computers with different instruction sets (say a VAX 6230 and an IBM PS/2) might run the same program, with exactly the same input–output behavior, but with a completely different set of machine code commands (the lines of 1's and 0's in Figure 1.4) being initiated in each case.

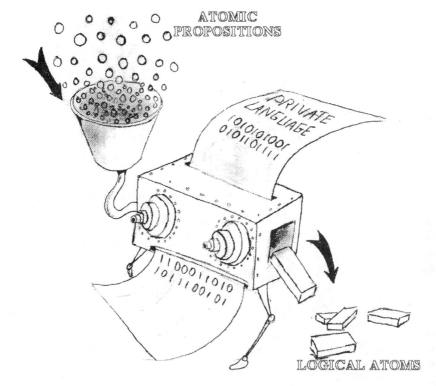

FIGURE 1-4

The first problem with atomic propositions is reminiscent of the ancient problems confronting Platonists: How many of these ideal forms/atomic propositions were there, what exactly were they, and how did they interact with reality? (We'll see these issues recurring in the Chapter 5 discussion of knowledge-based natural language processing.) The second problem is perhaps an even deeper one and it behooves us to give it some attention. We'll note that Neurath's notion of the *protocol sentence* ran straight bang into the same wall.

Any kind of positing of internal processing is going to run into the second problem. Essentially, how can any *private* language refer? The answer Wittgenstein gave is that it's impossible. However, AI systems based on this type of conceptual architecture seem to function at least in some domains. These domains are usually essentially static and admit of a parsimonious symbolic description. There must be some sense in which private languages are valid.

FIGURE 1-5

Wittgenstein (1967) begins his rebuttal of private languages with the quote from St. Augustine, referred to earlier, concerning how words refer and how children learn language. Yet the fact is that some words do refer (like book) and children can learn associating the sound and the object in these cases. Perhaps there are a multiplicity of different ways by which words can refer? We return to this point in Chapter 5.

We're anticipating a lot at this stage, so let's rewind a little. The primary aim of analytic philosophy is to restore clarity in language. Having done this, it is expected that many apparent problems in philosophy will turn out to be no more than linguistic conundra.

If natural languages like English prove to be hopelessly obscure, well, so much the worse for them. It may be necessary to distort them to create protocol sentences of absolute clarity, or even to invent a new language. In any event, the truths to be expressed through the medium of this language are all scientific truths. Moreover, science is a continuum from the hard sciences like physics on the right to the social and behavioral sciences (including psychology) on the left. The question arises as to how we can quantify mental life so as to admit of this type of description. We discussed one technique for doing this earlier when we examined the overt data associated with the wish to go to Portugal.

One key concept of the Vienna Circle was the *verification principle*. The scientific value of a proposition was identical with the mechanisms by which it could be verified. "I am hungry" potentially could be verified with respect to overt bodily activities; "God exists" can't be verified like that and so has no scientific value. Likewise, statements similar to "I feel a shadow has passed between us in this relationship" would have difficulty being verified. Consequently, and here we come to a really important point, a great deal of real mental life gets jettisoned with acceptance of the verification principle, along with much metaphysics and theology.

As we're going to see later, semantics in computational linguistics (elsewhere, it becomes very obscure indeed what precisely it is about, or what possible relation to the world it envisages for symbols) is often treated as the study of meaning, usually including how groups of propositions can acquire meaning through their logical combination. If the ideal language could be correctly designed, we could abandon semantics completely. The notion of *logical combination* would be superfluous; the semantic content of sentences could be obtained on the basis of syntax alone—that is, on the basis of the grammar of the language. (Chapter 3 includes an analysis of the appropriateness of the syntax–semantics distinction.)

However, we've seen that all attempts to create such a language failed. Even without the private language argument, the failure of Wittgenstein, Neurath, Schlick, and Carnap to come up with a single atomic proposition or logical atom was impressive. Moreover, another issue presented itself: What were the ultimate facts? Were they sense data, as Neurath thought, or something a little more ineffable, as Wittgenstein postulated?

All these arguments are extremely relevant to contemporary debate in cognitive science. We're going to review several attempts like the Churchlands' to reform our view of mind as radically as the logical positivists. It's worth pointing out one final paradox here: The Vienna Circle, although apparently radically materialist, ends up flirting with dualism. This ideal language contains all the truth, mental terms and meaning. It is to be distinguished absolutely from discourse or activity of any other kind. The old Cartesian mind–matter distinction has sneaked up on us!

The English philosopher Gilbert Ryle is our last stop on the journey to the present day. His analysis focused on analysis akin to our Portugal example, but without even the equipment to do brain scans. Consequently, on the one hand we simply have the English sentence "I wish to go to Portugal"; on the other, we have the overt behavior in buying the ticket, and so on. Ryle's philosophical behaviorism does a valuable service by showing that a certain subset of mental life can usefully be described in this manner. However, his account of activities like memory and perception is inadequate.

Cognitive science could play an enormous role in the philosophy of mind. The logical positivists and philosophical behaviorists were not being mischievous or deliberately obtuse in trying to quantify mental activity as they did. Rather, they were struggling sincerely with the problem of how to remain rigorously scientific while talking about mental life. Cognitive science has afforded new opportunities for doing that. In the first place, computer programs offered a practical hands-on example of how apparently mental, previously fugitive conceptual entities could be implemented.

In fact, a paradoxical situation arose with the advent of programs that performed tasks like "reasoning" about chemical structure. The AI scientists who designed the programs felt comfortable about using such words as *memory, thought,* and so on, in talking about their programs. Psychologists of the same period, who were steeped in philosophical behaviorism, were forced to eschew such words when talking about humans! One of the enormous advances resulting from Cognitive science is that the scope of mind, as scientifically studied, is now both our conscious experience and the unconscious processes that affect our behavior. We discuss this in considerably greater detail later. For the moment, let's leave the Reduced History of Philosophy with one final thought. The dialogue between science and philosophy is more complicated than may immediately seem the case. At first blush, it may seem that science eats into domains originally covered by philosophy, like physics and biology, turning them from objects of speculation into hard-edged sciences based on observation and experiment. By this token, it seemed in the early part of this century that science would encroach on the area called *mental life* in the same way. Quite the contrary has occurred: Instead of having a science that linked verbal behavior to overt acts in order to explain, for example, intent, we have one with a vastly richer store of valid data and method. Exactly what these are is the topic of the next section.

THE PHILOSOPHY OF COGNITIVE SCIENCE

Contrary to the usual practice of CS as it addresses this area, I deliberately emphasized philosophical epistemology, rather than the philosophy of mind, in the title of this chapter. The latter discipline will not be ignored; we consider it below. However, I consider that it has been on occasion accorded an overprivileged status in the field of cognitive science, at the expense of other disciplines. Its practitioners dominate the agenda of CS in the same sense, for the same reasons, and with much the same degree of benefit as that which occurs when lawyers dominate politics. Experts at debate, they can turn practice into theory and fact into fiction as their pet procedures dictate.

A good example of this is Fodor's argument about the nonexistence of a knowledge level in cognition (see below). This makes many semanticians and not a few AI workers redundant immediately. The only theory of semantics Fodor will accept is semantic functionalism, originally a behaviorist notion. But wait! Is it not true to say that AI systems that work with what their developers considered a knowledge level actually work reasonably well?

The concerns of the philosophy of mind (best expressed by Roberto Casati as the attempt to give a unified philosophical account of desire, feeling, belief, awareness, understanding, and action, which frankly doesn't leave much for the rest of us to do) are absolutist in a field where the set of base concepts must be capable of radical change due to empirical findings and cross-disciplinary fertilization. On a methodological level, the philosophy of mind should feel itself obliged no less than other fields to propose creative cross-disciplinary syntheses (as indeed Fodor did at one stage). Too often, its mode of argumentation is to follow lines of thought to absurd conclusions (*reductio ad absurdum*) by means, inter alia, of thought-experiments, and then pick through the carnage to find that, say, semantic functionalism or innatism has remained intact (shades of idealism!). Asked to give examples, they can't, but vehemently argue that the conclusion is correct. There must be something wrong.

I believe one of the problems is with the status of the thought-experiment in this field. We are from time to time asked to consider what it would be like to be a brain in a vat, receiving simulated sensory input; to have a precise double (beam me up, Scotty); or to live a completely socially isolated existence. It seems very likely that all of these situations (particularly the first) bear the hallmark of an implicitly Cartesian view of mind, and the arguments gain their impetus from precisely the Cartesian mindset we default to in this culture. Again, we find folk-psychological terms like "believe," "know," "meet in the flesh" mixed in the stew. One of the conclusions of CS, as it outflanks those who would set its agenda, may be that these situations are nonsituated and impossible. I am partly this brain you would place in a vat, but also partly this body, and I am interdefined in terms of my social contacts.

The approach taken in this book is not this kind of imposition of a definition of the domain and its methodology; it is rather an attempt to look across the disciplines which comprise cognitive science, intuit convergences, and suggest a vocabulary. The viewpoint here is that "knowledge" (extended, as we shall see in Chapter 2, beyond its definition as true justified belief) provides a good currency for trade between disciplines—when expressed in informational terms—it is an even better one. Campbell (1982) treats the latter concept of information in terms of redundancy in a message in an appealing way.

Philosophers of mind undoubtedly bring a useful set of skills to CS; they risk irrelevance and incorrectness by over-estimating their role as they "quine" (propose as nonexistent) representation, consciousness, the knowledge level, or whatever. A fair general rule for the quality of their work is this: If they criticize a research program, they should propose to substitute one as rich in its place. It is too early to say whether the eliminativists, or Searle, or Fodor are in fact correct; using the Cartesian deconstruction above affords one hint, the rubbishing of whole fields another, and the resulting framework a third. Searle and Fodor, brilliant critics though they are, are suspect under the latter two criteria.

The path to be taken in this section is as follows:

First, we're going to discuss the *res extensa/res cogitans* problem.

Second, we need to get a firmer grasp on what precisely we mean by *mind*.

Third, a framework, due mainly to Merleau-Ponty, which informs the treatment in this book of some issues in the foundations of cognitive science is outlined.

Fourth, these issues are reintroduced, in all their terminological glory, in the context of this framework. En route, we discuss the issue of what acceptable data for cognitive science are, and as a diversion, amuse ourselves with the canards usually treated as AI's contribution to philosophy (or vice versa).

We need to do some soul searching as indicated above at this point. Is such a superdiscipline as CS necessary? Could we not just work from a priori considerations like the philosophers of yore? We use Jerry Fodor's work to again answer with a definite *yes* and *no*, respectively.

Materialism or Dualism?

In a way, this section is a planned wild goose chase. In our discussion of Aquinas, it was pointed out that this statement of the mind–matter relationship is probably far too simple. However, like many other dichotomous expressions of philosophical issues, it can lead us to a wealth of insights. Moreover, this issue seems to be totally unresolvable, as framed in this way, and there is correspondingly no limit to the amount of debate that can go on.

The debate can often be very emotive in character. We find post-Enlightenment materialists, who insist that any notion of soul or spirit will throw us back into the mumbo-jumbo and inquisitions of the Dark Ages, ranged against dualists who, with some justification, argue that there is no way that we can maintain notions of intrinsic human dignity in a world of brute material fact. It has often been argued that Déscartes introduced his notion of the soul only under pressure from the Catholic Church. His successor la Mettrie found the courage, according to this account, to adopt Déscartes's framework in a purely material sense. This argument gathers strength from the fact that Déscartes destroyed copies of a potentially heretical physics tract he had written, when he heard of Galileo's difficulties. In fact, the normally sedentary Frenchman ran to the printer to do so. Yet the theoretical framework surrounding the existence and functioning of the Cartesian soul is substantial enough to allow that Déscartes was sincere in professing it.

Let's go to the matter at hand. Essentially, we'll find dualism a difficult argument to sustain because we can't work out how *res cogitans* could have any effect on *res extensa*. We'll find thoroughgoing materialism almost as difficult because of its lack of explanatory power for mental life (what IS consciousness, materially?) and the inadequacy of its notion of matter. In despair (!) we're going to examine the evidence from neuroscience and finish none the wiser. Having gone through this mill, we're going to stand back and guess which is the most appropriate viewpoint and end up in the mundane world of Heidegger and Merleau-Ponty.

Simply stated, Déscartes's arguments in his *Meditations,* which are in fact mental exercises, boil down to personal conviction that his experience of his mental life is of an utterly different nature to his experience of his body. He can, hypothetically at least, shut his eyes and deny he has a body: He can introspect, and discover in his inner (phenomenal) world some utterly certain experiences of a self, inalienably different to any physical experiences. This rock of selfhood, which both he and Berkeley were privileged to find, is the basis for the positing of the dualists' soul.

Try it out! You know who you are right now as you read a set of arguments against which you can readily define yourself in a book you've bought, stolen, or are just browsing through. Now forget about this book, with its distinct narrator's voice and offbeat illustrations and focus on finding this self, devoid of the definition those contents give it.

Well, at a guess, you don't share Déscartes's or Berkeley's divine nature. In fact, as you search for self as an object in your phenomenal world, you find yourself trapped in an infinite regress. The more you look, the less there is to look for. Moreover, as you separate self from its contents (for example, your attitude to this irritating Irish know-all), self seems to converge to the null set.

In fact, strangely enough, self seems a much more secure entity when in action, when defining yourself with respect to the world, than in introspection. So Déscartes's *Cogito, ergo Sum* needs to be nuanced and supplemented quite a lot: *Ago* (I act), *ergo Sum* is also true (see Chapter 8 for why).

None of which really undermines the central Cartesian insight: Consciousness is a mystery, particularly if we are thoroughgoing materialists. There has been a host of inadequate computational and cognitive explanations of consciousness in recent years, which I have exposed (Ó Nualláin, forthcoming), and which are commented on in Chapter 8. However, Déscartes's conclusion that some kind of spirit hovers around the brain, intervening when necessary, is unjustifiable. As spirit, it cannot affect matter. Moreover, his conclusion that we can introspect and find this soul in our experience of self is also incorrect. We discuss these matters at length in Chapter 8.

Remember, our main argument against Déscartes is the problem of A causing effects on B, if A and B are utterly alien to each other. This holds whether we regard mind as being of an utterly different type to matter (substance dualism) or containing an extra factor X (property dualism). You can gather your friends around over a few beers or tokes to consider the tension between this undoubted incompatibility and the equally indubitable mysterious nature of consciousness. As the night proceeds, a sensible soul might ask whether there is any relevant scientific evidence. Surely we can dam this torrent of words by performing an appropriate scientific experiment. If, using the brain imaging techniques we outline in Chapter 4, we track an intent from its neural activation infancy to its expression in overt action, can we then categorically insist that a physically describable circumscribed set of events has been noticed and that materialism has been established?

Well, no actually. Where did the intent come from? Moreover, overt action is preceded by an action potential in the neurons that are to initiate the act (see Chapter 4). Yet, even then, the issue is confused. This action potential does not inevitably lead to an action in all cases. Conscious intention can override the mechanism, even at this late stage. (I have discussed these findings in Ó Nualláin, forthcoming, and in Chapter 8; the original reference is Libet, 1985). In fact, the evidence from brain imaging of this kind is incredibly ambiguous, and one can remain in whatever camp one chooses after its analysis. It is rather like a discussion on which is the best football team, where loyalty is really the only arbiter. However, we can see the issue of the freedom of the will emerging, and we discuss this in Chapter 8.

Anyway, your former tennis player says, pouring another orange juice, that this is all a non issue. All this neural action potential is very clever, but we have fundamental issues of the conservation of energy to think about. Let's say we are, like the great neuroscientist John Eccles, Catholics and dualists. How can we, as self-respecting Nobel prize-winning scientists, countenance an interaction that seems to violate the first law of thermodynamics?

Quite simply, actually. First of all, in physics, Heisenberg's uncertainty principle insists that what we observe is not nature herself, but nature exposed to our method of questioning. In fact, the so-called "objective" properties of particles in a quantum physics experiment are as much artifacts of the act of observation as intrinsic to the particles themselves. The act of conscious observation seems to affect matter.

More fundamentally, Henri Margenau's work has established the existence of *probability fields* that consume neither mass nor energy. The speculation that Eccles favors is a soul permeating a probability field hovering around the brain waiting for action potentials in order to bypass the mind–matter distinction by initiating overt action in the world. It is an inviting picture, currently irrefutable, and Eccles and his soul will enjoy external bliss in heaven for it.

However, all that I wish to point out from Margenau, Heisenberg, and Eccles is that the mind–matter issue is infinitely more complicated than many standard texts make out (Churchland, 1988; Dennett, 1992; Flanagan, 1991; Jackendoff, 1987). The question phrased in philosophical terms is what it means for an event to have both physical and mental properties. As such, it is yet to receive an answer. The picture of matter that emerges from quantum physics resembles shadow rather than stone. Neither have the many neurophysiological experiments of varying degrees of ethics ranging from the appalling to the correct yielded any conclusions. We are going to have to look elsewhere.

I wish now to outline the viewpoint taken in this book. With Merleau-Ponty and Heidegger, we encounter an approach in which the mind–body problem is subsumed into a general view of how cognition in general functions vis à vis the world. Cognition is in the world, an expression of the more fundamental Being-in-the-world. We are mind–body unities, present in the here and now. I argue in Chapter 8 that the Cartesian *Cogito* does exist, but as an occasional, remote, and nondualist achievement. If a philosopher wishes to justify this position with respect to the area of philosophy dealing with such issues (metaphysics), we can point him to Aquinas's triptych of substance, act, and potency.

And so to other issues. First, what is mind and how can we study it?

In Search of Mind II

The first issue here is what permissible data are. We have noted the inadequacies of Ryle's approach, which attempted to include only verbal and overt behavior. With the advent of AI, the range of permissible data extended to include mental processes that could be formally described as a set of explicit procedures (algorithms)—for example, add a list of numbers by adding the first to the second, adding the result to the third, and so on. Let us call the total of all identifiable algorithms the *computational mind*. These algorithms may be doing extremely complex tasks for us, unconscious to ourselves. For example, as you read, Process A is focusing your eyes on this page and (to simplify) Process B is analyzing the sentences and extracting their meaning.

Consequently, we could decide that our search for mind should limit itself as already mentioned. Alternatively, we might decide that only processes that we could potentially become conscious of should form our data—that is, that the phenomenological mind is all we're concerned with. By this token, Process A, which is potentially observable (try it) is a valid datum, whereas Process B isn't. We lose Process B by this move but we gain a lot also: We can appeal to aspects of our experience that seem nonalgorithmic, such as our emotions on hearing music or the fluctuations in our consciousness itself.

Yet there is more to the study of mind than even the union of the sets defined by the data thrown up by the computational and phenomenological approaches. We shall see in Chapter 5 that a great deal of agonizing is currently being done in AI as to where to place knowledge-level descriptions. If we have a robotic system functioning in an environment, is it correct to project the knowledge-level description (that is, the attribution of mind) solely to within the robot itself, or to the combination of robot and environment? The current received wisdom is that this description is the preserve solely of an observer, and cannot be attributed to the robot alone but to the observer's perception of robot plus environment. Moreover, we shall find in Chapter 2 that there exists in cognitive psychology a canonical principle called the *principle of rationality*. This states, in essence, that the cognitive system will try to maximize the organism's adaptation to its environment. Where is mind now?

The answer I give is that mind is best considered as manifest in the principles underlying the interaction and increasing co-adaptation of organism and environment over time. A child learning to function increasingly efficiently in the world shows one instance of mind. A species adapting itself to a habitat over millions of years demonstrates another. In other words, mind need not be, as commonly thought, the preserve of conscious thinking beings.

Mind is externally present (immanent) in nature. One manifestation of mind is intelligence, and it is that with which we as cognitive scientists are most concerned. If we find ourselves focusing a great deal on conscious intelligence, it is because initially, at least, it promises to yield its secrets a little more readily and seems an extremely effective form of intelligence and manifestation of mind. Yet we hold onto a definition of mind that can encompass the dance of the bumblebee simultaneously with Einstein's discovery of general relativity.

The focus of this book is ultimately conscious intelligence. We are interested also in how conscious intelligence often is parasitic on the activity of unconscious processors, how the phenomenal mind rests on the shoulders of computational mind.

We accept a weak form of the information-processing hypothesis—that there exists an information-processing level of analysis of mind intermediate between neurophysiology and consciousness. This, as we shall see in Chapter 5, is considered the central premise of cognitive science. In its strong form (as expanded on by Stillings et al., 1987, for example) an attempt is made fully to characterize mind in this information-processing way. It is assumed that the system of informational structures can be decomposed, and the elements that form the result of this decomposition can be characterized intentionally. This characterization is often seen as a way of cashing out consciousness. The view on consciousness taken here is different; it requires embodiment and is a much more encompassing phenomenon than intentionality. Moreover, the information-processing level of analysis is not seen as in any sense privileged; it is interesting and useful, but no further commitment is made to it.

In the previous section, I outlined how the monism/dualism issue is viewed in this book. Let us now view how it stands on some other philosophical debating points.

Autism, Egocentrism and Intersubjectivity

In this section, I wish to outline one aspect of the general theory of cognition that informs this book. Intelligence and mind can be discerned in the interaction of the body-subject with its environment. Mind is to be considered in its immanent, computational, and phenomenal aspects. We hope eventually to shed light on the peculiar nature of conscious intelligence and such issues as selfhood and will. For the moment, however, we're concerned with a classification of the types of cognition that exist.

Cognition is conceived as comprising three modes: the egocentric, the intersubjective, and the autistic. Egocentric cognition is essentially cognition in which the view of oneself (especially one's body) is solely as subject (cf. our earlier discussion of Merleau-Ponty).

Perception of the world as one moves is a perfect example of egocentric cognition. We noted earlier that AI robotic systems, which attempt to function moving around a domain by continual updating of a representation of that domain have great difficulty doing this. How is it that we actually can manage to do this? Essentially, by combining the visual and somatomotor (feelings-of-movement) data in a way that extracts information from both. The posterior parietal cortex has been suggested as the most likely area for this combination (see Chapter 4). Yet there need not be any explicit data about oneself as another object in the environment here; thus, we call this egocentric knowledge. Let's note two areas in which this type of knowledge has been studied: the ecological optics of J. J. Gibson (Chapter 2) and Rodney Brook's mobotics (Chapter 5). Finally, Merleau-Ponty commented that one's knowledge of a new area, as expressed through one's language, is always initially egocentric.

He noted also that our primary experience is of being in the world with others, as a person among persons sharing a consensual (intersubjective) reality. Most recent work on child development shows an extremely early socialization (de Schonen, Burnod, & Deruelle, 1992). This consensual reality may be developed in some people in different ways than in others. For example, a musician may be able to discern that a guitar is out of time, whereas a nonmusician cannot; yet, what the musician hears is objective and potentially (among musicians) consensual.

Let's put that musician to work singing a song, which she has difficulty recollecting, in a warm auditorium. Her guitar slips out of time while she sings and she doesn't notice it, such is her concentration on the words. The musician is now in autistic mode with respect to tuning. Those of her audience who never noticed the difference in any case are in egocentric mode, and the weeping musicians in pain at the back are in intersubjective mode. We discuss in Chapter 8 how we can move from egocentric to intersubjective mode; for the moment, let's note that autistic mode signals the lack of conscious perception of a consensual object for one attuned to such an object.

In Figure 1.6, which shows a soccer match on TV, the crucial relations are as follows: The player in possession of the ball is using egocentric knowledge to remain in possession, to keep his balance, and so on. He is also, in intersubjective fashion, trying to

FIGURE 1-6

beat the goalkeeper. Myles has had too many beers and has watched too much soccer. All he sees are projections, without any authentic experiencing of what is really going on in the match. He is in autistic mode.

Which in turn leads us to ask: What is an object, anyway? For the tone deaf, what is a tune? The answer to be developed here is that an object is any (potentially) consensual experience that doesn't admit immediately of scientific disproval. The Flat Earth society consensually validates an object that can easily be shown not to exist. Musicians detect a difference in quality between REM and Beethoven's late quartets that can probably eventually be verified in terms of information theory (see Chapter 7).

This, then, is one aspect of the framework for the treatment of different types of cognition in this book. Let us see how it casts light on current controversies in cognitive science, and how they reflect this light. We'll call this aspect of our framework the

Mylesian position; the Nolanian position will unfold as the framework gets fleshed out in the cause of this book.

Some Current Controversies In Cognitive Science

In this section, we're taking the boat out into the stormy sea of cognitive science controversy. A strong stomach and nerves of steel are both basic prerequisites for this voyage, full of hurricane and pirate as it will be. The launching party will have as theme the notion of understanding and whether we can attribute this to computers. This topic will lead us to discuss the wider issue of the extent to which we can attribute mental states to computers in the first place. Then, in turn, we'll find ourselves discussing what it means for two mental processes run on different hardware to be equivalent. We discuss, in particular, whether we shouldn't just try to reduce the mental processes in question to their constituent parts. We then turn our minds to the issue of how and whether we really know what we mean by what we say and think, including about these issues.

THE CHINESE ROOM.   First of all, the launching party. We'll talk about whether a computer programmed with the appropriate knowledge structures can be said to understand a text that it processes correctly. This processing could involve paraphrasing the text, or translating it into another language (see the Chapter 5 discussion of scripts). John Searle's (1981) classic paper on this subject, one of the most reprinted scientific papers of recent decades, says that we must withhold predicating an understanding of such a system. We discuss just the bare bones of his Chinese room argument here: It is impossible to do any reading in the AI area without continually coming across his article.

Consider the situation depicted in Figure 1.7. A man sits inside a room, committed to a life of translating English to Chinese without knowing any Chinese (is this Searle or Beckett?). However, he does have a set of rules for the equivalences of Chinese and English words. Shown what appears a Chinese squiggle, he can match it with his tables of equivalents, and produce an English equivalent. The text in Chinese may be regarded as input, the text in English as output, to extend the computing metaphor. He might even have another set of rules by which he can, equally automatically, recombine the constituents of the English sentence in their correct order. Searle introduces many variations of this basic theme, in the manner of a picador at Pamplona: He is trying to goad his opponents in the hard AI (yes, computers *can* understand) camp.

FIGURE 1-7

Yet his argument boils down to a very simple issue: Because we'd be loath to suggest that the person in the room actually understands Chinese, and we must accept that he's working like a computer production system (see Chapter 5) in conjunction with his rules, are we not forced to conclude that computers cannot understand? We have seen that his target is the hard AI school, yet the soft and medium schools, although different in emphasis (for example, Sloman, 1992), also are part of Searle's prey. Replies to Searle from the hard AI school have focused on asking whether the system of man and rules together may be said to understand, and processor plus program be similarly assumed to understand. The level of vitriol in the debate has been staggering (for example, I was shocked to see the epithet "religious" being hurled at Searle by Douglas Hofstadter).

It is fair to say that Searle's instinct for the jugular is faultless. However, his position changed greatly over the years. His earlier paper (1981) was willing to grant that understanding was a property of programs unique to the human brain. After some deft footwork, he found himself stating that this type of position is in fact dualist. We're basically positing a contrast between a *res cogitans* (the program) and a *res extensa* (whatever the program is being run on, for instance a Turing Machine; see Chapter 5). We're attributing understanding, mental states, and so on, only to the program. His latest incarnation (1992) won't grant the syntactic operation inherent in programs any intrinsic physical reality; echoing Kripke on Wittgenstein, he declares that syntax is not intrinsic to the physics. (The views of this avatar on the CS enterprise in general we discuss in Chapter 5.) In my framework, understanding can be viewed correctly only in the context of a "situated" act of cognition. It is part of a life process. Note, parenthetically that understanding covers a multitude. Had Vernon Howell's mother managed to stop the siege at Waco, Texas before the carnage, we would have accepted that she understood David/Vernon. This extreme is empathy. The other extreme is understanding how $x^2 + y^2$ gives the square of the hypotenuse, where x and y are the other two sides in a right triangle. We see later that fully conscious acts have a privileged status in this framework.

Understanding is either such an act, or the recapitulation of such an act. Were an autonomous system like a Brooks creature to perform symbolic behavior like that in the Chinese room, we might concede that it understands. I have argued elsewhere (Ó Nualláin, 1992) that this cannot happen, given the current design principles of such systems.

Finally, Searle commented sardonically on the "courage" of such AI scientists as John McCarthy, who continue to predicate understanding of computers, beliefs of thermostats, and so on. Indeed, we can't stop them doing so. The moon can be a ghostly galleon, banshees can wail, poets can anthropomorphize the "cruel" sea and "kindly" sun. However, what is really important is that the problem of predicating understanding should be seen in a larger context as part of an overall theory of cognition, and that theory is one of the goals of this book.

EQUIVALENCES.   In this section, we discuss when we are allowed to attribute equivalence of process between two cognitive entities.

Example A: If we have a person calculating a payroll and a computer doing the same, with precisely the same eventual output, are we entitled to assume that they have followed the same steps? Example B: If we have a neural network (see Chapter 4) performing a memory task (perhaps remembering the months of the year in Swahili) and an American doing the same task, what criteria can we use to conclude a similarity in the nature of processing? Example C: If we compare the rule application sequence of an expert system (Chapter 5) and the stated sequence of logical operations by a human mathematician working on the same task, what are the grounds on which we are allowed to assume equivalence?

Well, I wish to spoil the fun immediately. What we're talking about in these examples is computational equivalence. (Let's note that in the computationalist cognitive science paradigm we explore in Chapter 5, the most relevant equivalence is at the level of *functional architecture*. The criteria we use in all these examples are:

1. Input–output behavior (obviously, this must be extremely similar). We also expect that changing the task (increasing the number of months!) will cause equivalent output changes in the two systems (amount of error).
2. Speed of processing. It is thus doubtful that Example A shows any sort of meaningful equivalence.
3. Where a meaningful comparison can be made with respect to intermediate processing, for example in C, we can infer that the mathematician's protocol is informative enough to assume equivalence.
4. We may decide, with Pylyshyn (1984), that true equivalence can be posited when one has established equivalence of functional architecture. Essentially, this involves establishing identity at the level of computer architecture. This position is arrived at after much careful consideration of the foundations of CS, and we mention it in this context in Chapter 5. We can reject it on the grounds that there are no good reasons for accepting the remainder of Pylyshyn's framework, unless it is considerably modified.

This, in turn, leads us to the question of what our methods of investigation should be in cognitive science, and the related question (again) of what are relevant data. The answer is that we're studying all aspects of mind, and consider everything from computational performance to input–output relations to protocol analysis valid.

Fine, but computational equivalence does not equal experiential phenomenological equivalence. According to the functionalist thesis, we are allowed to infer (almost) every type of equivalence from the functional one. I deny this, and am about to be accused of being religious, I think. What I wish to point out is that we do have privileged first-person (you and me) access to our experiences in a way that cannot be reduced to functional equivalence. In other words, consciousness is an issue here. I can bear the hounds baying as it looks as if I've put all aspects of personal experience outside the range of scientific inquiry. Quite the opposite: What I'm saying is that these problems of inaccessible data only arise in a Cartesian framework. When we accept that much of our experience is primarily intersubjective, and as such consensually valid (in the sense outlined in Chapter 8), there is no such problem about observables in a scientific sense—that is, in informational terms. That aspect of our experience which cannot be put in these terms is admittedly currently outside CS.

REDUCTIONISM.   There are various types of reductionism possible, ranging (rather like curry powder) from the mild to the very hot. In cognitive science, given the failure of Ryle's project, reductionism now concerns itself mainly with attempting to reduce experience to neural activity. However, we know remarkably little (see Chapter 4) about how neural activity results in the fully human symbolic/emotional vast palette of experience that we all enjoy. Consequently, reductionism can be usefully classified also with respect to the degree of hope involved about breakthroughs in neuroscience over the forthcoming decades.

The most hopeful reductionism is called *eliminative materialism*. The adherents to this faith live in hope for such radical breakthroughs in neuroscience that the folk psychology concepts of *belief, desire, knowledge* and—God forbid—*hope* itself can be abandoned (Churchland, 1988). This book is hopefully being read in a liberal democracy, and we allow people to believe what they like in such political systems. However, it is not scientifically valid to construct a science of cognition on such a poverty of neuroscientific findings, let alone prescribe what are valid constructs for viewing one's experiences on this meager basis. In fact, I believe it is valid to allow a construct like "intent" in cognitive science. Again, the telling argument is that it is quite definitely an integral part of the intersubjective realm. In fact, massive court cases can hinge on what the defendant intended at Time X, and a great deal of evidence can be adduced to buttress whatever the theory is.

Were it possible to reduce experience to neural event, we would be scientifically obliged to do so. However, the integrity of neuroscience, as a discipline, right from the time Lashley failed to find his engram (see Chapter 4) has been demonstrated in its ability to take on board findings that make its set task much more difficult. We are left picking through our experience to try to find clues to solve the main problems of conscious experience. In a sense, then, Merleau-Ponty's work in *The Phenomenology of Perception* is actually reductionist. It's reducing our experience of the world to its barest essentials, given the fact that we don't know enough neuroscience to get closer to the bone.

We should not be surprised, contrariwise, if the failure of our attempts to reduce conscious experience compel us eventually to transcend our experience. We should have the integrity to accept that through cognitive science our worldview may be changed in the direction of enlargement as much as reduction.

MEANING.   In this final subsection, we're dealing with several apparently unrelated issues. The first is again the question of privileged access to experience—that is, the extent to which you can claim that a given experience is yours, and yours alone. The next is what is known as the semantical problem: How do our names for these "private" mental states get their meaning? Related to this is the problem of how we can say that humans have mental states at all. We find ourselves asking how we can mean anything. Is there some kind of monitoring process in the brain that sees the symbol *dog* and means this quadruped with fur, claws, and so on?

I wish to argue that these issues are intractable only within a Cartesian framework. If we want to posit this monitoring process as the only mechanism, this unmeant meaner (see Dennett, 1991), we end up with Déscartes' schema. Once there, we're stuck very badly. So you've got this unmeant meaner within you that means things! How is it you can talk to me? Is mine of the same structure? Quickly, we're forced to concede, as the paradoxes multiply, that maybe we don't even have privileged first person access in the way we thought—as sole owners—to some of our experience. Mundanity insists that meanings are built up gradually from the subject's (dialectical) relationship with his or her environment. There is no absolute separation of the within from the without; the meanings define the relationship between subject and object (see Chapter 2 on Piaget). Moreover, just as there are different kinds of objectivity, ranging from egocentric perception to intersubjective elaborate symbolic behavior, so also are there different types of meanings.

Where then does the self come in, if there is no unmeant meaner? Essentially, in the preservation of relationships between subject and environment. The function of self as a cognitive system is the preservation of achieved relationships between the subject and its environment. (We explore this idea at length in Chapter 8.) Therefore, I agree that we don't have privileged access to our mental states and meanings in the legal way—for example, a householder can ask unwelcome guests to leave his property. If these mental states are valid (intentional) as distinct from neurotic, they are necessarily part of the intersubjective domain, as expanded on in Chapter 8. The meanings they carry are therefore potentially shareable. How then do they get their names? In the same way as *dog* and *house;* it's a matter for etymology, not the philosophy of mind. How do we know others have mental states? A better question: How can we possibly doubt it, given that the starting point for conscious experience and knowledge in the first place is the intersubjective world?

Therefore, in the framework here, meanings are artifacts of the dialectic between subject and world. So-called private mental states can often be properly studied as part of intersubjective analysis. Self's cognitive role is preserving subject–object delimitations. There is no Cartesian homunculus, or unmeant meaner. We are present in the here and now with others. Understanding in this framework is viewed as arising from the organism's attempt to achieve meaning. The debate on this issue in AI could not be more wide of the mark: Understanding is always the result of conscious effort, results in a sense of meaning where previously there was confusion or chaos, and as the result of an act of will is beyond the reach of any nonbiological system. The psychiatrist and concentration camp survivor Victor Frankl has written best on this role for understanding.

Conveying meaning to another person, as will be repeated, is a conscious and often willed action. Under the auspices of symbols I know to be intersubjective, I attempt to convey a certain point of view to you. Yet "I" am partly defined by this attempt (to answer T. S. Eliot's plaint that it is impossible to say what I mean, I am just what I mean) and cannot be other than conscious as it proceeds. Meaning in this sense is therefore tied in with intent and we should not find it any easier to formalize than the latter; any major criminal trial that attempts to intuit the precise "intent" of a suspect shows how difficult this can be.

If we can establish a separate domain within the intersubjective realm for value, we may find our theory of cognition mounting to an ethics. However, that would be the theme of a much larger and more important book than this one.

Fodor and Modularity.

In fact, according to Jerry Fodor, this book probably shouldn't have been written: One of his more celebrated edicts is on the nonexistence of CS. It is difficult to know whether Fodor fits best in this chapter or the next: His modularity of mind thesis (Fodor, 1983) is a set of prescriptions that cuts across both disciplines. As a compromise, he's in both. There is very little to argue with in Fodor's general approach to the mental per se. He argues, contra behaviorists, that mental events are causal, and that a paramount aspect of the mental is that it is intentional. He insists, in a more controversial vein, on the existence and crucial causal role of an innate "language of thought," the development of which is genetically predetermined and comprises all of cognitive development (see Chapter 2).

It is with the modularity thesis that we are more concerned here. Fodor makes a distinction in the large between modules (roughly speaking, fast, unconscious processes structurally similar to Example B on page 4, which are *vertical faculties,* and a *central system* that handles such global, nonautomatic processes as problem solving. There is much more of experimental import in the former than the latter. In fact, Fodor's law of the nonexistence of CS is predicated on the inaccessibility of central systems to the methods of investigation of CS. The most important characteristics of vertical faculties are the following:

1. They are domain specific. We can demonstrate, for example, that there is a distinct capacity for phonology (cf. Chapter 3) that is unrelated to any other aspect of language.

2. They are genetically determined. Taking phonology again, we find a universal pace and sequencing in phonological development, independent of the particular range of stimuli that the child is experiencing.

3. They are associated with distinct neural structures. A lesion in the posterior perisylvian sector disrupts assem-

bly of phonemes into words (Damasio & Damasio, 1992), leading to the obvious conclusion that this neural structure is related to that task. Near the sylvian fissure is the structure responsible for the grouping of words into sentences—that is, for syntax. The viewpoint of this book, contra Lakoff and Edelman (cf. Chapter 3) is that these points about the autonomy of aspects of the language faculty are well taken.

Fodor's terminology has proven a little confusing, in that he speaks a great deal about input systems, leading some researchers to believe that he is talking solely about perceptual processes. Let us keep it in mind that this is not the case as we continue.

4. The operation of input systems is mandatory: Once we know a language, we can't possibly hear it as noise again.
5. Input systems are fast, as anyone specializing in computer speech recognition can tell. Sampling must be done at about 40 KH$_z$ for CDs.
6. They are informationally encapsulated; that is, they don't "know" anything about the higher cognitive functions being executed.
7. Only the output of an input system is available to consciousness.

And so on. It behooves us to make a few points: First of all, as Jackendoff (1987) pointed out, the original modularity thesis doesn't allow for the existence of reading, because the visual module is communicating directly with language-specific lexical (word) information. Second, there must be more than one type of central system in order to cater to the different types of intelligence that exist (interpersonal, bodily kinesthetic, sport and dance), and so on. However, these are not the main issues I wish to confront, important though they are.

The principal issue is that Fodor makes claims that cover a variety of disciplines: developmental psychology (claim 2), neuroscience (Claim 3). In short, he needs support from the variety of disciplines that comprise CS. Second, even the glimpse we've just had at the range of nonvertical modules that might exist indicates that his caveats about studying them are not well-placed. In fact, it makes his work prone to trivialization. We could spend all our research time finding psychological processes conforming to his criteria for vertical, call the rest horizontal and thus beyond our ken, and leave it at that. We can regard Fodor's system as an interesting hypothesis about the nature of cognition that may or may not prove of heuristic value. It is a good example of the activity of philosophy of mind, as outlined above. Fodor's latest set of views are as provocative as ever. We already saw an outline; let's see the details. He refuses to admit the existence of a knowledge level in cognition. In conjunction with this is an insistence that all views of semantics dependent to any extent on the existence of such a level are just plain wrong. The knowledge is encoded on the lexicon and the development of cognition is manifest *a fortiori* in that of the lexicon. The only view of objectivity he will countenance is semantic functionalism; in the manner suggested by Skinner, reference is achieved only by lawful covariance between external event and sign. Asked for an example, Fodor is stumped. Sitting rather uneasily with this view is an unrecanted innatism; the words that are the concepts are learned by the unfolding of an innate germ of language. And, yes, Fodor will seriously argue that such concepts as quarks and black holes are pointers to innate such concepts. It is ultimately a mystical view; the child, from birth, is a microcosm of the universe.

Fodor takes time out to excoriate Ray Jackendoff and other sentimentalists of knowledge. (Were anthropologists like Hutchins not guilty of infinite regress, the issue would not arise; knowledge, a la Piaget in Chapter 2, is *a fortiori* internalization. However, this operation in turn requires a mind that can somehow divine precisely the salient features of the environment without previously being in contact with it.) Jackendoff insists that a word like "keep" will change meaning with change in the semantic field in which it's used. The key to their disagreement for Fodor is that semantic fields can't exist; for Jackendoff, it is the protean nature of words like keep. It weighs in the latter's favor that he does not return as empty-handed as his opponent, without examples.

Mind In Philosophy: Summary

We're now going to review the notions of mind that have surfaced in this chapter. We do so again in Chapter 9. As we review them, we'll again find that to propose a notion of mind is necessarily to posit a set of relationships between mind and world, subject and object. We conclude by restating the theoretical framework of this book with respect to these issues.

The first coherent notion of mind we encountered was the Pythagorean notion that such formal systems as number were the truest reality. The link between mentally representing a number and the external reality pointed to was assumed to be direct. Reality was coherent and best described in terms of natural numbers, which are easily mentally represented. The Pythagorean heretic who proved that the square root of 2 could not be expressed as A/B where A and B are natural numbers apparently met with a boating accident.

Platonism is even more extreme in its idealism. Even white objects were assumed to derive their color by reflection or participation in some celestial form of whiteness. The human mind functions in this system by coming into touch, gradually more directly as one's character improves, with one of these forms (we shall have a little to say on this in Chapter 8.) Both the Pythagorean and the Platonic schools were schools of ethics as much as epistemology, and indeed regarded the two disciplines as inseparable. Surprisingly, we've seen that several modern mathematicians (Gödel and Penrose being the best examples) are avowed Platonists. How else to explain our intuitions about infinite sets, other than by proposing their Platonic existence? They certainly don't exist on earth. With the Platonic school, we find ourselves discussing the notion of Nous, or mind as an ordering principle in nature. In modern terms, we can discuss this is organismic terms with respect to progressive adaptation to an environment, or in physical terms as stabilization of energy configurations, given the first and second laws of thermodynamics, the reality of dissipative structures, and so on.

Alternatively, we can focus on mind in the act of understanding. The Aristotelian/Thomist tradition tends to objectify knowledge, assuming a rigid contrast between a subject who knows expressed in a rigidly formalized entity called knowledge (the nearest analogue we have here to mind) and objects that are known. It is not denied in this book that such a dichotomization between subject and object can exist. What is proposed, however, is that it is an occasional achievement of the person, attained with some difficulty, rather than a continual state. We progressed to Déscartes, the modern formulation of whose philosophy is due to Eccles. According to the Cartesian framework, a totally self-conscious mind floats around the head, waiting to intervene by processing the neural signals that are completely automatically delivered to it. Obviously, this fits neither with our introspective experience, because our inner gaze fails to uncover this rock of selfhood, nor with the fact that a great deal of information processing is actually done peripherally, by the sense organs themselves (cf. the discussion on J. J. Gibson in Chapter 2). In fact, the absurdities that ensue when perceptual processing is treated as being informationally of the same type as higher order mental operations, such as deduction, are so striking that Berkeley managed to squeeze God into the computational processes involved.

When you subtract God from the Berkeleyan schema, you end up with Hume's notion of mind as a sequence of now loosely, now tightly connected states. Knowledge consists of sense data with *a priori* structures facilitating the development of laws of mathematics, logic, and so on. With Kant, however, we become aware that our explanation of formal systems like these must become a great deal more sophisticated. There is a tension in Hume's account between the barren wilderness that comprises mind and the neat structure of *a priori* knowledge allowing, inter alia, causality and logic. Our concept of mind must allow for purely internal processes that structure the incoming sense data in an informationally rich way (categories). The focus of our study of mind becomes the delivery of the structure of these categories through whatever means (psychological or computational) are available. The framework of this book acknowledges that in Kant philosophical epistemology reached a summit of some kind. What would remain to be done in cognitive science in a purely Kantian interpretative context is the following:

1. To unearth the processes of development of these categories and their formal structure at all stages of their development (Chapter 2);
2. To look at how knowledge is expressed by language, and indeed how on occasion it cannot be (Chapter 3);
3. To develop some plausible neuroscientific descriptions of mind (Chapter 4);
4. To review how the formal description of mind can and cannot be implemented computationally (Chapter 5);
5. To review mind in different species and across different cultures (Chapter 6);
6. To study mind in action. We need to look in particular at how symbol systems work. As they function, we see a coalescence of a formal system, some nonsymbolic opera-

tional knowledge, other ontological knowledge relating to one's role in the world, a model of the task, and finally, attunement to the emotional aspects of the situation. We find this coalescence common to the apparently disparate worlds of language, vision, music, and mathematics (Chapter 7); and,

7. Finally, we need to discuss how all the preceding steps relate to one's conscious experience of the world and oneself (Chapter 8).

THE NOLANIAN FRAMEWORK (SO FAR)

We're adopting the mundane viewpoint here for a few reasons. First of all, it seems impossible to explain cognition without an explicit theory of the body. Second, its treatment of the mind–matter controversy is not only a sensible way to view this intractable problem, but also leads one automatically to consider cognition as a subspecies of being-in-the-world. That's where we actually want cognition—it's not some disincarnate process of the soul, but a necessary accompaniment to being alive. Therefore, we find ourselves encompassing knowing and being in a single sweep. Moreover, we now have a neat way of treating what cognitive development really consists of. It's the process of coping, embodied, progressively better with a changing environment.

The Mylesian framework involves a tripartite analysis of cognition. With respect to a given task, we can be egocentric, autistic, or intersubjective. Unquestionably, this framework demands much research: We note from Gibson in Chapter 2 and Brooks in Chapter 5 what egocentric processing can involve. We cannot speak about pragmatic aspects of language in Chapter 3 without much reference to the reality of the intersubjective world. And we also note in Chapter 2 how to specify conditions about moving from the autistic to the intersubjective realm, and vice versa. Another new problem is that of attempting to characterize the egocentric domain in experiential terms, given that it is normally not experienced consciously. That was Merleau-Ponty's (1962) major achievement in *The Phenomenology of Perception.*

We are insisting, however, that the facts of experience that he made explicit are not currently reducible in any meaningful way to mere external data, be that data neurological or behavioral. Where fault lines exist in Merleau-Ponty's work, they tend to stem from the old philosophical mistake of construing perceptual and higher order cognition as being on a continuum, or in related fashion failing to see discontinuities between the egocentric, autistic, and intersubjective domains. In general, then, we find the Kantian framework with the CS research program it implies useful as a description of explicitly symbolic, representationalist cognition. For the interrelation of body–subject to world that precedes cognition, we find Merleau-Ponty's account of great heuristic value.

FURTHER READING

For premodern philosophy, the most worthwhile text is Copleston's (1962) mammoth *A History of Philosophy*. Copleston's account of the moderns is perhaps bettered by Ayer's (1982) *Philosophy in the Twentieth Century* and Passmore's (1966) *100 Years of Philosophy*. Needleman's (1982a) *The Heart of Philosophy* is a passionate plea for a return to concern with the great game of ideas in the activity of philosophy. Kenny (1973) is a lucid introduction to Wittgenstein. Steiner (1978) performs a similar task for Heidegger, and Meyer (1982) proposes a compromise between Wittgenstein's two incarnations.

• *two* •

PSYCHOLOGY

INTRODUCTION: WHY IS PSYCHOLOGY SO DIFFICULT?

What is psychology? The answer normally given is the science of mental life. This science has in the past included behaviorism, one of the central tenets of which is that the mental is nonexistent (philosophical behaviorism) or too difficult to try and study (methodological behaviorism). What is certain is that it's not a terribly successful science, if compared to physics or chemistry. We go to counselors with a great deal of skepticism-we tend to rely on concepts from the inherited wisdom of our culture, rather than scientific psychology, when searching for insights into ourselves and others. Let's be honest, we find psychologists, particularly academic ones, in general quite a weird bunch and tend to wonder what went wrong.

There are several formal difficulties with psychology as an empirical discipline. In the first place, the subject matter has the unpleasant habit of reading what you've just written about it and may even be perverse enough to change its behavior the next time round. In that, psychology belongs to social sciences like economics. A supposedly objective appraisal of a company's chances of survival, printed in the appropriate newspaper, can often deliberately be the death knell or resurrection of that company. Similarly, psychology's supposed descriptions of what one's inner experience or behavior should be often has the effect of self-fulfilling prophecy. We notice this once more in the Chapter 8 discussion of consciousness and self.

What we're trying to do in psychology is somehow to objectify what it is to have subjective experience. That's another difficulty. Anything we write down should be universally valid and compelling. We should be able to precisely describe experience and predict the motions of the currents of psychic life. Several attempts to do this have been made of varying degrees of scientific credibility and power. There is no denying the power of Freud's system: In his analysis of sexuality, he managed to hit a spot at which a lot of us are sensitive and to build an infrastructure that included a philosophy of civilization on this. Unlike Freudianism on both counts, behaviorism has little power in this sense and huge scientific credibility (Hudson, 1972). The major problem, then, is mapping significant areas of experience in a scientific and compelling way. In this sense, Merleau-Ponty's work can be viewed as significant psychology, or, more precisely, what we discuss later as phenomenological psychology.

Moreover, psychology has the opposite problem to the emperor of children's fable: It wears too many clothes, but the spectators are unwilling to say so. Let's be honest. Were our cognitive psychology powerful enough to describe the thought processes of creative artists and mathematicians, to take but two examples, then it would have the potential to be a kind of superart and superscience. Perhaps it might be on safer ground if it claimed to explicate these processes in retrospect. It should, moreover, tell us something significant about the processes of thinking through everyday problems to solution. Were it able to do this, we would say it had ecological validity. In other words, it should, inter alia, be able to handle the type of situated cognition situation we brought up in Chapter 1. To do its task, it may have to venture outside that realm classically considered "cognitive," as we do in the treatment of affect in this chapter.

Let's review some of this argument. Psychology should tell us something certain about our experience that we didn't know before studying it. That's a very difficult task, as it turns out, because that something is going to have to be universal and nontrivial. It's fair to say that no such psychology currently exists. People tend to go to religion, or to those paraphrases of an-cient wisdom known as esteric psychologies, for that kind of psychology.

What we're concerned with here is cognition and recommendations for computational description thereof, when appropriate. At the end of this chapter we should know more about what our hypothesis of situated cognition looks like, experientially and computationally. We have much ground to cover before we get to this point.

First, we describe the history of psychology, focusing on its incarnation as experimental epistemology since the mid 19th century. Second, we review the types of methodology that have proven valid during this brief history. We then proceed to discuss what is known about perception, and the extent to which it can be distinguished from cognition. Then follows what is by far the largest section in this chapter: The one dealing with memory. We find memory to be a multifaceted phenomenon. Memory is initially viewed in terms of information-processing theory. We need to know what kind of structure it has in these terms, and also what kinds of information it actually processes. We then discuss memory in terms of how its contents got there in the first place. What is learning? How does remembering happen? How does memory relate to the organism's life itself?

Perhaps the surest way of solving a problem is through memory: that is by remembering a previous, similar case and applying its lessons. I always leave my office keys in the door! Is this the only way? Which kinds of problem-solving experience are remembered, and which are forgotten?

Moreover, is there a pattern to this forgetfulness? If so, is it simply informational overload or is there a darker, upsetting type of process at work?

Finally, are we simply the sum total of what we remember? If you'd had my experience of life in its fundamental aspects, would you be writing this book? And, vice versa, would I be reading it? We then review the theme of mind in psychology. As previously mentioned, the situated cognition approach is then mentioned. Let's get on with history!

A BRIEF HISTORY OF EXPERIMENTAL PSYCHOLOGY

Psychophysics and Behavior

First, let's look at the word *psychology* itself. It is the *logos* (study) of the psyche or soul. For Plato, as for Descartes, the soul was immortal, indestructible, and totally other to matter. For Aristotle, the soul in all organisms is their animation. In fact, it resembles a set of skills more than any disincarnate mind. For example, we say in the Aristotelian framework that humans are rational by virtue of their souls. The soul is the form of the body, in the same way as the statue's form can be distinguished from the marble that comprises it. There is thus no need in the Aristotelian framework, as we noted in Chapter 1, for agonizing over mind–matter interaction. The unitary substance of the person, the psychophysical unity, can be conceptually separated into form and matter, with its form being the soul.

We've seen that a great deal of debate in epistemology used psychological evidence as a touchstone. Berkeley commented on how perceptions weave and bob. Hume introspected and found a chasm where he expected a soul. However, it is only from the early 19th century onward that psychology began to be studied experimentally. Essentially, the sense data began to be measured in some metric or other (for instance, auditory data in decibels, frequency of tactile stimulation in Hertz) and attempts made to calibrate the felt response.

Many of the pioneers were German: Weber, Fechner, Helmholz, Herbart, Wundt. Herbart and Helmholz produced theories of unconscious process in perception. The attempt to quantify perception and sensation was called *psychophysics*. Fechner produced the first mathematical formulation of the relation:

$$S = k \text{Log} I + c$$

where S is the intensity of the sensation, k and c are constants, and I is the objective, physical intensity of the stimulus. Several consequences emerge from this. It is the first ever relation of a measurable to inner experience, and as such is sometimes regarded as the birth-cry of experimental psychology. In fact, the date on which Fechner formulated it (October 22) is sometimes celebrated by psychologists as a birthday! Second, it is a logarithmic relation between the inner and outer, one of many such we will review in this chapter.

Finally, it is a type of Pythagoreanism. Interestingly, it derived from Weber's study of just noticeable differences (jnds). These were measures of the smallest differences in external intensities that could be detected. The notion of threshold, or jnd, is central to psychophysics. Let's note that none of these scientists were actually professional psychologists, because that appellation did not yet exist. The major figure from this era, Wilhelm Wundt, was a Leipzig professor of philosophy who gave scientific demonstrations in his extremely well-attended lectures. Wundt's early concern when he formulated a scientific psychology was in creating laboratory conditions in which introspection could be objectively studied. (Let's note that we're right back with our original problem of objectively describing experience in a consensual and compelling way.)

Wundt had that German immunity to boredom that many other peoples, including excitable Celts like me, in general do not share. His goal, a psychic atomism, was in intent not far from Wittgenstein's logical atomism. Complex mental states were to be analyzed into primitive sensations and primitive elements of affect. Let's take an example. In investigating the affective aspects of rhythm, Wundt set metronomes for various patterns of rhythm (an arhythm), then laid back and observed his feelings. He postulated that his reactions could be plotted as points (x, y, z) in three-dimensional space. In other words, every sequence had particular values along the pleasure, strain, and excitement dimensions. Wundt later abandoned his scientific work to focus on the residue of wisdom encoded in culture, or folk psychology.

Perhaps this change had something to do with the limitations of his initial methodology. How could he be sure that someone else hearing the same rhythm would have the same values (x,y,z) as he? A more complicated question in introspection then arose with what was called *imageless thought*. Whereas some experimental subjects (henceforth Ss) reported thought without images, others did not. It's possible that this issue can now be resolved with respect to the extent to which one does or does not function visually. In the fledgling science of experimental psychology, it was a catastrophe. In fact, it gave the philosophical and methodological behaviorism of J.B. Watson, which we look at presently, its earliest impetus.

First, let's look at the work of another excitable Celt, William James, brother of the novelist Henry, medical doctor and philosopher. James is not really a systematizer, let alone a psychic atomist like Wundt. His major significance is that his is the first thoroughgoing, presuppositionless, and scientific (that is naturalistic) study of conscious mental life (CML). He regarded nothing in CML as outside his scope, and eventually indeed published a book titled *The Varieties of Religious Experience*. A close reading of his massive *The Principles of Psychology* reveals his acquaintance with much supposedly "modern" research on perception and its difficulties.

James characterizes consciousness as essentially simple sentience or awareness. CML is, above all, purposive and dynamic. It is to James that we owe the definition of psychology as the science of mental life. His account of his own experience (for example in getting out of bed!) is often brilliant, his neuroscientific and perceptual knowledge are still surprisingly impressive, but he did not develop principled methodologies with replicable results. This too left the door open to behaviorism, which became the dominant force in American psychology for nearly half a century.

The first and one of the most thorough behaviorists was Ivan Pavlov, whose key work focused on the salivation reflex of dogs. Salivation is normally an unconditional reflex (UCR) to an unconditional stimulus (UCS) such as the showing of meat. Let's introduce a conditional stimulus (CS) in a bell ringing before the meat is displayed. We find, to our surprise, that the CS can produce salivation, a conditional reflex (CR), even in the absence of the meat, after a training period. We now have a basis for understanding how innate inner reflexes can be adjusted to respond to processes in the world to which they were not originally attuned. In short, we have the basis for a coherent methodological behaviorism.

Nor was this the only attempt in the early 19th century to reduce cognitive operations to physiological process. It was noted, for example, that plants move toward the sun with what's called a tropism. It began to seem that a combination of tropism and adjustment of reflexes, as postulated by behaviorism, might explain much behavior. It was left to Watson to supply the polemics for this new approach to psychology, which he did remarkably well. His career ended, alas, when he fell in love with one of his students, commenting to her in a manner that upheld his integrity as a behaviorist that all his responses to her were positive, and his major achievement in his later commercial career is said to be the idea of putting the candy bars beside the cash registers in supermarkets. It's perhaps significant that two of the most reductionist intellects of all time, Watson and Auguste Comte, both fell in love unexpectedly in middle age with major changes in their careers as a result.

Watson's and Pavlov's classical conditioning is not really sufficient to explain how we invent apparently spontaneous behavior not immediately related to reflex. My writing this book and your reading it are examples. B.F. Skinner provided the more powerful notion of *operant conditioning* to explain this sort of behavior. In Skinner's system, the organism emits behavior (operants), of which are rewarded by the environment. Ordering a beer is thus rewarded, putting your hand in the bar's cash register is not. We call the differential rewarding of operants their *reinforcement*. We can decide to reinforce continually, at intervals, negatively (by punishment), or not at all. Moreover, we can change the motivation of the organism by reducing its body weight (starving it). The classical Skinnerian experiment had a pigeon in a steel box with a green light. Its pecking at the light was the reinforceable operant.

Actually this schema is quite powerful. Essentially, it boils down to the statement that for every repeated piece of overt behavior there must be some kind of reward. Combined with classical conditioning, we get an apparently all-inclusive psychology that deals only with observables.

What of large-scale coordinated activity like performing a piece of music? The behaviorist view is that this is explicable with respect to successive attempts (approximations) at achieving it being differentially rewarded. We'll see in Chapter 3 that this can't explain language acquisition and in Chapter 5 that the CS notion of mind as computation over representations provided a powerful and antagonistic alternative metaphor to behaviorism. For the moment, let's note that behavioral therapy for destructive habits has its uses.

Phenomenological Psychology

The main problem with behaviorism from an experiential perspective is precisely its exclusion of experience. It objectifies behavior as readings on dials without allowing for the richness of subjective experience, or indeed the existence thereof in any real sense. It might perhaps be just as valid to start from an analysis of the essential facts of consciousness rather than from this analysis of behavior. In fact let's invert the whole picture (schema). Let's start from an analysis of our experience, setting aside (bracketing) even the existence of the external world for the moment, and on the basis of this analysis derive the formal structure of mind. In other words, what must the structure of mind be in order for the objects we experience to exist in the form that they do? In Chapter 1, we noted Merleau-Ponty's account of what perception must be in order for cognition to occur at all in the first place, and pointed out that it was a phenomenological exercise.

Merleau-Ponty stressed embodiment, agnosticism on the mind–matter issue, intersubjectivity, and a world that had meaning associated with it for the person. Phenomenology tries to ground its account at that level of experience at which there is no distinction between subject and object (see Nolan, 1992). What we need to do now is to draw out some of the psychological correlates of this viewpoint, and the psychological research that it can involve. We note also the difficulties it has and how they can be sorted out to some extent by the computational metaphor of cognition.

First of all, a sad story. We meet Edmund Husserl in his incarnation as an AI skeptic in Chapter 5. Edmund at first sight seems something of a failure, in that both his early "psychologistic" and later phenomenological projects ended badly. This was not through any lack of brilliance on his part, and his work throws up a vast amount of insights. His first project attempted to reduce mathematics and logic to psychological processes in the manner we criticized in Chapter 1. The conclusion that this reduction is impossible Husserl found convincing: However, Kant's proposal that cognition could only be treated by having the content of experience modified by the categories was one that Husserl could not accept. In his second, phenomenological phase he was far more inclined to attempt to unearth the nature of these formal systems by examining how these other contents entered his consciousness.

However, he eventually became stumped by the fact that their entry into his consciousness varied in nature as the contexts in which this entry occurred changed. To see a chicken in a farmyard is on thing; to see a chicken on someone's head quite another. Moreover, it is impossible to become aware of the precise computational steps by which we build up objects of any description. The former problem is one phenomenology shares with AI; the latter problem is one where AI can greatly assist phenomenology in building a science of Cognition.

Yet the fact that phenomenology allows data from the precise analysis of consciousness liberates psychology to make fine distinctions in experience. For example, there is a difference between the color red as paint on a wall (volumic red) and as fire (emissive red). Moreover, we can allow ourselves to study in detail the psychological structure of concepts that we know from our experience exist. For example, Michotte's (Thinès, 1977) work on causality varied the circumstances in which one object was seen to push another systematically and noted whether Ss attributed the movement of the objects to the pushing cause. The conditions for attributing causality were thus specified. This type of influence on the basis of a controlled experiments we call *transcendental deduction*: We arrive at a conclusion concerning the nature of the human mind from carefully controlled adjustment of experimental conditions coupled with analysis of Ss' response. Transcendental deduction is valid also in the Kantian framework.

The phenomenological position allows us to consider also the troubled question of human action. We agree that people are active with others in a world with intentional significance (that is, a world that is meaningful, or in which we seek meanings). Part of this significance is the fact that we are attuned to moral decision, and cannot in fact avoid it. Moreover, we can distinguish here between experience that is actively directed outward to an external world (authentic existence) and experience that is not (autistic or inauthentic existence). The gaps we have noted in Husserl's work still stand; however, we'll find that we can fill some of them in using computational ideas and that the phenomenological account raises questions that only it can answer. As such, it must be seriously considered in any final theory of cognition (Nolan, 1992, gives another description of phenomenology).

Cognitive Psychology

Perhaps this troubling problem of subjective experience can be handled in another way. In the incarnation of cognitive psychology (CP) as cognitive science, we find ourselves explicitly equating the brain with the computer, and mind as programs running on the computer (see introduction). However, CP had a long and mainly honorable history before computing, though it played second violin to behaviorism in most academic institutions until the 1960's. In its CS incarnation, we sometimes find ourselves equating processing of internal representation of the world with subjectivity.

However, such researchers as Bartlett, Piaget, and Wertheimer were willing to grant a major causal role to mental computations long before computing was either profitable or popular. We discuss all of these researchers later in the section on memory. The problem on how to persuasively base the speculations of these researchers (active from the 1920's onward) on firm, tenable foundations awaited computing. The concepts current in their time from information theory—such as describing the amount of data that could be held in one act of awareness as seven bits—were not quite hard-nosed enough for the perceived requirements of a psychological science. As mentioned, we discuss the major concepts of CP in the memory section.

Depth Psychology

Concurrent with the trend toward experimental epistemology in the late 19th century, a different approach was taking off. It emerged essentially from psychopathology, the study of neurotic and psychotic behavior. It has given rise to the secular religion of psychoanalysis, and in doing so acquired a bad reputation. We have seen that Herbart and Helmholz had already formulated a notion of unconscious (mainly computational) processes in perception. It was left up to Freud and his followers to complete the notion of the unconscious.

Freud's original work as a physician led him, after an unfortunate period of celebrating cocaine, to study with the hypnotherapists Charcot and Breuer. Among the symptoms that he noted was *glove paralysis*, a paralysis affecting only the area of the hand. Already, enough neurology was known to debunk any physiological explanation for this—it had to be a neurotic symptom. Freud spent a life's career plumbing the depths of the psyche to discover the origins of such neuroses.

We allude to Freud's theory as a theory of learning, and forgetting, on page 109. For the moment, let's note that his central concept was that of the libido, or life-force, of which sexuality was but one manifestation. The libido expressed itself through different channels and zones of the body as development progressed. It might find that an object in the external world offered release of tension. If so, it became cathected to that object. Primary process thinking released tension by producing an image of that object; secondary process found the person engaging himself authentically with the world in order to achieve it.

Sometimes the taboos of the family or society (for example, on incest) forbade even thinking of the object. Then the going gets complicated. We've had up to now an exercise in explaining motivation that could be handled easily in an experimental epistemology. The person may attempt to conceal his desire through the object by displacement (perhaps developing a lollipop obsession), reaction formation (hating the object in question), or whatever.

What was common to all neurotic symptoms was that they could be cured only by plumbing the depths of the unconscious. One method was the analysis of dreams, the Royal Road to the Unconscious; another was getting the patient to speak unthinkingly (to free associate) until the emotionally powerful matter emerged. Freud's phenomenology of mind proposed that the psyche comprised an energy system (the Id), the conscious self (Ego), and an unconscious moral principle (the Superego) that blindly took in (introjected) the moral imperatives of the society. It was assumed that energy had to be conserved (Freud lived very much in a world of Newtonian physics), therefore, the Ego could put its life plan into motion only by stealing energy from the Id.

Jung parted from Freud on the issue of the nature of the libido. He insisted that the psyche needed food of a nature other than the purely physical: It also digested the common cultural and spiritual experiences of humankind as expressed in its culture (archetypes).

For example, archetypes can be expressed in myths like those of Oedipus, Tristan and Iseult or indeed any of the classics. These myths had at least a twofold role: Not only were they to play on psychic structure in a way that would help integrate the experience of the myth into the society in question, but they were conceived also as introducing the person to ultimate concealed reality, the *mysterium tremiendens*. The prevalence and power of myth pre-empt the possibility that it can be dismissed in any meaningful theory of cognition.

Nor can the work of our third depth psychologist, Alfred Adler, be dismissed. He was wont to see human motivation primarily as striving for power, particularly over others. In this, he was following the philosopher Nietzsche (whose epistemology is not really developed enough to be taken seriously). Even an illness, according to Adler, is an attempt to acquire increasing power in the family through the attention the patient gets. If conceived as a process of requiring increasing mastery over an environment, the power motive is an informative one, and one that cannot lightly be dismissed for our cognitional theory.

Consequently, the going has become a great deal more complicated for us. We can dispute the details of Freud's account of the libido, but never the fact that there are unconscious processes that subvert our attempts to treat memory as a two-dimensional blackboard that can be looked at straightforwardly. Orthogonal to this blackboard are unconscious structures that, independent of our volition, write some items on it and erase others from it. Moreover, we have in Freud a worked-out theory of how libido motivates one to take an interest in the external world in the first place. In Jung, we find an inevitably intricate, convoluted description of the symbols that constitute archetypal experience. Jung is trying the extremely difficult task of objectifying experiences whose external symbolic expression is the map, rather than the terrain of their lived experience. We see this in the discussion of myth in Chapter 6. Finally, Adler at least does us the service of explicating what the organism's drive for greater mastery of the environment may correspond to at the social level. We sometimes label it *cunning*.

ON THE ROLE OF AFFECT IN COGNITION. But wait! Haven't we left CS far behind? Science requires some kind of objective tough-mindedness: We're apparently examining entrails in the forlorn hope of making useful predictions. Psychoanalysis and all that: That's all feelings, and everybody knows that they're vicarious, subjective and certainly irrelevant to cognition. Well, not quite everybody. In fact, a philosopher called Ronald de Sousa (1987) actually went so far as to write a book called *The Rationality of Emotion*, the title of which, as he explained, was assumed to be a joke or an oxymoron. One hundred twenty thousand closely argued words later, one is rather convinced by de Sousa. Let's attend to his viewpoint. If he's correct, and if emotion is of cognitive importance, then CS has been ignoring a lot of critical data.

De Sousa's criterion for rationality is success: If emotion can help us function more effectively in the world then it must be regarded as successful. Consequently, rationality subsumes both truth and objectivity, both of which are subordinate to it. How can emotions, in all their variety, help us in any way? De Sousa (1987) refers to the frame problem, Berkeley's formulation of which we examined in Chapter 1. I sit at a desk typing on a Sparc 1. I am in Ottawa, Canada, it is —10° outside, and I just spilled some coffee. So what? Well, let's try and work out some consequences of this. If the network crashes, I might lose my book. If Québec's terrorist FLQ reboot, they are likely to start in Ottawa. The coffee might jam up the keyboard. . . . In fact, I am attending to changes in none of these underlying process, though any of them might become of paramount importance. The frame problem at this level is the problem of significant change. De Sousa sees the cognitive role of emotion as ensuring that one remains focused on the task at hand. In this role lies its rationality.

Put another way, how do we know that information is relevant or otherwise until we retrieve it? de Sousa (1987) sees emotions as "adjusting salience among objects of attention, lines of inquiry and possible inference patterns" (p. 203). They "supply the insufficiency of reasoning" (p. 195). However, I spilt some coffee on my new clothes and I'm getting a little petulant about that. Surely this negative emotion disproves de Sousa's contention in itself: What could the cognitive role of such an immature response possibly be? It is here that the role of emotional education enters. Emotions derive their semantics (their relation to the world, in this case), from *paradigm scenarios*—from their characteristic responses to objects in particular situations. Children are taught the correct responses to objects as diverse as carrots, football and canine excreta. Once the responses are taught, the adult can give a name to the emotion that the child associates with the situation thereafter. De Sousa argues, I think correctly, that this process of emotional education can continue throughout life. He goes as far as to propose a general rule, which is to let your emotions be appropriate to the widest possible range of appropriate scenarios. For example, one's attitude to prostitution should not change as it is presented to one in different contexts, for example, simple exploitation by client or prostitute, or social work.

All this is very much worth the detour. Cognitive science badly needs a well worked-out theory of emotion such as that supplied by de Sousa. A good recent example of how pressing this need is was supplied by Herb Simon's (1994) foray into literary criticism, where he attempted to show that CS in its current state had much to offer Literary Criticism. There is one particularly striking line in this essay, where he claims it's unnecessary to propose a formal definition of emotion, because we have all experienced it.

Really? We all have also amply experienced vision, problem solving, cognitive development, reasoning . . . in fact, it's beginning to look as if we don't have to treat anything in CS formally. The treatment of affect must be put on as firm a basis as any other causal factor in cognition (see O'Rorke and Ortony, 1994).

Interlude: The Framework Here

Nolanism as psychology accepts the primary reality of experience. The vehicle that comes closest to fully expressing this as a theory of cognition is phenomenology. Consequently, in accordance with this position, we accept the mundane reality of embodied, intersubjective experience as primary. Yet this does not in the slightest preclude any of the following:

1. The possibility of learning by forming bonds between stimuli and reinforcements, in either the operant or the classical behavioral traditions.
2. The existence of hidden depths of psychic life best expressed (as they historically have been) in myths and archetypal symbols.
3. The existence of unconscious fast computing processes that form the elements from which our higher level perception and cognition can emerge.

With phenomenology, we distinguish between autistic (inauthentic) experience and authentic, intersubjective experience that simultaneously reveals the reality of both one's psychic world and the external world. We assent also to a dimension of egocentric perception and cognition. Finally, an open mind(!) must be kept for the reality of experiences that seem to reveal a transcendent reality and selfhood just as one's mind must be open to the possibility of reductionist explanation of all experience.

METHODOLOGIES IN PSYCHOLOGY

We now draw the ideas on the valid data for psychology together with ideas on its valid framework by prescribing the types of methodology that are valid therein. More than any of the other disciplines within cognitive science, psychology is dependent on controlled experiment. However, there are other methods used that also generate acceptable data.

The first such method is naturalistic observation. This may involve observing, in the manner of Piaget, the development of children through different hypothesized stages of cognitive prowess. Alternatively, it might involve observing the behavior of a computer program that implements one or another theory of mind. Related to naturalistic observation are correlational studies. For example, students who perform well on IQ tests also tend to perform well on exams. The trend in intelligence testing has been to assume a direct correlation between IQ and academic ability. This example, however, shows both the strengths and the weaknesses of correlational studies. The obvious conclusion seems to be that one's IQ is a causative factor leading to success or otherwise in exams. However, the IQ test was actually originally designed by Binet using success in exams as the criteria for scaling the IQ factor in the first place! In other words, the problem of cause and effect can be a great deal more complicated than it immediately appears.

Not so with the full rigors of experimental method. Here, the normal set-up allows one to isolate the precise effect of a single factor. For example, we might wish to determine the effects of alcohol on memory. We set up a task (for example, remembering a list of phone numbers), an agreed dosage of alcohol, and divide the Ss into two groups. The experimental group consumes the required level of alcohol, the control group none. We then can objectify the effects of alcohol in terms of success on the memory task. The objectification in question could also include factors like reaction time, or indeed anything measurable in this sense.

We looked at the technique of transcendental deduction earlier and found it could be used in phenomenological psychology. Let's observe it now in the more straightforward Kantian framework that is its natural habitat. A well-known experiment by Saul Sternberg involved Ss learning a list of single-digit numbers (e.g., 1, 3, 4, 5 . . .). The list was presented for just a second. After a 2-second delay, a single digit was presented and the subject had to decide whether it was on the original list, signaling the decision by pulling an appropriate lever. The aim was to discover what scanning method the Ss used. There were several different possibilities:

1. An image including all the digits in question.
2. Scanning through the list until the digit in question was noted and then stopping.
3. Scanning through the whole list, continuing even after the digit in question was noticed.

Now, each of these hypotheses leads to different predictions and can thus be directly tested. For example, if Hypothesis 1 is correct, the position of the digit in the list should not matter for the speed of reaction (that is, pressing the lever), nor should the length of the list be an important causative factor. As it turns out, Hypothesis 3 fits best with the experimental data. We have Kant's program of transcendental deduction given experimental flesh and bones in this type of experiment.

A similar experiment is Sperling's test of the memory trace. In this case, a large array of letters were momentarily flashed in front of Ss:

A G U S
T A I M
T I N N

If Ss were asked to list them afterward in total (whole report), no more than four or five could be remembered. However, if Ss were cued (perhaps by an appropriate tone) the instant the display was turned off about which row they had to list, an average of more than three could be remembered. This indicates that at least nine of the letters were available in some kind of short-term storage (iconic memory). A similar situation seems to hold for hearing (echoic memory). In short, it seems that we process vast amounts of data in the first instants after perception and these data fade extremely quickly. We shall have more to say on this below. (Luria's (1969) portrait of a man forced to remember everything is worth investigating.)

A further method is an extension of naturalistic observation to allow formal experimentation. For example, we've noted that it is valid simply to examine the input-output behavior of a computer program that simulates a cognitive process. We might find it possible also to vary the input and note corresponding covariance in output (see section on equivalences in Chapter 1). Alternatively, we can study an elaborate cognitive process like language and try to decompose it into elements (cf. Chapter 3).

We also might find it necessary, particularly in the case of language, to appeal to another source of evidence—native speaker intuitions. Lacking, as we do, a Grand Unified Theory (GUT) of Language, or a single comprehensive grammar even for our *lingua franca* of English, we find it necessary to ask the domain experts (that is, speakers of the language) whether sentences are grammatical or not as the only possible usable criterion. Moreover, we find it necessary to distinguish between these speakers' hypothesized knowledge of the language, as expressed in comprehension (their competence), and their often faulty (due to tiredness, information, or other factors) overload production performance. This hypothesized perfect linguistic structure is quite near to Plato's concept of ideas and their incarnation in the human mind. Moreover, like Plato's slave boy in the Meno, every human has this vast competence.

For the reasons given in the history section, we have omitted introspection. However, the type of phenomenological analysis achieved by minds as acute as Merleau-Ponty's must also qualify as a methodology. The type of data that they report must also be included. Again, the main criterion has to be consensual validation. We have not yet constructed a truly objectivist scientific psychology (and perhaps it is both impossible and undesirable). In order to ensure that we are catering for all the facts of mental life, we must allow data that, though collected experientially, are universal.

PERCEPTION

Perception and Cognition

The distinction between perception and cognition initially seems as well-defined as the distinction between seeing a tree and thinking about a crossword clue. However, things are in actual fact a great deal more complicated. In this section on perception, we discuss several different schools, each of which has a distinct viewpoint on the perception cognition issue. On the one hand, we're going to note that J.J. Gibson's school of ecological optics assigns to perception a lot of the higher order informational processes that might at first blush be considered the province of cognition; on the other hand, the constructionist account grants to perception only the task of supplying an informational characterization (in terms as basic as the binary code that computers use) of the scene viewed, with cognition supplying the mechanisms truly to process the scene, extract objects, and so on.

Related to this issue is the extent to which perception affects cognition, and vice versa. In a famous set of observations, it was noted that pygmies who grew up in jungle environments without sharp edges failed to interpret photographs, seeing black-and-white photos only as shades of gray (cf. Chapters 6 and 7). Is this a perceptual problem, a cognitional problem, or a problem of their interaction? Likewise, our language might predispose us to make certain fine distinctions in our environment (cf. Chapter 3) that are not immediately salient for speakers of another language. One North American aboriginal people—the Inuit—famously has about 14 (admittedly compound) words for different types of snow. Has cognition now affected perception?

We've noted that perception in Merleau-Ponty's schema is the background for acts of mind. Let's look at two other possibilities for characterizing the perception cognition relationship:

1. Perception is that which delivers the data on which cognition acts computationally (the constructionist account).
2. Cognition involves acts that are conscious or potentially conscious (remember our account of eye focusing as the latter in Chapter 1). Perception involved unconscious informational processes.

Therefore, such processes as syntactic parsing (see page 29) are perception according to Account 2 and cognition according to Account 1.

In fact, the debate is ultimately quite pointless. What matters is that somewhere in the long, intricate path from sensation much computational processing is being done. Whether this is called *perception* or *cognition* is really irrelevant. There is one sense, however, in which we could possibly use the distinction. We could reserve perception for acts that explicitly interrelate the subject and her environment, and cognition for (usually conscious) acts that allow the subject to transcend her environment by making plans. These plans, in turn, may explicitly involve changing the environment (I use this terminology in Chapter 9). We can then add that acts that formerly were cognition can become subsumed by perception. Let's consider tuning an instrument. It normally requires a conscious act of will for a beginner to detect differences of anything less than a quarter tone or so. Yet, once sensitivity enters the habitual structure of one's mind, it seems appropriate to place it more toward the perception than the cognition end of the continuum.

For some cognitivists like Jerry Fodor, this type of schema is unacceptable. We noted in Chapter 1 that he insists on certain insulating attributes of vertical modules, specifically that they be domain specific and informationally encapsulated. Perception is the province of these dumb, mutually independent vertical modules; cognition is the realm of a central system. In fact, as Jackendoff (1987) points out, Fodor goes to great lengths to separate the two: The reason seems to be to allow valid (veridical) cognition, immune to perceptual illusion. My feeling is that the burden of proof is very much on Fodor's side here. In order to establish his system, he needs to catalogue these modules (for example, phonology or syntax), demonstrate their encapsulation and indicate what is left for a central system to do. He then has to prove that no top-down influence from this well-defined central system to the vertical modules exists. Moreover, some of these modules are going to be multimodal; for example, motion data is represented with the aid of interactions between visual and somatomotor data (Trotter & Burnod, 1992). Head movements are registered by a variety of sensory modalities, including the vestibular. From an early age, children show ability to transfer knowledge learned in one sensory modality to others (Stréri & Lécuyer, 1992, show that from the time they are two months old, children can visually recognize objects previously only touched). The lack of top-down influences seems even harder to demonstrate: In vision, to take one example, the number of neurons carrying messages from central to peripheral areas of the cortex far outnumbers the reverse. We noted in Chapter 1 that the modularity thesis in its undiluted form doesn't even allow reading.

The form of modularity that seems tenable is at best one which allows modules to work across different sensory modalities and be identified with translation processes like those that integrate at the syntactic or phonological level. In fact, Jackendoff (1987) sees in this a way to allow greater freedom for the cognition–perception interaction than Fodor will allow. Undoubtedly, some of Fodor's notions, like those of encapsulation and domain specificity, are useful. However, it does seem that risk of trivialization is always there. More importantly, given volumes of corroborative data that, Fodor, in contrast to other researchers lacks, it seems worthwhile to continue doing CS in the hope of a more adequate theory of mind emerging.

Transduction and Encoding

Whatever one's position on the perception–cognition question, one must accept a separate stage at which incoming sense data are converted (transduced) into patterns of neural impulses that accurately encode the objective events mapped by the sense data. The precision of the encoding depends on the requirements of the organism. The human capacity for color vision is not shared by lower animals; conversely, bats are attuned to auditory frequencies that we humans will never hear. The palette of our sensory experience is structured initially by the evolutionary needs of the organism and, in the human case, secondarily by cultural development. For example, painters can detect gradations of color that nonpainters cannot.

Let's focus for the moment on the bare facts of transduction. Sense organs are cells spread over areas of the body that are specialized for the conversion of specific patterns of energy flow into neural event. The main senses are visual, auditory, olfactory (smell), tactile, gustatory (taste), heat, and various interoceptive and proprioceptive. Interoception focuses on inner sensation of the process of digestion. Proprioception involves feelings of movement (kinesthesia) and features feedback, particularly from muscle systems.

Much of the data used by sense organs is mechanical in nature. Obviously, touch and kinesthesia involve purely mechanical data. More surprisingly, auditory data are mediated by mechanical means. Sound comprises energy bursts that propagate through the air (or with less ease, other media such as water) as longitudinal waves. These bursts cause the eardrum to vibrate (see Figure 2.1), and these vibrations are transmitted through the bones of the middle ear (hammer, anvil, and so on) before reaching the basilar membrane. At this point, the frequency of the original energy burst is now being articulated as movement of fluid. This movement in turn causes hair cells to shear, resulting in bursts of neural activity which are processed.

In vision, however, the process is quite different. The hundred million cells in the retina (see Figure 2.2) divide into rods and cones, which respectively cater to black/white and color vision. Essentially, the transduction involves light falling on photosensitive material and electrical discharge causing neural activity. Moreover, a great deal of computation is going on at the retina in order to detect objects in the stimulus array. The outlines of objects correspond to points of maximal change of light intensity.

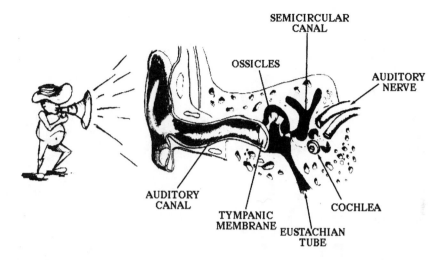

FIGURE 2-1

At the retinal level itself, without any reference to higher cerebral activity, a process (analogous to use of the Laplacean operator on a two-dimensional Gaussian distribution) implements detection of the outlines of objects.

The data are quite different for the other senses. The major point of interest with respect to cerebral activity is that in general, sensations that are close together in their energy profile have contiguous encodings in the cortex. The exception to this general rule seems to be olfaction, where the representation more closely resembles the formal neuron systems used in connectionism (cf. Chapter 4). *Topological mapping* is the name we give to the general rule.

Encoding is the process whereby properties of the initial energy patterns are preserved in neural impulses. Now that we've left transduction, the going becomes a lot more controversial. J.J. Gibson would play down the encoding and higher cortical stages on the basis that the information is already there in the sense data. We'll see that his analysis involves redefining the stimulus to involve structured sensation over time; for example, the sum of the varying perspectives on a chair as one moves around it is the stimulus for Gibson.

This argument of Gibson's can be extended to explain other perceptual constancies. We manage to maintain in our minds the real size of a football even as it is travelling very quickly away from us (size constancy). Gibson would argue that this realization is no

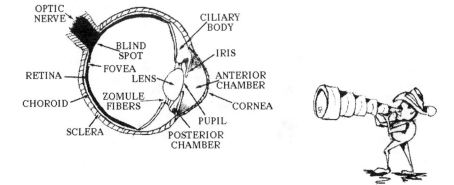

OPTIC NERVE

BLIND SPOT

FOVEA

RETINA

LENS

CHOROID

ZOMULE FIBERS

SCLERA

CILIARY BODY

IRIS

ANTERIOR CHAMBER

CORNEA

PUPIL

POSTERIOR CHAMBER

FIGURE 2-2

longer paradoxical if we bear in mind that the stimulus is the football moving over time in a certain context. Likewise, shape constancy holds for the chair we keep referring to color constancy is the fact that a car will somehow contrive to seem much the same color under a sodium arc light as in broad daylight.

The major uncontroversial point in this section, then, is the process of transduction from energy bursts to neural impulses. We can simulate this process mathematically by use of the Fourier transform. Fourier's theorem essentially states how any regularly occurring oscillation (like speech) can be mathematically mapped. Having done this, we have a tractable description with which to work computationally. We must bear in mind, however, that we lack a lot of the biological equipment with which nature simplifies these tasks.

Ecological Optics

The work of J.J. Gibson, the founder of this school, is enjoying a new lease on life in studies of vision. His study of such matters as optic flow—how perception of the texture of one's environment changes as one moves—seems in retrospect to have great heuristic value. Gibson's work is also extremely hospitable to the Mylesian viewpoint. Let's go through its main points.

First of all, Gibson stresses that the proper object for psychological study is the organism plus environment regarded as a single system. We've come across this point before in that we've established that mind can be studied only with regard to such a system, and we've added that we also have to study the development of organism environment interactions. I wish to flag how central this thesis is: In Piaget, we're going to discuss it as cognitive psychology; in neuroscience, as neural Darwinism (the notion that groups of neural processes compete with each other to have intercourse with the world, with only the winning group surviving to do so); finally, even with respect to the psychology of selfhood, we find a need for such an encompassing view of subject–object relations.

The organism is thought of as attuned to objective properties of the environment, rather than as driftwood in a tempest of stimuli. Let's take Berkeley's frame problem again. I move around the room, and my perception of my desk continually changes. How can I extract the desk itself from this flux? Let's change the issue completely, because this problem is almost intractable. Surely the stimulus that I process is actually the changing array of sensations, spread over time? Is it not reasonable to assume that there are higher order invariants that remain constant despite the dance of input data? In fact, Gibson devoted his experimental work to characterizing these invariants: One such set was connected with disappearing objects.

It's obvious that Gibson's position is analogous to philosophical realism. Objects are assumed to produce likenesses of themselves in one's brain in some sense directly (see Figure 2.3). The notion of objects being mediated by representations of themselves in the brain that structure how they are perceived is abandoned. We end up with Cartesian paradoxes if we posit the existence of these representations. There are obvious philosophical difficulties with realism, in that we find ourselves asking whether all possible perspectives on an object are equivalent objective properties of that object. In particular, how can error then occur? In psychology, we find ourselves asking how illusions such as the Müller-Lyer illusion (where two lines of equal length are perceived as being of different length because of their context) can occur, if we are so perfectly adapted to our environment. Gibson's answer to the problem of error is that it normally occurs within peripheral, as distinct from focal, vision; in distal, as distinct from proximal, perception. Illusions he dismisses as artifacts of contrived experimental set-ups that separate the organism from its environment.

The organism is not conceived of as particularly active in perception. It may, for reasons endogenous to (within) itself, decide to pick up one type of information rather than another at one speed rather than another. Quite simply, if hungry it will look urgently

FIGURE 2-3

for food. In the case of vision, the information is all there, objectively, in the light itself, and endogenous factors do not affect it.

In view of Gibson's (1979) lack of explicit reference to philosophy, the parallels with Merleau-Ponty are striking. For Merleau-Ponty and other phenomenologists, the world for the subject is as full of meaning (affordances) as it is for Gibson. Both groups also insist that three-dimensional space is not constructed by the subject, but given from birth. Gibson also refuses to make mind–matter distinctions, and likewise will not comment about mind in the abstract apart from an environment. In fact, we end up with a schema where again the problems of perception and cognition are inextricable from consideration of Being-in-the-world.

Like Merleau-Ponty, Gibson has difficulty in providing a comprehensive framework in which his brilliant work on the analysis of perception can be combined with a coherent view of higher order cognition. In Gibson's view, all potential uses of objects are said to be directly afforded. The pen affords writing, the car driving. A *reductio ad absurdum* of this viewpoint might claim that therefore blank sheets of paper should afford composition of *War and Peace*. It is here that the Mylesian framework attempts to redress the imbalance. Gibson's perceptual work, like Brook's mobotics in Chapter 5, is conceived of as a brilliant analysis of egocentric mentation (working of mind). The intersubjective level requires a different set of concepts.

It was assumed by many perception scientists that because of the alleged difficulty of experimental design that it provoked, Gibson's work was a heuristic dead end and neurophysiologically implausible. Both charges should be dropped. Gibson's framework insists that invariants should be described, but this is very much an empirical task at which he himself made much progress. On the neurophysiological level, it may seem at first glance implausible that objects can radiate impressions of themselves that inform the structure of processes in the brain. However, Karl Pribram's holonomic theory, which we outline in Chapter 4, allows the Gibsonian framework a neural reality. For Pribram, perception involves a coming into synchrony of the microprocesses of the brain with the activity of particular sense organs. Pribram allows that this synchrony may be mediated through action at several different levels (rather like Dyer's schema, which we explore in the section on connectionism in Chapter 4). He insists that a transformational realism of this sort is neurologically plausible and does violence neither to the integrity of brain science nor to the realist ethos.

Let's conclude by noting that Gibson's seems an extremely valid framework for egocentric mentation, and compatible in both its ethos and its specifics with Merleau-Ponty. Likewise, Gibson shares the French phenomenologist's difficulties in encompassing symbolic and perceptual mentation in a single framework. So far as their work is testable, it has in fact been verified. Children seem to have an intuition of 3-D space as early as can be ethically tested (Stréri & Lécuyer, 1992), their ocular movements (but not control) for object tracking are formed early, and higher order invariants do exist. However, children's symbolic behavior takes longer to develop and for that type of behavior we need to look at the work of Piaget.

The Gestalt Approach

We're going to find in our discussion of problem solving that the Gestalt approach has much to contribute to debate in that area. For the moment, we'll focus on what it has to say about the processes normally labeled *perception*. In the first place, Gestalt (whole group) psychology focuses on whole qualities in perception. Take, for example, our perception of the shape, in Figure 2.4 (a pub variation of the Kanisza triangle illusion): We cannot but see them as an incomplete circle, triangle, or star, rather than as a chaos of elements. Moreover, imagine Brahms' first symphony being played in D minor rather than its normal C minor. What's the difference between the two performances? Well, none actually, apart from that due to the specific qualities of the instruments. The "whole property" that dominates our hearing of the themes of the symphony (or indeed any melody, irrespective of the key to which it is transposed) takes precedence over the details.

FIGURE 2-4

Moreover, the Gestalt school argues that it is only with reference to whole properties that many apparently psychologically elementary processes have any meaning. We cannot even talk of generalization, a crucial concept for behaviorism, without some notion of a whole quality. Let's imagine that a Pavlov dog has learned to salivate to a tone of 256Hz. A tone of 240Hz is sounded and the salivation again occurs. In fact, it is found that generalization works for a large segment of the auditory spectrum. Gestaltists argue that even this shows a degree of concept formation, of the appreciation of a whole quality. Perception is seen as governed by laws of *Prägnanz* (good organization), which, for example, can correctly command the "closure" of the rectangle and circle in Figure 2.4.

The attack gathers even more force when directed at problem solving, as we note presently.

The Constructionist Approach

This approach insists that we construct objects from a chaos of shifting impressions. We have noticed time and again the paradoxes to which this leads with respect to both the frame problem and the Cartesian homunculus. Perhaps the failure of AI systems based on constructionism is the most telling argument against it— we dwelled on this point in Chapter 1.

MEMORY

We cannot ultimately separate memory, learning, the flow of consciousness, problem solving, and indeed identity, which is bound up to a large extent with one's lived experiences. Each single mental act involves many past such acts. Similarly, the field of consciousness for two individuals with identical external stimuli may be completely different. Their memories structure their experiencing of these stimuli in ways that result in vastly different subjective experience. An example to which we keep returning is the difference between a novice's and an expert's experience of music.

As mentioned, we are going to look at memory from a range of different perspectives. First of all, in what sense is memory a storage area, and what kind of store is it? Second, we talk about memory and learning. Third, we ask how we can creatively best make use of our lived experiences in problem solving. We mention behaviorism in passing. Fourth, in relation to this, we ask whether there are patterns to forgetting, to the inability to solve problems whose successful solution forms part of our past experience. Finally, we ask to what extent we are our experiences. That is, to what extent are we similar to others who have experienced similarly? This question has been partially addressed in Chapter 1; it will occupy us also in Chapter 8.

Memory as a Store

When viewing memory as a store, a computational metaphor is extremely useful. In computing, we make a distinction among storage media. RAM (random access memory), which is the primary workspace of the computer; and ROM (read only memory), which contains a few commands without which it is impossible to operate the computer. Similarly, we make a distinction in human memory between long-term memory, conceived of as backup storage, and short-term memory, which is a workspace. In the meantime, certain ROM commands remain continually present (for example, don't fall off heights, nothing can be in two places at the same time).

We need also note how our experience is conditioned by our memory of past events. Moreover, as we act on (effect) the world, our directives to our motor effectors have to be informed by feedback from our sense organs. Sperling's work showed that we process a great deal more data than we become aware of. The filtering process somehow presents a coherent world to us from the tidal waves of data processed. Were we forced to attend to this tidal wave, we would lose our ability to cope. At present, we're concerned with this filtering only in informational terms. In Chapter 8, we ask whether one of the principal cognitive functions of selfhood is actually to maintain a necessary distinction between relevant material (conceived of as meaningful) and irrelevant (conceived of as nonsense, or not even noticed).

Short-term memory (STM) is usually cited as holding about seven items (the seven wonders of the world, the seven tasks of Hercules, a seven-digit phone number). We can up its capacity, and the informational throughput of the whole system, by chunking. For example, Morse code operators gradually learn to chunk the dots and dashes into letters and these, in turn, into words. STM might also be divided into separate processes for linguistic and nonlinguistic knowledge.

In fact, arguments rage as to whether, and how, all memory can be analogously divided. Is there a visual as distinct from a verbal code in memory? Alternatively, it seems a priori likely that cognition is ultimately implemented by an unelaborate code of neural impulse (but see below and Chapter 4 to get a more complicated picture). Can it therefore be concluded that the language of thought is monolithic and simple, the yes–no (binary) answers given by neural firing?

Yet another possibility exists, and it is the viewpoint taken here. The brain, in its attempts to maximize adaptation of the organism to its environment, is willing and able to implement systems from a whole spectrum of different possibilities. These include visual (Kosslyn, 1994) and verbal codes, purely propositional (yes no) codes, codes that use spreading activation (by tagging neural impulses with cues as to their purpose and effectiveness), and purely symbolic systems. (*Codes* is meant in a broad sense here to include systems of production and transformation of representations.)

The evidence at the moment for the multiplicity of codes hypothesis comes from observation of the tagging type of neural firing, observation of the development of vision in infants that shows an opportunistic quantum leap from a probabilistic guess to a pure symbol at a critical stage, and the implementation of the hypothesis in the connectionist architectures discussed in Chapter 4 and in much greater detail by Dyer (1989). Brain science shows a lateralization of verbal and mathematical ability in the left hemisphere and spatial abilities in the right hemisphere in over 90% of those surveyed. Yet so little is known about higher level cognition that no final conclusions are near being drawn about its location.

Effectors can perform extremely complicated memory tasks like musical performance (cf. Chapter 7). Here we have enormously intricate interactions from a variety of sources. We'll finish this section by noting that many of these manual skills are unconscious. It would be impossible to perform music, or even drive a car, while being fully focally conscious of every movement. The degree to which we can become conscious even of verbal or analytic skills itself varies greatly from person to person.

Memory and Learning

It is generally agreed that it is impossible to study knowledge without taking its development into account (Kirsh, 1991). This goes as much for knowledge manifest in an organism's increasing adaption to and mastery of its environment as for knowledge implemented as computer programs. In this section we're going to examine some different statements of the learning process.

INNATISM. The first such notion states in effect that learning does not occur. The tradition of innatism, dating as far back at least as Plato, holds that knowledge acquisition is simply the unfolding of some inborn structures. Whether these structures are the property of an immortal soul free from the dictates of space and time, as Plato thought, or the protein-synthesis commands of the DNA double helix, as modern-day innatists like Chomsky and Fodor claim, is irrelevant to us here. Logically, the claims of the innatist position are independent of the precise implementation of the mental structures postulated (be it a soul, a brain, or a computer).

Essentially, innatism contends that acquisition of a concept on the basis of experience alone (claimed by empiricism as valid) cannot actually occur. Innatists insist that the concept must already be there in some germinal form. In other words, it is impossible logically to derive a whole plethora of abstract concepts (set intersection, logical inference, and causality, to name but a few) from experience. They must be innate. It will be noticed that most of these abstract concepts are handled by Kant in his notion of categories. Piaget, in turn, argues that even categories require development, but that this development involves species-specific interaction with the environment that is the lot of every human being. Consequently, we have in Piaget a synthesis of the innatist and empiricist position. The knowledge corresponding to categories is learned through interaction with the environment, but this interaction is inevitable (Furth, 1981).

Until recently, little was known about the infant's perceptual abilities. For every innatist like Merleau-Ponty, who posited a great deal of knowledge being present from birth, an equal but opposite empiricist like Locke claimed contrariwise. It was noted on page 73 that the current evidence seems to favor precocious abilities at least in the nonsymbolic sphere. An early capacity for depth perception in infants was demonstrated by a set of studies by T.G.R. Bower (1979) that featured an artificial visual cliff. Young children show surprising capacities for transfer of knowledge between perceptual modes (for example, an object previously only seen may also be recognized when being felt and not seen), categorization, and casual relations. Similarly, face recognition has been demonstrated in 3-day-old infants (de Schonen, Burnod, & Deruelle, 1992).

However, the situation is a little more complicated than this. This type of knowledge is egocentric and shared with precocious animals (some of whom are far advanced compared with human infants of equivalent ages; indeed, there may be a strong argument that human infants need to have as few as possible of their behaviors, as distinct from their sensory abilities, set in stone in order to learn optimally later). Children may demonstrate an ability to correlate an image generated by camera tracking of their leg movements with the proprioceptive data thus generated when they are as young as five months. Yet the same children fail to recognize themselves in the mirror until they are 19 or 20 months old (Baudonnière, Lepecq, & Jouen, 1992).

It seems that there is a discontinuity between the development of that egocentric knowledge and intersubjective symbolic knowledge that is uniquely our preserve. We discuss this implicitly in outlining Piaget's theory of development.

FREUD AND LEARNING. We've already discussed the major outlines of Freud's theory. In a later section we focus on phenomena like repression, which cause suppression of memories. The essential mechanism postulated for the positive process of learning is conceived of as cathexis. The range of objects that are cathected is gradually increased until something like the full adult awareness of the world emerges. The consequence we draw from this is that learning involves affect. The objects chosen often have intricate emotional meanings. Furthermore, they can be chosen with respect to the perceived needs of development of one's self, however, this self is conceived. Our cognitive theory excludes affect at its peril. Whatever the ultimate validity of psychoanalysis as therapy, the causal role of affect in cognition cannot be ignored.

THE DEVELOPMENTAL PSYCHOLOGY OF JEAN PIAGET.

Overview. Jean Piaget was born in Neuchatel, Switzerland in 1896, and died in 1980. His earliest paper, published when he was 11, was about the sighting of an albino sparrow. His formation was originally as a biologist, specializing in mollusks. In the early part of this century, a school of philosophy led by the great Henri Bergson (who had an exotic mix of Irish, French, and Jewish ancestry) focused on biology as a possible key to understanding some philosophical problems. Piaget quickly homed in on this approach.

From the biological perspective, knowledge must somehow increase the organism's adaptation to its environment. From the philosophical point of view, to study the development of knowledge in a natural setting seems a priori a worthwhile project. Piaget further argued that this development would reveal much about the essential nature of knowledge, as distinct from just amassing details about the vagaries of its development.

With this in mind, he began to study the cognitive development from infancy of his own and other children. This became his life's work. His first book, *The Language and Thought of the Child* (1926), secured his international fame before he was 30.

Piaget described his work as *genetic epistemology* and as such it is obviously relevant to cognitive science. His relevance is becoming greater rather than less as the years pass. Piaget's is the only fully worked-out theory of cognition that traces the growth of knowledge from an infantile state conceived of as unseparated from the environment (undifferentiated) to full adult logical competence. We've noted that it is currently accepted that intelligence, whether natural or artificial, cannot properly be studied apart from its development, which increases Piaget's relevance. Moreover, his insistence on viewing the growth of knowledge with respect to the exploration of an environment by an active organism gives his work a new urgency (cf. the short account of Brooks in Chapter 5). He alone this century has had the courage and genius to plot a detailed route from biology to logic.

Not surprisingly, given its scope, many of the details of Piaget's work are wrong. His experiments tended to be badly designed and used far too small a sample size, and like many others who have tried to replicate him, I've found myself disagreeing with his results, his interpretation of the results, or both. Earlier in his career, as we see later, he had an unhealthy obsession with logic. Interestingly, he later recanted, and proposed that psychology pursue an (unfortunately unspecified) "logic of meanings." He failed also to appreciate the autonomy and power of the human linguistic apparatus (Chapter 3). Were not his system flawed, there would be nothing left for cognitive scientists to do! Let's press ahead with a short description of his work.

A GLOSSARY OF PIAGET'S KEY CONCEPTS.

Equilibration: The tendency for an organism to seek both stability and a higher degree of adaptation to its environment. This was regarded by Piaget as the fundamental cognitive drive. Related to it are two more modern concepts: *The principle of rationality* insists that the cognitive system above all attempts to maximize the organism's adaptation. Maturana's *autopoeisis* today gives a more biological description of the same process (Varela, 1988).

Assimilation: This is the use of an old action or representation to deal with an object. It is consequently different to

Accommodation which adapts the cognitive system.

Decentration: This refers to problem solution by focusing on an aspect of the problem heretofore ignored for whatever reason. For example, you lose your car keys and you *know* that you gave them to your partner. You spend hours grilling your partner as to exactly when and where you gave them and refuse to budge on the issue. Suddenly you decenter and realize they're in your jacket pocket. This is an example of a type of decentration called

Subject-object differentiation: where Solution is achieved by considering oneself as part of a more encompassing picture, fleeing the egocentric domain.

Structures: These are (mainly) logical systems that are internally consistent and allow the subject to systematically deal with the outside world. Arithmetic is one such system. Piaget criticized the Gestaltists for assuming the existence of such systems without describing their genesis, and behaviorists for ignoring systems altogether (structure without genesis, genesis without structure).

Schemes: These are stereotyped sets of actions that perform particular tasks. A first example of such a scheme is the infant's looking for and finding its mother's breast. They must be distinguished from the

Schema (plural: *schemata*): a static memory structure reflecting some aspect of the world. An example is the schema that represents entering a restaurant. We remember that the stereotyped sequence of actions involves waiting to be brought to a table, perusing a menu, ordering, and so on. This notion was adapted by the Schankian school in its notion of a script (see Chapter 5). Bartlett produced an analogous concept.

Operational knowledge: This refers to knowledge that originates from one's physical interaction with the world. It begins with simple actions. These actions can then become internalized. For example, a child first might have to physically move around objects of various sizes in order to put them in order (seriate them). At a later stage of development, it is possible to do this by means of mental manipulation of symbols representing those objects. However, Piaget argues that a further internalization allows mental seriation of seriation, giving the operation of permutation. For Piaget, this kind of development is the essence of cognitive development and can in fact explain acquisition of language and mathematics, inter alia. Internalization of actions begets symbols in this manner, which is inadequate for language development (cf. Chapter 4).

Representation: With each stage in the development of operational knowledge comes also a distinct way of representing reality. Initially, the world may be represented only in terms of actions one can perform on it (enactive representation). Second, elementary mental images might be used (iconic representation). Finally, reality may be fully symbolically represented.

Innatism: We have noted that Piaget provides a via media between innatism and empiricism. He argues that there are certain ways in which a specific species must act upon the world. The knowledge arising from these experiences, though empirical in process, is genetically inevitable.

Conservation: This is almost as central to Piaget's work as equilibration. He argues that at a certain age, which varied from culture to culture but is usually around seven years, a quantum leap in cognition appeared. The child goes from conceiving of change as unidirectional and irreversible to seeing it as reversible. For example, Piaget argues that before conservation, if liquid was put in a broader beer glass, the child would assume that there now was less liquid. With conservation, perception becomes informed by abstract notions like mass, length, and quantity rather than by sensory impressions. Conservation is a milestone in cognitive development; with its advent comes number and a better logic as well as the notions of the last sentence. Let's examine number. For Piaget, it's conceived of as the operational synthesis of seriation and coordination. Until this synthesis occurs, number is inaccessible to the subject. Many of his experiments demonstrated, at least to his satisfaction, that children did not even have part–whole relationships until conservation. When shown a group of both somnolent and active cows, children would answer *yes* if asked whether there were more sleeping cows than cows. Similarly they agreed that there were fewer beads if a row of beads was compressed in length but more were removed.

Apart from egocentrism, to be presently discussed, conservation status is the most controversial of Piaget's concepts. The "sleeping cows" problem has been debunked as a linguistic confusion. Nobody has managed to get children to perform as badly as Piaget on the mathematical/logical/concept-formation tasks he uses. Yet there is a breakthrough in cognition around the age Piaget proposes, a fact that has remained intact through the voluminous discussion. Where Piaget seems to have erred is in his obsessive attempts to describe it in purely logical terms, and as the advent of a Kantian category. It may be more parsimoniously described as the child becoming able to reflect on her cognitive processes and detect that they are objectively mismatched to reality. We can describe it as a quantum leap in consciousness rather than logic (Flavell, Green & Rosch, 1986). The terms of description are examined again in Chapter 8.

Egocentrism: This term at first sight covers a much wider range of phenomena than our comparatively mild notion of the egocentric mode of cognition. We see in Chapter 9 how they're identical if we reinterpret autistic mentation to include also Piaget's notion of the egocentric. In Piaget, it referred to a tendency to take one's own view of things as the only possible view. As such, it should sound depressingly familiar. However, it also could express itself in adolescent messianism, the tendency of the recently pubertal to convert us all to their views now that they can themselves think. It has been misrepresented as willful ignorance (Sugarman, 1988)— what Piaget wished to point out was rather a state in which children failed in differentiating themselves from the external world. Sugarman's critique of Piaget is so pointed, and so explicitly directed at his notion of egocentrism, that we shall take some time out here to examine it.

There has been a great deal of experimentation on egocentrism. Children of 19 months *will* carefully turn an object around so you have precisely the same view of it as they do. However, Piaget's experiments showing children as old as eight making similar perceptual errors have been exposed as badly designed. This is not the main plank of Sugarman's accusations. Piaget, she argues, is in turn charging infants with egocentrism. In order to justify this charge, he must establish that the children have what amounts to full adult competence in the area in question, but for some reason choose not to use it. However, this is not Piaget's position, nor those of his fellow travelers like Polanyi (1958), whose conception of the child is also that of a body subject that sees herself as fused to an environment.

It cannot be too strongly stressed that what both Piaget and Polanyi are talking about is an infantile sense of lack of differentiation from the external world (see also Nolan, 1990), rather than some kind of perverse deliberate placing of oneself at the center of the universe. Merleau-Ponty considering his arm as an object (Figures 1.2 and 13.) is a differentiated act of consciousness; considering it as a subject is, in the Piagetian sense, egocentric. This point gains in importance because on it hinges a great deal of the main thrust of Sugarman's argument that there is no theory of mind in Piaget. On the contrary, not only is there a theory of mind, but also an elaborate theory of the development of mind. The later logicist excesses we duly castigate on page 106. However, Piaget's starting point, that of a body-subject gradually and simultaneously getting to know about the world and his role in it, is the best possible starting point for a theory of cognition. It is compatible with the mundane world of Merleau-Ponty and its notion of development through a life world (Lebenswelt), with the biological basis that CS ultimately needs, and with the theory of consciousness as progressively developing rather than as a given that we plumb for in Chapter 8.

Let's now try to tie many of these strands together in an account of Piaget's stages of development. We're going to quote a little from Piaget as we go to get an insight into his style of reasoning.

Piaget's Account of Development.   For Piaget, reality is by no means a constant array of unchanging objects. He explicitly denies the thesis that there are objects existing as such for the subject.   Instead he insists that knowledge arises from interactions that take place midway between the two (that is, between subject and object). His system can be viewed as an extraordinary analysis of the development of knowledge, using this single theme as key: "I only know an object to the extent I act on it."

We are then to examine Piaget's system as a "psychogenesis of knowledge starting from the original indifferentiations." The first of these indifferentiations is between self and world. Piaget posits the infant's lack of true selfhood. "The young infant relates everything to his body as if it were the center of the world." Yet no self-awareness at this point. The situation has been described by both Polanyi (1958) and Piaget as "narcissism without Narcissus." Only with the beginning of "coordination of actions" does self begin to differentiate itself from the world.

Piaget labels the stage of development described here as the sensorimotor stage. He addresses himself explicitly to the question of how the adult world of well-established subjects and objects develops from these beginnings. During the second preoperational phase, logic begins to be foreshadowed in "internal coordinations of the subject" and causal relations are similarly represented by "external coordinations between objects". However, there is not as yet any fixed independent external world.

We must interrupt our account at this point to consider the evidence Piaget has collected to support such remarkable claims. His experimental methodology is self-consciously informal and makes use of verbal protocols: "The surest method . . . is to analyze the proofs employed by the subject" (Piaget, 1958). These proofs often seem to involve failure by the subject to distinguish between his own actions and the objective workings of the apparatus. "(At the preoperational stage) the subject is most likely to explain the situation in terms of the totality of actions he can perform on the apparatus" (Piaget, 1958). The state of affairs at this point is summarized by the statement "the subject's physical actions still entirely dominate his mental workings." As yet, there is no mode of representing reality independently of possible actions upon it.

We have already encountered one of the core concepts of Piaget's system, his insistence that representation takes different forms at different developmental stages. At the next stage, that of *concrete operations*, representation is mediated through reversible transformations instead of conceptualized actions. The emergent competence corresponds on the temporal dimension to "the fusion into a single act of anticipations and retrospections" (Piaget, 1970). The emergent objective relationships allow new ability "to order . . . serially" and "observe frequencies objectively." The more veridical view of reality obtained emanates directly from a differentiation of subject from object.

In a further development, from the stage of concrete operations onward, subjects tend to describe stimulus situations in terms of possible transformations that can be performed on them rather than in terms of their perceptual configuration. "Every state is conceived of as the result of a transformation." The actual converges with the possible in an encompassing representational act.

However, as yet form has not been separated from content. The reversible system of operations that defines the concrete operational stage is not completely content independent. The acts of seriation, equalization, and so on, cannot be performed with equal competence on all materials or in a manner that disregards the subject's mode of representation of the material in question. Piaget points out that the critical difference obtained between types of materials that are earlier part of the subject's concrete operational competence and other materials stems from the fact that the latter category feature properties that are "less easy to dissociate from one's own actions." It is harder to conserve mass than length because it is harder to objectify.

Only at the adult *formal operational* level of thinking is there established an enduring differentiation between subject and object. Similarly, the symbolic mode of reasoning heralded by the onset of formal operations finally sets form apart from content. "Formal thought no longer deals with objects directly but with verbal elements." Experience is vastly broadened by the mental operations afforded: "It is now reality that is secondary to possibility" (Piaget, 1958).

We have come to the final point of Piaget's account of development, a point at which the complementary processes of interiorization and exteriorization have produced a system of mental operations that "at last frees itself from physical action and the universe." Only now can those actions Piaget stresses as mediating subject and object, which constituted the touchstone of our analysis, be disregarded.

It should be obvious that a stimulus situation that presents a problem at one level of development may not do so at another. One of the classical experiments in the Piagetian framework asks subjects at various stages of development to supply an explanation for the equality of angles of incidence and reflection. Every pool player knows that, in the absence of sidespin, these two are equal. At the preoperational stage, the only issue is that of practical success or failure (of the experimental manipulation—the central problem cannot even be conceptualized. Subjects at the level of concrete operations fail to arrive at a general law, which is only achieved at the stage of the formal operations.

The following section concerns Piaget's logicism. It can safely be avoided by those averse to logic—others may find it the most interesting part of Piaget's system. A line of asterisks welcomes the nonlogicians back.

****

Piaget's Logicism.   It was stated above that if Piaget had wholly succeeded in his goal of tracing cognitive development all the way from biological interaction to logic, there would be nothing left for cognitive scientists to do. Note that it is not being suggested that he totally failed; what is being argued is that the questions he asks about knowledge as a biologist, philosopher, and psychologist are the correct ones, and that many of his concepts, such as assimilation/accommodation, transformations, stages of representation, operational knowledge, and internalization of actions, are similarly appropriate.

However, he stretched himself a little too far. His eventual aim was to explain logic in action using the same set of concepts as for biological adaptation and psychological processes. Above all, he insisted the Kantian categories like logic and arithmetic had to emerge naturally and in a principled way from natural adaptive processes. His style of reasoning led him to describe many processes in logical terms that may be better described otherwise (see below for the discussion on symmetry). Specifically, he often attempted descriptions in a full-fledged and intricate logical formalism for processes that are much better described in other terms.

For example, he attempted to describe concrete operations in terms of *elementary groupings*, which lacked full propositional logic's power. He continued in his further speculation to describe preoperational thinking in terms of a *semilattice* with no capacity of set intersection. If all this leaves you at the starting post, don't worry; it's there simply to reveal the labyrinthine world of Piagetian logic. Instead of the kind of axiomatic system we describe for production systems (see below on problem solving), Piaget described his logic as an *operational algebra.*

His symbolism obviously demands explanation. He generally expresses binary logical operations as equations. The right-hand side of the equivalence sign represents the possible truth values of the two propositions under consideration. In any particular case, only certain combinations of truth values are valid. The left-hand side features the conclusion to be drawn. It must be pointed out that regardless of the equivalence sign, these statements are not equations. This point will become clear after we consider the example that follows. We're going to need logic for the rest of this book, so let's get used to it. ∧ means *and*, ∨ means *or*—(thunderstorms ∧ rain) means we can't have one without the other; (thunderstorms ∨ sunshine) means that there is incompatibility there.

Piaget claims that all adults possess a degree of logical competence that seems at first glance truly extraordinary. Adult logical competence has four components:

1. Actual situations can be represented accurately in their absence. This component follows necessarily from the fact that stimulus situations can be represented in propositional terms. "Reality is secondary to possibility . . . propositional thinking is essentially hypothetico-deductive" (Piaget, 1958).

2. Let, p, q, r, and s signify, respectively, three independent and one dependent variables. Subjects are informed that p is the result of a particular combination of q, r, and s. For example, the color yellow (p) might result from the addition of three chemicals (q, r, s). Piaget claims that all adults can apply combinatorial reasoning to discover what precisely is the required combinations or "generate a combinatorial system which corresponds to the observed facts" (Piaget, 1958).

This logical operation is symbolized $(p{\wedge}q{\wedge}r{\wedge}\bar{s}) \vee (p{\wedge}q{\wedge}\bar{r}{\wedge}\bar{s}) \vee (p{\wedge}\bar{q}{\wedge}r{\wedge}\bar{s}) \vee (p{\wedge}\bar{q}{\wedge}\bar{r}{\wedge}\bar{s}) \vee (p{\wedge}\bar{q}{\wedge}\bar{r}{\wedge}s) \vee (p{\wedge}\bar{q}{\wedge}\bar{r}{\wedge}\bar{s}) \vee (p{\wedge}q{\wedge}r{\wedge}s)$. Subjects form their judgements according to a combinatorial system and so this logical operation, Piaget argues, corresponds precisely to what's going on in subjects' minds.

3. The repertoire of logical operations attributed to adults includes a set of 16 binary operations. "We are not exaggerating when we claim that it is possible for subjects at this level to work in turn with each of the 16 binary operations of standard logic" (Piaget, 1958).

As we have already seen, these operations are bonded on two operations and the standard logical connectives.

At this point it is appropriate to illustrate by example. In one of Piaget's better known experiments, Ss are asked which variables determine the period of oscillation of a pendulum. The possible critical variables are weight (w), length of string (l), and impetus (i). Let q signify the periods increasing, q the periods decreasing.

We first of all examine the binary operation implication:

$(1=q) = (1^\wedge q) \vee (\bar{1}^\wedge\bar{q})$

It will be remembered that the right-hand side of the equation features the possible truth values of the propositions under consideration. In the same manner as q and $\bar{q}$; 1 and $\bar{1}$ (likewise w and $\bar{w}$) signify increase and decrease in the relevant dimension. It should be obvious that there are two possibilities—that the length and period should increase together, and that they should likewise simultaneously decrease. Consequently, a relation of implication holds between length of string and period of oscillation.

The binary operation *tautology* establishes that the weight of bob is independent of the period of oscillation $(w \text{ o } q) = (w^\wedge q) \vee (w^\wedge\bar{q}) \vee (\bar{w}^\wedge q) \vee (\bar{w}^\wedge\bar{q})$. The binary operation disjunction establishes that either the weight of the bob or the length of string is critical: $(w^\wedge 1.) = (w^\wedge \bar{1}) \vee (\bar{w}^\wedge 1) \vee (\bar{w}^\wedge \bar{1})$.

4. Piaget time and again insists that "one may find the roots of logical and mathematical structures in the coordination of actions" (Piaget, 1970). Thus, perhaps his proposal that a group of transformations isomorphic to the Klein four group forms part of the adult logical repertoire. I, N, R, and C stand, respectively, for identity, negation, reciprocity, and correlativity. This INRC group can operate both on combinations of two propositions and within itself. It goes without saying that the INRC group has a psychological referent: In fact, Piaget (1958) thinks it can be found in the child's reasoning. "We should not be astonished if we find this same INRC structure in the very reasoning of the child" (Piaget, 1958).

It is generally agreed that this *Vierergruppe* is an unnecessary appendage to the Piagetian system. It will suffice to take stock of the operations allow.

$I(p \vee q) = (p \vee q)$
$N(p \vee q) = (p^\wedge q)$

Likewise, the defining intragroup operations may be specified thus:

NI = N
CR = N
INR = C
CRN = I

In a further elaborate schematization, Piaget brings the INRC group to bear on the notion of logical proportions.

****

How much evidence is there for all this logical competence being attributed to the average adult? Extremely little, as it turns out. Moreover, Piaget's formulation is unwieldy in the extreme: We're going to note that the Gestalt tradition would solve the pendulum/bob problem hinted at here by invoking the elementary notion of symmetry. Finally, we'll see that most adults find it extremely difficult to reason with propositions in the manner just outlined. They can, however, perform tasks that are logically precisely identical if more content is supplied. Let's take the logical form, modus tollens, as an example.

1. If p then q.
2. Not q.
3. Therefore not p.

Dreadful, isn't it? However, look at this:

If the check is valid, it's signed on the back. The check is not signed on the back. Therefore, ?

Yes, that makes it a lot easier.

Logic seems useful in the psychology of reasoning as a descriptive tool rather than as a prescription of what's going on. It also serves a purpose as a model of the competence of the ideal human logician, as distinct from her performance (see Chapter 3 on this distinction in linguistics). Piaget's logicism is probably the weakest part of his system. Had he demonstrated logic's fundamental role in reasoning as he attempted to do, all the problems of formalization of mental process would have been solved for CS as much as for cognitive psychology.

Piaget and Mylesianism. Before discussing Piaget's relation to the framework here, let's note his relation to his philosophical antecedents and contemporaries. As a philosopher, he can be read as attempting to give a developmental account of Kantian categories as necessarily arising from the inevitable facts of our interaction with the world.

Nor is his framework in any way incompatible with Merleau-Ponty. We can view Merleau-Ponty's phenomenology of perception as the experiential dimension of the biologically based interactions that Piaget sees the organism as immersed in with its environment.

Merleau-Ponty wrote much on Piaget without really coming to grips with where Piaget can fill up the gaps in his own work. We noted that Merleau-Ponty has difficulties with explaining how symbols can arise from perceptual experience, a failing he shares with Brooks (Chapter 5). Piaget insists that symbols can arise from the internalization of actions. (In fact, he takes this argument a little too far in the case of language. I find his account of mathematical reasoning as internalization of action convincing, but we're going to see in Chapter 4 that he can't as easily explain language development). Where Piaget can best inform Merleau-Ponty is a location that is relatively difficult to access.

Merleau-Ponty places the subject in an intersubjective world and fails to note that there are many situations in which we make sharp distinctions between ourselves and the conceived external world of people and objects. Piaget describes how this separation can occur. Yes, the child's world is narcissism without Narcissus, fusion with an encompassing environment. However, we noted in the glossary entry on centration that subject–object differentiation actually can occur. Remember Archimedes rushing from the baths in Chapter 1! Cognitive development in the Piagetian and Mylesian frameworks features a myriad such events.

In fact, the intersubjective domain is characterized mainly by such events, which all of us experience. Yet what is intersubjective for one group may not be for another: A group of musicians may agree precisely on the superiority of Mozart over Salieri in a way that is caviar to the masses (at least those who have not watched *Amadeus*!)

Moreover, with Piaget's notion of operational knowledge, we can give the first hint of the metaframework of this book (which we'll call the "Nolanian system," a phrase coined by John Flavell in a conversation at Stanford on November 23, 1983, the day before Thanksgiving). It will be argued in Chapter 3 that the standard linguistics account of language must be supplemented by an account of this operational knowledge, and how it interacts with the formal system of language in idiosyncratic ways in particular contexts.

Conclusion.   Many of Piaget's concepts are still heuristically useful. First of all, his questions about knowledge as a biologist, philosopher, and psychologist are still extremely pertinent and cognitive science cannot properly proceed without confronting them. Second, we shall use the following Piagetian notions:

schemes and schemata, equilibration, conservation reinterpreted as an advance in self-awareness, operational knowledge, autoregulation of knowledge structures in interaction with an environment, different types of representation, and decentration with an emphasis on subject–object differentiation. I am fully aware of the lacunae in Piaget's experimental work: He also makes the same mistake as CS of ignoring affect and social factors. Given the tremendous scope and power of his project, it is not surprising that the great majority of his critics have, implicitly at least, adopted some or all of his framework (Donaldson, 1978). Perhaps that is the ultimate tribute.

BEHAVIORISM AND LEARNING. Some important aspects of learning can usefully be described using only the concepts of behaviorist psychology. The problems with this approach arise when it adopts a "nothing but" approach; that is, when no significant causal role is attributed to mental structures.

Our earlier discussion of Gestalt psychology featured an interlude where we spoke about generalization; for example, a stimulus may be heard as "the same" over a large band of the auditory spectrum. The other conceptual tools of behaviorism are reinforcement schedules, which can involve only occasional (interval) rewards (the most cost-effective), or continuous or negative reinforcement in behavioral therapy. However, behaviorists end in absurdity when trying to give a thoroughgoing externalist, stimulus response account of behavior that involves use of systems (arithmetic, language) by the organism. Besides this, we need an elaborate version of feedback, by which the organism can adapt its actions, even for simple behavior.

THE DEVELOPMENT OF INNATE SYMBOLIC SYSTEMS AND THE LANGUAGE OF THOUGHT. Language development does not admit of a parsimonious description in terms of behaviorist psychology (see Chapter 4). In fact, the death knell for behaviorism's domination of American psychology began with Noam Chomsky's review of Skinner's *Verbal Behavior*. In retrospect, it seems likely that Chomsky was motivated as much politically as academically. Skinner had outlined his blueprint for an ideal state in the fictional *Walden*, which featured precisely the type of state control over people's lives (by "enlightened" use of behavioral psychology) that Chomsky is known to loathe and fear. Whatever about that, the cognitive revolution in psychology then finished off behaviorism's pre-eminence.

It seems a safe verdict that language develops to some extent autonomously, and this as the consequence of the unfolding of an innate capacity. Moreover, it seems valid to say that all human languages fall within a certain narrow range of formal complexity (again, see Chapter 3). What I shall show in Chapter 7 is that the same situation seems to hold for the symbolic system of music, and may indeed hold for vision where the nature of the symbols is less clear.

In that chapter, a contrast is emphasized, for any cognitive act involving symbols, between the characteristics of the formal system involved (language, music), the operational knowledge implicit in the act, and the subject–object (ontological) relation therein (see Figure 3.4). What is important about this schema for the moment is that we cannot explain cognitive development as the development of any single symbolic system, whatever its power. We shall note a great deal of evidence concerning the role of operational knowledge in language development. Yet this in no way diminishes the importance of understanding the formal rules (the grammar) underlying our comprehension and production of language.

I fully realize that the word *ontological* is being used in a sense other than the classic philosophical one of Chapter 1 or the knowledge engineering sense in AI, where the ontology of a system list the types of entities used therein to map the domain in addresses. Laing (1969) uses "ontological" in precisely the "conceiving oneself as object" sense we need here. His concerns, which will briefly border ours in Chapter 8, is to explain mental illness in phenomenological terms above all as alienation from self. It is not my intention to claim any direct link between linguistics and psychopathology yet.

We discussed previously Fodor's (1983) modularity hypothesis. No discussion of innatism would be adequate without reference to Fodor's (1975) notion of cognitive development as the unfolding of a "language of thought." It behooves us also to clarify exactly what Fodor is attempting. We have cited him as an antagonist of CS, which is in at least a limited sense unfair, and need to get a firmer purchase on what he is saying to understand where this notion of a language of thought fits in his work. In fact, he is not a priori an opponent of CS. His hostility is directed solely at its more ambitious project of characterizing *everything* about the mind. In fact, Fodor has little or no difficulty with the notion that the projects of CS and of the philosophy of mind should overlap; he is skeptical, however, about the prospects of CS ever formalizing anything other than the basically syntactic operations performed by vertical modules. The horizontal modules that comprise the intentional system are of a different nature, and beyond our purview.

One of Fodor's starting positions, methodological solidism, is classical CS: Computation over representations comprises cognition, and therefore there must be a language of thought in which representations are couched for cognition to occur. This language of thought is innate: from birth we already possess the complete set of representations, and the world with its apparently "busy and boundless fancy" is actually just painting these representations by numbers. Learning is impossible the type of logical law exemplified by modus ponens previously cannot be extended to other more nuanced cases, as already discussed.

Innatism, like absolute idealism, is more or less irrefutable. So you once had concept X and now you've got concept Y. But Y is logically distinct from X! You can't possibly have learned it as an extension of X! However, there are at least two major caveats here: One is that different types of representation of a problem can have huge effects on its solvability; (we see a demonstration of this below); second and returning to an idea from Chapter 1, how is it that only Archimedes of his contemporaries discovered specific gravity? Remember, Lonergan's account of insight insists that it is a function of both internal and external factors. We must allow the environment in somehow. We can explain this particular phenomenon by insisting that Archimedes had simply unearthed the applicability of innate concepts like equality in a new context. The result, however, is a new concept that passes into the habitual structure of the mind. The notion of an innate language of thought, then, like that of modularity itself, risks trivialization; it might reduce to a very limited set of context-independent operations (like modus ponens) applicable to thought in every conceivable context. Finally, just as we concluded earlier with Jackendoff (1987) that there must exist a variety of horizontal modules, so can we also insist on languages of thought applicable to personal and athletic skills as to the purely intellectual ones that are Fodor's focus.

SUMMARY.   We have received a vast range of learning mechanisms, from agglutination of connections between stimuli and responses to growth of systems like language and logic. All of these are important, but the use of structured knowledge like logical systems gives an extra dimension of power. Let's now look at how these systems can be used in problem solving.

Memory and Problem Solving

To what extent is memory involved in problem solving? Or do we often create new solutions to problems, be they crossword puzzles, satisfying our sexual needs, or getting ahead in our careers? We begin this section by looking at Max Wertheimer's (1959) approach to these issues. We find that he distinguishes between different types of problem situation and different types of solution process. For a large subset of problems, the surprising thing is that solution depends on a precise specification of the problem! For other problems, like artistic creation, the situation is different.

We discuss the neat problems first and note deduction as a type of solution mechanism. We then go to the opposite extreme and ask whether sometimes we aren't just making statistical guesses about solution. Finally, we discuss neat types of solution that are yet not dependent on deduction. These types sometimes involve subject object differentiation like that used by Archimedes.

TYPES OF PROBLEM AND TYPES OF SOLUTION. Wertheimer's (1959) is the most sophisticated account within psychology of the process of problem solving. Let S_1 represent the situation in which the actual thought process starts and S_2 the end of the process. Wertheimer stresses that solution and problem are part of a single coordination. "The thesis is that the very structural features in S_1 . . . lead to the operations dynamically in line with the essential requirements" (Wertheimer, 1959). He points out three different types of problem. The first is represented S_1 . . . S_2 (or . . . S_1 . . . S_2 . . . if one insists on looking at the problem in the context of the individual's life-space). This closely resembles crossword puzzles. Other convergent thinking, the second type, represented S_1 . . . , resembles open-system thinking or scientific discovery. The achievement here is the realization that a problem actually exists, "that the situation is not in such good order" (Wertheimer, 1959). Finally comes the type of discovery characteristic of art rather than science. The artist begins by envisaging some features in an S_2 that is to be created.

The central issue in Wertheimer's work is the distinction between "fine, clear, A-type" solutions and "blind, fortuitous, B-solutions." The former type involves a restructuring of the problem according to the Gestalt *Prägnanz* laws. "A new, a deeper structural view of the situation develops involving changes of the functional meaning of the items." In this process of reconstruction, the role of individual items is changed according to their role in the new structure. Think of how two letters in a word look before and after you have solved a crossword clue.

Wertheimer's demonstrations are mainly mathematical rather than scientific in nature. Solution is normally effected by the perception of rhorelations between aspects of the stimulus ensemble. The accounts he gives of scientific discoveries involve more sophisticated rearrangements. Moreover, scientific discovery involves a preparatory period during which an ill-defined sense of incompleteness of a research area resolves itself into concentration on a particular region. (These two types of account correspond respectively to $S_1 \ldots S_2$ and $S_1 \ldots$ in the previous schematization.)

An example of an A-type solution procedure is the process by which children derive the formula for the area of a rectangle from that of the area of a square. For Wertheimer the derivation emerges from a consideration of "how parts fit together and complete the area . . . a realization of the inner relatedness between their fitting together and whole features of the figure" (Wertheimer, 1959). A^2 is the area of a square, where A is the length of any side. Let L and B respectively represent the length and breadth of any rectangle. According to Wertheimer, solution proceeds from the restructuring of the rectangle into $L \times B$ squares of unit area.

We've seen Gestalt psychology stress the role of whole qualities in perception. Wertheimer gives a detailed account of the role of whole qualities in problem solving. Symmetry is one such whole quality not reducible to a relation of relations. Wertheimer uses a purely mathematical example to illustrate the role of symmetry. The sum of a series $1 \ldots n$ can be obtained by multiplying the sum of the extremities $(n + 1)$ by the number of pairs (n divided by 2 for even numbers). Only by grasping the necessary symmetry of the series and then becoming aware of the inner (rho) relation between form and task can the formula be understood. The symmetric form in question emerges from the realization that each pair in a restructuring of the stimulus material adds to $n + 1$. There are (n divided by 2) such pairs for even numbers. The two quantities are slightly different in the case of odd numbers but the role of symmetry is the same.

The nature of restructuring should now be clear. Restructuring plays a considerable role in scientific discovery but must be preceded by focusing upon a certain region in the field under investigation. Galileo's discovery of inertia stemmed directly from a dissatisfaction with the contemporaneous accounts of acceleration. Having experimented with the change of quantational acceleration with increase in slope of a plane down which an object rolled, he began to consider the complementary concept of quantational deceleration. The two pictures together furnished a previously inchoate situation with the whole quality of symmetry. Galileo's discovery of inertia corresponds to the schematization . . . S_2 we used earlier to describe artistic creation. However, the main achievement was, as Wertheimer puts it, to get a clear, clean structural insight against the sophisticated background. Galileo's main achievement lay in actually defining the problem.

The procedure of restructuring the problem as a *sine qua non* of solution will be re-examined in detail in a later chapter. For the moment, however, centering is the most relevant to us of the procedures. Wertheimer defines centering as "the way one views the parts, the items in a situation . . . with regard to a center, a core" (Wertheimer, 1959). It refers particularly to the process of conceptualizing one's needs as part of a situation rather than as the meaning of the entire situation. Such a transition between viewpoints "may lie in the deeper requirements of the I itself" (Wertheimer, 1959). At this point we are near one of the main themes of this book.

For Wertheimer, conceptual confusion is often the direct result of miscentering. He points out, moreover, that "the problems of centering are ignored in traditional logic and psychology."

Centering can be a restructuring of the stimulus ensemble. What of the process of viewing one's desires as part of an encompassing situation? There is one passage from Wertheimer (1959) worth quoting at length at this point:

> The role of the merely subjective interests of the self is, I think, much overestimated in human actions. Real thinkers forget about themselves in thinking. The main vectors in genuine thought often do not refer to the I with its personal interests . . . problems often remain insoluble so long as one focuses on one's wish or need.

The sympathy with Piaget's description of cognitive development as progressive objectification of the external world is obvious. This process of differentiation between subject and object is not formalizable in logical terms, as Wertheimer (1959) points out. It will be reintroduced in Chapter 8.

We have now considered the variety of processes that Wertheimer cites as contributory to the creation of novelty. What of his viewpoint on the question of whether problem and solution are in fact complementary, in the sense outlined earlier? He is explicit on this point.

> S₁ contains structural strains and stresses that are resolved in S₂. The thesis is that the very character of the steps, of the changes, of the operations between S₁ and S₂ springs from the nature of the vectors set up in these structural troubles. . . .

In other words, unresolved tensions within the problem (S₁) already imply the steps required for solution (S₂).

PROBLEM SOLVING AS DEDUCTION.   It would, of course, simplify matters greatly if we could regard all problem-solving behavior simply as logical deduction. We have spent a long time (rightly, as it turns out) agonizing about problem definition and problem solution. Let's go to Disneyland (or EuroDisney) for a moment and imagine that in this fantasyland all reasoning proceeds like this, using the logical terminology we have already introduced:

If *p* then *q*.
p.
Therefore, *q* (modus ponens).

We construct systems that comprise structured sets of such rules:

If the jets play the Sharks, the Jets win.
They're playing.
The Jets are going to win.

We have similar rules about the Dolphins, Cod, Mackerel, and so on. Eventually, it becomes a trivial matter to decide who is going to beat whom. We need just refer to our table to figure out exactly what's going to happen. We call such a table, combined with its principles of operation, a production system.

Fodor's argument on innatism, in the context of production systems, essentially boils down to this: Let's say that the child has learned modus ponens. Now consider this as the second premise: The Jets have just lost. The conclusion, from another reasoning schema called modus tollens, is that the Jets did not play the Sharks. However, let's rephrase the opening premise as "It can't happen that the Jets and Sharks play, and the Jets lose." By changing the representation, we have catered for both schemata.

This could well be the way that the situation is represented in the language of thought. If, however, we extend the situation by introducing qualifiers like "sometimes," Fodor would argue that we are on different ground, and need new innate schemata to explain how the reasoning form is learned.

A serpent may occasionally enter our Disneyscape. It asks: Does the brain really process propositionally in this matter, or does it construct mental models mapping this knowledge? This serpent's importune query can take up volumes of cognitive science journals (the Johnson-Laird vs. Rips saga; see Rips, 1990).

Alternatively, we can simply note that propositional logic systems, as outlined, seem on the balance of evidence to have some psychological reality. Whether they're actually implemented as spatial mental models, or solely as intricate systems of propositions, we can assent to their causative functions. Sensible people, we remain with this point of view pending further evidence on exactly what types of codes the brain is capable of.

PROBABILISTIC REASONING.   Given what we know about the brain, we shan't be surprised if through our fairly complete ignorance a ray of light concerning the adaptive nature of thought occasionally shines through. Neurons can have hundreds of thousands of connections with each other (cf. Chapter 4). It seems extremely unlikely that the neural language of thought is an all-or-none affair. Rather, aside from the possibility of different levels of code, thought should work probabilistically. We should constantly guess at what's going to happen next in order to function effectively in the world.

Let's recall Sperling's work (see p. 70). A first guess at the proper interpretation of a stimulus array is the entire array. This gradually gets further and further focused until we come up with the interpretation we need. Consider language process (cf. Chapters 3 and 7). Evidence suggests that immediately upon hearing an ambiguous word like *bank*, we activate it in all its contexts. Our current context of action results in just one of these being chosen. This choice is a probabilistic process. We can conceive of much everyday living as problem solving, particularly if we allow for probabilistic reasoning. In Chapter 5 we look at the Bayesian approach. For the moment, let's note that neurons' connections seem admirably suited to implement probabilistic processes. Moreover, the facts of the activities of all sensory and symbolic modalities (language, vision, and so on) seem to confirm its importance.

"FINE" SOLUTIONS. We've had a taste of Wertheimer and know what he means by A-type solutions. What we must do now is spell out the consequences in terms of subject object relations.

For Wertheimer, fine solutions are given by rho relations between subject and object. Once more, what precisely are rho relations? Wertheimer speaks of "the kind of inner relatedness which is outstandingly reasonable because of the rho relation, the fitting together of requirement and result" (1959). However, they are easier to recognize than to define. We noted several of them earlier.

Let's return to symmetry. Piaget claims that formal operational thinking is a prerogative for solution of a problem involving symmetry: "The idea of an equivalent amount of work half-understood during stage III [formal operations] provides the explanation of the phenomenon of equilibrium" (Piaget, 1958). For Piaget then, an understanding of equilibrium is not achieved until adulthood. Wertheimer denies that and adduces empirical evidence to support his viewpoint.

The Piagetian system here must be faulted for a certain inelegance. It is forced to posit an inordinate amount of sophisticated logical operation in explaining, for example, how a child comes to equilibrate the sides of a balance. Let p and q represent, respectively, increase in weight and in distance from the midpoint; $\bar{p}$ and $\bar{q}$ represent the respective decreases. The same propositions must be asterisked to describe the corresponding factors on the other side of the balance. Operations from the INRC group are required to implement the equilibrating process: I $(p \wedge q)$ = to increase weight and distance simultaneously on one side. This is not by any means the whole story. The major lesson is how cumbersome Piaget gets on these matters.

For Wertheimer, on the other hand symmetry is "an outstanding whole quality... in turn an outstanding inner relation with the stability of the whole—a rho relation". He points out that symmetry is a universal element in preoperational children's conceptual structures and so cannot require any system as complex at the INRC group. An experimental situation closely resembling Piaget's found in many children "very soon a considerable tendency to focus on the middle" (Wertheimer, 1959). Wertheimer extends his argument to scientific discovery, remarking that "structural symmetry in dynamics played a significant, important role in Galileo's thought processes and in modern physics."

Such pronouncements are outside our range of interest here. Nevertheless, there can be no question but that the notion of rho relation affords a more parsimonious description of adult reasoning on problems involving symmetry. Piaget's system cannot explain the competence young children showed on Wertheimer's symmetry problem.

Another type of fine solution involves the introduction of a new concept: We have seen that Galileo added deceleration to what was already postulated about acceleration and managed to square that particular circle. Yet this new concept has a symmetric relation to the old one! Perhaps mind in nature also invented symmetry at some stage (as you read this page, I hope, with both eyes open).

WHY SOLVE PROBLEMS, ANYWAY?   Or rather, why create them for oneself? What precisely is that factor within us that forces us out in the world, often into unprecedented and unpleasant situations, going to trouble to make trouble? We discuss this in Chapter 8.

If our conceptual structures are incomplete so is the universe itself. The paradoxical search for novelty against a background of stability seems common to humans and nature.

A science of cognition that ignores affect, conation (including will), and social factors can explain how problems are solved once they have been defined. However, it is clear to us now that this is only the beginning. We need to know, for a given person, what she is likely to perceive as a problem in order to predict anything significant about her future behavior. We would like to know something about the problem-solving style she is likely to adopt. Finally, we might find that some people are more driven to seek out and solve problems than others. In fact, it might be said that our exclusion of affect, conation, and social factors has robbed our science of much of its significance and explanatory vocabulary. In short, it now lacks ecological validity.

There are several different accounts (with wildly varying degrees of subtlety) of motivation in psychology. It is the practice of this book in such cases always to take on board the most encompassing viewpoint, the perspective from which all other views can be seen as special cases. Abraham Maslow's work affords such a perspective. It posits a hierarchy of needs, starting from the biological ones of air, water, food, and sex. Only when the earlier ones on the list have been fulfilled can one focus on fulfilling the next. Maslow suggests that the next set of needs relate to expansion of one's competence on some way, that is, to self-actualization. This competence can be a matter of understanding more as much as being able to do more; it may in fact relate ultimately to knowing precisely what one's real nature is. For example, the desire to achieve competence at a musical instrument is also that to know what one's expression of one's self will be in the world opened up by this new expertise. We return to this in Chapter 8; for the moment, let's ask ourselves why Archimedes was at all attentive to the external effects resulting from his body's immersion.

That type of phenomenon we can treat with an extension to the vocabulary and concepts of cognitive science that allows a causal role to subject–object differentiation. Let's end this subsection by noting that what people live for has a profoundly causal role on their cognition. This raison d'être has so far been better handled by the structures of myth and religion than by affect-free reason.

Memory and Forgetting

First of all, let's focus on easily quantifiable types of forgetting. If, in the manner of the late 19th century psychologist Ebbinghaus, we learn one list of nonsense syllables and shortly afterward learn another, we will find that they interfere with the recall of each other (proactive and retroactive interference, as we go forward in time). All such interference is catered for by a construct known as the *fan effect.*

Another type of forgetting is the myriad data items we ignore in our perceptions from moment to moment. We've noted that the self–not self distinction is extremely important in the preservation of a coherent information flow. In this context, let's briefly refer to the puzzling phenomenon of clinical autism. Child prodigies exist who can play extraordinarily complex music by ear, draw extremely detailed cityscapes or, in the manner of Raymond in *Rain Man,* instantaneously count a heap of spilled matches. Yet they cannot function normally socially. RAM assigned to social processes in normal humans has become dedicated to symbolic activity of some sort. Is the genius of Mozart therefore essentially his capacity to maintain a foot in both worlds?

The recent bestsellers *Nobody Nowhere* (Williams, 1992) and *Somebody Somewhere* (Williams, 1993) are written by a sufferer of clinical autism. The single most remarkable aspect of her accounts is precisely the different conception of the relation between subject and object from the one that "normal" people are accustomed. This is exactly as the stance on the relation between consciousness and self taken in this book would predict.

We've noted that Freud's theory allows suppression of painful memories. However, this repression is just the tip of the iceberg. *Psychogenic fugue* is the phenomenon whereby one forgets all details of one's social being. Multiple personalities (often the possession of an individual who was physically abused in childhood) may or may not know of each other. These kinds of phenomena sit more easily with a fully worked-out, ecologically valid psychology than millions of experiments churned out about memorizing single sentences (we revisit this theme in Chapter 8). We find ourselves asking questions like:

- To what extent are we solely the result of our experiences?
- Can social selfhood actually be abstracted from the subject's total experience of the world?
- What are genuine human similarities and differences?
- Which experiences are central, and which are peripheral, to consciousness?

MIND IN PSYCHOLOGY

We have briefly analyzed many of the huge variety of approaches to mind that form psychology, including those that reject the usefulness of the concept of mind. We remain with our definition of mind as manifest in the organism's interaction with its environment. En route, however, we have become aware of data about behavioral conditioning, the cognitive function of self, the metaphysics of subject–object relations, and the abysses revealed by depth psychology that give us pause before we come to any too easy conclusions. Moreover, it has become obvious that we need to complement the notion of mind as immanent with an articulated theory of symbolic functioning. In other words, we cannot treat all mentation as simply the picking up of affordances.

The starting point for our theory of human cognition is that of the human organism immersed, embodied, in a life world. A prior intuition of the existence of an external world, including the intersubjective domain and three-dimensional space, is assumed in the manner we saw Merleau-Ponty demonstrate in Chapter 1. To understand cognition we must understand its development; to understand its development is also to plot the growth of consciousness through successive differentiations and integrations.

This chapter began with a statement of the central problem of psychology: the mapping of significant areas of human experience in a scientifically valid manner. We then proceeded with a history of experimental psychology, referring also to depth psychology and phenomenological psychology, before discussing the types of methodology that time has proven valid. This analysis is then related to the nolanian framework: We find that its prominent accent on consciousness makes phenomenological psychology a valid medium for the delineation of experience. We went on to discuss the relation between perception and cognition and found that allowing perception the role of the background for acts of cognition means that a given act of mind may change from being included under the rubrics of the latter to that of the former.

Human cognition cannot possibly be discussed properly except with respect to its development. We used the concept of memory to elucidate aspects of learning, problem solving, information processing, and forgetting. Piaget's is still the most comprehensive theory of cognitive development. Its many shortcomings can be justifiably attributed to the sheer scale of what he attempted. In fact, its concern with philosophical epistemology, its emphasis on situated cognition, and its biological reference are making it look surprisingly modern again. Paradoxically for CS, its major fault—the logicist obsession—gives it a computational accent. We discussed Piaget's work critically before salvaging those concepts like operational knowledge that together with the very questions he asks, are not the most valid notions in Piaget.

Our analysis of problem solving led us back to the world of affordances, as represented by Wertheimer's analysis of types of solution. We found that the processes of problem specification and problem solution converge. Moreover, one type of "fine" solution requires a relaxation of subject–object dichotomization. We contrasted a logicist, representationalist examination of symmetry with one that considers symmetry a rho relation, one at a level of description other than that of that dichotomy. Consideration of solution of problems cannot proceed for long without a theory of motivation; that is, without a theory of why one sets problems for oneself. In other words, we need to take into account affective and general motivational factors once more.

This chapter has focused on cognitive psychology, including findings from fields within psychology that are often mistakenly treated as irrelevant to cognition. A fully articulated CS would encompass cognitive psychology—it is as well to point out that a science dealing with knowledge should set boundaries for what we know and consequently what parts of our experience are authentic. It has been argued in this chapter that affect is also knowledge: that knowledge cannot be understood except with respect to cognitive development, nor cognitive development except with reference to the development of consciousness: that only a phenomenological approach to psychology can bear the massive burden of the research project suggested by this requirement: finally, that in terms of our personal experience of the world, we should not be surprised to find it enriched by rigorous scientific analysis.

FURTHER READING

Gardner Murphy's (1972) is still the most readable history of early experimental psychology. J.R. Anderson (1989) is a very strongly cognitive-scientific account. Bolton (1979) gives a good introduction to phenomenological psychology. Chapters 2 & 3 in Stillings et al (1987) complement the account here well. Neisser (1976), though out of date, is lucid, and worth a read.

• three •

LINGUISTICS

INTRODUCTION

This chapter is a very brief introduction to linguistics. There are three principal aims herein, apart from the obvious one of outlining a discipline which has historically been central to cognitive science:

1. To discuss language generically as a symbol system, like music and math.

2. To point out that a full description even of linguistic behavior requires consideration of operational knowledge.

3. To consider how the notion of situated cognition can be related to symbolic behavior through the idea of context. This argument is very central to the whole book, so let's look at it in outline. Essentially, it is argued that the relation between the layers of language (syntax, semantics, and so on; see Figure 3.16 on page 167) varies between tasks and with changes in the degree of restriction of context—that is, with the situation. Meaning is regarded as the province of an embodied person, not a particular layer of language. In terms of the theories to be discussed, we're concerned with finding a *via media* between formal grammatical theories of language and the alternative cognitivist approaches thereto.

Our path is the following:

First, we ask why such a discipline as linguistics exists, and what it sets out to study. We introduce the different levels of language. The context in which we discuss linguistics is its relation to computation. Consequently, there is a computational linguistics strand running through this chapter.

Second, we discuss the major schools within linguistics, starting with what has become known as the Chomskyan revolution. The going in this subsection is unavoidably a little technical; however, the area is interesting enough to be worth the extra effort. We discuss the crucial concept of formal language theory before proceeding to other linguistic theories.

Third, we discuss the role of nonlinguistic knowledge in our use of language. This discussion encompasses both the evidence from child language development (ontogeny) and language as a phenomenon in evolution (phylogeny).

This leads us to a discussion of the pervasive role of context. Initially, the effect of context is examined in syntax/semantics interaction.

We then discuss the multifarious uses of language, particularly as implemented in computational linguistics systems. An optional discussion of this latter topic brings us on to the summary of the role of context and of mind in linguistics featured at the end of the chapter.

WHY LINGUISTICS?

We are about to enter a minefield—linguistics is the most fractious discipline in. this book, and the one whose controversies are fiercest—so, it makes good sense to ask "why bother?" Surely there is an easier way to approach the apparently natural study of language than to discuss a discipline whose stated mission of supplying a formalization of language has led to the formation of dozens of mutually antagonistic camps, whose basic conceptions are often couched in highly baroque mathematical formalisms? Can it be possible that natural language, the capacity for which except in rare cases is part of our common human inheritance, needs such a complex apparatus for its description? Amazingly, the respective answers are no, there is no easier way, and yes, it does seem that every verbal human being is the possessor of a structure whose complexity rivals anything in the universe.

We've noted already that behaviorism failed completely to give an adequate account of language. Not for the last time, we are confronted with a powerful systematically structured system that doesn't yield to atomism of any kind. Essentially, a full behaviorist account of language would have to explain every event in the child's acquisition of language in terms of the child picking up, in a passive and unsystematic way, words and grammatical rules from an environment that readily affords such. On the contrary, it seems nearer the truth that the child actively explores her linguistic environment, and discovers grammatical rules almost in the manner of a scientist unearthing new laws of nature. Indeed, the child's linguistic environment is generally impoverished and does not feature the kinds of systematic rewards for correctness and punishment for mistakes behaviorism needs.

At the opposite end of the spectrum, Piaget's attempt to consider language development only as yet another manifestation of the coming to fruition of a general cognitive apparatus also fell short of the mark. Language, we're going to note, interacts with nonlinguistic knowledge in its development (ontogenesis), but also has autonomous rules of progression. In fact, the development of the linguistic expression of conceptual structures can strongly depend on how readily available this expression is in the language in question. The interaction between thought and language is a tangled web that we consider at some length later. Let's also note, parenthetically, that Saint Augustine's attempt to explain everything about how words get their meanings simply in terms of denotation is a doomed, quixotic, and quasi-behaviorist exercise. We have already seen the quagmire into which Fodor is led by taking semantic functionalism on board.

The diversity of human languages also gives pause. We consider in the next section (cf. discussion of $a^n b^n$) how in their heterogeneity, these 3,000 or so languages can yet have their complexity neatly quantified. Amazingly, in these formal terms the complexity of all languages falls within a very narrow band of frequencies in the spectrum of complexities that formal languages can have. In fact, artificial languages like Esperanto may have failed largely because of their simplicity: The genetic code seems to require something meatier. There are no irregularities in Esperanto, and it seems that this is as much an impediment as a support in its attempts to become accepted. Every natural language has idiosyncrasies—let's look at two such. The Gaelic *cailín* (quite familiar in its anglicized version of *colleen*), meaning *girl*, is in fact masculine. Characteristic Irish perversity (and maybe perversion)? The Germans wouldn't do anything like that? In fact, the German *Fraulein* is also a gender-bender—it's neuter.

The phenomenal learning capacity visible in children's learning acquisition has led to the generally accepted conclusion that some kind of innate language acquisition device (LAD) is at work. We've noted that this, *inter alia*, in turn has led researchers like Fodor to a thoroughgoing innatism. For him, the development of conceptual structures is identical to the development of a language of thought, which must be similar in some fundamental fashion to ordinary language.

More interestingly, the issues relating to what form an innate grammar must be, and the conditions whereby incoming strings of words can be decided on as conforming or not to that grammar, have launched a thousand separate research projects (rather like Marlowe's Helen!). We have noted that natural languages fall within a certain limited range of complexity: Likewise, work like

Gold's (1967) demonstrates that there are no guarantees that an arbitrarily chosen formal language can in fact be satisfactorily learned. The other 999 papers deal with issues like equating the recognition of strings in a language to proving that solutions within finite time exist for particular classes of problem. Alternatively, they use the resources of set theory to demonstrate that considered simply as sets generated according to some formal principle of generation (i.e., algorithm), the classes of formal languages fall into naturally occurring categories here as well. Further–flung speculation maps this notion of algorithmic production to conscious experience through various types of physical process. Thus recognition by a grammar and computability, listability, and the nature of the physical processes inherent in consciousness come together conceptually in a manner we discuss in Chapters 5 and 8.

It should not surprise us, given the titanic scale of a native speaker's linguistic knowledge, that we are better off appealing for judgment on matters linguistic to such a speaker than to our incomplete linguistic formalisms. We call the thought structures by which an adult native speaker can (normally unerringly) decide on the acceptability of linguistic samples that speaker's *competence*. This perfect structure might contrast with the occasionally Dan Quayle-ish standard of "performance" due to issues like tiredness, alcohol, the necessarily more difficult process of being a speaker rather than a listener, or whatever. We'll conclude this section by noting the levels at which native speakers can display their knowledge. (A native speaker of a language, roughly speaking, is one who has learned that specific language in infancy— *infans* = not speaking.)

In the first place, the speaker might decide that a given word doesn't sound like X, where X is English, German, or whatever. The German *zwei* does not sound like English, nor does the French *roue*. We call this the *phonotactics* level. The Gaelic *ngui* is a *morphological* pattern that could not appear in English: We simply won't have words that begin like that! Morphology also deals with issues like the normal additions of -*ed* to create the past tense and of *s* to create the plural. Alternatively, it *does be* obvious that this clause is a Hiberno-English construct, unacceptable to users of standard English. That is a *syntactic* judgment. "Pigs sprout green wings daily" has something *semantically* wrong with it, and if I now tell you I'm about to stop writing and go out for a beer, you might decide this is irrelevant and therefore *pragmatically* wrong.

So far, then, we've noted the following points:

1. Linguistic knowledge, the birthright of almost every human being, is one of the most complicated structures in the universe.
2. The grammatical theories that reflect this linguistic knowledge are correspondingly complex. We'll find that the field of linguistics is still in flux.
3. The process whereby children learn languages can be described computationally in the same terms as the process of deciding whether certain strings are acceptable or not. Moreover, we might find ourselves, along with Penrose (1989), pushing roots into areas of complexity theory and the deterministic nature (or otherwise) of physical processes that will gain purchase in Chapter 5.
4. Given the incompleteness of our formal linguistic theories, we find ourselves relying on native speaker intuitions for decisions on correctness, in all their fallibility.
5. For spoken language, conventional decisions on correctness are formulated on the phonological, syntactic, semantic, and pragmatic levels. As we discuss written language, we'll encounter a more complex structure.

****

COMPUTATION AND LINGUISTICS

The relationship between linguistics and computation is a complex one. The trend to rigorous formalization of natural language grammars in linguistics (Chomsky, 1957) coincided with the development of third-generation computer languages similarly characterizable by productions (see the later section on Chomsky). However, "parsers" (see end of this section) for natural language (e.g., Earley, 1970; Tomita, 1986) and for computer languages are to a large extent different. The degree to which purely syntactic parsing (e.g., Marcus, 1980) can be useful will also be discussed later.

Thompson (1983) supplies a framework in which the relationship between linguistics and computation can informatively be commented on. He proposes the schema shown in Figure 3.1.

The terms *linguistics, psychology,* and *philosophy* have their normal meanings. Linguistics we can define as the attempt to give a formal characterization of a grammar or a language (in

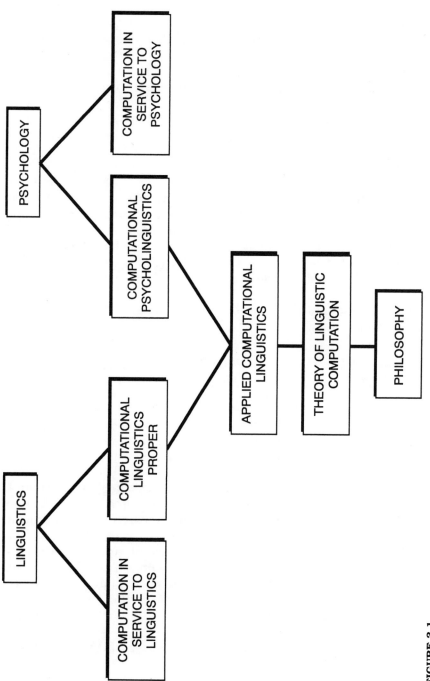

FIGURE 3.1.

Chomskyan linguistics, these are identical); that is, a description couched in logico-mathematical terms. Computational linguistics is considered as the attempt to give a computational characterization of a grammar. The models developed therein can be of service to linguistics (e.g., Karttunen) as can the technical apparatus afforded by computers' number crunching in speech labs, and so on. Psycholinguistics research attempts to explicate the cognitive activity inherent in language, often doing so in computational terms.

We have already mentioned aspects of the philosophy of language in Chapter 1. Theory of linguistic computation is a description of the communicative process in the abstract. Applied computational linguistics (ACL) is the instrumental use of language processing (Thompson, 1983). Informed discussion of ACL requires prior attunement to the issues raised in the other subfields suggested by Thompson. Wahlster (1986) suggested the following guidelines as a *sine qua non* for an ACL system.

1. A subset of the output or input is coded in a natural language (NL).
2. Processing of this subset is based on knowledge about syntactic, semantic, and pragmatic aspects of natural language.

One of the best statements of ACL's achievements has been given by Grosz, Sparck-Jones, and Webber (1986). It should be noted, as for example by McTear (1987), that the building of these systems will often incidentally explicate some aspects of language processing by humans. The central commercial application has proven to be NL interfaces to databases. Recent global economic trends have led to increased commercial interest in machine translation (MT), and speech processing research is also a growth area.

It is necessary briefly to outline the current status of ACL systems before considering the relevant findings from other disciplines. Grosz et al. (1986) make the following points, which still hold, with example systems being cited from the 1993 edition of the national software registry.

1. Semantic techniques have proven successful within very restricted domains.
2. Syntactic parsing is now, up to a point, a textbook affair with several good parsers commercially available (Disco,

a chart parser; UBS, a unification-based parser; and several GPSG parsers are available).

3. Discourse interpretation has handled concepts like language actions and intentions quite well (e.g., McTear, 1987).

4. Language generation has found difficulties in formalizing the interplay of linguistic and conceptual elements but some limited success has been achieved (Charon).

5. The problems thrown forth by anaphoric reference and metaphor are only beginning to be dealt with (SLG features anaphor handling).

Wahlster (1988) adds the following:

6. Morphology packages are now readily available (e.g., Morphix-3 and PC-Kimmo).

7. "Language-independent" knowledge representation packages have been developed (e.g., Kodiak).

8. Likewise limited language generation and user-modeling packages (e.g., GUMS) have been produced. Several good integrated systems, which include syntax and semantics (*inter alia*) exist, e.g., ANLT (Grover et al., 1993).

Finally, research on speech processing recently has been progressing quite quickly. Despite occasional exaggerated claims (e.g., Fujimoto et al., 1987) the following is the state of the art:

9. Speaker-dependent voice processing systems with vocabularies of up to tens of thousands of words are quite readily available. Research on speaker-independent systems using such techniques as grammatical representation of structural constraints on phoneme selection is proceeding with some success. Likewise, probabilistic methods are working well for projects like the current Darpa research.

We need a definition of parsing. It is to be considered as the use of any linguistic techniques whatsoever to derive a representation useful for the application in question. The representation can therefore be a database call (Boguraev, 1983), a conceptual dependency (CD) net (Schank and his school), a knowledge formalism (see Chapter 5), or whatever is appropriate for the task in hand.

****

THE MAIN GRAMMATICAL THEORIES

The Chomskyan Revolution

We shall now examine the trend toward formalization in modern linguistics. It is worthwhile briefly to examine the origins of this trend. The notion that linguistics is a science and should therefore report on objective phenomena in the context of a theory relevant to the data is comparatively recent.

Bloomfield's work on the description of language, which superseded earlier prescriptive attempts, is a crucial work here. From the early 20th century, American linguists have sought to describe spoken language rather than fit written language into a set of categories. It has become *description* rather than *prescription*.

It is in this later American tradition that Chomsky's seminal work (Chomsky, 1957, 1965) is firmly placed. This work has had enormous influence on philosophy, psychology, and linguistics, as well as the NLP paradigms we will consider in Chapter 5. Lyons (1977) described these consequences well. This despite the fact that it is difficult to see precisely where Chomsky's early work was a substantial progression from that of his contemporary peers, who also had examined the formal devices like finite-state automata that we are about to investigate. In fact, his two major methodological dictates, that of isolating language from other cognitive systems and insisting on the modular encapsulation of syntax, may look like errors in the long term.

Before discussing Chomsky's work, two remarkable properties of language must be mentioned. The first is that language is infinitely creative. Every native speaker of a language can formulate and understand an infinite number of sentences. These sentences may in some cases include strings of the form $a^n b^n$ that a finite-state machine cannot recognize without great difficulty (Gazdar & Mellish, 1989). These can be seen in sentences with relative clauses where the number of head verbs must equal the number of such clauses—The cat *who sat* on the mat, *which was* on the floor. . . .

Second, language possesses duality of structure (Lyons, 1977). Each level has its own rules, which linguistics theories must try to describe. These two main levels we've referred to as the *phonological* and the *syntactic*. Phonology, as has been pointed out, studies how sounds combine to form the elements of language. At the syntactic level, language is considered as the combination of meaningful units.

However, for his early work on formal grammars, Chomsky did not consider phonology in any detail. It is this work that is of most consequence for NLP and that we will now outline.

First of all, what is a formal grammar? To say a formal grammar is a system that generates a formal language is hardly enough. Chomsky would add that the goal of linguistic theory is a formal grammar that would generate all and only the sentences of natural language. Thus, the key idea in Chomskyan linguistics is that of a generative grammar.

For Chomskyan linguists, a grammar is essentially a set of rewrite rules that generate the sentences of a language. This is the essence of generative grammar. The formal languages generated by formal grammars exhibit certain properties in common with natural language (i.e., recursivity, ambiguity, duality of structure, creativity). We discuss these in Chapter 7 in conjunction with other symbol systems like music.

Other vernacular terms acquire new usages in our attempt to formalize language. The vocabulary V = a, b, c . . . is a set of tokens that forms the elements of the language. A sentence S is a string (e.g., aabc) of these tokens. The language L consists of all such sentences S, each of which is a string over V. We shall also use constructs like NP (noun phrase, e.g., *the fat cats*), and VP (a verb like *saw* or a phrase like *saw the fat cats*).

To introduce the next notion, that of productions, let's consider a tennis example. For example, to beat Jim Courier, you have to (among other things!) gradually force him out on his backhand side before playing a crosscourt. Let's write out this tactic as a grammar. We need at least two backhand (b) side shots, followed by a forehand (f) side one, for a successful rally, which we'll designate S.

Therefore, bbf, bbbf, bbbbf, etc., are successful winning rallies. We want to be able to generate these and only these rallies; if we find ourselves generating losing rallies (e.g., bf), we are guilty of over-generation. We need to introduce another entity, "E," to safeguard ourselves. E is a nonterminal, a term which I shall shortly define. Our rules are:

1. S → bE
2. E → bf
3. E → bE

If E = bf (rule 2), then by rule 1 S becomes bbf and we success-fully leave Jim scrambling. To generate the more complicated rallies, we use the fact that E is defined in terms of itself (that is, recursively). By rule 3, we can put as many bs as we want in front of "bf" before invoking rule 1.

What about the rules for generation of language? First, a dis-tinction commonplace in computer science compiler theory be-tween terminal and nonterminal elements must be introduced. Terminal elements (that is, lexical items) are the words that ulti-mately appear in sentences. Nonterminals are constructs like S, VP, and so on. The total vocabulary $V = VT + VN$, where VT is the set of terminal elements, and VN is the set of nonterminal ele-ments. Rewrite rules consist of a left-hand string, which must contain at least one nonterminal, and a right-hand string, which is the result of the rewrite. Let capitals denote elements of VN, lower case elements of VT. The following are valid rewrite rules:

$$A \rightarrow a$$
$$Aa \rightarrow a$$
$$ABC \rightarrow abc$$

It has been mentioned that a grammar in the Chomskyan sense consists of a set of such rewriting rules. There are five basic types of formal grammar that we will examine in order of increasing power. We re-examine this notion in the larger context hinted at here in Chapter 5 (see Figure 5.4 on p. 248).

The first, the Type 4 grammar, is also known as the finite-state grammar. This type has been used for many compilers and NLP programs. It is best to illustrate with an example from everyday language that shows both the structure and the limitations of finite-state grammars (see Figures 3.2 and 3.3). Obviously, this grammar can generate the likes of "The man bit the dog." (We're being purist in having five types; most categorizations, including that used in Chapter 5, call this Type 3.)

This kind of system clearly lends itself well to programming. Its expression in computational terms (like Backus-Naur form) is a trivial operation. However, as Chomsky (1957) proves, it is not powerful enough for ordinary language. The detail of his argument need not concern us but it relates to the A^nB^n structure we noted with its recursive ethos.

On the other hand, it is only recently that tangible evidence has come forth (e.g., Shieber, 1984) to question the validity of Type 3 grammars as a model for natural language. Both Type 3, or con-

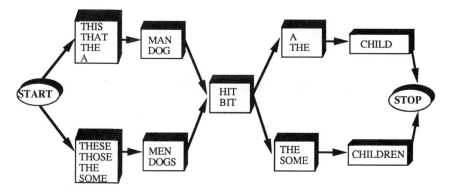

FIGURE 3.2.

text-free grammars, and Type 2 context-sensitive grammars are examples of phrase-structure grammars (PSGs).

PSGs introduce nonterminal vocabulary elements. All phrase-structure rewriting rules are of the general form X → Y. Type 2 grammars derive their additional power from rules of type X → Y/AB. This rule can be expressed as follows:

X is rewritten as Y if A precedes and B follows X.

It will make our task of examining parsing systems easier if we have a short look now at the types of production rules that produce these bracketed sentences. Obviously, there are other issues within PSG of which homonymy—for example, *bank*, which has several meanings, depending on whether one means the bank of a river or a commercial bank, is homonymous—is the only one relevant here.

Here is a PSG system that generates the same type of sentence as the previous Type 4 grammar:

    S   → NP VP
    NP → Art N
    VP → V NP
    Art → the, that, these . . .
    N   → man, men, dog . . .
    V   → hit, bit

Context-sensitive PSGs are certainly of sufficient power for NL generation. To these, Chomsky (1975) added the idea of

FIGURE 3.3.

transformations, which we consider later. Type 1, or recursively enumerable grammars, and recursive Type 0 grammars are likewise outside our present scope, being, as we shall see, too powerful for NL. We discuss these in connection with the work of Turing and Penrose in Chapter 5. They are similar enough, for all practical and indeed several impractical purposes, to be taken together as Type 0, which is what we do in Chapter 5.

However, Chomsky's distinction between deep structure and surface structure is one that was, for a time, central to linguistics. It is relevant here, particularly for semantics-oriented NLP systems. Deep structure is an internal representation of the meaning of the sentence (here Wittgenstein would disagree as we saw in Chapter 1. In fact, Chomsky eventually disagreed with himself on this point. Deep structure arose from the moment—which we shall henceforth refer to as "the incident"—when Chomsky decided to widen the scope of his linguistics in a new standard theory (Chomsky, 1965) that would treat semantics with the same formal rigor as syntax. The incident's consequences were that Chomsky retreated back into syntax.

Therefore, for some, linguistics turned from a prescriptive discipline into an attempt to mathematically characterize grammar. Chomsky's (1957, 1965) work has been massively influential in the field of NLP. That an innate system of at least the formal power of Chomsky's Type 3 grammar could be universal was a notion that excited many researchers in other fields. Grammars for human society, architecture, myth (Campbell, 1982), and a jazz musician's improvisations (Johnson-Laird, 1988) are but a few of the speculations that emerged. Earlier, we considered the long rallies in clay court tennis as displaying this type of structure.

It is apposite to reintroduce a distinction between Grammar and grammar. The former is the totality of a speaker's linguistic knowledge; the latter is syntax. Chomsky can be faulted, at least to some extent, for overemphasizing the latter at the expense of the former. Thus, semantics is not treated formally with anything like the same thoroughness as syntax. Indeed, it is sometimes argued that Chomsky's major contribution has been providing the first framework in which phenomena like tough movement can be discussed. Tough movement is a phenomenon that manifests itself in sentences including a small set of adjectives (for example, tough, hard, easy). It was found, using Chomsky's analysis, that the subject of such a sentence as "The party was hard for Bill to leave" is not "the party," but rather the clause "for Bill to leave the party." The same goes for the sentence: "It's easy to beat Jim Courier."

The attack on Chomskyan deep structures was two-pronged. Generative semanticists insist that there is no clear-cut distinction between syntactic and semantic rules and that the lexicon can take a role in grammar. Interpretative semanticists, on the other hand, move deep structure closer to the level of syntax. Chomsky's own later writings have tended to favor this conclusion, which seems to have won. It may be argued that the demise of doctrinaire Chomskyan linguistics has been salutary. *Vive la différence!*

However, even agrammatical strings of words (e.g., talks IRA impossible), which obviously don't conform to any formal grammar, may yet be successfully processed. The transition from the laborer's single word "Slab" to full use of syntax is, Wittgenstein argues, of a quantitative rather than a qualitative nature. It is unquestionable that we inherit grammars of a certain complexity. Yet processing can sometimes successfully occur without recourse to the rules of these grammars.

The general model due to the Chomskyan theory of transformational grammar, then, is the following: deep structures (which arise mysteriously from a black box called *semantics*) and comprise entities like (*Mary is eager*) (*Mary pleases someone*) are transformed into surface structures by transformational rules. These syntactic structures are in turn relayed to phonological rules and so we gladly hear "Mary is eager to please." The syntactic structures are treated using the resources of formal language theory. As has already been mentioned, the major difficulties that arose concerned the role of surface structure in determining meaning. A quantifier like *some* completely alters the meaning of

"Women are dishonest"

to the completely politically and semantically correct.

"Some women are dishonest."

Yet it was difficult to cater for the pervasive influence of such quantifiers by reference to deep structures alone. Thus the confrontation between generative and interpretive semantics, which, as has been mentioned, is seen to have been resolved in favor of the latter. But where does this now leave us in our efforts to express a Grand Unified Theory of Language (GUTOL) in formal terms?

The Counter-Revolution

The problem outlined above about the role of quantifiers, combined with other lacunae, halted transformational grammar's advance. One critical issue we have raised is where exactly semantics fits in the schema. One possibly viable option is to introduce a level of logical form intermediate between meaning and surface structure. I shall argue later that all this is rather pointless; in the meantime, let's look at the paradigm (Government Binding; GB) that proposes this idea about logical form.

The first innovation in GB, which was formulated by Chomsky himself, was a tendency to put much more weight on the "dictionary" entries of words themselves—the lexicon. Second, in keeping with Chomsky's stated preference for rules that worked across all the languages of the world—his desire for a Universal Grammar—the syntactic rules, such as they were, were couched at a higher degree of abstraction than the relatively language-dependent notions of noun phrase or verb phrase. Look back on our phrase-structure grammar (PSG) in the preceding section. The GB statement of the first three rules would be:

$$S \rightarrow \bar{\bar{N}} \ \bar{\bar{V}}$$

$$X \rightarrow \text{Specifier } \bar{X}$$

$$\bar{X} \rightarrow X \text{ Complement}$$

We wish this to generate "The company with which we've done business." There doesn't seem, so far, to be any major gain in efficiency. However, let's examine this rule. In general, $\bar{\bar{N}}$ is going to take the role of an NP: We are told that it comprises a specifier followed by $\bar{X}$. Thus, we end with "The $(\bar{X})$." $\bar{X}$, in turn, can be rewritten as "company" with complement standing for a prepositional phrase such as "with which we've done business." This general schema, slightly adapted, will work for VPs as well.

In general, sentences and verb phrases are conceived of as governed by a head, in particular a head verb, with an accompanying description of the agent and patient of the verb. Thus, "John broke his elbow" would be formulated:

gov	agent	patient
broke	John	elbow

(In Gaelic, which like 19% of the world's languages is verb–subject–object [VSO] order, that sequence is preserved for the normal language: Bhris Seán uilleann). What has happened to the determiners (his, the, etc.)? In NLP systems that use GB, these items are featurized at another level of description. Thus, *elbow* would have associated with it a marker indicating it had a determiner equal to *his*. GB theory has proven an extremely rich formalism, and the attendant notions like $\bar{X}$ syntax have computational implications. Moreover, the idea that a symbol functions by virtue of head items, which at various levels ($\bar{\bar{X}}$, $\bar{X}$, etc.) structure the subsidiary elements in their vicinity, is useful even for such systems as disparate in function as music and vision. In music, we find that from themes' development subthemes are introduced, which in turn become the head items for further development. In vision, it's been speculated that recognition of shapes can best be done computationally (neurologically, no one is quite sure) with respect to similar rules of well formedness. According to this framework, we view a body by breaking the components down with generalized cylinders. The torso is one such cylinder, the head another the arms another: the S in the rule

$$S \rightarrow \bar{\bar{N}} \ \bar{\bar{V}}$$

corresponds to the whole body, with $\bar{\bar{N}}$ being a significant item like the torso, $\bar{\bar{V}}$ the head, and so on.

It's clear that GB theory operates at a rather stratospheric level, is rather imprecise in places, and allows much room for particular interpretations. Not so the formalisms that have been developed in the framework, or on the fringes of computational linguistics *per se*. Here, the necessity for computational precision has forced linguists to come up with much more detail. A common tool of this particular trade is the use of features. Originally used for phonology, where for example the presence or absence of a vocal chord *hum* as one pronounces a sound yields the categorization *plus or minus voiced* (for example, the *z* in *zebra* is voiced and the *s* in *silence* isn't); features are now a common part of syntax. For example the verb *broke* has the following features: Its category is a verb, its tense is past tense, and it expects an NP argument (e.g., an elbow). If we incorporate features like these into a PSG formalism—and note that the argument feature allows sentence constituents to interact—we have the beginnings of a generalized PSG (GPSG). This system has proven computationally useful and is psychologically not implausible.

Alternatively, we may decide to put a huge burden on the lexicon, thus specifying much of what is handled by syntax in conventional theories. Categorical grammar is such a system.

In introducing his functional unification grammar (FUG), Kay (1985) insists that language must be considered as a system for transmitting and encoding ideas. FUG is a grammar-writing tool, and is too powerful for NL in its undiluted state. Karttunen and Kay (1985) have shown how FUG can be applied to an extremely inflected, relatively free-word-order language like Finnish.

The sentence *Esa luki kirjan* (*Esa read the book*, where *kirjan* is *book*, *luki* is *read*) can be legally written in any of the 3! (= 6) possible orders in Finnish. Phrase-structure rules are not appropriate here; subject and object relations are not given by word order. However, word order can have some influence. The sentence given above tends to be interpreted as active, whereas *Kirjan luki Esa* tends to be interpreted as passive. Other orderings may stress, for example, that it was a book, not a newspaper.

Thus, structural configuration and prosodic contour are important for Finnish. FUG may be applied here to express the functional descriptions necessary.

Lexical functional grammar (LFG) distinguishes between rules about a word's syntactic role (c-rules) and its functional role (f-rules—for example, is it subject or object). At the end of the analysis of a particular sentence, the two descriptions must be interrelated. LFG has proven computationally extremely worthwhile. Other computational formalisms include relational grammar, tree-adjoining grammar, and definite clause grammar, where the computer language Prolog is used to optimize the use of PSGs.

We've looked extremely briefly at the most currently influential alternatives to transformational grammar. Yet, by their authors' own admissions, none of these systems give a comprehensive account of all language. In the following section, it will be argued that the reason for this is the effect of nonlinguistic operational knowledge. We need, in this context, to look at the development of child language. We then briefly look at supporting neuroscientific evidence for the Nolanian viewpoint, and at cognitive linguistics, the theory of linguistics most compatible with neural Darwinism.

LANGUAGE DEVELOPMENT AND LINGUISTICS

Thought and Language

Chomsky considers his work to be a theory not just of linguistics, but relevant also to psychology and philosophy. Chomsky is the current high priest of linguistics. I use this term deliberately and not pejoratively. It is ridiculous to exclude his politics from a discussion of Chomsky, and his claim that his intellectual and political activity are a unity forces question about his continual claims on moral high ground. Not even his many critics would deny that Chomsky still is the most influential linguist, if not the most correct. So, to find out about language, ask Noam. Yet he has continually failed to explicitly acknowledge the shortcomings of his work, even when, as has often happened, the criticisms leveled have in fact forced him to change his mind. This autocratic attitude is precisely the politics that he criticizes so brilliantly. Yes, his intellectual and political activities are complementary: One is a precise mirror image of the other.

Some of his more excitable disciples (including Fodor) have argued that the ontogenesis of the language of thought is coextensive with the ontogenesis of mind, and less controversially, that epistemological issues can be greatly clarified by proper attention to language's role. There still are those who advocate the path of linguistic determinism-that is, the notion that thought *is* language, or at the very least informs it greatly. This thesis attracted many followers this century and is entitled the Sapir–Whorf hypothesis after its main protagonists, Edward Sapir (an anthropologist and linguist) and Benjamin Lee Whorf (an insurance official for whom linguistics was a passion).

The kind of experimental evidence used to support this hypothesis focused on languages where certain concepts might be extremely strongly or weakly encoded. For example, the Zuni language has an impoverished color vocabulary, but by contrast, the Inuit people have an enriched snow vocabulary (admittedly of compound words), and the Gaelic language has a rich palette of words for fog and rain. Native speakers of Zuni might be shown a set of colors A . . . D and, after a delay, asked to match a new sample against one of the remembered array A . . . D. Their failure to do this as well as English speakers was seen as indicating an inability to encode these color concepts due to a restricted vocabulary. This type of result supports linguistic determinism. We're going to see evidence later from child development for the alternative cognition hypothesis.

Piaget, we have noted, insists that language is a species of thought. Let's try to reconcile these opposing viewpoints in some sense. What is thought, and what is language? We need to look at their evolutionary development in order to fully answer this question.

Signaling systems exist throughout the animal kingdom. One of the best known is the dance of the honey bee. A bee, having gone out to reconnoitre an area, performs a dance for the benefit of her colleagues on her return. Some superb research has demonstrated that the dance unfolds according to certain definite grammatical rules and comprises an account of where the richest source of pollen in the neighborhood is. Let's note two things about this:

1. Mind in nature, manifested in the structured interaction of a variety of components: the bees' need for food, the flowers' need to reproduce.
2. The structured "language" of the bee's dance.

Thought as problem solving also exists throughout the animal kingdom. A classic set of experiments by the Gestalt psychologist Ivo Kohler showed that chimpanzees were able to solve the problem of reaching a bunch of bananas by pulling up a chair to extend their reach. This is quite clever, and you and I both know people who wouldn't think of this, even if given a millennium to do so. So why not try to teach chimpanzees language? Their vocal apparatus is not all that good, so let them learn American Sign Language (ASL). Surely . . . ?

Unfortunately not. Nim Chimpsky (yes, even in the 60s and 70s Chomsky had his vitriolic critics) and colleagues managed to pick up a few hundred signs for various things and some primitive rules for the combination of these signs. Indeed—and this shouldn't surprise us given what we now know about the necessity for human nonprecocious (altricial) development—at 12 months of age the average chimp had more to say than the average baby. However, the general consensus is that there is a bottoming out due to an inability to truly refer to objects in the external world, independent of strong inner physical reactions incited by those objects (a banana, for example, will get the digestive juices flowing). We can, if we like, say that the language tokens have connotation (they mean something in inner idiosyncratic terms) but not denotation.

Where does this leave us? We accept that language and thought exist quite far down the evolutionary scale. However, ingenious attempts to teach an animal with which we share 99% of our DNA anything beyond the rudiments of language have failed. We'll begin outlining our overall perspective by noting that these results would not have surprised the Russian psychologist Vygotsky. In his masterpiece *Thought and Language* (1962), he argued that the two were distinct in evolutionary terms. It is only with humans that thought becomes linguistic and language conceptual.

Perhaps I should now put the first of my cards on the table. If thought and language interact in this way, and their interaction is in some way idiosyncratic, as I argue here and in previous work (Ó Nualláin, 1993), a GUTOL is an impossibility. The GUTOL would have to include, along with its formal system, operational knowledge, the whole of the intersubjective domain, and the forms imposed on experience by mythic and archetypal experiences.

The Evidence From Child Development

We've noted that the most useful viewpoint to have on children's linguistic development considers the children as research scientists in search of general laws. Even an infant's solitary mean-ingless babbling is directed experimentation (and not, as one of my students told me, the child's training to be a professor). In fact, per-haps unlike that of lecturers, the child's babbling is highly struc-tured. I have already noted the voiced-voiceless (e.g., /d/ versus /t/, /v/ versus /f/) distinction. In general, the evidence seems to corroborate the following:

1. The child is actively experimenting with such distinctions.
2. If a distinction appears early on in the child's babbling, it tends to be a correspondingly universal feature of the world's languages.

The voiced–voiceless dimension, one of the child's first forays, is quite universal over all human languages: The distinction between the vowel sounds in the French *rue* and *roue*, inaudible to many nonnative French speakers, appears much later.

As soon as the child has mastered the phonetic system and begins to produce strings of words in the native language designate, other regularities appear. The one we must look at here is the expression of thought structures through incomplete syntactic forms. (In the heyday of developmental linguistics, thousands of postgraduates waited fretfully to record the next utterance of a snot-nosed child rather like a neophyte waiting for her guru's next oracular pronouncement.) One such thought structure is posses-sion. Interestingly, it appears in English before the child has mas-tered the syntactic form:

That John, dog
That Dada nose

In general, old syntactic forms are used to express new concepts. This single fact gives the lie to the strong form of the Sapir–Whorf hypothesis.

However, the situation is a little bit more fraught. For example, negation, which is simply expressed in languages such as English and German, is more difficult in French:

I am *not* working
Ich arbeite *nicht*
Je *ne* travaille *pas.*

Meanwhile, Japanese and Irish people just can't say no. In Gaelic, you can only deny a specific proposition, rather than say *no:* This has in fact infected our English to the point that *yes* often means *no* in Dublin, which leads to interesting date rape trials. One can answer *Nil,* meaning *there is not,* but not specifically *no.* In Japanese, there are different forms for negation. Even in English, however, there are different forms for negation as rejection (don't), nonexistence (there isn't) and denial (he didn't). Nonexistence is expressed by its correct form only after being long established as a cognitive category. If we accept negation as the root concept, which most developmental psychologists of the 1970s did, we accept that here is a manifestation of autonomous language development. In general, the conclusion from this field was that new forms express old meanings, and new meanings are expressed through old forms.

SOME SUPPORTIVE NEUROSCIENTIFIC EVIDENCE. In order to support our notion of the separation of thought and language, it's going to help greatly if we can find some corroborative neuroscientific evidence. Damasio and Damasio (1992) supply just that. They posit three structures related to the language faculty, evidenced by dysfunctions specific to the brain areas assumed responsible for each structure:

1. A large number of structures in both the left and right hemispheres (cf. Chapter 4) process motor and sensory interactions with the environment and categorize them. The pathology associated with this is that patients with lesions in the V2 and V4 areas of the cortex can neither see nor imagine colors.
2. A specific area near the sylvian fissure in the left hemisphere allows for the correct formation of words and sentences. Such dysfunctions as dyslexia are characteristic here.
3. Interlinkages between (1) and (2). The pathology here results from damage to the temporal segment of the left lingual gyrus. Patients can perform color-selection tasks correctly but will say *red* for *blue.*

We can look on (1) as operational knowledge and (2) as purely linguistic knowledge. So far, the evidence is in our favor.

COGNITIVE LINGUISTICS.   It is the viewpoint of this book that language must be described in its own formal vocabulary as well as being interrelated with operational knowledge for full understanding of its role in cognition. George Lakoff's work may be regarded as perhaps a misguided attempt at Piaget's project to fully realize language as a species of the more general notion of thought, or what Edelman (1992) refers to as *embodied concepts*. For Edelman (1992), following Lakoff (1987), both syntax and semantics depend on a prior set of schemas like that of *container, center-periphery,* and *source-path-goal*. Even syntax yields to these schemas: syntactic categories are manifestations of the container schema (undoubtedly, Lakoff would be sympathetic to Piaget's notion of relativization as a manifestation of the general procedure of insertion). The head/modifier relations we saw exploited in GB would be an exemplar of the cognitive universal center-periphery.

It is Lakoff's approach to semantics that is perhaps more instructive. Let us take just one of the five types that Lakoff proposes of a general construct called *idealized cognitive models* (ICMs); that is, propositional such models. These last consist solely of base-level concepts (entities, actions, states, and properties). When associated with linguistic elements, we get a new form called symbolic ICMs. These provide the mapping required by conventional semantic theory. It's worthwhile to pay a little more attention to Lakoff's theory. It is the one that Edelman favors as his pet theory of situated, embodied cognition, and it provides one possible out from the troubling problem of grounding.

First of all, it is compatible with aspects of the ethos of the preceding section. The knowledge encoded there under Category (1) is seen as the basis for ICMs. Apart from the propositional, there are other types of ICMs, including the metaphorical. All that is necessary for communication is that we should concur, if not agree(!); "The act of communication is the intending of the object as being what it is for both under the auspices of a symbol" (Edelman, 1992, p. 245). This is precisely the viewpoint on meaning we arrived at in Chapter 1 starting from quite different considerations.

There are some even more telling points made by cognitive linguists. We shall see in Chapter 5 that some constructs like spatial prepositions are viewed as outward projection of the body and its activity. The notion that Edelman emphasizes, that concepts arise from the brain's categorization of its own pattern of activity, is formulated thus by Mark Johnson:

An image schema is a recurring dynamic pattern of our perceptual interactions and motor programs that given coherence and structure to our experience. (Johnson, 1987, p. iv)

These image schemas, as mentioned above, include container, center-periphery, and so on. Were cognitive linguists to concede formal autonomy to syntax (as in Figure 3.4, where the symbol dimension fulfills this role) their stance would seem to me valid. But why should there be a privileged cognitive apparatus of this nature? We are back to the Chomsky versus Piaget debate, which Chomsky is seen to have won. Essentially, the evidence from phenomena like English past tenses and plurals as well as analysis of the formal language complexity of natural language points to a

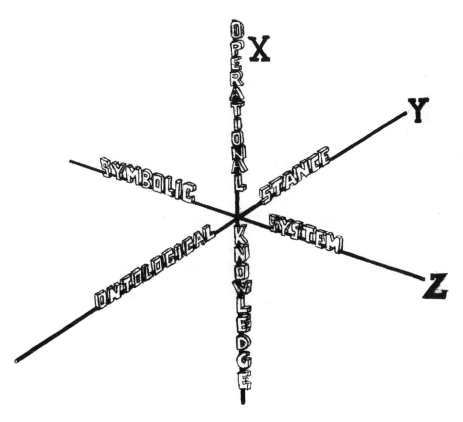

FIGURE 3.4.

mechanism of a sophistication and consistency other than that to which we are accustomed.

A *via media* between the formalists and cognitivists can be found by admitting the autonomy of syntax; there may also be analogous syntaxes of music and math. It is as complicated as it needs to be for the conveying of thoughts, the main business of language. Every use of language has values along three dimensions, of which the syntactic (which to simplify we express as "symbolic") is just one. Let us now examine context.

TOWARD A DEFINITION OF CONTEXT

It's time now to draw some of these strands together. We hypothesize evolutionarily distinct strands which we will simply label (oversimplifying somewhat) as "thought" and "language," which weave together in the course of child development. We can identify this substrate of thought with many different types of knowledge, including the Piagetian notion of internalized action that we term *operational knowledge.* These separated strands form a tapestry of various hues and various knits. These hues and knits we're going to call *contexts.*

Consider the sentence *I love you.* Is that crystal clear, or what? Now consider it in the following contexts:

1. Mother Thérèse of Calcutta speaking to the poor of the world.
2. Two lovers speaking.
3. Ross Perot speaking to Bill Clinton.

We obviously now have, superimposed on the words themselves, a whole plethora of other considerations to do with intentions and situation; in short, with context. That simple sentence can express the Greek notions of agape (1) or eros (2), or the notion of brutishly contemptuous sarcasm (3).

Let's take this a stage further. For the situation envisaged in (2), the speaker could be understood speaking in initial letters (ILY) or, at a guess, backward (YLI). In the schema of Figure 3.16, all that's necessary for full extraction of meaning is social context and letters.

Similarly, the sentence

"Tighten the nut on the bicycle in the garage!"

can be a request to get a simple job done, or alternatively a heart-felt plea to a child to get himself and his bicycle out of the house (quickly). The technical problem illustrated by this example is called *prepositional phrase attachment*. What is significant about it for our purposes is that there is no way by which we can resolve the ambiguity therein on linguistic grounds alone; the context must be taken into account.

With this in mind, I suggest that context in language is precisely the interaction of linguistic and other knowledge. Our tapestry includes different hues and different weaves as context changes. In other words, the laws interrelating nonlinguistic and linguistic knowledge are going to vary greatly as context changes. Not only that, but we can restrict a context, as in (2), and our apparently clear-cut stratification of language disappears. Letters (Level 2) seem to interact directly with social context (Level 8) without any regard for intermediary stages. In short, as context is restricted the levels of language collapse into themselves. (See Figure 3.16 on p. 167)

That, therefore, is the reason why linguistic models that attempt to separate syntax, semantics, and so on, by putting them into neat, separate boxes simply don't work. In fact, it might be argued that this is basically a Cartesian error: It is talking about this abstract entity called *language* without reference to how it is actually used in the world (see next section). Syntactic relations, in a sufficiently restricted context, can give the type of information normally viewed as semantic.

Let's take an example. We can use extremely similar systems to perform a syntactic parse of a sentence and to perform a full analysis of meaning, if the latter task is being done in a sufficiently restricted context. Both tasks involve traversing nets. In the former, we use a computational device called a transition net; in the latter, we adapt this (only slightly) to form a transition tree. If you care to take my word for this and don't feel disposed to follow some computational linguistics technical details, you can safely skip the next section.

****

Transitions and Syntax

What is a transition net (TN)? How can TNs capture syntactic structure? A TN is a series of nodes connected by arcs. These arcs can be traversed if a condition attached to the arc is fulfilled. The condition may be appearance of an NP or, as is the case with semantic grammars, a specific word or series of words. In any case, the traversal of an arc may require traversal of an entire subordinate net or tree.

An example will illustrate. A fragment of English can be defined as follows:

S   → NP VP
NP → det common Noun
NP → proper noun or pronoun
det → a, the
VP → V NP

The corresponding TN looks as shown in Figures 3.5 and 3.6 (which includes also the possibility of adjectives).

Augmented TNs have registers that retain records of features or partially completed parse trees. Each of these registers has an

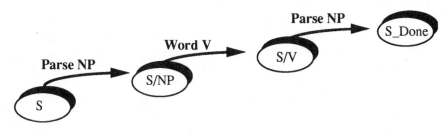

FIGURE 3.5.

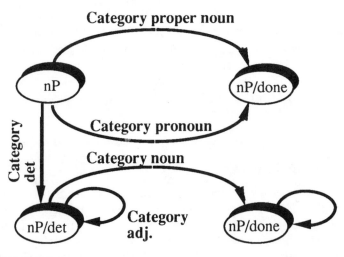

FIGURE 3.6.

action associated with it. The register may, for example, note the fact that the subject of a sentence is plural. In generation, this action will transform the verbs correspondingly. Obviously, the augmentation adds considerably to the power of the grammar.

We have suggested an ATN structure for a subset of English—noun phrases (see Figure 3.6). This by no means models all English noun phrases.

It should be noted that *category* first tests whether the incoming phrase is of a certain type, and then removes the phrase from the input if the test succeeds (Figure 3.7). *Parse* follows a network right to its end.

Parse is used in the same way in both ATNs and AT trees—as a directive to traverse a subnet. We now add four basic types of operations in net and tree traversal of language representations. We have looked at *Parse.* The second, SEQ, is appropriate for items like determiners that require only one test. Graphically, it looks like Figure 3.8, which is a seq over NP and VP).

Either can be used when two nonjump arcs (jump arcs do not need a constituent to be traversed) emerge from the same node. An example is the one-step traversal of jumps that consist of either a proper noun or a pronoun (Figure 3.9).

A noun may have a number of modifying, informative adjectives in front of it. The test for such items is optional, as represented in

FIGURE 3.7.

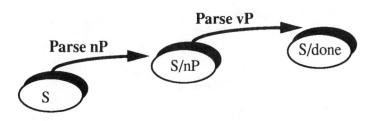

FIGURE 3.8.

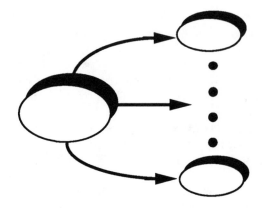

FIGURE 3.9.

Figure 3.10. A full parse of the "man bites dog" sentence is given in Figure 3.11. (I hope that Figure 3.3 elucidates the above explanation!)

TRANSITIONS AND SEMANTICS.   It should be clear that the term *semantic grammar* is almost silly, yet it is still used for that application of AT trees (ATTs) in which the transitions can be specified semantically. Thus, to take but one example, instead of specifying (Parse NP) we can now do (Parse OBJECT).

ATTs differ from ATNs in the following respects:

1. Arc transitions may require specific words rather than syntactic elements.
2. Arc transitions may be specified semantically. In this chapter, we should not be surprised by a syntactic relation yielding semantic information. When an object is not specified, it is preceded by an upward triangle in the top-level description (see Figure 3.12).

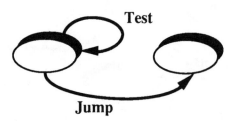

FIGURE 3.10.

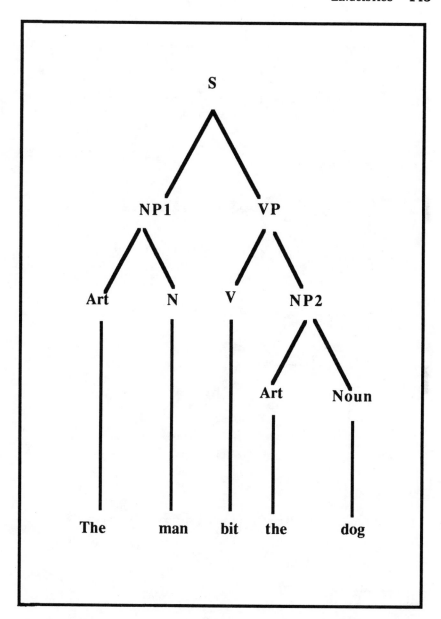

FIGURE 3.11.

3. Values are attached to the trees so specified, and these
    values normally form the basis for computation of the
    parse-result.

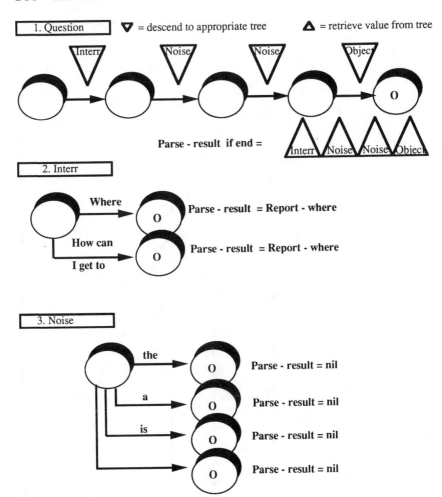

Alternatively, these "Noise" words may simply be ignored.

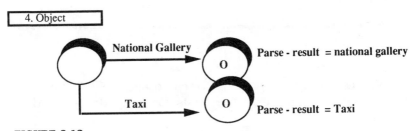

FIGURE 3.12.

4. These values are terminal elements in the vocabulary. Our formalism specifies such values with a downward triangle in front of the name of the tree that these values are intended to replace.

5. TTs do not allow backtracking.

6. ATNs allow more than one arc per mode.

As an example, let us look at Figure 3.12, which is a small subset of a semantic grammar system.

The system can handle the following grammatical questions:

Where is the national gallery?
Where is the taxi?
How can I get to the national gallery?
How can I get to the taxi?

It can also handle several ungrammatical questions, of the type that speakers of Hebrew (which often does not use the verb *to be* in the present tense for interrogatives, and, often, omits articles) may ask, for example:

Where taxi?
Where the taxi?
How can I get national gallery?

This facility is due to the jump arc at the bottom of 3 in Figure 3.12 that's marked "noise."

The value attached to the top tree—question—is a search procedure specified by the subordinate trees. Let us take the sentence "Where is the taxi?" as an example. The result is, in whatever programming language is being used, a database query for taxi.

How is this achieved? First of all, we see that question, the top tree, requires the values being brought up from the results of traversal of the lower trees.

1. Inter results in Report-where (in the sample here).

2. Noise twice results in nil, because it does not add any information.

3. Object produces taxi.

Therefore, we've looked at two systems of almost identical computational structure. The ATN produces only a syntactic parse;

however, the same mechanism in a more restricted context can elicit the semantic relations necessary to answer questions.

Had we restricted context a little further, single words might have sufficed; further still, and single letters might have done. This is our first venture from the world of grammatical theory into language use. We've already found a new use for the regularities of structure treated by syntax. The central plank of the argument in this book is that mind can be studied only *in situ,* as an organism's interaction with its environment. We should not be surprised if we are surprised again by the polymorphism of language-thought interaction.

Consequently, we abandon the syntax-semantics dimension, as conventionally considered at this point. To correctly study language, as is the case with cognition in general, we must consider person and environment together. The meaning derives from their interaction, not rabbits plucked from a semantics black box.

****

THE MULTIFARIOUS USES OF LANGUAGE

Let's widen our net (I'm tempted to say broaden our context) a little by looking at the things we do with words. It is standard linguistics at this stage to distinguish between the information conveyed by a string of words and the intention that same string attempts to realize.

> Would you like to keep on reading until you understand the argument?

can be interpreted at one level as an inquiry about what might please the reader, and at another (the perlocutionary) as a warning against jumping to premature conclusions. However, the situation is even more complex than that. Let's recap the argument of the previous section before we elaborate on precisely how complicated the situation is.

The notion of a fully realized formal GUTOL has been abandoned. The essential reason is that linguistic knowledge interacts with nonlinguistic knowledge in idiosyncratic ways peculiar to specific contexts. Moreover, the stratification of language into well-defined levels ranging from the wholly conceptual (semantics and pragmatics) to the wholly structural (syntax) is now seen as artificial. Syntactic relations in a sufficiently restricted context can yield meaning, as indeed can a simple string of letters given further restriction. We need to look at what task is being done, and how restricted the context in question is. For the moment, it's worth noting that there might be a useful distinction between meaning (for a user of language) and semantic relations (which the speaker might use as a means to give meaning).

Let's now look at a set of possible tasks:

1. Syntactic analysis. It may be the case that all we want to do, as in the manner of schoolteachers, is determine whether a given string is grammatical or not.

2. Using syntactic methods to derive semantic information in the manner of semantic grammars.

3. Mapping to a scheme comprising a model of a set of actions. We've noted in the discussion of Piaget that certain such stereotyped schemes must exist.

4. Mapping to a set of logical atoms. A good example of this is reading about the politics of a country, other than one's own, in a foreign language newspaper. Somehow, all the familiar characters are there!

5. Processing of agrammatical strings such as *Hotel arson explosion* or even initial letters (*ILY* in a marriage proposal scene).

We have at least two orthogonal axes on which these tasks can be plotted:

1. Degree of restriction of context.

2. The specificity of the output. For example, do we want a single fact or a motor sequence?

Not entirely coincidentally, all these tasks have also been computationally attempted. We have already seen how syntactic analysis and use of syntactic methods are done. Mapping to a scheme is done by the system developed by Schank and his colleagues. Mapping to a set of logical atoms has been attempted by a variety of researchers, particularly Nirenburg (1991). Processing of agrammatical strings is an application of word expert parsing (Small & Rieger, 1982), where linguistic knowledge is all encoded at the lexical level.

This vast spectrum of language use, coupled with our findings on ATNs and TTs, have led us to abandon the received wisdom of absolute syntax–semantics (as meaning) separation; the distinction is obviously often inappropriate for computational purposes. To understand language, we must consider the language user in her environment. Meaning derives from this interaction of speaker and environment, not by appeal to a semantics black box after a syntactic parse: "In order to carry out referral, a formal representation must become an intentional one . . . this requires a consciousness and a self" (Edelman, 1992, p. 238).

At the very least, we must separate semantics and meaning. We can sometimes usefully view the semantic level as a theory of the domain in which the person is embedded. This theory can be expressed in image schemas (or some other consensually validated mentalese), or if the domain is the clearly laid-out suburbs of Wittgenstein's "city of language," a formalism like set theory. It can trivially be proven that these representations can be described using the resources of predicate calculus; this does not commit one to a belief that predicate calculus is an appropriate psychological model. On occasion, the semantic level can be bypassed entirely, as we've already seen; derivation of meaning is a different if overlapping issue to semantic analysis.

Readers lacking an interest in computational linguistics can safely proceed immediately to the section beginning on page 171.

****

LINGUISTICS AND COMPUTATIONAL LINGUISTICS

We've already found it useful, in considering the relation between syntax and semantics, to make reference to computational linguistics techniques. The syntactic act of finding the main structural components of a sentence, we found, would in a restricted context afford semantic information. To show just how much more complex the situation gets when we move across languages, let's consider the sentences (from Carbonell & Brown, 1988):

John took the cake from the table. He washed it.

Normally, the referent of the *it* (the anaphoric reference) is resolved only with reference to semantics (tables, not cakes, are normally washable) or pragmatics. We call the latter activity *discourse interpretation.* However, let's look at the translation of this sentence into other European languages:

John a pris le gateau de la table. Il l'a nettoyé*e.*
John nahm die Torte von der Tisch und er putzte *ihn.*
John cogio el pastel de la mesa y *la* lavo.
John ha preso il pasticino de la tavola e *la* ha lavat*a.*

Only in English, therefore, is it necessary to analyze beneath the syntactic level to semantic or other levels in order to resolve the anaphor in question. Indeed, in the Italian example, the necessary information is (as underlined) available twice. CL has been extremely useful in highlighting issues like this. It has, on occasion, not only forced linguistics to give more computationally tractable accounts of its theories, but also introduced rigor where there might have been only vagueness followed by polemic.

Applied Computational Linguistics

OVERVIEW. The applications considered in this section fall into three main teleologically derived categories. Other applications—for example, text generation and text scanning—are not as relevant here.

1. Natural language (NL) interface to databases.
2. Machine translation.
3. Speech processing.

For historical reasons, we shall deal with MT first. In all cases, it will be noticeable that the systems described here work well only within sublanguages.

Some AI work, (e.g., Schank and colleagues) has been concerned with building NL understanders. The representations therein produced may be used for either Task 1 or Task 2.

MT is historically significant because it exposed for the first time the difficulties inherent in NLP. The early English–Russian work (Weaver, 1955) foundered because of an underestimate of the inherent complexity of language. The translation produced tended to be massively ambiguous because of a failure to formalize the knowledge involved in the area, and thus disambiguate. Weaver's inspiration that symbols could be crunched like numbers with techniques like statistical semantics was attenuated in scope. Yet the perceived relative failure of other NLP techniques has recently led to a comeback for statistics (see Chapter 5).

Analysis of English-Russian equivalents of the words *coach*, *lose*, and *set* yields a 2040-way ambiguity when the number of different meanings each of these can have in Russian is multiplied. Moreover, Russian often omits articles (Nirenberg, 1987). The result is great difficulty in achieving the desired bidirectionality from English to Russian and vice versa. With that in mind, we shall now consider what actually has been achieved.

MACHINE TRANSLATION.   Both Nagao (1988) and Tucker (1987) describe the variety of approaches for MT. The algorithmic details we considered in Chapter 2. It suffices for the moment to distinguish between:

1. The commercial approach, which uses a well-defined sublanguage in a commercially viable area (e.g., weather forecasting).
2. Approaches that concern themselves with more sophisticated text, different categories of text, and improving quality (Nagao, 1988).
3. The AI approach, which treats translation as problem solving.
4. Probabilistic approaches (cf. Bayes in Chapter 5).

Within these approaches different techniques (considered later) may be used. The first or direct approach does not construct an *intermediate representation* (IR) but maps direct from source to target text. A great deal of preprocessing of idioms and prepositions is first necessary. The Georgetown MT system (Toma, 1977) and its close relation, the EU's SYSTRAN (Zarechnak, 1979) are two instances here. The latter in particular has proven quite effective (Tucker, 1987) but pre- and postediting are necessary. In other words, someone has to clean up both the input and output texts.

Transfer-based systems attempt to catch more subtle constructs by producing an IR (such as the syntactic parse we already noted). Taum-Meteo is a highly successful semantic grammar system with a near-100% success rate. The Taum group produced their system in response to a need for translation of the weather forecast between English and French. Metal works in the telecommunications domain with a 45–80% success rate.

Nirenburg and Goodman (1991) attempt knowledge representation (KR) in a manner analogous to early Wittgenstein. All such systems must eventually address themselves to the problems inherent in the "logical atomist" ethos if they intend to venture outside restricted contexts. Recently, Nirenburg shifted his attention to the fuller KBMT framework. With the recent ratification of NAFTA and further translation requirements from the EU—particularly for documents like fire regulations where translation is mandatory—it looks as though MT will capture an ever greater share of the $25 billion worldwide translation market.

NL INTERFACES TO DATA BASES. It should be noted that NLIs are to date the most commercially successful application of CL. We outline the historically most important systems before looking at criteria for their assessment. There is a general consensus (Bates, 1984; Grosz et al., 1986; Hendrix & Walker, 1987) about the appropriate criteria.

Woods' (1969, Woods, Kaplan, & Nash-Webber, 1972) work on the lunar rocks project was the first to establish a definite paradigm within NLP syntactic parsing (that is, ATN theory and method). This paradigm has been examined above.

Woods's system answered questions in a very narrow contextual range. Burton and Baum (1976) addressed themselves to the issue of how to specify the domain of knowledge in a manner that did not require analysis at the level of conventional syntax (S, NP, VP, and so on). The resulting method, the semantic grammar (SG), was used by Waltz to answer questions about planes, and we've looked at it at length.

However, it was Hendrix and his associates (Hendrix, Sacerdoti, Sagalavicz, & Slocum, 1977; Hendrix et al., 1978) who first developed programs that allowed people to write their own natural language interfaces (NLIs) without, so to speak, reinventing the wheel. From the time of their LIFER project, constructing an NLI became a matter of writing applications for a general parsing machine.

It should be mentioned that considerable difficulties still remain. Thompson (1983) comments that a skilled programmer with considerable knowledge of language structure remains a prerequisite. In the same vein, Grosz and colleagues (1986) comment that the domain analysis to create such a grammar and the design of the grammar itself still require expertise in NLP.

LIFER consists of a set of language specification functions and a parser. Hendrix (Hendrix et al., 1977) comments that it attempts to emulate certain procedures performed by technicians. He adds that the use of an ATT, rather than an ATN, leads to several new properties.

LADDER (Hendrix et al., 1978) is one application of LIFER. It answers queries on naval data and consists of three parts. It is the first, an NL parser, that we are most interested in here. Intelligent data access (IDA), the second component, commences the access of data. FAM handles the management of files.

INLAND's major innovation is its ad hoc grammar for its finite set of queries. This type of grammar allows questions of these forms:

How many ships are there with length greater than 300 feet?

What is the length of the Kennedy?

Where are the Nina, Pinta, and Santa Maria?

IDA breaks these questions down into search patterns (e.g., ((Noun; e.g., Kennedy) (?length))).

Harris (1984) wrote a system called INTELLECT with a specifically commercial application, also based on SGs. Like Schank, he founded a company (Artificial Intelligence Corporation). Winston and Prendergast (1984) described INTELLECT, which answers questions about the Fortune 500. Recently, Harris has produced English Wizard, a follow-up system.

Hendrix's successor to LIFER, called Q + A, is described in Kamins (1985). It consists of three components:

1. a nonrelational database access system
2. a text editor
3. an NLI system called Intelligent Assistant (IA), which helps in the creation of domain-specific applications. IA has a built-in 400-word vocabulary, a database, a dictionary, and an interactive knowledge-acquisition program that allows the user to add lexical knowledge. The vocabulary includes 250 nonterminals.

Q + A is the first system we have examined that features a programming language other than Lisp. In Q + A, the syntax is expressed as Lisp data structures and the semantic routines as Lisp procedures, but the parsing algorithm is implemented in C and assembler (Hendrix & Walker, 1987). Compilation into custom p-codes to run on a virtual machine speeds execution. We find cause to comment on virtual machines in Chapters 4 and 8.

Q + A has been enormously successful, becoming one of the top five best-selling software products in the United States (Wahlster, 1988). However, Wahlster (1986) notes the lack of flexibility in the grammar and the restriction of the NLI to database access. Both problems are due to limited space.

TEAM (Martin, Appelt, & Pereira, 1984) features a schema translator in Prolog, and its other components are in Lisp. It runs on Symbolics LM-2 Lisp machine. Domain-dependent components include the lexicon, conceptual schema, and database schema. These must be rewritten in full for each new application. The domain-independent component includes the following:

1. A parser and grammar.
2. Semantic translators, which convert sentences into BSF (basic semantic form), which is a CD-like representation.
3. Pragmatic and scope-determining processes.
4. The previously mentioned schema translator.
5. A basic vocabulary and taxonomy.

This distinction between domains will be featured again in the forthcoming appraisal of systems.

APPRAISAL OF THESE SYSTEMS.   In their introduction, Grosz and colleagues (1986) propose the following eight categories for use in appraisal of systems:

1. *Modularity.* This concerns (a) the separation of domain-dependent and domain-independent knowledge, and (b) the separation of the processing modules (e.g., syntactic and semantic modules).
2. *Integration.* The extent to which the information from each module is brought together into a single analysis.
3. *Problem factorization.* Related to modularization. This issue concerns the extent to which each module is performing its task. Is the syntactic module operating purely formally, or is it inappropriately required to do reference evaluation?
4. *Transportability.* Moving between domains.
5. *Habitability.* Does the system allow for human error (e.g., misspelling, elliptical input)?

6. *Extensibility.* Ease of transportability and of extending the allowed language.
7. *Speed.* Of response.
8. *Veracity.* The extent to which the human cognitive function is modeled.

This category is fairly irrelevant, insofar as we know very little about human LP and the small amount we do know suggests that the representation paradigm is to some extent inappropriate.

Wahlster (1986) introduces a ninth category:

9. *Transmutability.* The extent to which the system can adjust to different types of usage.

Schank stresses a commercial *sine qua non:*

10. *Updatability.* Can the system be adjusted to react to quick change (as, say, in the stock market)?

Harris (1984) would insist that NLP systems be able to interface with other computer processes (e.g., graphics, databases). We will term this:

11. *Compatibility.*

Speech Processing. Few areas are more prone to hyperbole. However, in recent years Apple's Plaintalk and IBM and Dragon's systems have brought this technology in an advanced form into the marketplace.

The more enlightened work in this area—for example, HWIM (Bruce, 1982) and HEARSAY (Charniak, 1985)—has indicated the necessity to include other linguistic and nonlinguistic knowledge. The identity of the word input in human hearing seems to be guessed by a weighting of the evidence from these various sources of knowledge. Thus, we return to the central fact that language is massively hypothesis driven. It is unlikely that the transduction from longitudinal waves to shearing of hair cells, which is the basis for human audition, yields information as massively complex as that required by a pure engineering approach (Allerhand, 1987). However, context can be so specific that a single phoneme could activate a scheme.

HWIM includes 13 different types of knowledge, ranging from the acoustic-phonetic to the strategic (Bruce, 1982). By contrast,

Allerhand (1987) simply considers the discrete time-varying signal that must be mapped onto a symbolic form. His own solution, like Carson's (1988) is to formalize grammatical constraints on the sequence of phonemes allowable. We've discussed these constraints with respect to native speaker intuitions on phonology. The latter may yet win out, if the research projects based on statistical approaches can be said to be part thereof.

LANGUAGE "UNDERSTANDERS."   The scare quotes are deliberate. A problem with ACL is the degree to which people are willing to attribute intentionality to the CL systems. This argument appears in Chapter 1, has been flogged to death elsewhere, and we won't worry any further about it.

What we will discuss here is a series of systems that develop IRs that can be used for paraphrase, DB query, or translation. Wahlster (1988) stresses that knowledge representation (KR) is a crucial issue here. Our full discussion of KR is in Chapter 5.

KRL (Bobrow & Winograd, 1977) focuses on descriptions of objects. Both McDermott (1981) and Wilensky (1987) fault it for its lack of denotation. And Winograd has abandoned this quest. The more successful KL-ONE (Brachman & Schmolze, 1985) insists on frequent use of structured inheritance nets as well as of descriptions. A parser has been developed in this framework. Woods (1984) describes a use of KL-ONE for NL interface to databases.

Wilensky (1987) adduces a set of criteria that, he claims, demonstrate limitations inherent in all KR systems to date. KODIAK, his system, focuses on the "relation" notion. However, two points should be noted. First, KODIAK opens the floodgates for a proliferation of concepts; indeed, Wilensky concedes that the number of concepts will exceed the number of words. Consider, for example, how *mind* is used in this book.

This is due to its attempt at context-independent KR. Secondly, KODIAK is not really language independent (pace, Wahlster, 1988). For example, Wilensky subsumes *owner* under *legal entity*. There is no such concept in Gaelic: *sealbhdóir*, the nearest analogue, cannot appropriately be used as a legal term. The highly specified nature of Wilensky's relational networks will result in many such malapropisms. Translation requires cultural attunement. On a higher level, the notion *view*, which Wilensky introduces, may well be language independent.

Wilensky (1987) takes CD to task for its epistemological inadequacy. CD (Schank, 1975, 1982; Schank & Leake, 1986) is based on a minimalist interlingua (IL). Schank was greatly influenced by case grammar (Fillmore, 1968) and perhaps by Richen's work. His IL consists of 11 verbs (e.g., *Move, ingest*) that can affect the numerically indexed (– 10 – + 10) states of health, anticipation, and awareness.

This choice of primitives seems to be arbitrary, to some extent. The basic concept underlying the verbs is *trans* (movement). However, there are many verbs in every language (like *awaken, réveiller, tuer, dúisigh*) that express changes in health, anticipation, and awareness.

The knowledge encoded in its pristine form (Schank, 1975) corresponds to the Piagetian sensorimotor and preoperational stages. Piaget claims that after these, there arise the concrete operations (from about 7 to 12) and formal operations (12 onward) stages (Piaget, 1958, 1970, 1972). At the latter stage, we've seen that a system of logic is available, as well as a capacity to reason hypothetico-deductively.

Schank does not even begin to consider the questions Piaget tackles. Therefore, Schank's choice of primitives is arbitrary and his epistemology hopelessly inadequate. However, his later realism (Schank & Abelson, 1977) allowed production of some functional systems. A final caveat must be entered because of Schank's implicit tractatus-type theory of language (Wittgenstein, 1922). Indeed, one of his core entities is the picture producer (PP), a direct evocation of early Wittgenstein. If early Wittgenstein is, in fact, incorrect, this evocation is unfortunate.

Riesbeck's request-based system (Birnbaum & Selfridge, 1979; Riesbeck, 1975) uses a production system to parse. Words (concepts) have associated test–action pairs, or requests.

As parsing proceeds, a concept list and a request list are both built up. Requests can test for the presence of lexical items or ordinary properties of the concept list. For the concept *Fred,* the test is T; the action is Add (PP - Class (Human Name (Fred)) to C-List. Eli, the more refined of Riesbeck's parsers, has been optimized by Gershman (1982). It is used in most of the Schankian systems now to be described.

Cullingford's SAM (Cullingford, 1981) was a series of programs designed to understand stories. The context of the stories, not surprisingly, was extremely specific; for example, diplomatic incidents. Eli was used, as already mentioned, to produce a CD representation of the text. Certain invariant points of interest were expected:

1. The events.
2. The *dramatis personae.*

These invariants were recognized by scripts and demons (see Charniak et al., 1987). Business considerations dictated that SAM should decrease its typical run-time from 16 minutes. Even before the arrival of the present generation of computers, FRUMP (De Jong, 1982) took about 2.5 seconds to perform a similar job of understanding. Moreover, it produced summaries of input text in English, French, and Chinese.

FRUMP first analyzed the text to find out what kind of story was involved, then filled in the holes in the frame (see Winston & Prendergast, 1984) associated with that story. Typically, the stories were taken straight off the UPI newswire. At this point, Schank began to set up Cognitive Systems, Inc., to exploit the obvious commercial potential of such systems.

Lebowitz's (1978) integrated partial parser (IPP) is a further text-understanding system that functions in much the same manner. Its major innovation is the ability to recognize types of stories seen previously. As has been mentioned, Schank's (1986; Schank & Leake, 1986) current work extends this ability to learn from experience. He attempts to extend the understanding and creativity of such systems by refining their explanations (XPs) of new phenomena. Since his resignations from Yale and Cognitive Systems Inc., he seems more interested in education than NLP.

Lehnert's QUALM (Lehnert, 1982) cleared the ground for Schank's later analysis of XPs. Eli is again used to produce a CD net of the question. This CD net is then placed into one of the 13 conceptual categories that Lehnert herself devised. (Three such are causal antecedent, goal orientation, and request). Inferences now further constrain the question specification. The resulting structure can interrogate any story with a representation in scripts or plans. Scanning mechanisms can derive the correct information. Wilks (1976a; Wilks & Sparck-Jones, 1983) has also produced some parsers based on purely semantic analysis. The general method is to map from semantic templates to a preseg-mented input text (Wilks, 1976b). The templates are the used, for example, for English–French translation.

Two of the problems Wilks faced were AI standards. The first is the problem of disambiguating the word *pen* where the context seems equally to suggest *writing instrument* and *playpen*. The second is the one-to-many problem in translation. For example, the French *de* may mean *of* (*le livre de Jean*) or *from* (*il le jete de la fenêtre*).

PATTERN MATCHING. Techniques that match patterns in the input text to stored templates in order to build the requisite representations of the input come easily to the mind of computer scientists when faced with NLP. Thus, Weaver (1955), it has been seen, speculated that even context could be determined by statistical semantics. Only with 1980's skepticism (and computing power) did statistical methods make a comeback.

Early English–Russian translation work used pattern matching with rudimentary syntax (Charniak et al., 1987). The output texts were massively ambiguous (Pierce, 1966). Reasons that suggest themselves include the poor syntactic coverage (once the sublanguage had been left) and disambiguation, both of referents and of word senses. However, in a sublanguage, syntactic constructions tend toward relative uniformity (Grishman & Kitteredge, 1986); anaphoric reference is a great deal of the time to the last object, even in the general, nonsublanguage case. Moreover, we have seen that gendered languages afford more scope for anaphoric disambiguation (see above). Finally, Wittgenstein (1967) indicates that word sense ambiguity occurs particularly when the word is outside its native language game.

In introducing his request-based parser, Riesbeck (1975) stresses that one should not rule out use of pattern matching. Indeed, request-based and word-expert parsing (Small & Rieger, 1982) also require prior definition of words, much like key word parsing. Pattern-matching methods have a healthy robustness.

However, pattern matching fails for complex questions. For example:

Wie weit ist es vo(r)(n) (Object 1) zu(r)(m) (Object 2)?
How far is (Object 1) from (Object 2)?

For this type, we need a semantic grammar. A variety of Ockham's razor holds in NLP: Never use an inappropriately complex method! With that, we'll end our survey of the field.

Computational linguistics (CL) has been extremely useful in its highlighting of issues like this. Through CL, linguists have been forced not only to give tractable accounts of their theories, but also to introduce computational rigor at points where it might otherwise have been lacking. The result has been salutary for everybody involved.

Philosophy of Language (Reprise)

We introduced the major questions about language and knowledge in Chapter 1. Some issues about the role of myth in personal development were introduced in Chapter 2.

We shall use a further argument from Jeremy Campbell (1982) to close this section. He argues that myths, legends, and so on can potentially be understood by computers. This flies in the face of any sensible conception of myth. Consider the following classic Irish legend from the Fianna cycle:

Fionn, the leader of the Fianna, and Diarmuid, his *protégé*, are both in love with Grainne. Diarmuid elopes with Grainne to the wilderness. While Fionn is giving chase to Diarmuid, a wild boar severely injures the latter. Fionn has healing powers, and need only sprinkle water on Diarmuid to cure him. Instead, he spills the water on the ground.

Let us now consider a CD representation of the main points of this story.

1.	Diarmuid	D-Prox Grainne	4.	Action:	Throw
2.	Fionn	D-Prox Grainne		Actor:	Boar
3.	Action:	PTRANS		Object:	Boar
	Actor:	Diarmuid		To:	Diarmuid
	Object:	Grainne		From:	Boar
	To:	Wilderness		Health (Diarmuid) = -8	
	From:	Fionn	5.	Action:	PTRANS
				Actor:	Fionn
				Object:	Water
				To:	Ground
				From:	Fionn
				Health (Diarmuid) = -10	

Diarmuid, as you may have guessed, is now dead.

Understanding, Pitrat (1988) argues, is achieved when the program "has made a representation which does not depend on any natural language." CD form fulfills this requirement. The story of Diarmuid and Grainne fits into a general category of "love-magic and forest themes" (Joseph Campbell, 1968—no relation to the other Campbell) whose antiquity "goes back far beyond Celtic times." It is an archetypal tale of love and jealousy.

Were a program to be supplied with a Piagetian scheme for the preceding structure, could it be said to understand such stories? Joseph Campbell would think not. For him, myth's functions include "the shaping of the individual . . . to his social group" as well as fostering "the centering and unfolding of the individual" in accord with both his natural and his social environments.

We have now left that realm of discourse in which an unembodied representation could be said to constitute understanding. True comprehension of myth requires not only a model of the world, but participation and growth in the world. Campbell is obliquely reiterating the Dreyfus and Dreyfus (1988) argument that the central difference between natural and artificial intelligence lies in the relation of reality to the model thereof. Bateson (1979), who we discuss in Chapter 5, would agree, insisting that a story is above all a "pattern of relatedness" of the reader to his environment. This relation is immediate and cannot be achieved by a model.

Like parsing in the CL tradition, literary criticism analyzes texts to derive representations. However, the representations so derived are by no means as clear-cut as database calls or CD nets. For example, Anthony Burgess (1989) may say of Waugh's *Brideshead Revisited:* "It is a work of propaganda for the Catholic cause . . . here everything is almost cabalistically predestined . . . God wins . . . God has to win."

Donoghue's (1986) analysis of the language of Joyce's *Ulysses* and *Finnegan's Wake* give some indication of how far CL is from literary understanding. The ground shifts beneath our feet immediately: "To Joyce, language always seems to offer itself as a counter-truth to the truth of reality" (ibid). We are no longer even interested in representation, so what exactly is happening? Because "language is not responsive to transitions" a new technique must be developed to model the nondiscrete nature of reality.

In *Finnegan's Wake,* "the words are confounded by taking to themselves diverse linguistic affiliations and echoes from 50 or 60 languages" (Donoghue, 1986). The difficulty of parsing such text is a point that need not be labored.

A more general point about any literary analysis is that the representations produced are of the type that programs cannot even potentially understand; that is, those that refer directly to the embodied reader's relation with his or her social and natural environments. It is possible, however, that some hermeneutics techniques such as deconstruction (Donoghue, 1986) may at some stage prove useful to CL. Above all, the emphasis in literary criticism on determining the context in which the writer is working in order to fully determine meaning is instructive.

In summary, then, the foregoing discussion indicates that there is no possibility whatever of a general computationally tractable formalization of language. CL should use a great variety of techniques, not just computationally convenient algorithms with a mathematical excuse. Rather, NLP can be done only within specific contexts. When semantic techniques are used, as Pitrat (1988) points out, the primitives chosen will include many applicable only to this particular language game.

Theory of Linguistic Computation

Thompson (1983) reserved this term to describe the communicative process in the abstract. Two questions arise naturally in this context. The first is how to formalize the expectation-driven nature of human language processing. The second relates to the interleaving, or otherwise, of syntactic and semantic processing, and we've laid this particular bogeyman to rest in the general linguistic context. Let's look at it in CL.

Even the origins of the use of the word *semantics* are shrouded in mystery (Tamba, 1988). It is generally credited as Breal's (1897) innovation. It can refer to properties of words that, for example, preclude ideas dreaming. (The sentence for which Chomsky may be remembered most is "colorless green ideas dream furiously.") Smith and Wilson (1979) point out that the logical entailments of a sentence can be divided between those that are justified, semantically and pragmatically, and those that are in fact extralinguistic.

That human cognition is in general massively hypothesis- and expectation-driven has become clear to researchers in CL (apologies for Figure 3.13), psychology (Kelly, 1955), and even management theory (Moynihan, 1974). Schank and Riesbeck have demonstrated that much linguistic performance, in particular lexical disambiguation, can be modeled as the filling by later words of the roles suggested by the requests from previous works. Kelly's construct theory (Kelly, 1955) insists that people always actively construe their situation. Finally, the managerial theory of cues proposes that people normally line up several hypotheses simultaneously; the one actually chosen is that for which there exists the most statistical evidence.

In this same vein, Halliday (1975) points out that language-learning for children is *a fortiori* a voluntary activity: It is "learning how to mean." Previous structural descriptions of the process are inadequate. Halliday's description takes a functionalist view, and insists on taking into account how the child actively tries to participate in the system of shared meanings in his or her society.

Both Lesmo & Torasso (1985) and Lytinen (1986a) have addressed the issue within the framework of CL. Both point out

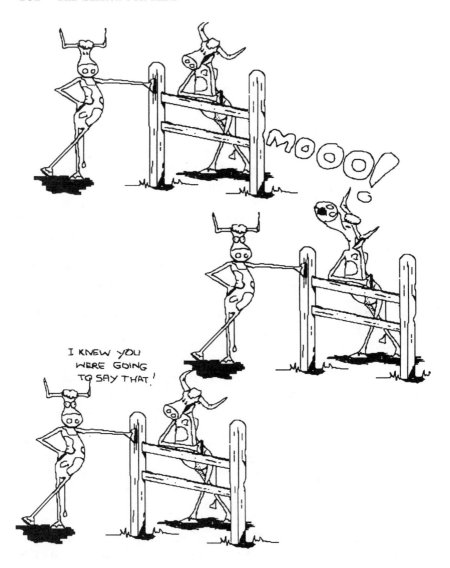

Language comprehension is massively hypothesis-driven!

FIGURE 3.13.

that parsing can be greatly speeded up by judicious interleaving of syntactic and semantic components. An example is prepositional phrase attachment.

In the sentence "He saw the lake with a telescope," the attachment of *with a telescope* can be either to *He* or *the lake* on a purely syntactic parse. It is the semantic component of the system that can decide that it should normally be to *He.* This is a simple example, and the increase in efficiency gained by interleaving can be great for complex sentences.

Lytinen (1986a) agrees with interleaving in this manner, and adds that the use of nonlocal syntactic checks is also helpful. This seems to the author a more sensible proposal either than Wilks and Sparck-Jones's (1983) desire to totally eliminate any independent syntactic component, or Marcus's (1980) attempt to parse purely syntactically.

Yet there seem also to exist cases where the syntactic analysis is implicit, if it in fact occurs at all. Consider Wittgenstein's laborer shouting "Slab!" instead of "Give me a slab!" It seems that here the missing words and syntactic construction are supplied by the context. Moreover, agrammatical strings can yet yield meaning. One such *hotel arson explosion* is a near-classic in CL literature.

However, the situation is more complex than that. If the NLP task is that of understanding an extended text, two cognitive acts come into play.

The first act is the act of domain determination. The knowledge brought to bear in this first act is essentially word meaning (Walker & Amsler, 1986) and syntax. No operational knowledge of the type modeled by Schank's (1982) "scripts" is yet used.

The author argues that syntax is more predominant at this stage than later on in the act of comprehension. Once context has been determined, operational knowledge comes into play. Moreover, syntax and semantics interact in the manner described by Karenina Lytinen (1986a).

We've seen that the situation can be more complicated still. Wittgenstein's laborer utters only a single word; and we assent when, in Tolstoy's *Anna Karenina,* a marriage proposal is successfully carried through using only the initial letter of each word.

Let us retrace our steps. I argue that in reading any text, a two-stage comprehension process is evident. The first stage involves domain determination. In this stage, syntax and isolated word meanings are paramount. In the second stage, once the domain is determined, the interaction between syntax and semantics becomes a great deal more systematic. Lytinen (1986a) gives a good description of their interaction in the second stage.

Yet that is not quite the full story. Agrammatical strings of words can evoke full acts of comprehension: Context can be so restricted that single letters can suggest whole words (the *Anna*

Karenina proposal scene). Moreover, the interaction of syntax and semantics seems quite different in the first stage of comprehension than their interaction in the second stage. We discussed that point in a broader sense earlier in this chapter; we do so now within CL.

Finally, when context is considerably restricted, syntactic processing may seem at best implicit.

The author intends to give an outline for a preliminary explanation of these phenomena. First of all, however, let's look at one final relevant set of findings.

McClelland and Rumelhart (1986) describe a connectionist structure for language (see Chapter 4) in which inhibitory and excitatory connections exist between elements of language. These elements can range from orientations of letters to single words. It is claimed in this approach that reading behavior can usefully be considered as the attempt to find statistical evidence for a particular word. Look at Figure 3.14 of Myles as Hercules: Certain readings are being suppressed, others facilitated. As Myles reads, he processes "the bee's knees," not its competitors, "the cat's pajamas" or "dog's dinner."

In fact, what we need to reconsider at this point is: How many levels of language are there? The conventional account (Jackendoff, 1987) would depict four, as in Figure 3.15. However, our current analysis would suggest at least eight, as in Figure 3.16, for written language with a correspondingly complex layered system for spoken language.

It is this author's opinion that McClelland and Rumelhart's (1986) approach is essentially correct, and can fruitfully be extended. Human processing of language, the author wishes to argue, can be considered as above all the attempt to find statistical evidence for a particular interpretation of text. The evidence may come from any, several or all of semantic, syntactic, phonetic, pragmatic, orthographic, or operational sources. The interpretation may be a Piagetian scheme, a Schankian script, or a requested piece of information represented by a single word.

The two major issues dealt with in this section are the expectation-driven nature of human language processing, and the relation of syntax and semantics in such processing. The author believes that as the expectations vary in nature, so does the relation of syntax and semantics. It is now time to look again at the overall model that the author wishes to propose.

From McClelland, it adopts the notion that language processing involves the collection of statistical evidence for a particular inter-

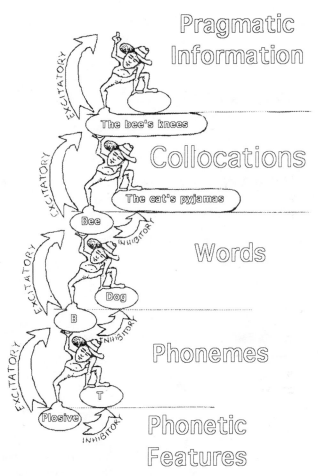

FIGURE 3.14.

pretation. However, McClelland and Rumelhart's (1986) work does not venture outside the purely lexical area. The model here claims that the network also includes schemes, syntax, semantics, and so on. The final interpretation may be choice of one scheme over several others just as easily as choice of one word over its rivals.

The precise weighting of the evidence from syntactic, semantic, lexical, orthographic, and operational sources depends, *inter alia*, on the degree of restriction of context. Lytinen (1986a) takes for his corpora grammatically correct and literate sentences. However, let's again mention *Ily* in a marriage proposal scene. Alternatively, try *lecture student confusion question*. It is obvious that in, for example, the emotional nexus of a marriage proposal scene, a single

Perception   Production

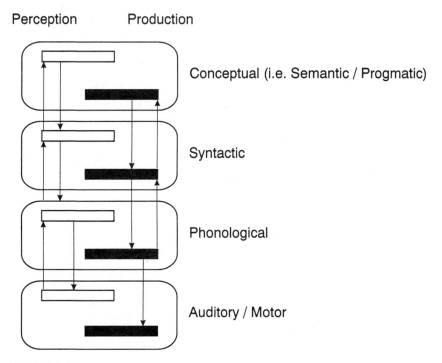

Conceptual (i.e. Semantic / Progmatic)

Syntactic

Phonological

Auditory / Motor

FIGURE 3.15.

phoneme can trigger a whole script. Syntax, if used, is very much implicit here.

Syntax deals with the regular combination of words. There is some evidence (Campbell, 1982; Johnson-Laird, 1993) that it is a manifestation of a more general underlying cognitive ability. The author wishes to claim that its importance in language processing, and its interplay with semantics, both depend on to what extent context has been restricted. When, in Stage 1 of language comprehension, context is relatively unrestricted, syntactic knowledge is paramount. However, in Stage 2, context may be so restricted that syntax is at best implicit.

The model offered here explains a range of phenomena. On the one hand, it is no longer a surprise that agrammatical strings can yield meaning, and that, at one extreme, a single phoneme can activate a script. On the other, the varying degrees of interaction between knowledge from syntactic and semantic sources are now explicable.

The model is tentative, and much work remains to be done. McClelland and Rumelhart (1986) report evidence for their theory.

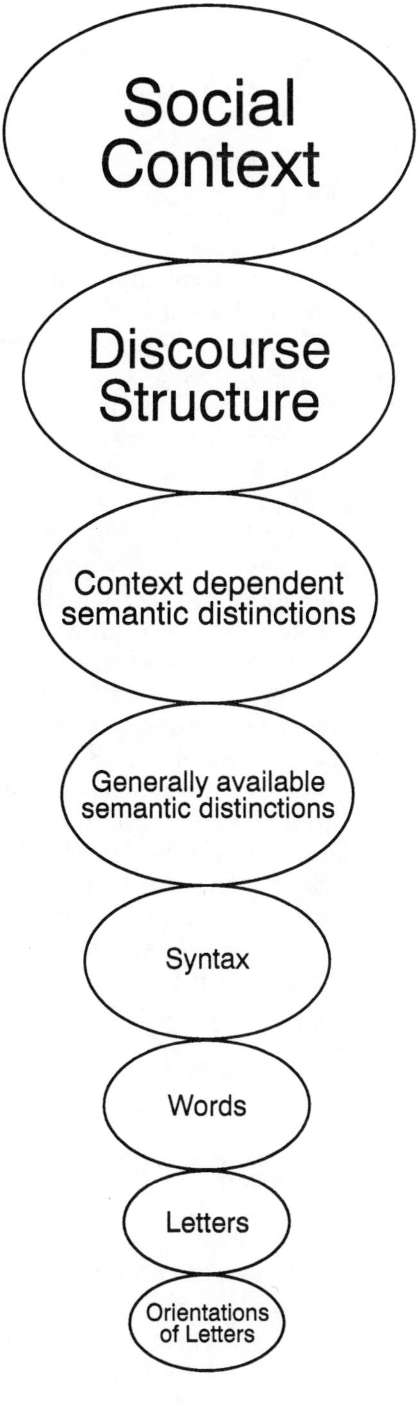

Social Context

Discourse Structure

Context dependent semantic distinctions

Generally available semantic distinctions

Syntax

Words

Letters

Orientations of Letters

FIGURE 3.16.

They found psychological subjects could more easily find *k* in a word (e.g., ankle) than in a meaningless sequence of letters. Thus, they claimed, the notion of excitatory links between letters and words in an hypothesized neural network gains support. The author envisages research that examines how subjects differentiate between word senses on the basis of different underlying scripts, and guess at the identity of acoustically underdetermined phonemes on the same basis, *inter alia*.

The consequence for ACL is, above all, a justification of the use of a variety of techniques. If the context has not yet been determined, word meaning or key word analysis is necessary (De Jong, 1982; Walker & Amsler, 1986). For a relatively restricted context, the relation between syntax and semantics seems well handled by Lytinen (1986a). At a further point of restriction, minimalist interlingua systems (Schank, 1975) and template matching (Weizenbaum, 1976) seem to work.

Thompson's (1983) setting aside of theory of linguistic computation for the study of the communicative process in the abstract makes it relevant to consider nonverbal communication here. Along with unrestricted speech processing and textual comprehension, Wahlster (1986) puts human communicative competence on the pantheon of goals unattainable in CL. Human communicative functioning is, we have seen, expectation driven, and the minuscule channel capacity (Miller, 1968, puts it at 25 bits per second) is compensated for by massive parallelism.

When is NL more appropriate than mice, icons, and so on (WIMPS) for nonmachine interaction? Some researchers have reviewed work on interface design, but in a specifically psychological framework. (Rules proposed include a restriction on spoken output to a maximum of 5 seconds.) Bates (1984) tackles the problem head on. NL communication is more appropriate, he argues, when the following considerations are paramount:

1. The task is relatively undefined.
2. There are no clear indications as to the limits of the system.
3. The existing interface is pitched at too high a level for the actual users.

Woods (1984) outlines a system combining NL and pointing for large, multivariate tasks like (Woods' scenario) World War III.

Unless at least some of the previous considerations are relevant, computational linguists can, depending on their original background, return to teaching French or Cobol programming, as soon as the EU and other funders of MT programs cease laying golden eggs. WIMPS may possibly eliminate Considerations 2 and 3 for interface work; the critical issue is Consideration 1.

In summary, then, Thompson's insistence that the milenniar parser should be massively expectation based is correct, as is his claim that the field of NLP has yet to address this requirement.

Cognitive Psychology and Computational Linguistics

It will be remembered that the model advanced above distinguished between two stages of language processing, which differed with respect to the presence of operational knowledge only in the second. Let's now recap Piaget.

Piaget, we've seen, insists that knowledge is formed by interactions between the subject and object that define the limits of both (Piaget, 1926, 1970). The resulting knowledge has active elements called *schemes* (Schank, 1975) scripts are a rough analogue), and static, representational elements called *schemas*. For Piaget, it is incorrect to suggest, as Wittgenstein (1967) does, in his refutation of private languages, that knowledge can be gained only by the process of mapping private sensations onto words.

The ontogenesis of language, Piaget claims, is a subset of the more general process of the ontogenesis of thought. This relation of set to subset is valid even for syntax (Piaget, 1926); the child can master relative clauses only with mastery of the more general motor operation of insertion, according to Piaget.

In Piagetian genetic epistemology, as we saw in Chapter 2, there are four stages through which humans must progress to arrive at adult logical competence. With the advent of each new stage, the individual's mode of apprehension changes.

At the opposite extreme to Piaget, we found the Sapir–Whorf hypothesis (Vygotsky, 1962). For Whorf, our conceptual apparatus is limited absolutely by the distinctions suggested by our language. However, we've seen that this hypothesis is simply not tenable, given the evidence against it from child development.

Piaget insists that knowledge is the result of interactions midway between subject and object (Piaget, 1971, 1972). He insists, moreover, that private languages (in the sense of representational schemes and schemata), can exist, and are referential because their origin is through these kinds of interactions, not idiosyncratic, nonreferential mental process. Piaget will also allow logical atoms, of a sort. However, they will resemble the ultimate thought elements of the *Tractatus* (Wittgenstein, 1922) only after infancy. In infancy, they will more resemble sucking reflexes, and so on.

It is at this point that we saw developmental psycholinguistics, in general, and the work of Vygotsky (1962), in particular, become relevant. With Vygotsky, we've seen claims that language and thought (Piaget's operational knowledge) have distinct evolutionary roots. Birdsong, for Vygotsky, is nonconceptual language; rats' maze solving is nonlinguistic thought. Only in human children after infancy, he claims, does language become conceptual and thought acquire linguistic expression.

Consequently, the existence of a two-stage process in language comprehension makes more sense. It is only in the second phase that operational knowledge features develop. Thus, the success of Schank's later script-based systems (De Jong, 1982; Schank & Abelson, 1977) now seems explicable. In them, the context is chosen, then a script representing the relevant operational knowledge is applied.

Wittgenstein (1967) was correct to renounce his earlier contention that there is a context-general calculus that can relate language to the world. The relation between knowledge structures like scripts and the relevant linguistic expression thereof varies between context. The underlying operational knowledge may be as different for two words as a screwdriver is from a hammer.

Let us again take stock. The author believes that the arguments of the later Wittgenstein (1967) need to be answered, and has chosen this ground—cognitive psychology—in which to answer them.

Piaget (1926, 1971a, 1971b, 1972) provides us with counterarguments, but burdens us with the task of fitting operational knowledge into the system. The author considers that one can so fit it in the notion of context. Also, Piaget's overemphasis on the operational at the expense of the linguistic needs to be tempered by findings from developmental psycholinguistics. Finally, it should be emphasized that the relation between knowledge structures and linguistic expression varies between contexts.

To write a successful CL knowledge-based system for a given application is to specify that relation for the particular context. Schank's most successful systems grew from this realization. After earlier attempts in microcontexts with a minimalist interlingua Schank and Abelson (1977) declined to separate form from content. For each application, each context, the rules of relation of operational and linguistic knowledge had to be redrawn. This makes the development of knowledge-based ACL systems the extremely difficult but not impossible task that it is.

For the next section dealing with psychology and CL, there are mainly disparate findings to report. They both await much more research activity.

COMPUTATIONAL PSYCHOLINGUISTICS.   Kay, as chairman of Coling 88, deplored the lack of research in this area, citing only Kaplan as a noncloset computational psycholinguist. Kaplan and colleagues explored garden paths in relative clauses. Miller (1968), whose work focused on the psychology of communication cited earlier, suggests in a finding with which the reader may now agree that human language processing becomes difficult after the fourth relative clause. Kaplan's earlier work (Kaplan et al., 1971) focused on developmental psycholinguistics. It has been suggested from time to time that machines could learn in analogous fashion to children, but little progress has been made.

Johnson-Laird (1983) adduces findings due to Marslen-Wilson that show that the simple presentation of a word activates it in all the possible contexts in which it might appear. This author insists that resolution of the exact meaning of the word awaits further evidence from the input text. We now have an analogue in NLP to Sperling's work on iconic imagery.

Finally, Thompson (1983) insists on the relevance for this area of putting the world in the machine. Much work remains to be done on precisely what kind of hypotheses the human language understander lines up, what kind of evidence is sufficient to resolve the issue, and so on.

****

The Active NLP movement

It is a consensus that NLP, considered as the general task of analyzing an arbitrary text in order to derive output for arbitrary ends (be they translation, data base interface, or whatever) is extremely difficult. Wittgenstein's major achievement might be said to be proving that it is impossible. One way to ground the area is analogous to that taken by the active vision movement. This program redefined computer vision studies as task-oriented from their original definition in terms of producing a 2-D representation of a static external world. Active NLP looks at language as it is used in the context of real tasks, rather like Wittgensteinian language games. Inevitably, the degree of restriction of context will often resemble that found in sublanguages.

The integration of natural language and vision is a case in point. Systems are included which, like ours (Ó Nualláin et al., 1994 a, b, in press), attempt to construct arbitrary scenes on the basis of NL descriptions or, *inter alia*, attempt an interlingual representation of spatial descriptions or visualize the primitives used in KR formalisms like CD. Dialogue in this new area has proven hard to establish between the different practitioners.

The task for the computer in our system consists of the incremental interpretation and reconstruction of verbal scene descriptions as they are spoken (or initially, typed) by a human user. The idea is to allow a person to give a very sparse description of an environment that he wishes to create a model of, and to have the computer system instantiate (that is, create according to the specification) and display an almost photo-realistic, three-dimensional model that is consistent with everything the user has said so far, and whose additional details are in some sense typical for the domain. As the user's description proceeds, some of the details and parameters of objects in the scene that will have initially been given default or randomized values will change to the specific values mentioned by the user. New objects can be introduced into the scene by simply mentioning that they are there, and these new objects too initially will appear in canonical orientations, in "reasonable" places, and with sizes, colors, and other attributes taking on values that are randomly distributed around appropriate norms. The defaults, of course, often will be inappropriate to the model that the human user has in mind, but as (s)he continues to specify salient details of his or her own view of the world, the computer's internal model (and the screen view) change correspondingly, and new subsidiary defaults come into play. Of course, most of the detail is registered subsidiarily (in Polanyi's, 1958, sense; see Chapter 4) if at all.

A user's description of a scene might proceed as follows. The visualization window on the screen is initially black, and the system waits for the user to begin.

User: You are standing on a suburban street corner.

(Immediately a scene appears, consisting of typical suburban houses with lawns, sidewalks along the edge of the street, trees, and so on.)

User: The house on the corner has a red door, with green trim around the windows.

(Scene adjusts to fit the new descriptive detail. Note the phrase "on . . . corner" occurs again, with a different interpretation because the dominating node is a house rather than a person.)

User: Walk down the street to your left, which is Rowan Crescent.

(A street sign appears, with the new name on it, and the scene changes to reflect movement of the observer. The database is incrementally instantiated to include additional detail re-quired to fill in the scene. The compass-point orientation of streets is still undetermined.)

Implementation of the system is not yet complete, but we have a version running on a Sun workstation that supports dialogues similar to those shown. We are using the Alvey Natural Language Tools grammar and parser (Grover et al., 1993) for syntactic and semantic analysis of the English input; we are building the domain models and translation mechanisms in CLOS (the Common Lisp Object System); and the graphical visualization facility is currently implemented directly in Common Lisp with some use of CLOS as well.

The system investigates several different themes. One is the postulated common semantics (in the "model" sense above) of language and vision as a "language of thought" mechanism for grounding. The data we have so far from our project establishes a set of relationships between the logical form expressions produced by ANLT and the naive physics of the streets and blocks worlds. We believe that we shall have to experiment not just with different domains of application but also with different semantic formalisms in order to derive principles of relation. The isolation of these principles is important enough to justify the effort.

Another is the active NLP theme of assessing how far NLP can be taken in a computational environment and the investigation of the limits of that environment. We have prepared well with respect to the tools used and task chosen; undoubtedly, however, we shall come across some limitations to our approach.

LANGUAGE AND OTHER SYMBOL SYSTEMS

Let's note the following facts about language once again.

1. All natural languages are within certain precise limits of formal complexity.
2. All natural languages (NL) can be in some sense described in formal grammars.

3. All NLs have a recursive structure; for example, we find a sentence embedded within a sentence in an utterance like "(He said) that (He was going)."

For NL, substitute *music,* and these statements seem also true. It will be argued in Chapter 7 that the same state of affairs could well hold for vision also.

ON THE NOTION OF CONTEXT

Two extremely evident trends within CS are of relevance here. The first is the recent emphasis on situated cognition à la Brooks (1991); the second is the acknowledgment from those such as Slezak (1993) that context is not just another entity (along with, for example, information capacity) that can be introduced, as if from outside, in order to explain behavior. On the contrary, we are embedded in contexts continually, and it is in fact entities like *language* that, considered in the abstract apart from their actual use, are misleading. One of the concerns of this chapter has been to acknowledge the truth of these two ideas in an overall theory of language processing.

In this chapter, we have strongly distinguished between two types of cognitive act: that of context determination and that of processing within a context. Only the latter process features operational knowledge. We can usefully refine our vocabulary here. It is better to call the initial act domain determination, and acts that further restrict the discourse content can be termed acts of context restriction. These acts cause the levels of language to collapse in a manner that allows, for example, direct interaction between the pragmatic and syntactic levels. It is this type of interaction that must be examined by theories of situated cognition, which are by definition theories of the effects of context.

A final speculation: We spent a long time, while clearing the ground, examining the relation of syntax and semantics. Syntactic relations, we argued, give semantic relations in a sufficiently restricted context. Yet there undoubtedly are occasions where a neat semantic theory of a domain exists. For example, the theory called model-theoretic semantics is trivially true if we are talking about set theory. We are now right back to the position we advanced in Chapter 1, that different types of objectivity exist, all valid for their own types of application. In Chapter 8 we begin to discern the cognitive role of self in our schema. So far, it is clear that context has been added to the Nolanian schema as a major player. Self will be found to be intertwined with context.

SUMMARY: MIND IN LINGUISTICS

Computation and linguistics have defined the boundaries to the discussion in this chapter. We first of all reviewed the main theories of linguistics. All seemed in some way incomplete. We noted that for Edelman the notion of formal linguistics is itself an aberration. In any case, it was established that we could not equate mind with any such formalization of whatever power—cognition involves interactions between language and thought. We reviewed how these interactions developed both ontogenetically and phylogenetically. Having established this strand of the argument, we began to examine the relation of syntax and semantics. This, in turn, led us to question the conventional notions of the stratification of language as valid ideas of language processing.

What we've been most concerned with is finding a *via media* between formalists like Chomsky and skeptics like Edelman. Our final position is that use of language involves exploitation of a formal symbol system, interaction of this system with operational knowledge, and intersubjective knowledge of oneself as an object in the world. Neuroscientific evidence currently exists for the first two points. Moreover, we found cause to greatly amplify the part played by context in linguistic behavior.

FURTHER READING

Modern Linguistics by Smith and Wilson (1979) is a good introduction to Chomsky's earlier work. *Natural Language and Computational Linguistics* by Beardon, Lumsden, and Holmes (1991) is well explained and features Prolog examples. Gazdar and Mellish's (1989) *NLP* is available in Lisp, Prolog (the language of choice in the case of this book) and POP-11. From philosophy, Austin (1962) has greatly influenced CL, as has Montague (1974), though the latter text is difficult. Dowty, Karttunnen, & Zwicky (1985) is a good collection on parsing, particularly in an FG framework. Finally, Kelly (1955) deals with *construal*.

• *four* •

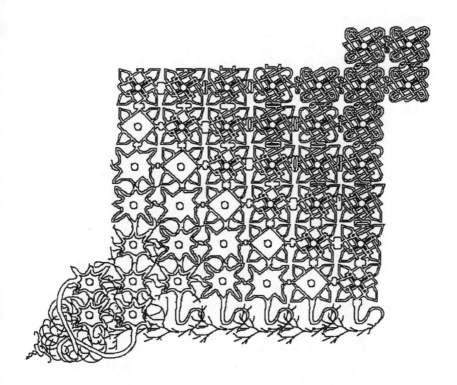

NEUROSCIENCE

THE CONSTITUENT DISCIPLINES OF NEUROSCIENCE

The brain has been slow to give up its secrets. Like all the other areas of cognitive science, neuroscience, were it truly successful, would pre-empt the necessity of separate consideration of its confrères. Had we a full neuroscientific account of cognition, the description of each of the other disciplines would be seen as subservient. For example, let's imagine that we had a full neurological account of the processes implicated in *modus ponens*. We could then explain ability to perform this logical operation purely in terms of brain nerve cells (neurons) firing. Inability to perform modus ponens properly in certain circumstances could, by the same token, be explained with respect to neural aberration. That description would take priority over the psychological account, which might explain performance errors in terms of attention lapses, alcohol ingestion, and so on. The purpose of the psychological account would simply be to translate the primary neurological account into its own terms.

Similarly, linguistics issues could be resolved with respect to the workings of a complex neurally implemented formal system. The fundamental motive of ethnoscience would simply be an *a posteriori* rephrasal of why neural system A had different nuances than neural system B. Every subdiscipline within cognitive science aspires to be the whole of the subject. Neuroscience fails just like all the others. However, here the case is slightly more complicated. The ambitions of neuroscience are higher than those of the rest, in that it would claim to afford a description of cognition at the physical level as well as the symbolic, which none of the others care to try to do. Insofar as this is the case, the fall to earth is more precipitous; we know very little about the hardware that supports cognition after a century of modern neuroscience.

At this stage, neuroscience covers a multitude of subdisciplines within itself. Neuroanatomy deals with the gross structure of the brain. Neurophysiology deals with its physiological functioning. Cognitive neuropsychology attempts to map cognitive function onto anatomical location or, failing that, functional groups of neurons. Nor is the Christian virtue of hope absent from neuroscience; a set of eliminative materialists, the neurophilosophers, await the resolution of philosophical questions, past, present, and future, in the advent of neuroscience. (Now we see as through a glass darkly, then shall we see face to face.)

This chapter, on the other hand, focuses on what is currently known and what is likely to be known about neuroscience in the foreseeable future. We start off with the investigative methods of neuroscience. Until recently, much of our knowledge about neuro-science stemmed from brain injury either accidentally or deliberately inflicted.

Among the most appalling incidents in the history of science was the experimentation conducted on "subhumans" by the Nazis and in mental hospital on patients by doctors in the so-called civilized world. What makes things worse is that nonintrusive techniques are now available, and very little was found out through the other research, experimentation for which barbaric is not nearly an adequate epithet.

We then spend some time focusing on gross neuroanatomy. It will help to briefly discuss the biological development (epigenesis) of the brain. As we discuss anatomy, we find ourselves at times forced to locate functions across gross anatomical divisions. This forces a discussion of which and to what extent psychic functions are localized and which are globalized. Following this, we summarize our knowledge and then our ignorance.

The computational paradigm variously called *parallel distributed processing* (PDP), *neural networks*—which don't really exist yet—and (a term also used here) *connectionism* was originally neurologically inspired. It may yet have much to say on how symbols arise from the apparently chaotic calculations of billions of neurons. We discuss connectionism first as experimental neuroscience. We then introduce the major conceptual construct therein, the formal neuron. This leads us to a discussion of connectionism's neurological and psychological validity. We then speak about the learning paradigms current in connectionism. One of them, competitive learning, leads us down old pathways of evolutionary theory.

A central problem remains: How do symbols arise? Alternatively: what is a symbol, that we should know it? Do we have a binary system of neural impulse and full symbol, or (the more likely conclusion) is there a continuum in existence? Another issue is the experiential correlate of subsymbolic PDP. Michael Polanyi's notion of subsidiary awareness is advanced as an hypothesis here. We then discuss connectionism, *per se*, as a computational tool and to our surprise find the technique of Archimedes quite useful.

We then discuss the brain as a computational system. As such, it is quite different from its rivals in Chapter 5, and helps proper consideration thereof. Finally, by way of tying together some of the strands of our consideration of neuroscience, we discuss the work of Gerald Edelman.

THE METHODOLOGY OF NEUROSCIENCE

Lesioning

We've already looked at the old-fashioned way to do experimental neuroscience: Select a subhuman, tie him down, and cut away that part of the brain for which you wish to establish a function. If a particular function doesn't survive the procedure, the tendency is to localize it in the lesioned area. However, this methodology tends to have technical drawbacks together with its definite whiff of absolute moral evil. For a start, few cognitive functions are localized enough to yield to this type of investigation. Secondly, invasive neurosurgery is still an inexact science. Finally, the subhuman is likely to have averse reactions to the procedure he has had to undergo, and may be unwilling to undergo it again. Electroconvulsive therapy (ECT) has sometimes been observed to use the fact that chronically depressed patients will act extremely happy in order to avoid having to endure once more a large voltage being established across the space between their ears. ECT's origins are in the abattoir; yet it may be useful in some types of mental illness (the existence of much of which has itself credibly been doubted). The original inspiration was cows' frenzied response to a blow on the head.

Two further cases of doubtful neuroscience are the "discovery" of the pleasure centers in the ungeate nucleus of the brain by an American neurosurgeon and Penfield's localization of specific memories in anatomically distinct cortical areas. A video of the American (deliberately unnamed here) smiling happily and interrogating a female subhuman still exists. The subhuman has, Skinner-style, a panel from which she can choose one of three buttons. To the neurosurgeon's pleasure, she continued to press the one that resulted in stimulation of her ungeate nucleus. She described it as the "sexy" button. His conclusion that this resulted in stimulation of a pleasure center is correct, but it was far more likely to be his than hers. Moreover, it has been known since the late 1970s (twenty-odd years after that research) that morphine-analogous hormones called the endorphins, located in the nerve terminals, evoked perhaps by electrical discharge, also regulate pleasure. In like fashion, Penfield's work, which involved stimulation of cortical areas until patients found themselves remembering items as specific as sunny days beside the river, recently has been called into question as well, and it never has been replicated. Had Penfield's findings been corroborated, they would constitute outstanding evidence that memory is *localist*, that is, that specific memories can be very strongly associated with specific neuronal groups. The strong version of the alternative *distributed* hypothesis is that memories are spread all over the cortex.

The neuroscientific search for localization of function has also had some spectacular successes. The earliest such was around 1860—Broca's implication of an area in the left hemisphere of the brain in language. If damaged, one becomes speechless (aphasic) to varying degrees; some recovery can be achieved only if the trauma occurs in infancy. Indeed, language in its two main manifestations (spoken and written) has been a happy hunting ground for neuroscientific ambulance-chasers in that specific pathologies for complete loss of speech (aphasia), writing (agraphia), and reading (alexia) have been identified as often correlated to specific neuropathology, perhaps the result of a stroke cutting off the blood flow to the area. Dyslexia, dysphasia, and dysgraphia (which is commonly and wrongly called dyslexia) are milder symptoms.

Look at Figure 4.1. The brain's symmetric form requires communication between the two hemispheres (HS) through the corpus callosum. This section has no other known function than that of telephone exchange and was occasionally removed in cases of severe epilepsy. (Let's note, *en passant*, that the nerve fibers descending from both hemispheres cross over, resulting in the left hemisphere's (lhs) controlling the right side of the body, and vice

**Corpus
Callosum**

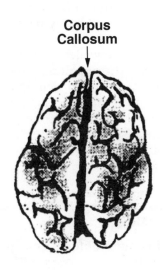

FIGURE 4.1.

versa.) Broca's localization was confirmed by this procedure. An image shown only to the right hemisphere (rhs) could not be verbally identified (the rhs has a very limited, often obscene vocabulary), except in the extremely rare cases where speech is located in the rhs. Moreover, it does rather seem as though, in the normal case, spatial and musical reasoning are located in the rhs. However, at some point in the 1960s, speculation began to go seriously off the rails. Two minds! Two consciousnesses! One version of this hypothesis casts the lhs in the role of an interpreter of all experience, more or less carrying on a monologue to explain the world to itself, sometimes with destructive consequences. One such example is if a patient suffers a biochemical imbalance leading to depression, the interpreter deepens the depression by inventing a story to explain it. We should remember this quote from one of the patients used in these investigations as we discuss this issue of fragmentation of personhood in Chapter 8:

Are you guys trying to make two people out of one?

Typically commisurectomy patients would be asked to perform separate tasks with right and left hemispheres, while perhaps also listening to a commentary on the soccer World Cup in the left ear, and the U.S. open golf championship in the right. Most psychology textbooks include a rather benign diagram of the setup. The conclusion must be that personhood, as distinct from self (see Chapter 8), is unitary, despite terribly contrived experimental setups that would tend to fragment many people with perfectly intact corpora callosa.

Lesioning, then, has not revealed as much as one might have thought, and far less than the appalling ethical standards of many of the experiments might seem to demand as justification. The ultimate reason seems to lie in the fact that the brain does not localize function spatially as neatly as one might wish. We discuss that at length later. We also discuss later some localizations suggested by the different lobes in Figure 4.2—for example, the occipital lobe handles visual processing.

Positron Emission Tomography (PET) and Magnetic Resonance Imaging (MRI)

Certain isotopes of common atoms emit positrons. Oxygen-15, far less common than the O_{14} we love and breathe, can be traced after an injection into the blood stream by tomographic methods. An example application is tracing the neural activity correspond-

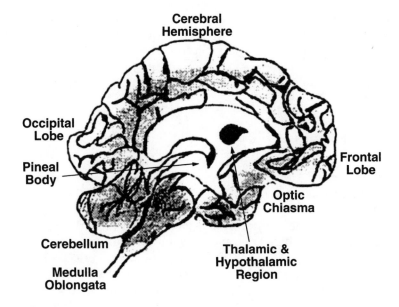

FIGURE 4.2.

ing to eye movements. The major feature to track is going to be the oxygen debit in inactive parts of the brain that don't have an appropriate blood flow. PET can be usefully supplemented by the high resolution imagery afforded by MRI. These techniques taken together are extremely effective.

EEG

Again, this is a method with a past vulnerability to 1960s excesses. The electrical activity of the brain was first crudely measured at the start of the 19th century. About 20 years ago, it was found that experienced meditators showed ability to create surges in the (alpha) brain wave forms associated with sleep. The followers of Maharishi Mahesh Yogi, in particular, claimed a scientific charter for their technique. It is not my intention to deny the beneficial effects of meditation, but the particular result quoted in the newspaper publicity of synchrony of the two has not been replicated.

EEG can, however, particularly assist psychological experiments. Take the following list of words:

Dollar   Penny   Bob

For an American, the word *Bob* is likely to provoke an anomalous reaction, manifest in a jump in EEG activity registered. For a middle-aged Irish or British person, the registered anomaly is more likely to be *Dollar*—bob was commonly used for the coin whose present-day equivalent is the 5p. EEG is a relatively crude technique.

Other Techniques

It is possible to use other nonintrusive techniques for neuroscientific research. Tracers and dyes might differentially stain certain types of neurons and not others. Retroviruses are being experimented with.

In particular, the pseudorabies virus together with anatomical tract tracing and dies are revealing much concerning neuronal architecture and pathways. Other recent promising techniques include patch-clamp recording and intracellular monitoring. Single-neuron monitoring is of obvious intrinsic interest. Rat studies using this technique have been credited with helping sufferers of epilepsy. This technique has produced one finding of extreme interest to us (which incidentally makes Smolensky's work—see below—seem a little narrow in conception) in that neurons seem to vary greatly from simple to hypercomplex in the specificity of the information encoded.

In a classic finding, a cell in the primate cortex was found to respond only to a primate hand. This gave rise to speculation about the existence of *grandmother cells*—cells hard-wired to respond only to that loving face (Hofstadter, 1979, 345-8). This type of monitoring of single neurons may reveal much more.

Counting

Well, this actually hasn't been done yet. In fact, the number of neurons in the brain is variously estimated at 10 billion or 100 billion, with most textbooks splitting the difference and plumping for 50 billion. Recently, Jacob T. Schwartz (1988) upped the ante to 1,000 billion neurons. However, he was bid down by another article in the same collection (Cowan & Sharp, 1988) that chose the miserly 10 billion figure again. Yes, it's perhaps a little premature to create a neurophilosophy without performing some arithmetic: Our ignorance of the brain starts with the number of neurons, and develops from there. A word of warning: you've lost a few hundred since the start of this chapter, given that we lose thousands a day.

One estimate of the number of connections (Edelman, 1992) suggests that someone counting the connections in one brain at a rate of one connection per second would take 32 million years to complete the task. A neural section the size of a matchead contains about 1 billion connections. I could be bound in a nutshell, and consider myself a king of infinite space.

Double Dissociation

This technique is strongly related to lesioning. Essentially, if a specific lesion in area A causes inability X but not inability Y, and one in area B causes only inability Y, the conclusion is that area A is correlated with ability X and B with Y. For example, if a lesion only in Broca's area causes problems in speech but no visual deficiencies and one only in the occipital cortex causes the reverse, one tends to make the obvious attributions.

GROSS NEUROANATOMY

One Brain or Two?

We have already discussed the split-brain school that attempted to posit separate consciousnesses (in the case of Penrose, 1989) or indeed "selves" in the two hemispheres of the brain. A more useful type of division is perhaps that between the neocortex and the rest of the brain. The neocortex was formed over the past half million years in an unprecedented evolutionary explosion. It is difficult to quantify or understand the evolutionary pressures that gave rise to it. (Incidentally, the speed with which human language developed indicates that it may have used previously existing neural hardware, the type of kludge-like solution that nature has often used in the brain.) The rest of the brain is known as the limbic system and is in evolutionary terms a great deal more primitive. It is important to remember that these ancient structures survive intact in a perhaps uneasy alliance with the neocortex. As humans, we find another of Socrates' metaphors surprisingly neuroscientifically apt. He conceived the person as in a chariot driven by two winged steeds. One attempts to fly toward the heavens; the other's goal is to enmesh and entangle in the earth. So, as proponents of this perhaps insightful dichotomous view of the brain would also claim, Janus-faced, our brains run simultaneously on codes of pure intellect and pure hormone. Thus the necessity for constructs like myth.

Transmission between neurons is achieved by substances called neurotransmitters going across the cleft between two neurons (see Figure 4.3). Normally, the cleft (synapse) yawns across the space between the dendrite of one neuron and the terminal bouton of another. Let's say that transmission is from neuron A to neuron B. We call the A side of the cleft the presynapse and the B side the postsynapse. Such membranes, which have been optimized for transmission, are specially thickened and have certain special receptor molecules. Many different types of neurons and of neurotransmitters exist. It certainly does not look as if Nature chose to limit herself in any way with respect to the types of codes that the brain might use.

Approximately forty percent of the brain's consumption of energy (which has a similar percentage of demand on the energy of the whole body) is devoted to maintaining the electrochemical possibility of neural transmission.

Neuron B is thus kept at a resting potential of –70 mV by ion pumps in which potassium plays a leading role. Electrical

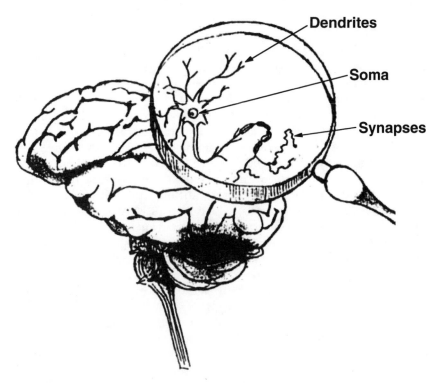

FIGURE 4.3.

impulses (or action potentials) travel down the axon of A and on reaching its terminal produce a calcium influx. This influx causes the neurotransmitter to fuse with A's membrane, thus releasing the chemical message (for example glutamate) into the cleft. This in turn bonds to a receptor molecule on B, causing an ion channel to open. The consequent ion exchange will create an action potential in B if transmission is successful, resulting in B's membrane becoming positive. It may however be the case that A is acting as an inhibitor, causing B's potential to decrease to –90 mV. Finally, transmission for a particular neuron can occur a maximum of only about 200 times per second. It will attempt to transmit the impetus to the next neuron in the sequence before settling back to its normal polarized state. With at least tens of billions of neurons in the brain, all of which can have hundreds of thousands of connections with each other, the chains of command are webs of an intricacy beyond our current comprehension. (We noted in Chapter 2 that they seem ideal for probabilistic reasoning.)

This neurophysiological process is chemically mediated (mainly by sodium) but inevitably the ion exchanges have electrical effects that are transmitted along the chain of command, activating action potentials as they go.

We have examined neural transmission in some detail for a number of reasons. The first is to compare it with transmission of purely electrical impulses in computing. There, communication is currently achieved through conventional electrical circuitry etched on semiconductor material. The only limits applicable to computational hardware mechanisms are the speed of light and heating effects inevitable in electrical process. Neural mechanism, on the other hand, has a limit in its speed of around 100m/s (versus around 300,000 km/s for the speed of pure electrical transmission). Yet the programs implemented by neural systems perform tasks that are way beyond the capacities of current computation. The pattern-matching task achieved with every human glance is at least 10 years distant from current abilities of computers. The consequence is that the brain is seen to operate with a different architecture than the computer. If it is to perform tasks of such a complexity so quickly, it must have an ability to work *in parallel.*

Let's explore what this means. In Chapter 3, we noted that language admitted of at least these separate levels: The conceptual, the syntactic, and the phonological. Each has its own laws of combination of units. Now, we can imagine that using nonparallel *serial* architecture, the relation between these levels is pretty clear. For example, we might assume that the conceptual level awaits input from completion of the syntactic analysis. Yet this is both linguistically and computationally absurd: Many sentences admit of hundreds of different syntactic parses, and it is lunacy to conceive of these as being sequentially presented to a conceptual homunculus until he decides on the appropriate reading. Moreover, interleaving of the syntactic and conceptual analyses can cut down on the number of parses, often by a factor of hundreds. No; what must be happening neurologically is parallel processes simultaneously exploring the conceptual and syntactic levels, here making a guess based on previous experience with a similar text or utterance, there simultaneously checking the syntactic wellformedness of a chunk of the phrase with respect to that hypothesis. The processing is being done massively in parallel, with regard for neither the exigencies of pure syntactic theory, nor the requirements of possible-worlds semantics. In accordance with the principle of rationality, the brain will use whatever parsing strategy and whatever degree of parallelism are necessary to get a meaning clear enough to proceed to the next speech or other behavioral act.

Second, connectionism is based on an idealization of the rather rugged system used in a neural transmission called a *formal neuron*. The ideas of neurons and connections are honored in this idealization; the complexities that arise from the concerted action of billions of such neurons are not. Yet connectionism has claims to neural validity of its own aside from its efficacy as a computational formalism. These claims rest on functional equivalence (see Chapter 1); we're going to note that connectionist systems have memories that are more like humans' than computers', and that their pattern-recognition competence has the same profile. In particular, like ourselves, connectionist (PDP) systems can perform much better if asked to complete "Shall I compare thee to a summer's day? . . ." than if asked, unprepared, to recite Sonnet 18 from the Master. The former process we call *associative content-addressable memory* (ACAM or CAAM), and the latter is look-up memory and would involve retrieving Sonnet 18 from a standard computer memory.

Neural Epigenesis and Evolution

Cells seem to specialize into organs in accordance with the instructions mediated through the fields that dominate these organs. It seems rather as if the orders that command a cell to specialize into a liver rather than a kidney cell are mediated through force fields that resemble the magnetic fields necessarily generated by an electric current. At a sufficiently early stage in embryonic development, any appropriately relocated cell will specialize as commanded. However, at a later stage, a liver cell will refuse to become a kidney cell if transplanted.

Not everything actually is known about how learning is implemented neurally. Thousands of rats gave their lives in attempts to prove that a rich sensory environment gives rise to increased numbers of connections. In fact, connectionism is quite successful in implementing learning solely as changes in connection strength. More recent work focuses on the phenomenon just noted of cells' ability to change (transmutability). If true, it provides an extremely rich metaphor for learning, one with exciting consequences in terms of cerebral functioning. Could learning something be akin to setting up a field that appropriately alters the very nature of neurons? Alternatively, molecular modification of proteins might occur, in particular the process called *phosphorylation*, which modifies proteins on transmitter receptor molecules and ion channels on cell membranes. Yet another alternative is a process called *long-term potentiation* (Fischbach, 1992), which is a long-term enhancement of synaptic transmission and currently favored as a mechanism for learning and memory in the hippocampus and other areas. It is not yet well understood, but may be important in development.

A second striking fact about fetal/neonatal development is the massive death of neurons that occurs shortly after birth. This, among other phenomena, has given rise to neural Darwinist speculation about competition between neurons. This is discussed later. Could it be the case that groups of neurons compete among themselves for functional roles? Again we find the principle of rationality acquiring evolutionary and neurological echoes.

Finally, let's mention the nature of the brain–body unity itself. The nervous system must be more than a crossroads for the incoming (afferent) neural impulses carrying information about the external world and the efferent impulses that cause action on that world. There must be periods of quietude, switches between connective patterns; in fact, a whole patchwork of different knits (yet again!) To understand the brain–central nervous system (CNS) nexus, we must take into consideration that it functions in a living body immersed in a world with certain definite sensory qualities. Indeed, the capacity for movement itself provided many of the neural developments that give longitudinally segmented organisms an advantage over radially segmented ones like the sea urchin.

Again, we find it impossible to discuss a system coherently without reference to the life world (the environment as it relates to the organism) from which it springs and without which it has no meaningful function or structure. To discern this meaning, it is necessary yet again to consider evolution over a long time period. This biological hypothesis fits in extremely well with the situated cognition view we outlined first in Chapter 1. The possibility of a biologically based epistemology, glimpsed by Bergson and Piaget, seems increasingly indicated with our increased neurobiological knowledge. Moreover, the purely philosophical consideration of Heidegger and Merleau-Ponty also correctly placed us in this life world.

Gross Neuroanatomy Itself

We must view the brain as part of an encompassing nervous system (NS). The central nervous system, rightfully considered, comprises the brain on one hand and the spinal cord on the other. The brain, we've noted, can be subdivided into the advanced neocortex and the rest, the limbic system. The other part of the nervous system includes the somatic and autonomic (ans) systems, used for body homeostasis—for example, digestion and blood pressure regulation.

The cortex is divided into lobes by fissures. To the front are the frontal lobe and frontal motor area. The former facilitates emotional response, the latter voluntary motor activity (later we consider involuntary). The fineness of the motor response required is proportional to the area of frontal lobe allotted. It is located just below the central fissure.

Sensory information is relayed to (a) the (touch) parietal lobe at the parietal lobe beyond the central fissure, (b) the temporal lobe below the lateral fissure (sound), and (c) the occipital lobe. The limbic system is part of the primitive brain and is concerned with lower functions. The hypothalamus is involved with the regulation of appetitive behaviors. The reticular formation is a network of nerves running from the mid-brain to the limbic system. It monitors arousal. The Hippocampus has a vital role in STM. We've seen that there is another nervous system as well as the CNS, called the peripheral nervous system which originates in 31 spinal and 12 pairs of cranial nerves. This can be broken down as represented above:

1. The somatic nervous system feeds to striped muscle and sensory nerves from receptors.

2. The ans is a motor system for smooth muscles and glands. We can consider the stress reaction as an example of its functioning.

Realism and Cerebral Functioning

Over the next two sections, we shall look at neuroscientific evidence for the viewpoint on cognition being promoted in this book. The first question relates to how we can justify Gibson's ecological optics and other such theories that posit a direct, anticonstructionist view on perception. In fact, we have already encountered some of the critical concepts. First of all, we can sensibly view the competition between neurons as attempting in a neural Darwinist way to recognize or respond to something in the external world. Secondly, and more significantly, we can coherently view the act of perception in terms of processes within the cortex synchronizing themselves over the time with sensations at the sense organs. In other words, direct nonmediated perception of the external world is possible if given time. A resonance between neural event and sensory activity can be set up. Nor need we ignore the fact that the neural activity will be a transformation of the incoming sensations. The main part, that it is a direct impression rather than a construct, remains intact.

Karl Pribram has outlined a *holonomic* theory of brain function around this central idea. His earlier, more radical contentions also assumed that the brain reflected the external world precisely as a laser does. A laser image of an object is distributed globally throughout the representation. Damage to part of the representation affects the resolution of the image, which is yet wholly preserved. The early Pribram contended that neural representation was precisely analogous and totally distributed. This view he has now modified, allowing localisms as well. The notion of synchrony between neural process and physical sensation remains intact.

Mylesianism and Cerebral Functioning

Let's now take preliminary stock of neuroscientific findings that are compatible with the ethos and specific aspects of the framework proposed in this book and in particular with Mylesianism.

We needed, first of all, some neural hardware mechanisms that could support a realist epistemology and have just outlined them. Indeed, we can also define the objects of the intersubjective domain in these terms. (Can it be that our discourse about higher symbolic items has neural constraints that require that my neural events when discussing "justice" be similar to yours? Remember how we learned that concept: It took plenty of examples, followed by a person-to-person pedagogical experience with a respected elder. This is just speculation, yet it is not, in effect, at all incompatible with Edelman's perspective described later.)

More to the point, we're espousing agnosticism on separate perceptual modules. We wish, in a further development, to be able to reserve the word *perception* for cognitive acts maintaining a stable relationship with an environment (and *cognition* for acts that transcend that environment) without totally losing the original meaning of the words. We wish to be able to "receive" a mismatch between a muscular effort and a dart that misses the board (visual and somatic "perception"), or indeed that Bill Clinton never recovered from his presidency's poor start although he won the NAFTA vote. The neurological evidence is on our side here; for example, as well as the role already advocated for it, the parietal lobe coordinates visual and movement information. (Likewise, the auguries from psychology are good: Infants can show intermodal transfer as we described in Chapter 2.)

A great deal of weight falls on the shoulders of egocentric knowledge. We need it for tracking objects, for moving in any way successfully in an environment. Recent evidence (Berthoz, Israel, & Wiener, 1992) has shown that there exist neurons in the hippocampus with exquisitely directed roles. For example, some allow for the movement of the body in particular physical contexts like corners. This is precisely the kind of potentially nightmarishly complicated task (cf. the frame problem) where we need special-purpose hardware to perform the calculations unconsciously, "egocentrically." The posterior parietal cortex is another location of this hardware. Similarly, we find that tracking objects, another task where the frame problem can easily manifest itself, is handled by the oculomotor reflex, which can if necessary also come under voluntary control. This is also a Gibsonian invariant.

The thorny problem caused by different perspectives on an object may yet be unravelled neurally as it has been mathematically. We find also that our agnosticism about monism and dualism gains greatly in strength from analysis of the neuroscientific evidence, which can be read as supporting any or no viewpoint on the issue.

Cerebral Functioning: Globalizations and Localizations

It's time to put another ghost to rest. A huge literature has grown up around the issue of whether cerebral function is localized (that is, if there is one function per area of the brain) or global. Perhaps the high-water mark of the former school was Gall's *phrenology*, where the faculties of man were assumed located to such a specific extent that one's character expressed itself as bumps in different places on the head. Psychological personality testing involved essentially running one's hand over the subject's cranium. Lashley's search for local subroutines or engrams involved teaching rats to run mazes, excising areas of the cortex, and noting the disimprovement in performance. To his surprise, he found that no all-or-none relationship existed. What rather seemed to happen was that the disimprovement in performance was directly proportional to the quantity of the cerebral area excised regardless of the particular location. Lashley was led to believe that all memories were stored globally over the entire cortex. We noted Penfield's work, which seemed to suggest the opposite, in the introductory section of this chapter.

Hubel and Wiesel (1962) won the Nobel Prize for work that again seemed to suggest localization. Only in the past few years has it been called into question. Briefly, what they seemed to have established were banks of cells in the occipital cortex of the cat, differentially attuned to lines of varied orientations. One bank would be attuned to vertical lines, another to lines at 5° from the vertical, and so on. Let us conclude this discussion by emphasizing that the weight of evidence suggests that both local and distributed function is used. The former is epitomized by "grandmother" cells, the latter by Lashley's (1942) brain-ablated rats.

The conclusion, yet again, is that the brain will cohere to whatever form is necessary in order to optimize its adaptation. In another twist of the screw, it must have the capacity to give hardware support to formal systems as complex as language, music, and mathematics.

One of the best established localisms is topographic maps of incoming sensory transductions of energy. Essentially, what this implies is that two incoming stimuli of similar energy profile should eventually stimulate adjoining areas of cortex. Two mutually distant stimuli should, contrariwise, activate mutually remote regions of the lobe devoted to the relevant sensory information. By this token, orange and red should be mapped onto adjoining areas of cortex, distant from violet. One exception to this general rule seems to be olfaction, where calculations of the particular smell seem to follow neoconnectionist (PDP) formal neural principles rather than topographic principles.

Whatever the specifics of the principles, there is little doubt that the brain performs many of its calculations informed by spatial representations over groups of neurons. The cortex can be viewed as sheets (lamina) of neurons, piled one over the other. Let's focus for a moment on the parietal lobe, where fusion of information from visual and movement sources has to occur. The activations of neurons over a given Cartesian space might represent the act of throwing a dart, or reaching for an object. It seems plausible indeed that the brain has optimized algorithms for coordinate transformation over that space in order precisely to calculate the trajectory of an arm. Such algorithms may also calculate items as disparate as which particular type of carpet one is feeling, or which particular note one is playing on an instrument.

Probabilistic reasoning plays a massive role in being-in-the-world. We don't passively receive the world; we actively form hypotheses to construe it, and do this continually in every sensory modality and symbolic system. Moreover, our guesses are to different extents confirmed or not from moment to moment. You didn't expect to find Louis Armstrong mentioned in this sentence. We need to be able to maintain the integrity of our guesses in the face of incomplete and sometimes of contradictory information. A three-wheeled car is still a car. Best guesses are confirmed or not probabilistically, allowing us the kind of ability to function in the real world that AI systems still so markedly lack.

Moreover, these guesses have massive neural support. If one analyzes a sensory modality like vision with respect to the neural support, it turns out that the vast majority of the hardware involved is carrying (top-down) information about the hypotheses being lined up. The bottom-up information concerning the sensory information itself is viewed only through the context supplied by top-down information.

Our ignorance of how the brain supports higher level cognition is impressive. It is possible that the kind of state-space transformations we have already discussed are used for much cerebral process. In this framework, phonetic discrimination, to take but one example, is achieved by laminar decomposition of the language's phonology and calculation over a 3-D Cartesian space. Those who believe that the brain is an extremely complex structure with simple principles of operation (e.g., Churchland, 1988) will hold this to be true. However, it's also possible that the brain is capable of a multiplicity of different modes of operation, implemented over qualitatively different structures. Much of the exciting research on that area comes from PDP. Let's pay it a visit.

CONNECTIONISM (PDP)

Look again at the opening page of this chapter. The Celtic design is actually a single line folding over itself, intertwining with offshoots of itself that yet now are perceived as others. See how the neural pattern becomes a pattern from the Book of Kells . . . the emergence of symbols from neural activation is infinitely more mysterious than this. We have learned little about it from conventional neuroscience and should be grateful for clues from any other source. One of the main justifications for PDP research has been its sustained assault on this question. Consequently, our discussion of PDP will first focus on its role as experimental neuroscience.

We begin by briefly discussing its central theoretical construct, the formal neuron. Of more interest to us in this section, however, are PDP's claims for psychological and neurophysiological validity. These claims are quite considerable in the former case but are not without their critics. In the latter case, there obviously is an enormous difference in scale between and PDP system attempted to date and the human brain. However, the performance differences due to lesions are impressively similar. Moreover, the neural Darwinist notion we explored in the previous section has a neat PDP correlate in the notion of competitive learning. We must then return to our central theme, the emergence of symbols from the concerted activity of groups of neurons, and here we find surprising results. The bridge to considering PDP as computer science is glimpsed as we briefly consider methodological issues and the relation to Gibson's work.

As an interlude before entering into the computational domain that extends also over the whole of Chapter 5, we attempt to map PDP considerations onto conscious experience. If indeed PDP is more than a metaphor for neurophysiological process, what are its experiential aspects? What is the relation between massively parallel neural function and subjectivity? We find a surprising analogy in Michael Polanyi's work on tacit versus explicit knowing, experienced respectively as subsidiary versus focal awareness.

This brings us to one of the major new computational paradigms of the past decade: PDP as computer science. As a cognitive science paradigm, it has become so powerful that CS is often identified in terms of, "Oh yeah, neural networks." Its power is such that biologists and physicists have joined psychologists and linguists, together with other cognitive scientists, in exploring the ramifications of PDP. As neurobiology, PDP has an obvious attraction. As physics, the thrill is more subtle, yet deeper: It has been found that knowledge can be viewed in this paradigm as particular configurations of an "energy landscape." Moreover, learning can be usefully described in the thermodynamic terms of a ferromagnetic core seeking a stable configuration. The process of learning can be looked at *en courant*, as a path being negotiated through the energy landscape in an attempt, surveyor fashion, to find the lowest valley.

As computer science per se, a host of interesting problems emerge. Why and in what ways is a variable in a computer program (which is like our old friends x and y from high school algebra) different from a variable in a PDP system? It is easy, using such an algebraic variable system, to support (an NLP system that caters for the type of recursion epitomized by this bracketed sentence within a sentence). However, this recursive capacity, along with several other characteristics of algebraic variables, does not come altogether naturally to PDP systems. We end this chapter by introducing further computational considerations related both to brain and PDP systems, which ease our passage into Chapter 5.

Connectionism as Experimental Neuroscience

The notion of a formal neuron is generally attributed to McCulloch (1989) and Pitts. This notion is simple in the extreme. On page 186, we hypothesized neuron A connected to neuron B. Let us imagine that the threshold of neuron B, a measure of its polarization, is 10 units. Then the impetus required for it to fire must equal or exceed 10. We calculate it by multiplying the threshold of A by its strength of connection to B. In real PDP systems, we are going to have N neurons with threshold Ti and connection strength Ci connected to B. The impetus arriving is a summation over all of them $(\Sigma\ Ti\ Ci)$.

So much for formal neurons. What we are focusing on here is PDP's case for psychological-neurological validity. It rests on the following planks:

1. The CAAM paradigm is psychologically more plausible than lookup memory.

2. Lesionability is possible for PP systems with some of the same results as for biological neural systems. Indeed, we even find evidence that specific speech disorders like dysphasia can be induced by lesions on PDP systems.

3. Learning is adaptive rather than all-or-none.

4. Knowledge representation (KR), particularly in distributed connectionist systems where a single concept may be distributed over several nodes, yields high interaction between different items. We have time and again noted how activation of a single word brings up all its contextual occurrences as well before the correct one is chosen. This can easily be modeled with PDP systems. Both human and PDP memory perform well in complex material with an inherently strong semantic organization.

Let's take five. Myles in Figure 4.4 is using localist representation. Each mode represents a particular concept. Standard KR is of this nature. However, in distributed KR, as in Figure 4.5, the neuron may be doing something very strange indeed! Here, we end up with the scenario where a single item may be represented over several neurons, and conversely a single neuron may be representing several items.

There are, however, a few serpents in this particular garden of psychoneurological validity. We have already discussed how conventional algebraic symbols contrast with PDP "symbols": The former seem to be to some extent used by the brain. For example, music and language exhibit recursion at least to some extent. The learning involved in PDP often resembles a long slow swim through a marsh rather than the straightforward additions to production-type systems (cf. Chapter 2) of which we are all capable. Pattern recognition comes easily and in a psychologically plausible fashion to PDP, and concept formation does not.

We discuss computational specifics in a later section. One such specific, that of competitive learning, is relevant right here. Normal PDP systems involve a teacher's correcting incorrect guesses made by the system and adjusting "weights" of connections in accordance with specific algorithms in order to converge to an optimal solution. An alternative framework presets neural groups to compete with each other for the "right" to recognize a particular pattern or evoke some such chain of events. A related notion is that of attractor neural networks, where the

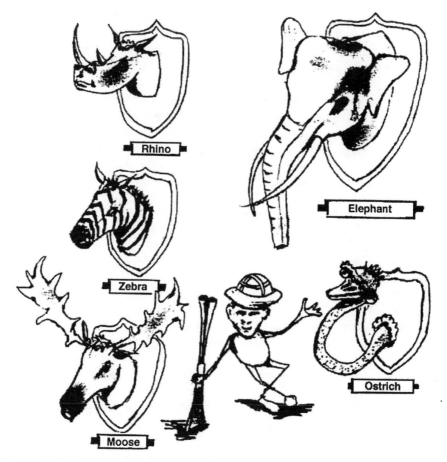

FIGURE 4.4.

mathematical vectors representing input patterns are conceived of as being differentially attracted by different locations in the energy landscape. Here we have notions that lend credibility to the construct of competition between neural groups, winner-take-all networks. The fact of massive neural death in early infancy, already noted, suggests a somber fate for the losers.

SYMBOLS AMONG THE NEURONS.   "I wish I had said that," said Oscar Wilde on hearing a particularly witty epigram. "Don't worry, Oscar, you will" was his rival Whistler's reply. The title of this subsection is due to Touretzky and Hinton (1985), who described therein a

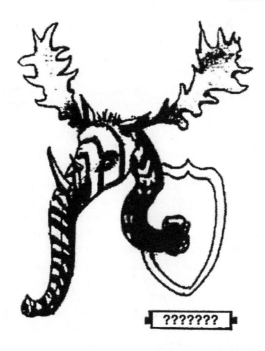

FIGURE 4.5.

production system with a PDP architecture. However, its slow learning curve gave rise to the "Touretzky tarpit" phrase, another mot of which I am envious! A related famous statistic is a matter of 2,232 samples before such a system learned exclusive disjunction which we discuss below (XOR; see Figure 4.6). The single line cannot correctly separate the "true" from "false" cases, with input expressed as 1s and 0s. Thus, symbols don't seem to thrive among the neurons—is there an alternative way of conceiving the relation between explicit symbol and neural activation? Might we not be better off postulating a gradual ascent from the latter to the former, with several well-defined watering holes en route?

To ease our entry into the consideration of this section, let's focus on the neurophysiological phenomenon of "pacemaker" neurons. All neurons fire randomly on occasion, as if warming up. The firing of pacemaker neurons, however, has been found to conform to certain specific preferred temporal patterns. Recently, it has been postulated that these patterns could be used as tags to indicate the significance of other patterns of neural firing. In other words, the message occurs in a medium of context supplied by analysis of the firing of pacemaker neurons. This is quite a breakthrough: We now have neural communication occurring at two different logical levels. Moreover, the notion that neural computation takes place only through the operation of spatial coordinate transformation in an interlaminar state-space must be abandoned. The addition of temporal sequences admits the possibility of several different types of neural code.

It is apposite right now to reconsider another of the problems of cognitive science whether cognition is best conceived of as neurally implemented in only one (propositional) code or in two (i.e., logical and spatial). The advocates of the former point of view (e.g., Pylyshyn, 1984) normally rested their case by making a claim for

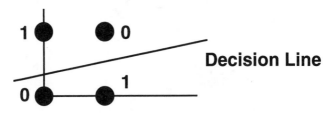

Exclusive Or Problem

FIGURE 4.6.

digital, computer-like neural transmission. This now seems far from the truth, but so too does any opposing view claiming only for a "spatial" language of thought combined with the propositional one. It does rather seem as though the brain is capable of supporting a variety of codes, now pure coordinate transformation, now including temporal sequences also, now perhaps making reference to grandmother cells and symbols structured according to formal rules of interrelation. Kosslyn (1994) adduces brain-imaging data that conclusively demonstrate the existence of a spatial (or imagistic) code.

Dyer (1991) described PDP systems at various levels from the neural to the fully symbolic, proposing interlevel mapping algorithms. The details of his excellent work need not concern us here. Of much more relevance is his concession of PDP's urgent need for full symbols. He argues, moreover, the neural process often builds upon unfinalized, distributed probabilistic guesses at symbols before they resolve their boundaries. Children's early behavior shows evidence of "distributed KR," guesses at colors or shapes that gradually solidify into explicit symbols, which can later be built upon. The conclusion is inescapable that neural activity admits of a multitude of forms, with symbolic activity having pride of place in terms of its effectiveness.

Parallel Distributed Processing as Tacit Knowing

This section is, *inter alia*, an overture for the overall cognitive architecture to be outlined in Chapter 9. Part of its motivation is a wish to resolve some of the tensions just mentioned for example, symbol or not. The work of the philosopher and scientist Michael Polanyi is discussed. It is argued that Polanyi's schematization of conscious experience provides a basis on which the perennial dichotomy of symbolic versus subsymbolic can informatively be discussed and such antinomies as those that arise from the frame problem be looked at afresh.

Polanyi seldom makes reference to computing, and it is at this point that the main theme of this section emerges. Polanyi's distinction between explicit and tacit is seen as analogous to that between high-level explicit symbols and low-level distributed symbolic patterns. The notion that focal consciousness, or explicit awareness, may be best regarded as a virtual machine is introduced and seen to be consistent with some relevant data. However, we shall see in chapter 8 that it doesn't go quite far enough.

THE NECESSITY FOR BOTH THE SYMBOLIC AND SUBSYMBOLIC DIMENSIONS.
Cowan and Sharp (1988), at the end of an excellent survey of
connectionism and its history, open a methodological front on
the classical (PSSH) position. They characterize the classical AI
methodology in these terms: "First specify the context, next
describe the logic of the desired behavior, and then try to achieve
it by using various heuristics" (p. 113). They argue that this
approach results in that context-dependence that is the bane of
AI. Connectionism, they argue, can sidestep this stumbling block.
We should note the analogy with Gibson's work on perception: In
subsymbolic PDP work, as in ecological optics, the subject–environment relation is intimate.

However, for Cowan and Sharp (1988) the future success of
neural nets hinges on an ability to simulate a "primitive attention
mechanism" (p. 115) in the manner of Handelman, Lane, and
Gelfand (1989), to take one example. They conjecture that the top-
down and bottom-up approaches will eventually merge under the
umbrella of "experimental epistemology" (or at least be a part
thereof) (p. 116) and insist that progress in the area awaits further
knowledge of how ideas and intentions can be realized neurophysiologically.

Some of Smolensky's (see below) (1990) more recent work down-
plays PDP's neuromorphic claims and allows it to be judged on its
experimental success as a research paradigm. In a reply article,
Wilks (1990) emphasizes that the jury is still out on that score. Let
us now review the evidence for the prosecution.

Papert (1988) argues that the "cost of holism" can be great for
some tasks. Touretzky and Hinton (1985) have shown how a high-
level classical description can be translated down to a parallel network; however, the computational cost is astronomical.

It is at precisely this point that Polanyi's approach can prove
most useful. The computational cost of thoroughgoing connectionism is too high, yet the lack of psychological veracity in classical AI
is too glaring an omission. Polanyi's schema allows us to look at
classical, symbolic description as valid, precisely because it is
supported by subsidiary processes. Either component in isolation
is incomplete. Thus, the problem of the computational cost of connectionism that Papert notes no longer seems as intractable as it
once did. Let us now look in more detail in Polanyi's work.

THE WORK OF MICHAEL POLANYI. The following account is taken from
Polanyi's two major works. *Personal Knowledge* (1958) inveighs
against objectivist "scientistic" notions of knowledge, insisting that

the research process cannot be divorced from the personal commitments of the researcher. Both here and in *Knowing and Being* (1969), Polanyi is concerned with giving a coherent psychological analysis of the growth of knowledge, and in the process proposes a very specific outline of the structure of waking consciousness. Polanyi's interrelated conceptions of knowledge and consciousness provide a hospitable venue for the symbolic–subsymbolic debate.

The distinctions that Polanyi makes between focal and subsidiary awareness are parallelled by a dichotomization between explicit and tacit knowing. He is concerned with awareness as essentially cognitive, so awareness and knowledge are treated as one.

Let us fòcus on the nature of focal and subsidiary awareness by referring to specific examples. Subsidiary awareness is of the impress made by the hammer on the palm of the hand; focal awareness is of driving in the nail. Subsidiary awareness is of the particulars that constitute an object; focal awareness is of the object. Nor is subsidiary awareness to be identified with the "fringe of consciousness." As one writes, Polanyi argues, one's subsidiary awareness of the pen is by no means compromised or incomplete, though one is focally aware of the content of what one writes.

Every act of consciousness has these subsidiary and focal components, and tacit knowing is based on the former. Indeed, this dual structure of awareness, Polanyi insists, is why humans do not fall prey to the frame problem: The fluctuating, changing objects are monitored subsidiarily to yield solid percepts at the focal level. We may add to this the special-purpose hardware that implements processes like the oculomotor reflex.

Yet, at moments of creation, it is tacit knowing that predominates. Moreover, tacit knowing is capable of self-correction. Ultimately, Polanyi argues, all knowing is tacit in nature, or based on tacit knowledge.

Let us draw the analogy out explicitly. Tacit knowing as structure and subsidiary awareness as process can be usefully modeled by PDP systems with a capacity for some autoregulation. Yet, as we have seen Cowan and Sharp (1988), there must exist also a focal, perhaps top-down component. At this point, let us examine the cognitive architecture that forms the central postulate of this section.

A PROPOSAL FOR A MIXED COGNITIVE ARCHITECTURE.   Polanyi's schematization distinguishes between a single focal and myriad subsidiary elements of awareness. It also provides a framework for the problem of embodiment in emphasizing the subsidiary nature of body awareness in the manner we have seen so much of in Merleau-Ponty (1962). Let us now look at Polanyi's work in a computational context.

The analogy between top-down and focal has been dwelt upon. Subsidiary awareness we can regard as treated by PDP systems. Where does all this get us once the neatness of the metaphor loses it novelty? What follows is one speculation as to what the consequences of Polanyi's formulation would be for current AI.

The first point is that subsidiary awareness can cast new light on the frame problem (Pylyshyn, 1987). The fluctuations of objects are handled by autoregulating subsidiary systems. The next point is that subsidiary systems can address the problem of context change. We can regard the myriad subsidiary systems as monitoring a stimulus environment until a salient change occurs. Moreover, the word *myriad* is used advisedly. We again note Marslen-Wilson's findings, that the presentation of a single word activates it in all its possible contexts for a short time, though only one of these contexts finally is chosen. We witnessed analogous findings in Sperling's experimentation in Chapter 2.

Therefore, we can regard subsidiary systems as active content-addressable neural nets that spring to life and enter focal consciousness once they are sufficiently determined by the environment—that is, once the content reaches that certain threshold at which the auto-associator "fires." In the meantime, until they so enter, they actively monitor stimuli and can act to preserve the integrity of a scene despite change in the manner described in the previous section. Moreover, such connectionist systems have at least a degree of neurophysiological plausibility.

What of focal consciousness that doesn't seem to have any hardware support? Bateson (1979) has characterized this type of consciousness as a shortcut to implement specific goals and notes its lack of place in a natural scheme of things. In fact, the best analogy for focal consciousness in computer science may be an adaptation of the notion of a virtual machine. We comment at length on Bateson in Chapter 5. Let's plunge into computing. We'll be there for awhile.

One specific example springs to mind of virtual machine use, and it's all the more fortuitous that it is at least vaguely AI. The designers of the best seller Q + A (an integrated software product including a database and NL interface) were confronted with a difficult problem: How to build an NLP system with decent linguistic coverage that could work on the slow CPU and limited memory of an IBM PC. The answer was to compile the syntax rules and semantic functions into customer p-codes. Hendrix and Walker (1987) explain, "A p-code is a machine-language instruction, but for a virtual machine rather than the physical hardware. The p-codes are executed by an interpreter and emulates (sic) hardware of a different design" (p. 254).

The result was enormous savings of space. Obviously the notion of virtual machine is an extremely common one in computer science (Lister & Eager, 1988) but here the analogy is particularly apt.

Therefore, we bring the analogy a stage further: Focal consciousness comprises top-down processes that though supported by and dependent on subsidiary processes, operate by completely different rules on the same hardware. Moreover, the same process can be implemented by PDP or top-down systems as Touretzky et al have shown: The latter is much faster. Smolensky's (1988) notion of a virtual rule interpreter parasitic on the truly causal subsymbolic processes is analogous to Polanyi's schema (see below).

There is no question but that this involves a new type of cortical computation from that which PDP systems attempt to simulate. However, Gregory Bateson (1979) vehemently argued over the course of more than a quarter century that focal consciousness was precisely that. In conclusion, it does indeed seem that Polanyi's distinction between the focal and the subsidiary, between the explicit and the tacit, may provide a vocabulary with which one can usefully discuss an enormous range of phenomena, psychological and computational alike. In particular, to reiterate a point made earlier, use of this vocabulary may shed much light on the symbolic–subsymbolic debate, although perhaps not fully explaining aspects of focal consciousness.

PDP as Computer Science

HISTORY OF PDP AS A COMPUTING PARADIGM. A historical approach is by no means inappropriate here. The ground breaking work of McCulloch and Pitts, mentioned earlier, led inevitably to a huge upsurge of interest in the area. The fact that the model of the neuron that was being used was a near-grotesque simplification failed to turn away the faithful. Their central argument was that any neuron could be described in binary form using the resources of the then-burgeoning science of information theory. Such description could lend itself to computational implementation.

During the 1950s much research was done on pattern recognition using the "peceptrons" inspired by the earlier breakthrough. The central notion was simple: A photosensitive surface was directly connected to an output layer of neurons that could, for example, if hooked up to a speech synthesis unit, output the word *seven* if a shape with seven items were presented, *four* if a different shape were presented, and so on. Research on PDP has always been highly mathematical in its analysis. A formal proof was established that these perceptrons could learn to recognize anything that they could potentially recognize (the perceptron convergence theorem). As always happens in AI, a serpent entered. Frank Rosenblatt, one of the major practitioners, was the first to notice it.

Perceptrons work by classifying patterns. As we note below, that is only one of a number of principles that can inform PDP computational processes. If looked at visually, the only kind of classification of which perceptrons are capable is drawing a line between accepted and unaccepted patterns, as viewed mathematically. This allows them to distinguish X and O, but not C and T. (The former pair are linearly separable, the latter are not.) Likewise the group of patterns that comprise successful exclusive disjunction (1 and 0, 0 and 1, 0 and 0—see Figure 4.6; in the notation of Chapter 2, p and $\bar{q}$, $\bar{p}$ and q, $\bar{p}$ and $\bar{q}$) were similarly outside its scope. A classic book by Minsky and Papert (its arguments were recently resurrected in Papert, 1988) collected a number of such proofs. PDP was seriously ailing.

Like all history written by the (erstwhile in this case) victors, the Papertian account fails to emphasize the solution tentatively proposed by Rosenblatt to this problem of *linear separability*. Briefly, as expanded in McClelland and Rumelhart (1986), it involves adding a hidden layer(s) between input and output. Now patterns that are separable only by planes (sometimes hyperplanes in *n*-dimensional hyperspace) could be classified. However, the convergence theorem cannot be proven for this case. Following the work of Rumelhart, Touretzky, and Hinton, and physicists such as Hopfield, PDP acquired the sheen it still possesses as (at worst) a fascinating mathematico-physical formalism. PDP systems have, with varying degrees of success and credibility that decrease as we go across this list, learned to recognize patterns like faces, pronounce English, assign roles to actors in sample sentences (featuring prepositional phrase attachment), and form the correct past tense for a large range of English verbs.

PDP implementations can be software simulations, where each neuron might be represented by a function in a high-level programming language, accepting as values for its parameters the inputs from neurons below it in the net, or alternatively actual hardware design, where every neuron corresponds to a separate processor. What all the various implementations share (Arbib, 1987) is at least one of the following features:

1. Use of networks of active computing units, each restricted to a simple functional structure.
2. Parallelism: The neural reality thereof certainly gives pause.
3. Encoding of semantic units over groups of neurons.

FUNCTIONAL CLASSIFICATION OF PDP SYSTEMS. We review an architectural classification later. An appropriate functional classification would distinguish the following types:

1. *Pattern classifiers.* These would categorize patterns 1 . . . N (be it a set of faces or speech sounds) correctly by outputting responses 1 . . . M as required. The best example is Nettalk (Sejnowski & Rosenberg, 1987), which learned to pronounce some English text. Most conventional neural networks perform tasks like this, occasionally on content as abstract as stock market trends. The success of these systems often involves extremely complex interactions between thousands of neurons in the net. They can perform in complex, unpredictable ways and include as a special case:
2. *Auto-associators.* Here, the task is that of recognizing the very pattern that the network encodes ("Shall I compare thee . . ." should evoke the rest of Sonnet 18 in an auto-association).
3. *Pattern transformers.* These would be expected to transform one pattern, like an English infinitive, into another, an English past tense.
4. *Inferencers.* These could supply rules of semantic relation to handle issues like ambiguity, the bane of NLP. So far, this can be done only with extreme difficulty.

PDP AND ARCHIMEDES. Aleksander and his colleagues (see Aleksander & Burnett, 1983) developed several visual systems with a connectionist-inspired architecture. We are concerned only with the realization of Archimedean subject–object differentiation attempted in these systems, so the technical discussion will be brief. Their major initial insight was that recognition of shapes like faces on an all-or-none basis was an extremely fragile technology that could be improved greatly by partitioning the faces into, say, 32,768 distinct parts. The task would be perhaps that of recognizing which of 16 different stored images corresponded most precisely to an incoming stimulus. Their first solution was to allow each stored face to "vote" on how many of its 32,768 neurons corresponded to the incoming stimulus. The face that got the most votes from its constituents was seen as the winner.

Now let's imagine that two of the faces are those of identical twins, and one has a mole on the upper left cheekbone. The mole might be sufficient to distinguish them in most cases, but let's now allow them to wear (or not, as they choose) glasses, moustaches, and indeed toupees. Aleksander and his colleagues found that this kind of problem in a milder form could be solved by adjusting the initial training period. Instead of simply training discriminators to respond to static shapes, the discriminators would be taught to respond over a succession of trials to a pattern comprising both the static shape and its own response to that shape. The added information afforded by its own action greatly enhanced the formal power of each discriminator.

And so back to Archimedes. He notices some definite effects due to his body's volume and invents hydrostatics in the process. Unquestionably, his ability to notice his effects on the world in subsidiary awareness increases his computational power. Suddenly that subsidiary awareness becomes focal as he remembers his promise to King Hiero of Syracuse. It will be argued in Chapter 8 that this monitoring of one's effects is more than a simple feedback mechanism or indeed a servomechanism. In fact, it will be maintained that it is part of a larger process of attempting to realize oneself through the world, an attempt that holds as true for symbolic domains as for physical.

COMPUTATIONAL PARADIGMS IN PDP.

The perceptron.   We have already looked at this in some length. As a learning automaton, it is limited in the extreme. The learning algorithm is elementary. If the system initially fails, the weights of connections are adjusted to an extent directly proportional to their strength.

Backward error-propagation (BEP) This remains by far the most popular PDP algorithm. Essentially, it describes the computational process required to adjust the weights of the connections in cases where there are one or more hidden layers between input and output (see Figure 4.7.) As noted above:

1. The relationship between input and output is not linear. This means, given an input of magnitude x, we can't assume the output will be some linear function of x.
2. Patterns represented by input vectors that require n-dimensional space for correct separation can be handled with BEP.
3. There is no guarantee that the solution found will be optimal.
4. A great deal of the engineering involved in getting a BEP system to perform a specific task used to be *ad hoc.* Someone would decide on the fly just how many hidden layers and how many neurons in each, though this has been addressed by various authors—including Fahlman.

Learning is implemented by changing the weights at each level in such a fashion as to minimize error. Moreover, we may *a priori* decide the rate at which the system should learn: Ideally, slowly for tasks that require fine discriminations (for example pronunciation), quickly for other tasks, such as distinguishing X from O. (A full mathematical treatment of BEP can be found in McClelland & Rumelhart, 1986, pp. 322–326. The BEP algorithm can also be found in a simplified form in Johnson-Laird, 1988, where it is arithmetically expressed.)

For the n-layer BEP situation, we have to consider the transformation of the input vector iterated several times. Again using our

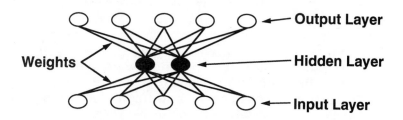

Backpropagation Network with Two Hidden Units

FIGURE 4.7.

vector notation, we consider the weights as plotted in an x-dimensional weight space. We need to establish that the delta rule can, at least with some simplifying assumptions, perform a gradient descent on the error in the situation BEP requires. Essentially, we have to establish that the error measure of E in Equation 2 below, differentiated with respect to weight, is proportional to the change in weight prescribed by the delta rule. Let's look at how the two major entities are calculated:

1. Output values from each neuron are computed by the application of a sigmoidal function. Let xj be the input to neuron j.

$$Y_i, \text{ its output} = \frac{1}{1+e^{-x_j}}$$

2. The total error of the network is calculated at each trial:

$$E = \frac{1}{2} \sum_i \sum_j (y_{j,i} - d_{j,i})^2$$

where j is an output unit subscript, i is a pattern subscript, d is the desired and y the actual values of the output unit's activity.

BEP is neurologically implausible. Moreover, psychologically speaking, we don't learn only in cases of error. Hinton has recently been experimenting with self-supervised BEP, which would counter both objections.

Hopfield nets and Boltzmann machines.   John Hopfield's current work involves issues as disparate as simulating slugs in neural networks and making radical claims about the nature of consciousness. (He contends that consciousness is potentially available to computers.) His earlier work proposed one brilliant physical analogy for both the structure and process of groups of neurons. Let's dwell on this structure process point for a moment. Neurons can be seen, in concerted action, as cohering to certain distinct structures. Conversely, individually active neurons might group together into structures whose stability depends precisely on activity of the neurons therein. From 10,000 feet, moving ocean waves look like static features of a seascape.

Ferromagnetic cores are another case in point, and they are the physical analogy that Hopfield initially suggested for brain structure and process. They comprise lattices of individual atoms, each of which has a particular magnetic orientation. Yet the ensemble is stable, despite the activity of each of the individual members. Indeed, there is a succession of such stable states of the lattice, leading to one of minimum energy. In Figure 4.8, the current state of the lattice (or neural network) can be represented as a point in the (wavy line) energy landscape. Starting at point A, the ball must move until it gets to point M, a stable state. However, we're back at a BEP-like problem—we don't know if this is the optimum state. For that, we need the addition suggested by Boltzman machines which we discuss presently.

KR is done in Hopfield nets by the energy landscape described above. The local minima facilitate CAAM. Let us continue the physical metaphor. The cooling of ferromagnetic cores was, unsurprisingly, discussed at length in the Los Alamos H-bomb project. Essentially, what they needed to do was to give the wavy line a tug, as if it were a rope attached at one end to a wall, and allow the ball bearing to settle into an absolute minimum. Learning is thus implemented as finding an absolute minimum of an energy landscape. One application has been approaching the traveling salesman problem, that is, the NP-complete (see Chapter 5) problem of plotting the optimal route through a set of cities for a salesman. The trick in simulated annealing, the Los Alamos technique, is to flip the spin of one of the atoms and view the result. If it's more stable, stick with it; otherwise, revert to the initial state.

Adaptive resonance theory (ART). Like BEP, ART is used mainly for curve fitting. However, unlike BEP it acknowledges that explicit teachers don't occur in nature. *Both* BEP and Hopfield/Boltzmann architectures require teaching to a degree unrequired in ART. The categories to which incoming features are judged to be similar

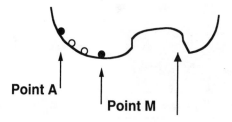

Point A

Point M

Energy Landscape with Trajectory of State Space

FIGURE 4.8.

compete with each other: ART is unsupervised learning (see Figure 4.9). Many notions from biology are used in ART, making the claims for neurological plausibility (neuromorphism) all the stronger. Indeed, the component neurons seek to emulate the membrane properties of neurons by obeying nonlinear differential equation descriptions. A locality principle prohibits interaction except between adjoining neurons. ART works well in distinguishing items of different categories.

Self-organizing maps (SOMs). Again, the structural principles here are drawn from biology. In particular, the SOM uses an analogy from processes at work in the mammalian cortex that convert sensory signals into features. In SOMs, each neuron is connected to its section of the environment via a set of fibers that may be excitatory or inhibitory. The neurons are typically arranged in a two-dimensional lattice (like those in BEP, but without the input output pointers). We discussed topographic mapping earlier. We can achieve it in SOMs provided that excitation across the neurons varies in a regular and continuous fashion with the sensory input signal. What essentially we're trying to achieve in SOMs is that the probability distribution of the input set will be reflected in that of the output set.

Sigma–PI learning (SPL). Again, this technique is used for learning continuous maps and the technique gives PDP expression to Gibson's notion of organism-environment interaction.

Earlier, we noted Cowan and Sharp's appeal for alternative AI methodologies to those that premap the domain and then act on

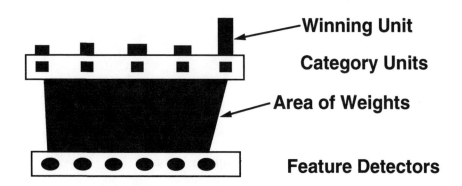

ART Attentional System

FIGURE 4.9

it: With this type of architecture, this appeal has been heard and responded to. Essentially, SPs work by function approximation for any type of reasonably continuous function. The teacher input is the correct values ($f(x \ldots z)$) for input values $x \ldots z$ (see Figure 4.10).

Conclusions. We have examined the major computational PDP architectures. With the last two, we entered the domain in which Gibsonian subject–environment relations attained computational expression. In this, even more than in its exciting helter-skelter of physicobiological models, PDP shows signs of becoming an importantly innovative approach to major issues in cognitive science.

PDP AND SYMBOLS. The final two PDP architectures we looked at are PDP at its most radical, potentially most informative, and most removed from the world of conventional symbols. It is indeed possible that they are good neurobiological models for primitive perceptual processes; however, we're going to need some other principles of operation in order to support full symbolic cognition. PDP systems can be said to fall down on a number of points here. In the first place, form is not wholly separate from content in these systems.

The major issues in the inadequacy of PDP for full cognition relate to the nature of symbols. These at least are problems for PDP (there may be more) versus GOFAI (good old-fashioned AI).

1. Symbols are variables in GOFAI, which treats them using conventional algebraic methods, but it is difficult to achieve this in PDP.
2. Recursion (we noted this above). In conjunction, we can note that recursion leads to (potentially) infinite generative capacity.

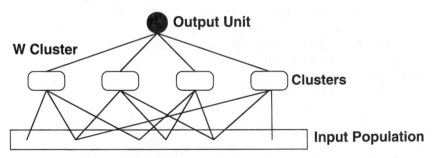

Format of Sigma-Pi Unit

FIGURE 4.10.

3. Memory management. The notion of a variable occupying a discrete address with changing tenancy does not come easily to PDP, except (obviously) at the computer architecture level.

It rather looks as though these aspects of symbols are unavailable to higher animals as well. These and other aspects of symbolic behavior are often lumped together under the general umbrella term systematicity (see below). It is perhaps disingenuous to continue using this *contra* PDP. Let's, for example, cast our minds back to the discussion of Piaget in Chapter 2. There we saw that humans have difficulty with forms of *modus tollens*. Unless the content is adjusted to something to which they are accustomed, they tend to get the inference wrong. Is this altogether different from PDP systems that can function only in one specific domain?

Paul Smolensky (1986, 1990) has made a sustained attack on the symbolic–subsymbolic issue while engaged in his main pursuit of attempting to formulate mathematically rigorous foundations for CS. He does not doubt that the mind is, in a real sense, a computer; he sees the major issue as that of fully describing symbolic behavior in the necessarily subsymbolic language of neural function. Language is the ultimate test of validity of this account; most attacks on PDP have focused on its inability to deliver systems that can plausibly emulate human performance on such tasks as derivation of past tense forms of verbs. More generally, the requirement of systematicity in its original form insists that PDP systems should manifest the same grasp on distributional regularity as humans; to say, for example, that X loves Y, where X and Y are human, immediately allows one to construct the syntactically correct (if not pragmatically inevitable) "Y loves X."

Smolensky's foundation for CS is the principles of Harmony Theory (HT). The cognitive system is viewed as an assembly of atoms with a capacity to draw inferences consistent with the knowledge in these atoms. HT can specify the well-formedness of the activity (that is, harmony) of any such system *vis à vis* others given the same input data. It is thus, in a sense, the PDP correlate of measuring the degree to which a system obeys the principle of rationality. Harmonic grammars allow sentences that satisfy a set of soft constraints identifiable as the grammar. Smolensky has demonstrated that each level of the Chomsky hierarchy is emulable by a class of harmonic grammars. If we allow ourselves to rank the constraints, with constraint i stronger than the sum of i+1 to n (that is, stronger than any below it), we end up with that extension of HT known as optimality theory that has proven particularly powerful in the case of phonology. Time will tell whether other phenomena of language will surrender as easily to this type of analysis.

Smolensky has been much concerned with the objections of systematicity. He is willing to concede an explanatory role, but no causal one, to the rules of grammar. To understand his reply to these objections in detail requires some immersion in linear algebra; it suffices for our purposes again to note that all the basic units in PDP systems, be they incoming–outgoing patterns of activity or the units in the net itself, are described mathematically as vectors. The instantiation exemplified in the X,Y example above can be handled by "tensor product" of vectors. It is important for Smolensky's formalist purposes that such solutions be consistent with the formalism chosen; it must hang together as a single mathematical system. Therein lies the greatest strength and weakness of his approach. The neural reality of entities like hypercomplex cells indicates that nature sometimes takes short cuts to the same goals HT trudges toward. Smolensky will himself admit that much work remains to be done in circumscribing the space in which his systems even begin to learn, given their current slowness. The size of the space involved suggests that modified innatism may be mathematically inevitable for those in the PDP area (as accepted in McClelland & Rumelhart, 1986). Of more significance for our purposes is the ignoring of experience itself that the "mind–computer" equation requires. The integrity and ingenuity of Smolensky's research initiative will no doubt eventually lead him to confront this issue.

It is the thoroughness of this work that gives one pause. Smolensky has demonstrated how formal languages at each level of the Chomsky hierarchy can be realized without any *deus ex machina* notions like hypercomplex cells. Any resulting systems will be as yet implausibly slow, but nonetheless successful. One possible synthesis allows that symbolic cognition is initially of the nature Smolensky describes, but that in its equilibration drive the brain can abstract from its own activity and compile the symbolic behavior down into ever more complex forms, for example complex neurons. This fits well with how we learn language and other symbolic skills.

While on the topic of emergence and GUTs of cognition, it's apposite to note the claims of theorists of complex systems. Essentially, they posit as a property of systems that at certain points "at the edge of chaos" order emerges, manifest in ideas, increasing returns in economics, consciousness, and so on. The pell-mell of connection activity in the brain makes it a complex system *par excellence*. However, much more needs to be known about the precise conditions that foster order as an immanent property in this fashion.

THE BRAIN AS A COMPUTING DEVICE. We have already noted several issues here: The slowness of neural impulse, the parallelism, the sheer scale, the astronomical number of connections, the redundancy that gives rise to lesionability, the top-down context effects, the variety of types of KR, the variety of codes. Let us finish by noting the brain's enormously rich connection width and its contrast with the computer on each of the following characteristics of current computers: their extremely narrow channel responded to by a very fast CPU working together with a large, fast, normally inactive memory.

We've found also that the very structure of the nervous system requires consideration of biological evolution. PDP has been extremely fruitful in suggesting tentative hypotheses about neural process ranging from its support of high-level cognition to low-level organism–environment coupling.

THE VICTORY OF NEUROSCIENCE: THE WORK OF GERALD EDELMAN

Edelman believes in CS perhaps even less than Fodor does, though, as we shall see, for quite different reasons. Edelman's (1992) path toward the Holy Grail is the following:

1. A theory of brain and consciousness (which we review in Chapter 8).
2. A theory of perceptual and cognitive categorization.
3. A theory of meaning based on embodiment.

Psychology, he uncontroversially insists, must be grounded in biology. What *is* controversial is his claim that enough neurobiological data already exist strongly to constrain cognitive psychological theory.

We mentioned neural Darwinism, significantly called neural Edelmanism by Francis Crick, in an earlier section. It is apposite now to explain it in more detail. It is a thoroughgoing evolutionary account of how survival of the fittest acts in the brain. Each neuron may have excitatory or inhibitory connections with its neighbors. The unit of selection is the neuronal group, featuring both types of neurons. Edelmanism distinguishes two stages in the path to full cortical form:

1. In the embryonic stage, selection among competing neuronal cells and their processes determines anatomical form and patterns of synaptic connectivity.
2. At the postnatal stage, selection among neuronal groups without change in the anatomical pattern shapes the behavioral repertoire.

Edelman's notions are quite minimalist. Topobiology, which determines organ epigenesis, and re-entry complete the set. To explain the latter, we must first realize that neuronal groups differentiate into maps of different parts of the stimulus array. One such map might handle form, another color. Re-entry is a process whereby these two maps would form connections with each other on presentation of a stimulus that was evoking reactions in both, in a manner similar to Hebbian learning. Therefore, a given object which, apparently problematically, registers in two maps, would evoke the correct response in the correct part of each map, with a strong connection between the two developing. This is Edelman's solution to the binding problem. The ethos of this schema is similar to some of the more biologically based PDP systems. Edelman extends his system to conceptual thought via a notion of a concept as manifesting the brain's higher order recognition of its own patterns of response, a notion we saw in Chapter 3's treatment of cognitive linguistics.

Many of Edelman's conclusions are very compatible with the framework here; particular, his qualified realism and selectionism (that is, his emphasis on survival of the fittest). He has harsh things to say about CS and we need to see why. In the first place, he rightly argues that CS must be properly biologically based. However, the brain is not a computer. Anatomical maps are not fixed, there is a huge variety of different types of code, and the wiring of the brain is near-random. Moreover, brain structure *does* matter.

He characterizes CS in the classic computational terms (or, to be precise, as methodological solipsism) we discuss in Chapter 5: Mental representations with a regular syntax are related to the world by the semantic assignment of symbols to objects in classi-cal categories (Edelman, 1992, see also Stillings et al, 1987). However, Edelman adduces numerous arguments against this, some of which we've come across time and again in this book:

1. The world is not composed of objects in classical cate-gories. The work of Rosch, *inter alia*, has demonstrated that neither is our categorization classical.
2. Thought and meaning are embodied.
3. Consciousness is required to explain meaning.
4. The merely syntactic operations of computation can't give a mind–world relation (but cf. the end of Chapter 3).
5. Language is communicative (that is, intersubjective).
6. The functionalist notion of programs as mind is incom-patible with evolution; for example, the world is not an infinite Turing tape (cf. Chapter 5.)
7. Moreover, cognition gets its content only with respect to evolutionary history.

Much of this fits very well with this book. However, as has already been noted, syntax in a restricted context can give mean-ing. Moreover, Edelman's account of language is simply not ade-quate. He does give an account of mind with respect to neuroscience.

Summary: Mind In Neuroscience

Edelman provides us with an opportunity for a short curtain call. His work synthesizes several themes. We have been concerned in this chapter with an introduction to the discipline. This involved first of all categorizing the different subdisciplines therein before going on to the methodology of neuroscience. After reviewing gross neuroanatomy and being duly impressed with the sheer scale of the brain, we proceeded to discuss neural functioning and how learning might be implemented, about which much is currently conjectured. The notion of interneuronal competition is a leitmotif here.

We found it possible to maintain the Mylesian position in the face of the neuroscientific evidence. The mild realism is supplied by Edelman and Pribram and the processes involved in egocentric knowledge seem to have a correlate in, for example, the action of certain neurons in the hippocampus and parietal cortex. One major source of interest was topographic maps in the cortex for most sensory modalities, with the exception of olfaction. Another interesting point was the extent to which the hardware of the brain seems appropriate for the support of probabilistic reasoning.

We reviewed connectionism under a variety of headings: as neuroscience, as computer science, and as a theory of tacit knowing. The accusations of a lack of systematicity were seen as being a little less damning than might at first seem to be the case. We classified connectionist systems with respect to both their architecture and their use. It was indicated that the more biologically inspired such models are the most interesting. In their minimalism and selectionist ethos, they resemble the work of Edelman, with whose critique of CS and proposal for a theory in mind in neuroscience we closed the chapter.

The lessons for our overall theory of cognition are clear. The notion of a body-subject active in exploring the world has now acquired a neuroscientific echo and seems in evolutionary terms to be valid. Nature, profligate as ever, allows massive death of neurons so that the survivors can better map themselves onto objects both in the world and representing the body-subject's interaction with the world. Another core dynamic principle, re-entry, resolves the binding problem. There is no passive impressing of objects at the level of interneuronal dynamics; the realist interpretation is appropriate only at a higher level of description. The paradigms emerging in neuroscience are embedded and equilibriating in precisely the sense we need for the Nolanian framework. The difficulties with full symbolic behavior can best be explained in the schema hereby allowing a general syntactic (a "syntax of thought") system available to all forms of cognition, be it linguistic, musical or kinesthetic (for example, dance often conforms to a grammar).

The notion of a body-subject active in exploring the world has now acquired a neuroscientific echo and seems in evolutionary terms be valid.

FURTHER READING

Edelman's (1992) *Bright Air, Brilliant Fire* is a provocative and readable introduction to neuroscience. The collection of articles on mind and brain in the September, 1992 edition of *Scientific*

American is worth your attention. The collection in McClelland and Rumelhart (1986) gives much detail on connectionism. Churchland (1990) explores how algorithms may be neurally implemented. Gray (1987) and Margenau (1984) are useful for those still interested in monism–dualism.

• *five* •

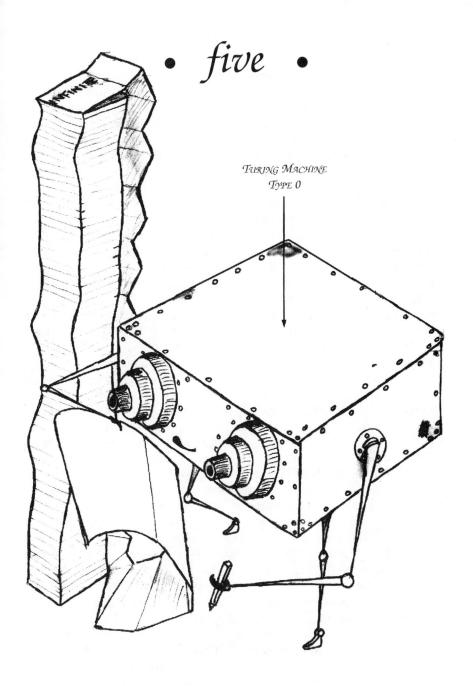

TURING MACHINE
TYPE 0

ARTIFICIAL INTELLIGENCE

This chapter is intended as an analysis of what AI can tell us about mind. *En route,* we discuss the main techniques of AI at a general level. Production systems were introduced in Chapter 2, parsing in Chapter 3. There is no need, for our purposes, to concern ourselves with the implementation of specific algorithms in specific programming languages. Several good texts that do this already exist (cf. end of chapter). All those texts tend toward claim jumping a little bit. Inevitably, a text that makes reference to the foundations of AI must (if only implicitly) make philosophical assumptions; a text that (as most AI texts do) treats connectionism must refer to neuroscience; a text that focuses on knowledge-based (KB) NLP must concern itself with issues in compositional semantics. Finally, a text on a subject that breathes life into previously theoretical issues in epistemology by incarnating them as computer programs will necessarily claim an urgent importance for that subject that can hardly be denied.

Consequently, it is unsurprising that the consensus view of cognitive science is that it is a species of the genus AI. I have argued throughout this book that this is not the case, yet it is important to see where this misperception came from. Essentially, cognitive science acquired some of its initial impetus (and funding) from the success of AI programs. This, in turn, led to an overemphasis on computation in the conceptual armory of CS. One consequence was the notion of CS as the search for algorithms in all its subdisciplines, and the identification of these algorithms with mind. In psychology, attempts were made to discuss cognition mainly as reasoning, and reasoning solely as computation. In linguistics, the process of NLP was seen as a *deus ex machina,* an autonomous self-contained parser blindly applied to every text. Neuroscience as CS has focused on neural algorithms to a damaging extent distinct from their application—we'll see in the next chapter that the categorization processes all of us as humans elicit from our culture has been viewed as a computer program.

Not that there is anything amiss with the search for algorithms, *per se.* The problems arise when this search becomes divorced from questions about the environment in which these algorithms are applied, and—even more importantly—in interaction with which the algorithms acquired the specifics of their structures. Separation of algorithm from environment is a specifically Cartesian pathology. We discuss this issue in the first section on AI and CS.

If this is the first chapter that you, a computer scientist who wonders what all the fuss is about, have perused, I can understand your misgivings. Yet another failed philosopher trying to make a tainted buck by criticizing the honest implementational work of AI! The normal career path here has been to scan through the input-output behavior of AI programs (most such philosophers are programming philistines), dig up a dead European white male who said something vague about knowledge in a foreign language, let him loose on the (inevitably limited) program, and show that the 99.9 (recurring) percent of human behavior that the program fails to emulate is due to its lack of situatedness, or hermeneutics, or encephalitis. Well that's not my style. Like you, I've had in the past to make my living as a programmer, and greatly admire the classic AI programs. AI has taught us a huge amount about cognition and epistemology precisely because of the ingenuity of those programs. It has taught us as much by its failures as its successes, because we know for sure now that, for example, if a researcher as technically good as Terry Winograd says NLP is a very difficult task for a computer, we are unlikely to say otherwise if we attempt the same task.

So let's stick to people who criticize AI from the inside. This will include philosophers who attempted something like AI before computers (for instance, Wittgenstein in Chapter 1) and found it impossible on theoretical grounds, computer scientists and mathematicians who struggled with the concept of computing and found it had certain inherent difficulties, and linguists who confronted the awesome formal system that is language and withdrew overwhelmed. All these various personages left a flag at the point where they stopped their ascent. They also left an account describing how they attacked the particular face of the mountain to which they addressed themselves. That line of attack is the technique they introduced to AI. The final camp marked by the flag affords a view of just how complicated the task is. Thus, the second section in this chapter, the promenade down the hall of skeptics, will leave us greatly the wiser about the techniques as well as the limitations of AI.

We then reintroduce the computer science theme of the last chapter. What type of computer science is AI? It has had an influence on computer science (for example, the invention of time sharing) through its huge computational overheads: Can it have more? What has actually been achieved in AI considered as software engineering—what software products can be pointed to? We've looked at NLP in Chapter 3: Is there a general categorization of AI software that holds as true for vision as for automated reasoning as for NLP?

The high-water mark of AI as cognitive science was reached sometime between the 1970s and the 1980s. At that stage, it was imperative for any cognitive psychologist worth her salary to indicate some kind of computational process, normally filched from AI, for her theory. This trend still to some extent continues today, and we need to discuss it before focusing on the theory of mind as treated in AI. This topic is currently in ferment and we are going to find, to our considerable surprise, that the view of mind emerging from AI is as close to the Greek *Nous* as any metaphor centered on (mind) = (programs running on a brain).

AI AND COGNITIVE SCIENCE

What Is AI?

Let's attempt a definition. If we don't define our terms at the start of the argument, we could well be accused of obfuscating basic issues:

> AI is that aspect of computer science that attempts to make computers perform tasks which we would consider indicative of intelligence if performed correctly by humans.

Well, programs that play good chess are still generally considered AI, however, programs that calculate a large payroll quickly, and thus conform to the terms of this definition, are not. Indeed, AI is now focusing a great deal on tasks like walking and understanding simple sentences, which we tend to regard as not particularly indicative of intelligence. We're wrong in so regarding them. Under the type of close scrutiny on which AI insists, these tasks turn out to have massive information-processing requirements. Thus, let's try:

> AI is the study of intelligence as programming.

This may or may not be an improvement, but we'd better define programming pretty loosely. It's going to include conventional software engineering at one extreme and the kind of PDP architectures and agonizing over the nature of symbols we noted in Chapter 4 at the other. If at first you don't succeed:

AI is an experimental biology of intelligence, concentrating particularly on being-in-the-world as information processing.

This allows PDP to return to the fold and takes into account such work as Brooks', but it's not going to be much use to such practitioners of applied AI as expert systems builders.

A fair general rule about AI systems qua human cognition seems the following: If you find an intellectual task enormously difficult but possible (for example, expert chess playing), AI systems can do it brilliantly. If you find a task only occasionally difficult (grammar checking), AI systems can do it badly. If the task is so easy that you don't even consider it a task (conversing), AI systems do it extremely badly or not at all. Insofar as we find a task difficult, we tend to reflect on it and abstract principles to deal with it. We can usually find an algorithmic description for these principles. Not so with processes like pronouncing a language correctly, where we've had the help of 4 billion years of evolution. AI investigative methods can often abstract some subset of processes like articulation or vision (for instance, the syntactic analysis of scenes we noted in Chapter 2), and through computational analysis, enlighten us greatly about them. However, the full functioning of a sensory modality or motor faculty in the real world is a quantum leap more difficult and usually far beyond the scope of current AI. Let's stop trying to define it precisely. Its very *modus operandi* is going to change as it switches from well-defined areas like deductive reasoning (in the discussion of GPS below) to the world of computational neurobiology (such as the final PDP systems in Chapter 4). If you need to ask what AI is, you'll never know.

The emergence of subsymbolic AI, especially subsymbolic connectionism, has made the task of distinguishing different levels of analysis of AI programs more difficult. Back in the halcyon days of good old-fashioned AI (GOFAI), the following analysis seemed correct: An AI program can be described as the knowledge/logical level (KL) with respect to its KR formalisms, at the algorithmic level with respect to the specifics of their implementation, and at a final specifically computational level. Unfortunately, this triptych does not work for PDP systems, where the KR often directly informs and is directly informed by the specifics of implementational and computational architecture. One interesting aside is that the KL is now identified with an observer's perception of the functioning of the AI program rather than any supposedly objective mapping of the domain (cf. the discussion in Chapter 4 of

Cowan and Sharp). We discuss this at length at the end of this chapter and find it compatible with our organism–environment view of mind.

Perhaps AI stands to the rest of computer science as philosophy does to its own offshoots. Psychology, originally a daughter of philosophy in its incarnation as experimental epistemology, struck out on its own to lay claim to its own domain: In that it followed its siblings, physics and the other hard sciences. Similarly, lacking another compelling metaphor for intelligent behavior, computer science has frequently found itself forced to turn to human intelligence when looking for models. However, once the technology deriving from this analysis has been established, it is more likely to be discussed on its own terms than those of AI. Consequently, we can't define AI in terms of the content of its investigation.

What of its methods of investigation? We can distinguish here between at least three separate issues (Partridge, 1991):

1. The principles of program development. In that, AI is not terribly different from conventional software engineering.
2. The principles relating to satisfactory input–output behavior.
3. The scope of the findings emerging from it.

With respect to AI's attempt to abstract the relevant computational principles applicable to a particular domain, we find ourselves with a Wertheimer-like (cf. Chapter 2) two-level classification:

1. "Fine" solutions involving a parsimonious monolithic analysis; for example, the notion of competence grammar.
2. Solutions that involve the interaction of a (sometimes massive) number of different processes. It should be clear from Chapter 3 that NLP, considered as a general task, will admit only this type of solution.

These types of considerations, taken together, should allow us to firm up what our notion of AI is.

To finish this soul-searching section, let's briefly mention the kind of issue currently debated in AI. It should be clear at this stage that the GOFAI versus subsymbolic (SS) debate (where SS includes both mobotics and the later PDP architectures we reviewed) is raging. One of the tasks the discussion at the end of this chapter sets itself is to resolve it, in the sense of providing an overall framework in which it can sensibly be discussed. This framework can perhaps gain in credibility from its links with Merleau-Ponty, whose catch-cries of situatedness and embodiment (in French *incarnation*) are echoed loudly in the SS world. As we discuss the attribution of the KL level of the designer or observer, we find ourselves referring to *stances.* Mind in AI is a much more fascinating and multihued issue than even the dreams of its pioneers might have suggested.

The Reduced History Of AI

Most good stories involve the hero having X, losing it (or not realizing he has it), and getting it back for keeps. This goes for the story of Christian salvation as much as any airport bookshop romance. Many writers on the history of AI have been forced into this framework. I invoke the reduced Shakespeare company again to allow these writers their say with a 30-second history. We'll then step back and cast a colder eye.

THE 30-SECOND HAMLET.   Once upon a time, a group of brave, clever, but misguided young men wanted to build machines that would emulate human intelligence. They had some limited initial success on tasks like machine translation, pattern recognition, and automated reasoning. Being very young, they got extremely excited and told all the military and other funding agencies to give them more money because they were on the verge of creating a real artificial intelligence. However, some wiser, older men like Pierce (1966), Lighthill (1972), and Minsky and Papert (1969) proved that the young men were, as we said, misguided. The young men, now older and wiser and with considerably reduced research grants, became seriously concerned about issues like KR, and by the early 1980s had regained some commercial credibility.

The End

THE FIVE MINUTE HAMLET.   The success of early AI did go to its practitioners' heads. We discuss its general principles below. However, just as Rosenblatt anticipated Minsky and Papert, so also neither the Pierce nor the Lighthill report were the big news they're often portrayed as. For example, the Pierce report, in the manner of the failed philosophers justly denigrated in the last section, took the contemporary MT systems to task on the basic grounds of their incompleteness. One such system, Systran, is still in current commercial use nearly 30 years later (Toma, 1977). The frame problem "discovered" in the Lighthill report had been revealed by McCarthy years before (Pylyshyn, 1987). So let's leave victor's history and victor's justice aside for a while and try to get inside the minds of the admittedly hubris-stricken but nonetheless brilliant early AI researchers. GPS provides a perfect example of GOFAI.

GPS (Partridge, 1992) consisted essentially of the following:

1. A set of procedures that classify the difference between present state (S1) and goal state (S2).
2. A set of operators to reduce the relevant differences.
3. A procedure for assessing compatibility between S1 and operator.

We have met such a system before in Chapter 2. Now, this type of architecture works superbly on tasks like solving differential calculus problems where the crucial skills lie in correctly categorizing the problem (Is it trigonometric or algebraic? If the latter, is it a divisor–quotient problem?), then progressively converting it to tractable form. However, even aside from the issues related to situatedness, GPS must be re-created almost in toto to be applicable to another area of application. For the second time, we find that the syntactic level that can allow only for regular combinations of symbols has sacrificed power for generality. Yet, once the domain has been properly mapped, the power of these systems is awesome. By the end of the 1950s, Bertrand Russell had occasion to congratulate the writers of a neater proof in mathematical logic than he had been capable of at his peak.

The central tenet of early AI was the Physical Symbol Systems Hypothesis (PSSH), which is that a physical symbol system such as GPS was adequate for supporting all intelligent behavior. We have seen in Chapter 4 how fraught this hypothesis has become, both as a methodological recipe and as a theory of intelligence. However, a science that had in its infancy managed to out-Russell Russell was perhaps due a Promethean fate. The early spectacular successes of PSSH had a contrapuntal line in the PDP of Rosenblatt and Kohonen. Given this explosion of achievement, anything done in the 1960s was inevitably going to be perceived as a relative failure. Therein, I think, lies the problem, of which the Pierce and Lighthill reports were but a symptom, not a cause. Finally, it is true that the 1960s and 70s witnessed a growth of interest in KR and that credibility returned in the 80s. We review current trends in AI below.

****

Foundational Issues: Cognitive Science And Computation

Even at its nadir, AI was still exciting. It was still able to provoke intense debate even on relative nonissues like whether "computers" could "understand" (cf. Chapter 1). To see a computer program translate even a toy sentence, convert even an isolated spoken word into text on screen, or decide what wine you should have with the snake at lunch is impressive in the extreme. By the time CS was beginning to get its funding from institutions like the Sloan Foundation, it was inevitable that it be heavily influenced by AI. At that stage, AI was very Cartesian: Its central paradigm was the notion of cognition as computation over a set of representations built up from different sensory modalities. I wish to take this opportunity to discuss the extent to which this idea has (perhaps excessively) influenced CS and why the central issues of CS have to be resituated in a much larger concept of mind than currently obtains. Let's look at some of the main texts in the area.

It is fair to say that there exists a great deal of confusion among nonspecialists in the area about the precise nature of CS. Different sections of the academic community hold widely varying conceptions of its nature. For psychologists, it consists of that aspect of cognitive psychology that attempts to give a computationally tractable account of mind. For computer scientists, it is at present vaguely identified with neural networks. In terms of funding, much of its cash comes from its links with AI, which increases the confusion.

For Gardner (1985) the scope of CS is quite clear: "[CS is] . . . a contemporary, empirically based effort to answer long-standing epistemological problems." Indeed: "Today, CS offers the key to whether they can be answered" (p. 6).

Pylyshyn (1984) is even more explicit: "Many feel, as I do, that there may well exist a natural domain corresponding roughly to what has been called 'cognition' which may admit of such a uniform set of principles" (p. xi).

For Pylyshyn, then, cognitive science is on a par with disciplines containing such a set (for example, "chemistry, biology, economics or geology") in having a precisely specified subject area: "The domain of cognitive science may be knowing things . . . informavores" (p. xi). The biochemistry analogy of the introduction is apposite; "knowing things" are to play the role of the gene, and epistemology is a critical theme.

Stillings et al. (1987) were even more forthright and Jamesian: "Cognitive science is the science of mind" (p. 1). Like both Gardner and Pylyshyn, they stress the interdisciplinary nature of the enterprise of CS, and focus on the disciplines of psychology, linguistics, computer science, philosophy, and neuroscience in their account of the area. Johnson-Laird (1993), whose earlier incarnation was as a cognitive psychologist, gives this definition, which sets off the first alarm bells: "Cognitive science, sometimes explicitly and sometimes implicitly, tries to elucidate the workings of the mind by treating them as computations" (p. 9). The disciplines of psychology, artificial intelligence, linguistics, anthropology, neurophysiology, and philosophy are again seen as the most relevant.

Let us pause for a moment to take stock. There seems to exist a consensus on at least these basic issues:

1. Cognitive is the science that deals with cognition, especially knowing. Yet—and here comes the knot in the wood—it has aspirations to deal with mind *per se.*
2. As such, it must accommodate findings from a variety of disciplines.

To return to the current theme, we noted that instead of focusing on organism-environment interaction over time, a jarring algorithm as *deux ex machina* note was apparent in CS. This note is heading toward crescendo. Gardner (1985) supplies the most complete characterization of the methodology of CS. He predicates several features of CS (38 ff) from which we can learn much about excessive computationalism:

1. The acceptance of a symbolic level, a level of representation. This point is amplified considerably by Pylyshyn (1984), varying on the same Cartesian theme: "I will suggest that one of the main things cognizers have in common is they act on the basis of representation" (p. xii). It should be pointed out that this is the keynote of AI in CS: If the representationalist ethos is accepted, then the domain becomes computationally tractable. If it can be established that humans work from symbolic representations, then the task of CS becomes that of implementing these representations as programs, and CS seems *a priori* quite a feasible enterprise. We've already found cause to attack representationalism on philosophical (Chapter 1), perceptual (Chapter 2), and methodological (below) grounds. The latter set of objections is going to force us, if we wish to save face as representationalists, to admit that such

work as Brooks' requires that a variety of types of representation types other than the centralized, symbolic, and manipulable ones of GOFAI exist.

2. The use of computers. As Gardner points out, CS could have emerged at any point since the 1940s, but acquired its initial credibility and impetus from the later success of computing.

3. The playing down of the influence on cognition of affect, context, culture, and history. This de-emphasis can also be contested on various grounds, which we've discussed at length in Chapters 1, 2, and 3. Above all, this playing down excludes the necessary theory of motivation from the theory of cognition. However, as cognitive science reaches for the mantle of "science of mind," its adherents research affect (O'Rorke & Ortony, 1994), consciousness (Chalmers) and social factors (Halley, 1992).

4. The interdisciplinary ethos. Gardner describes CS as being bounded on its extremes by neuroscience and ethnoscience. Its core comprises cognitive psychology, AI, and large amounts of both of linguistics and philosophy, which is obviously in keeping with the structure of this book.

To complicate the situation, some AI researchers, flush with the success of their systems in microworlds, feel disposed to hold forth on topics as diverse as selfhood, consciousness, the nature of the soul, and freedom of the will (Minsky, 1987, is a fine example), still holding fast to their original, restricted set of computational considerations. Winograd (1990) argues that this is a dangerous trend. Nor is this disease confined to computer scientists. Johnson-Laird (1993) has an equally wide range of interests and an equal lack of appreciation for the complexity of the issues he raises. Indeed, in true Messianic style he offers eternal life through simulation of personality (p. 392). The broadcaster and neurophysiologist Blakemore (1988), in his popular TV series on the mind, within the space of two pages (pp. 270-272) first of all emphasizes the autonomy of moral issues, and then claims that they also fall within the domain of neurophysiology. There is a very serious problem here that we discuss under the heading of selfhood and consciousness in Chapter 8.

It is worthwhile again detailing what one version of the current foundation for CS, as understood and taken to task by Edelman, actually looks like. The essential assumption is that there is an a priori order in the world that can be read by a mind like a Turing tape is read by a computer. Mind is the set of programs run on the brain, and just as the particular computer is unimportant, according to the functionalist doctrine of multiple realizability, because the private language can do the mapping, so too is brain structure (see Edelman, 1992, for counterarguments). Cognizers operate with syntactic processes on representations. Semantic interpretation maps articulated functional states onto some domain of intended interpretation. Human thinking, which may be described as cortical ratiocination, involves goal-driven behavior over semantically interpreted structures.

It is also worthwhile considering another aspect of the foundations of CS, as suggested by Pylyshyn (1984). In Chapter 1 we mentioned his notion of functional architecture as the touchstone for equivalence. He insists, moreover, that the choice of the structure of transducers is of critical importance for the science of cognition. They must act on physical, not symbolic, entities; thus the violence of the attacks on Gibsonians from Fodor and Pylyshyn. Their insistence that there are no constraints on affordance is well taken. Part of the task of this book is to supply a via media.

Gardner regards CS as epitomized by such work as Marr's on vision, or Johnson-Laird's on reasoning. However, it is difficult to see how such issues as affect (de Sousa, Chapter 2) and consciousness can be handled. Let's sound a few sour notes.

We discussed several more of Edelman's reasons for suggesting the whole enterprise is ill-founded in Chapter 4. Here are yet two others, which should by now be familiar.

1. The exclusion of affect and consciousness, which Pylyshyn admits is likely, diminishes the science.
2. Only one type of objectivity, that which obtains when a neat semantic characterization of the domain exists, is allowed for in this schema.

We discuss the new foundation again in Chapter 9.

Edelman's position on meaning—the insistence that it requires consciousness and embodiment—is a distant echo of the work of Michael Polanyi (1958) and all the more secure for this resemblance. The accent on consciousness is expanded on by Searle (1992), who finds it scandalous that a science allegedly concerned with mind should ignore its conscious aspect. Moreover, Searle insists that neither materialism or dualism is a tenable, or indeed a coherent position. However, Searle is after bigger game; the limitation of inquiry in the sciences of mind to two levels, the neurophysiological and the phenomenological. This is in explicit contrast to the central tenet of Cognitive Science, as proposed by Dennett (1993, p. 195): "There is a level of analysis, the information-processing level, intermediate between the phenomenological level and the neurophysiological level."

Several good reasons exist for preferring Dennett's account of this particular event to Searle's. The first is that having abandoned one level of analysis, there does not *a priori* seem to be any good principled reasons for not abandoning others. For example, the neurophysiological level can successively be reduced to levels in which the explanatory frameworks of chemistry and subatomic physics are the most relevant. Secondly, Dennett's central tenet does not strongly constrain cognitive science; it can be interpreted as signalling that such a level is interesting and important without requiring one to buy into the notion that it is intentional and cashing out consciousness in this way. Thus interpreted, this tenet sits easily with the viewpoint on the study of mind outlined in this book.

The most recent thorough attempt to found cognitive science on classical lines is due to Barbara Von Eckardt (1993). Her argument on cognitive science is in itself powerful enough to merit attention; however, she explicitly denies that cognitive science is in Kuhnian crisis; rather, she says, it is an immature science with an implicit set of commitments that her book succeeds in making explicit.

Immature science is exemplified for Von Eckardt by notions like the fluid theory of electricity. A paradigm change, on the other hand, could be provoked by a phenomenon like black-body radiation. Let's imagine that physics had continued to ignore black-body radiation, and had continued along its long-accustomed path; such was the case for the Ptolemaic universe. Is this self-blinkering not precisely analogous to the past attempts in cognitive science to establish a science of mind without consciousness, affect, and social factors? What we have in these attempts is an almost willful ignoring of explicanda in the manner of the Geocentrists. The ignoring of these factors has a history corresponding in its complexity and controversy to the cosmological issue, and by coincidence converging in the latter respect on the same individual. It was in fact Galileo's distinction between "primary" and "secondary" qualities that first exiled much of mental life from the scientific framework. It behooves us for the moment to consider Von Eckardt's exemplary account of cognitive science.

The central issue is this: If cognitive science really is to become the science of mind, it must include affect, consciousness, and social factors. Yet the foundations laid by Von Eckardt do not admit these factors any more willingly than do those laid by Pylyshyn; they can perhaps later be confronted (1993, p. 341).

Von Eckardt does not relax this tension, nor is it her intention to do so. On the contrary; she is concerned with making explicit the assumptions with which cognitive science researchers have to date implicitly been working. In fact, her book can be read in this light as a rather more thorough demolition job on conventional cognitive science than that of which Searle, Edelman and their cohorts would have been capable.

Let us first consider her characterization of cognitive science as an immature science, rather than one in crisis. She is unwilling to accept that cognitive science is capable of crisis for two reasons; first, it is too immature as a science; second, Kuhn's notion of a paradigm is poorly formulated. She is only willing to accept his notions of a "disciplinary matrix" and "exemplar." In fact, cognitive science is to be viewed as a research framework, perhaps the precursor to a new science.

Let's consider the latter point first. The notion of a "paradigm" at least has the virtue of being generally recognizable; more importantly, we lack any more appropriate phrase to capture scientific revolutions like that involved in the transition from classical to quantum physics than "paradigm change." Here, the term is being used on this "as if" basis; such alternative formulations to Kuhn's as Laudan's need a similar concept. Secondly, though cognitive science may be immature in the sense Von Eckardt describes, the attempt to construct a science of mind is not. It has recently gone through stages where the major foci of study were the philosophy of mind, introspectionist and then behavioral psychology, and cognitive psychology. It is in this science of mind tradition that many of us, including the present author, are working; for the moment, we are content to call ourselves cognitive scientists. (It is to be hoped that we can widen the terms of reference of the field to the point that Searle and Edelman can enter. Indeed, Searle suggests that his new neurophysiological/phenomenological field should be called cognitive science. Consequently, in contrast to the iconoclastic Edelman, he is a reformer.)

For Von Eckardt is proposing that cognitive science be considered "an approach to the study of Mind" with no expressed limitations (p. 15). These limitations enter only when she is outlining the metaphysical and methodological premises of her discipline. Suddenly, mind becomes "the human cognitive mind/brain" (p. 50) that consists of a set of cognitive faculties, for methodological purposes best considered as absolutely distinct from each other; the same purposes will require the exclusion of consciousness, affect, and social factors. It need not be emphasized that we have now left the study of mind; the field being described so thoroughly could perhaps be described as computational psychology. All the more so, since the two central assumptions are computationalism and representationalism. The functionalist ethos of modern mind science, with its insistence of multiple realizability of mental process, also permeates her discussion. The discussion of representationalism is superb (p. 143 ff) and the introduction of different types of representation via Pierce's distinction between index, sign, and symbol may save the concept from attacks like those of Stich. However, the tension between cognitive science as the science of mind and as something rather less has not been relaxed, nor will it be by Von Eckardt.

Whether deliberately or not, Von Eckardt does us a service by pressing the attack on this point. She refuses to allow its domain be simply propositional attitudes, as Fodor would prefer; Pylyshyn's *ne plus ultra* for the discipline is identified as unencapsulated faculties, before being rejected as too confining. However, her own analysis would suggest that the current de facto limitations of cognitive science will not allow it to handle many phenomena causative in human cognition; she has little more than aspirations to offer on that score. Finally, her analysis suffers from its complete ignoring of the anthropological component of cognitive science, and the lack of detail on several of the other disciplines constituent of Cognitive Science. The constraints she sees neuroscience imposing on cognitive science are strong (p. 330); yet she refrains from referring to Edelman's conclusions, as noted above.

Von Eckardt, then, has out-Searled Searle in her criticism of cognitive science. An alternative path to constructing a foundation for cognitive science, and the one I have taken, is first to review those disciplines that claim any province of the science of mind. Common themes, when they emerge, allow the construction of a common language as Halley (1992, p. 1) advocates, rather than its imposition, *de haut en bas*.

Consequently, then, AI has exerted an ambivalent influence on CS. It gave the area its initial impetus, but biased its research toward representationalism to the exclusion of many relevant formative influences on cognition. Moreover, the pronouncements of brilliant AI researchers on philosophical issues have often demeaned both themselves and the topics on which they're holding forth. Perhaps the most subtly malign issue, however, is the exile of the mind from world implicit in the computational metaphor. The anti-environmentalist consequences I have discussed elsewhere (Nolan, 1992). Even in engineering terms, as the brilliant work of Brooks (1991) has indicated, the metaphor seems incorrect.

In fact, CS has doomed itself to failure as a coherent science even of cognition by this exile. The very structure of the nervous system has been formed by organism-environment interaction, constraining the nature of the computations that can take place (Chapter 4). Language considered as a closed system is inscrutable; considered as a channel of interaction with the world, it reveals many of its secrets (Chapter 3). Perception is the hopeless analysis of a chaos of shifting impressions, until we take into account the mutual influences of organism and environment (Chapter 2). In Chapter 1, we discussed the philosophical absurdities that arise from separating mind and world; there are more such to follow in the next chapter.

Mind, then, is not a set of algorithms, nor any such box of tricks. It is, however, visible in the ordering principles manifest in adaptation over time. With the increase in the organism's computational powers, those principles become more informationally complex. Yet we cannot understand this complexity in terms of the computations alone; we must find ways of characterizing the environment correctly. I have discussed the notion of context as one such characterization in Chapters 2 and 3 and shall continue the line of argument in Chapter 7. Gibson's notions of affordance and optic flow have a similar intent. These characterizations might yield a more intellectually correct as well as a more technically accomplished cognitive science. Let's now summarize the viewpoint of this book before focusing on the techniques of AI:

1. We explored the current debate about the domain and methodology of cognitive science and found a tension between the received foundations and current science of mind ambitions of the discipline. The tension is exacerbated by critics who fault the subject for its reluctance to address consciousness, affect, and social factors and in so doing elevate itself in accordance with its current ambitions.

2. The viewpoint taken here is that addressing these issues still allows a coherent discipline to exist. Social factors can be handled by informational characterization of subject–environment relations (as done in, for example, situation semantics), affect by studying its informational role, and consciousness by examining projection of informational distinctions (see Chapter 8).

3. These moves extend the discipline as required, while also allowing it a neat demarcation line from other disciplines. It can act as a reservoir of interdisciplinary knowledge while accepting that, for example, the analysis of social trends (as distinct from how they are processed by the individual) is not within its scope; likewise, those aspects of applied experientialism dealt with in consciousness studies are not informationally salient in a way we can currently characterize and so not now within its own remit. The manufacture of those new tools for thought and action called *cognitive artifacts* is an engineering problem; the issue of their fit with human needs and abilities is an applied cognitive science issue.

4. At an individual level, several distinctions (for example, egocentric versus intersubjective), arise naturally in the analysis of cognition, as does the notion of the importance of the Lifeworld, and so on.

5. At a guess, the core subjects of cognitive science will remain cognitive psychology and those aspects of philosophy, anthropology, neuroscience, ethology, AI, and linguistics that have specifically cognitive reference. They will remain in competition with each other in the sense that at any time only one of them will be perceived as having the most promise.

Perhaps a term like *Noetic Science* (inspired by the Greek term for knowing) might better capture the interdisciplinary attempt to study the mental in so broad a context. At a guess, however, we're stuck with cognitive science as a term just as we were with AI.

****

SKEPTICS AND THEIR TECHNIQUES

Figure 5.1 features unflattering and often wholly inaccurate depictions of our skeptics.

Ludwig Wittgenstein and Slot Assertions

Wittgenstein we have met already in Chapter 1. His life he described himself, while dying of cancer, as "wonderful," and I take his word for it. What is certain is that it was exceptional even in the company of the many other eccentrics here in the Hall

FIGURE 5.1.

of Skeptics. He was born in Vienna in 1889, a scion of one of the wealthiest families in Europe; having given away his vast inheritance in his early 30s, he spent the latter part of his life as almost an intellectual vagrant, at one point asking (and being refused) permission to live with a Connemara peasant's family. Intellectually, he was in turn an aeronautical engineer, a mathematical logician, a general semantician, and an all-purpose iconoclast. His careers were successively those of a professional philosopher, a much-decorated infantry soldier in the Austrian Army, a professor of philosophy (in his Ph.D. exam, his *Tractatus* was described as a work of genius, and thus certainly adequate for the award), a hospital orderly, a spurned would-be medical student in Dublin, and an intellectual dharma bum. (Monk, 1990, provides a superb account of his life and work; Derek Jarman's film is both instructive and moving.) Like Alan Turing, he was homosexual, or whatever the politically correct word is at the time of reading. Either through guilt or lack of interest, he remained mainly chaste.

Wittgenstein's lifelong obsession, we learned in Chapter 1, was language and its relation to the world. Like all of us, he wondered whether there was an order in the world *a priori*, or whether we imposed order on it. That his philosophical scholarship was rather poor (Kant's response to this question we have already noted) was an advantage in this case. The naiveté led to a sense of adventure, and the *Tractatus* took the philosophical world by storm. We have already viewed logical atomism as computer science *per se* and in the immediately preceding section as cognitive science—what remains for us to do now is to view it as AI, or more particularly as NLP. It may not be altogether fair to Wittgenstein to extend the scope of logical atomism beyond language: It is a theory of language's relation to the world.

Schank and Abelson (1977) we have already remarked on as unconscious disciples of Wittgenstein. In its pristine form, conceptual dependency (CD) attempted to map all of language onto the following main verbs, which we've mentioned in Chapter 3: PTrans, MTrans, ATrans, Propel, and Mbuild, which could have their purposes achieved by the action of the subsidiary verbs: attend (i.e., focus on), speak (make noise), move, grasp, ingest, and expel (the latter two are generic terms for actions performed to and by anything animate). The use of these verbs, we noted, can effect changes on states of health, anticipation, and awareness. Even this minimalist approach has hidden layers of complexity. Schank and his followers outlined what it meant in terms of them for item A to cause item B, and a multitude of other relations. The resulting NLP systems, as we've noted, were capable of paraphrase and translating sentences like

Der Rat verabscheidet den BeschluB

to

The Council adopted the resolution

if the CD "requests" that mapped the verbs onto CD primitives were worked out at length and mappings set up between the nouns. That of course is quite computationally expensive, and to set it up to translate our old friend (Chapter 3):

Johann nahm die Torte von der Tisch und er putzte ihn.
John took the cake from the table and washed it.

involves a completely separate language-engineering task.

Nor was Schank's the only such *Tractatus*-type attempt. Sergei Nirenburg and Goodman (1991) have produced a number of similar systems. Interlingua is the Holy Grail of NLP—were an adequate interlingua to be found, the task of intertranslating the world's 3,000 (or so) languages would be simplified to writing 3,000 parsers to map the source languages to the interlingua, and 3,000 generators to map from it. The truth is that because of the inadequacy of logical atomism, we're more likely to have to specialize the mapping from each source language *i* to each target language j, with N the number of languages, resulting in a number of programs calculated by $N^2 = 9,000,000$. Moreover, the addition of semantic primitives to this latter type of transfer-based system is a mixed blessing, as many MT systems have found.

None of this would have surprised our Ludwig, who began to attack formalization (even of mathematics, let alone language!) with the zeal of a convert. In fact, like many of his equally technically brilliant companions in our hall of skeptics, Wittgenstein inveighed strongly against what he saw as the dehumanizing effect of science's effort after general laws. This should give us pause: Chomsky spends some of his time campaigning tirelessly for the violently politically oppressed; Gödel and Penrose are Platonists; Turing was convinced of the reality of telepathy; Husserl sought a science of transcendental self; Winograd directed a society for responsible computer professionals, concerned *inter alia* that trigger-happy expert systems should not make the final decisions about starting WWIII. Indeed, it does rather seem that the malign features of computer science cannot be blamed on its true founders. The truly reductionist seem to be divided roughly between the eschatologically (awaiting the end, like David Koresh!) reductionist (Minsky grew up in a community that saw itself as descendants of Rabbi Loew of Prague, who famously was reputed to have built the first robot, or Golem), those technically incompetent philosophers who saw AI as a chance to make provocative statements, and fine AI writers like Tanimoto (1990, p. 6) who are cheesed off with the redundant philosophers of the first section in this chapter.

Wittgenstein was part logician and part mystic in his early work. His later comments on language centered on the doctrine of language games—inventing imaginary situations in which language is used for a tight practical purpose. In these language games, activities and reactions are clear-cut and transparent. These might include a construction worker shouting "Slab" to indicate "Give me a slab!" Again, let's note that context has obviated syntax and semantics—the lexicon is feeding straight into the pragmatic level. For logical atomism's analysis, the later Wittgenstein substituted conceptual investigation with the analysis of words like *intention* and *will*.

The later Schank showed a similar realism. His scripts refuse to try to separate form and content *à la maniere de* his early work. Chapter 3 features a script for a myth like that of Diarmuid and Grainne. AI naive physics research focuses on precisely which primitives are relevant for particular contexts, and which primitives are context general. I have done some preliminary work on this problem. Such concepts as *animate, gender, location,* and *event* are utterly general: However, *composite* and *unitary* are far less general. Finally the kinds of distinctions that might underlie the conversation of, for example, two expert computer programmers without needing any explanation (that function's a kludge) are less general still (refer back to Figure 3.16).

With Wittgenstein, therefore, we become au fait with the logical atomist approach to KR and the problems thereof. Essentially, we have to decide for ourselves which logical atoms are appropriate for which applications without being able to appeal to any general laws. Our next skeptic, Edmund Husserl, is going to lead us to the same destination via an interesting object–attribute–value (OAV) route. Wittgenstein's KR we can, by contrast, describe as slot assertion (SA) or predicate notation. In formal terms, OAV can actually be described by SA predicates, and (to spoil the story) shares its formal limitations along with its epistemological limitations, as we shall now see.

Edmund Husserl And Frames

Edmund Husserl was born in Proswitz in 1859 and died in Freiburg in 1938. Husserl, according to victor's history, was supplanted in his chair at Freiburg by Heidegger after the latter opportunistically joined the Nazi party, a move that led him eventually to the Rectorship at Freiburg. As usual, the story is more complex. Whatever the truth about Heidegger's motives, the early Husserl was, like the early Schoenberg, a fervent German chauvinist as well. I have discouraged my illustrator from doing amusing drawings on this subject.

In Chapter 1, we followed Edmund's career through its early psychologism to the latter phenomenology leading to his interest in the transcendent. Of most importance for us is the phenomenological stage. For Husserl, one of the major issues in this discipline was that mental representations of any type of object had to provide a set of expectations (that is, a context) for structuring incoming data. If expecting a car to be the next object, we expect that it will have certain default attributes (an internal combustion engine, four wheels, doors). These default assignments Husserl called the *predelineations:* The object at the top level he expected to be invariably the same, even if certain of the default assignments turned out incorrect (an invalid's three-wheeled vehicle is still a car). For Husserl, the beliefs expressed in the predelineations in their relation to the facts defined the context.

Now we come to the sad part. How many such contexts are there? Grey, blue, electric, BMW. . . . Husserl's rueful final comment was that he was a perpetual beginner in phenomenology. The multiplicity of these "contexts" (we use the term differently) and the impossibility of predicting which one was next together constitute the most pathological manifestation of the frame problem.

By coincidence, the Husserlian object can be captured neatly in OAV. We expect a car (Car 1) to have the following profile:

(Car 1 Country of manufacture Japan)
(Car 1 Color Brown)

Note the consistent object–attribute–value sequence. The top level object is "Car": The OAV notation captures everything we need to know about it. Our default assignments allow us to predict certain stable features about cars. They are likely to have four wheels, and less likely to be manufactured in Japan, which means that "4 wheels" is a worthwhile default assignment. However, to try to calculate all the defaults that are likely to be necessary from moment to moment is a horrendous task computationally. The frame problem rears its head once again.

In fact, OAV can be described in predicate calculus (PC) if the separate propositions in PC can be interrelated. For example:

(Color Brown)
(Number-of-wheels 4)

can all be housed under a data structure called "Car." The problems with logical atomism and these with OAV have the same origin (aetiology). In fact, that supposedly higher level KR systems like frames (and their near relative semantic nets) can be described in PC means they all have the same problems. Wilensky (1987) comments on this and adduces the following desiderata for KR systems:

1. They should be capable of mapping any domain (that is, they should be epistemologically adequate).
2. Each construct of the KR system should have a direct referent in the world (denotation).
3. If possible, the KR system should be uniform at the epistemological as well as the algorithmic level across all

domains. This will lead to economy of processing. Unfortunately, this is a pipe dream. Syntactic regularity can give semantic relation only in very restricted contexts. Wilensky proposed that his millenniar system should work for everything.

4. Psychological plausibility. Thus, any system dependent on modus tollens better beware!

Wilensky proposed the banner heading Cognitive Representation Theory (CRT) and KODIAK as a system conforming to these Principles. Unfortunately, the number of concepts in a CRT system will, by Wilensky's own admission, exceed the number of words in the text (cf. Chapter 3). There seems to be no escape.

We humans manage to line up a myriad hypotheses at various levels and nature has gifted us a computational architecture that can process in parallel fashion to determine whether these hypotheses are confirmed. The attempt to emulate this computationally runs slap bang into the frame problem. Even the act of processing a simple sentence has hidden pitfalls. If there exist two possible parses for a sentence (and usually there are many more), in the absence of a neat semantic routine allowing instantaneous disambiguation the parser must search through many possible parse trees. This search problem achieves pathological proportion when, for example, the traveling salesman tries to plot an optimal route through 100 different cities. AI has developed many routines to ameliorate search: It helps greatly if there is a readily calculated estimate of distance from the goal state at all points.

There was a time in AI when GPS-type architectures in conjunction with search routines defined almost the whole discipline. Recently, genetic algorithms that view tentatively proposed solutions as the attempt of a generation to reproduce have come very much to the fore. Again, we depend greatly on an evaluation function, continually calculable over the whole search space.

We leave Edmund in his later career, attempting to view his experience in terms of a transcendent self experiencing transcendent objects. It is time to hurry onward to the homosexual father of computing.

Alan Turing And Computability

Turing is credited with assisting in breaking the Enigma codes during WWII. Again, let us beware of victor's history. The Enigma codes, a commercial venture of the 1920s, were actually decrypted in the early 1930s in Germany by a commercial rival and their adoption, even in elaborated form, by the Nazis is something of a mystery. (I promise that this is the last mention of the Nazis, who seem to be cropping up everywhere in this book.) Turing, Emil Post, and Alonzo Church all achieved their initial fame by proposing solutions to Hilbert's *Entscheidungsproblem* (roughly translated, the decision problem). To understand Turing, Post, Church, and more importantly computing and its limitations, it behooves us to concern ourselves with Hilbert.

In the early years of this century, Hilbert challenged his peers to determine whether there existed a generally effective mathematical procedure; that is, an algorithm that could solve everything from NLP problems to differential equations to calculating a payroll. If it existed, a formal device (a computer) embodying this procedure would solve every problem. (Historically, the Sufi mystic Ramon Luil, the Franciscan Roger Bacon, and the philosopher Leibniz dreamt of the same thing.) Think about it! It must be pretty content-free; if it embodies any considerations relevant to, for instance, differentiation, it has ruled itself out of court for everything else. It must be pretty powerful, and yet reasonably simple. We can never prove that it's precisely correct: The "proof" of the Turing–Church conjecture is that any opposing views have been established as formally identical. In fact, the wild surface differences between Turing's and Church's formulations conceal their formal identity. This has led Penrose, inter alia, to propose that computability is a Platonic form.

Turing's solution resembles Emil Post's. Computing, he argued, can be conceived in terms of the following components:

1. An infinite tape (yes, beyond the rings of Saturn, as in Figure 5.2).
2. A read head to read a program of instructions.
3. A write head capable of rewriting 1 as 0, 0 as 1.
4. An automaton that can move the tape.

We can also allow the Turing Machine (TM) to stand up, as shown in the diagram on the opening page of this chapter. Amazingly, a TM can be constructed to calculate any mathematical function, given sufficient supplies of time and masochism.

Is there a solution to the *Entscheidungsproblem?* On the contrary, what Turing established was that given any arbitrary (TM(N), it could not be established whether the TM would ever halt or not. (Cantor, who created the diagonal slash argument that

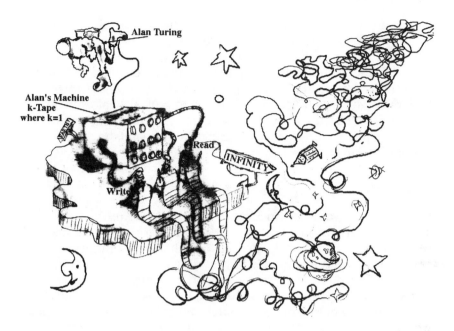

FIGURE 5.2.

Turing used, went insane, Turing committed suicide: I leave Turing's proof as an exercise for the reader.) Consequently, there exists no generally effective mathematical procedure. Yet hope springs eternal: We can still construct a universal TM (UTM) that can simulate the operations of any individual TM. It is stretching matters only a little to see the UTM as a computer and the TM as a program running on the computer. Turing's result indicates that there may exist problems that are not solvable in finite time.

Let us recall Chapter 3. An efficient NL parser was capable of $O(N^3)$, where N is the number of words in the sentence; that is, the time taken to parse was proportional to the cube of N. In like vein, we can talk of (P) problems soluble in polynomial time (N^K); (NP), or nonpolynomial; and NP-complete, which may be more difficult still. Many NLP problems are NP-complete.

Astonishingly, the connection between TMs and language cuts even deeper. We can regard the acceptance of a language by a grammar as the possibility of solution of a problem in finite time. (Some interesting results indicate that there is no guarantee we can learn a Type 1 grammar). We can speak of P, NP, and NP-complete languages, all of which are encoded in TM formalism. Moreover, we can establish that it can't be proven that any randomly chosen Type 1 language can be recognized in finite time (another exercise for the reader). If an extraterrestrial should talk, we might not understand him: His language could be Type 1.

Finally, to end this section with some light entertainment, here is the Turing test described implicitly in the discussion of Searle in Chapter 1. Well-trained Dublin barmen don't even see their customers. If Myles and friend are judged to be identical over 50% of the time, we can, as Figure 5.3 suggests, assume they're running the same program. Here, too, Turing was pessimistic, but only in the short term.

Gödel, Completeness, And Decidability

Kurt Gödel was born in Brünn, Austria-Hungary, in 1906 and adopted American citizenship in 1948. He's dead. He is actually responsible for the breakdown of formalist mathematics and we refer to him again in Chapter 8.

Turing decidability is the property that any proposition produced by a PC-type system should be provable to be a valid theorem of the system or not to be such. PC is in fact semidecidable: We can establish that we can prove that any theorem is a theorem, but not that a nontheorem is such. Yes, I've thrown you into the deep end of Gödel's work, which directly echoes Turing's. Gödel's fame arose from his demonstrating the following about any system

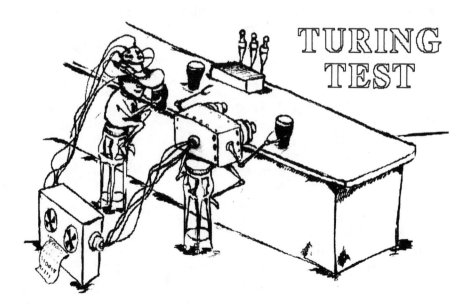

FIGURE 5.3.

with at least the formal power of arithmetic:

1. It cannot demonstrate its own consistency.
2. It will contain propositions that can neither be proven nor disproved in its own formal machinery.

Reasoning as numerical calculation therefore has formal limits, the transcendence of which limits we'll see that Penrose equates with the emergence of consciousness (cf. Chapter 8). We can interpret Gödel's result as an implicit criticism of systems like SOAR (Partridge, 1991, p. 437-443) which in any case have huge KR difficulties. Gödel established that the set of recursive functions is calculable. In that he echoes the Turing–Church thesis. Techniques exist to convert mathematical problems into pure or partially recursive form. We met recursion already in Chapter 3, along with Noam Chomsky, our next skeptic.

The Chomsky Hierarchy

Recall the classification of grammars in Chapter 3. Well, you've read the book, here's the diagram (Figure 5.4). You will recognize the bottom level, the TM, which turns out to be precisely formally equivalent to a Chomsky Type 0 grammar. (Our former Type 0 and Type 1 are both now regarded as Type 0.) Context-sensitive, Type 1 grammars feature a finite tape with read and write heads. Type 2 or context-free grammars have a stack, a computational device allowing recursion and a read head. Type 3 can be implemented simply as a regular grammar. We have remarked that all natural languages fall somewhere between Type 2 and Type 1. In fact, another abstract system called an *indexed grammar* can parsimoniously handle all NL expressions.

Why is Chomsky a skeptic? Again, because of his insistence that language is unique (*sui generis*), the unfolding of the LAD. We have already discussed the shortcomings in Chomsky's theory. Obviously, this skepticism is even more true of Fodor, who sees all cognition solely in terms of the unfolding of an innate language of thought.

Roger Penrose And The Last Emperor

Penrose's (1989) book at a stroke followed Searle's (1980) article into the nether regions (*anus mundi*) of AI infamy. Frankly, it is in this reaction (e.g., Sloman, 1992) that AI begins to show some hypersensitive colors. We'll meet Penrose again in Chapter 8 as a wholly inadequate theorist of consciousness. His book is an attack not on the discipline of AI but on the intellectual position called AI, which he identifies as the unreconstructed proposal that

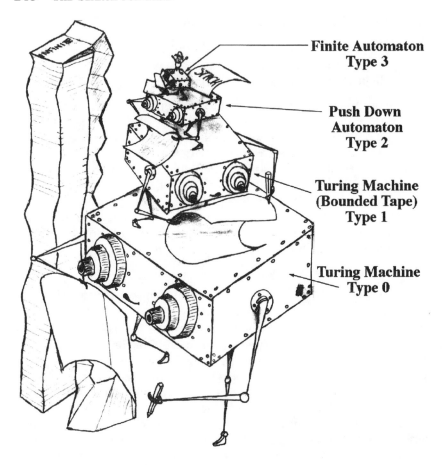

Finite Automaton
Type 3

Push Down
Automaton
Type 2

Turing Machine
(Bounded Tape)
Type 1

Turing Machine
Type 0

FIGURE 5.4.

computers can have mental states. His book is a brilliant attack on a straw man. On completing it, you will have a firm grasp on the main principles of computability, quantum mechanics, cosmogony, algorithms, nonrecursive mathematics, set theory, and neuroscience, without really knowing why.

Penrose as skeptic is discussed in Chapter 8. As creative theorist, he brings our arguments about the identity of language recognition and computational complexity a few stages further. He proves that we can justifiably bring in set theory as well. Algorithms generate recursive sets, the recognition of which is in general possible. Nonrecursive sets seem the province of conscious experience. Moreover, these nonrecursive sets (particularly those that are recursively enumerable) describe the physical neurophysiological processes that are occurring in conscious experience. Indeed, Penrose regards his own (nonrecursive) tiling theory as a valid theory also of how conscious experience "tiles" new neural pathways in the nervous system. Most physical processes are straightforwardly algorithmic. Penrose argues that because of its meta-Gödelian nature (cf. Chapter 8), conscious experience must transcend this. He will not allow that computers are conscious—only at least a half-brain can be. With Penrose's nevertheless brilliant book, we find an extraordinary confluence of themes from mathematics, neuroscience, and physics. His more recent work is influenced by the conjectured possibility of coherent quantum states in the "cytoskeleton" of cells.

Terry Winograd

SHRDLU are the 7th to 12th most commonly used letters in English and the title of Winograd's (1972) early system. It involved a simulation of a robot arm on screen shifting blocks around in accordance with NL instructions. Frankly, apart from the neat Prolog-like planning of actions, little distinguishes the NLP from the ATTs described in Chapter 3. The context is so restricted that the syntax, semantics, and pragmatics are inextricable.

Yet SHRDLU was an outstanding technical advance in its demonstrating that NLP was possible in that kind of microworld: Winograd's (Winograd & Flores, 1986) later work was outstanding for fully acknowledging that microworld principles would not generalize.

In fact, the catch-cries of situatedness and embodiment have yet to be both reflected in Winograd's technical work: For that, we must refer to Brooks (1991). Brooks couples organism and environment by implementing robots that are minimally preprogrammed, being directed only to explore. Their computational architecture features embedding of finite state automaton (FSA) (cf. regular Type 3 grammars) one within the other. Ideally, a Brooks creature has sensors, FSAs, power supply, and minimal program all on board.

Brooks and his followers have had outstanding success in solving the perceptuomotor frame problem we first referred to in Berkeley by means of egocentric knowledge, built up by active interaction with the environment. Brooks, however, goes too far in stating that symbolic action, consciousness, and intelligence will emerge inevitably for reasons the Chapter 1 discussion of Merleau-Ponty made clear.

Bayes And Probabilistic Reasoning

Being the last will and testament of the Right Reverend Thomas Bayes, born in the year of Our Lord 1702 in London and recently deceased in Tunbridge Wells, 1761:

I labored a lifelong with mathematics, that I may establish first the truth of Isaac Newton's calculus, and the divinity of Christ. Being able to maintain myself by my clergyman position as a secure English nonconformist, I thought with myself that I should better myself through the hand of God as manifest in chance. I declare to my God that I resolved that the probability of event a given the occurrence of event b equaled the probability of a (a priori) multiplied by the sundry probabilities of b given a divided by the probability of b (a priori).

$$P (a/b) = \frac{P(a)\ P(b/a)}{P(b)}$$

—Disgusted, Tunbridge Wells

In fact, Bayesian probability is very much back in fashion, particularly in NLP where all else seems to have succeeded only slightly, and within NLP particularly in speech to text applications. Let us consider the task as that of mapping phonemes $b, \ldots b_n$ onto text $a, \ldots a_n$. We need to establish:

1. The relative probability of occurrence of text items $P(a)$.
2. The language model as described by $P(b/a)$.
3. The relative frequencies of $b_1 \ldots b_n$.

That established, we can ignore syntax, semantics, and pragmatics (in fact NLP in general) and look on the problem as purely an engineering one. This has been done with remarkable success, for example in military (DARPA) projects. A similar approach might be used for MT; that is, simply regard translation as intermapping of words occurring with identical frequencies in source and target texts. Finally, it has been found that one need only take into account frequencies of patterns involving three words at a time (trigram model) for optimal use of this approach.

Bayes' work in probability theory has been the subject of numerous attacks, which is why he merits inclusion in this section. However, it seems to work well, whatever its theoretical shortcomings.

David Marr And The Syntax Of Vision

Marr's work involving a primal sketch of the syntax of the scene is well described in Partridge (1991). For Marr vision was above all algorithmic, yet he insisted that a deeper level of analysis than his was necessary. Once we go deeper, by for example including the types of KR mentioned earlier, we abandon generality for power. We shall notice this trend in expert systems as we already have in NLP.

Myles And Postmodernism

Postmodern novels allow the narrator to write about a character who writes about the narrator. We find ourselves in a strange loop or tangled hierarchy (Hofstadter, 1979; Figure 5.5). The link with Gödel should be clear. Let's note that our waking up from one level of recursion is, according to Penrose, the epitome of a conscious act.

In his incarnation as Flann O'Brien (1939), Myles wrote the first fully realized postmodern novel. It becomes difficult at times to tell who is narrating, and the characters are allowed to plot against the life of Trellis, the original narrator, whose life is saved by the accidental destruction of the manuscript by his maid. In the Gödelian framework, we can regard the tale narrated by one of Trellis's characters as one system. Trellis's tale is the most encompassing system. Decisions on the truth or otherwise of a particular segment of narrative, or from whom it originates, would fall under the category of processes that Penrose suggests is nonalgorithmic.

What Would Descartes Think
Of Being Called A Skeptic?

Another exercise for the reader. Hint: How can *res cogitans* affect *res extensa?* And how could this possibly be implemented?

AI AS COMPUTER SCIENCE

In his superb IJCAI Computers and Thought lecture, Rodney Brooks (1991) comments on several aspects of conventional computer architecture:

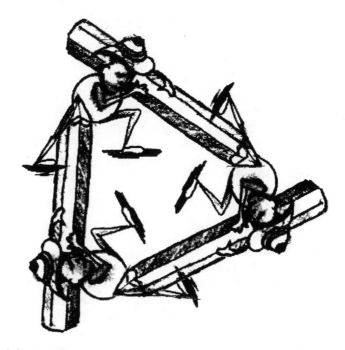

FIGURE 5.5.

1. He conjectures that alternatives, such as protein folding, must be considered. If a protein is deformed from its standard configuration, it automatically regains it, often in a matter of seconds. This reforming procedure is massively informationally rich, and might support the kinds of process necessary for cognition.

2. He comments that computing involves an extremely fast processor operating over a very narrow bandwidth with a large, almost wholly inactive memory. We saw in Chapter 4 that the brain differs on all of these points.

Parallelism is currently very much on the agenda for AI as computer science; however, the comments that Brooks makes are perhaps deeper. His epistemological emphasis is very much on situatedness and embodiment. Yet again, I wish to flag the following limitations in robotics qua epistemology:

1. It is oversanguine to expect consciousness simply to emerge.
2. Fully symbolic behavior must be supported by a specific architecture.

Chapter 7 reveals the goods on these particular issues.

We have just glanced at objections by Turing, Gödel, and Penrose to AI on the grounds that its programs are formal systems and necessarily incomplete. Moreover, in Penrose we find that this incompleteness relates to AI programs being supported by physical processes that are, in his definitions of these terms, "algorithmic" and thus "computable." One alternative suggested is the *quantum computer*, a computer based on only partly deterministic physical processes. It has been conjectured with some credibility (Penrose, 1989) that these computers can theoretically reduce NP-complete problems to P in some cases.

AI As SOFTWARE

The theme of this section is that it is possible to plumb either for syntactic-level generality or KR-level power, but one must be sacrificed for the other. Moreover, the use of probabilistic reasoning seems to help greatly. Development of the area awaits advances in machine learning, which seem a little over the horizon at this stage. I refer the reader to Partridge's (1991) analysis both of this topic and the specifics of the AI systems, which I discuss only at the most general level. In a later section, we consider the notions of context, syntax, and semantics in AI.

NLP

We have looked at length at NLP qua computational linguistics. As AI, we've seen that the turning point was Winograd's SHRDLU, which established that:

1. Success was possible for NLP in a restricted context.
2. However, this context was a microworld and it became obvious that it was a formidable task to develop context-general principles.

So the situation remains. The algorithms have become more efficient (Tomita, 1986); the applications include NL interfaces of increasing coverage (Hendrix & Walker, 1987) and interlingua-based machine translation systems of ever greater sophistication (Nirenburg, 1987). Yet even these successful systems remain tied to specific domains and there do not seem to be any principled ways of fitting a system to a domain. Much is left to *ad-hoc* improvisation and trial and error.

In fact, the state of the art in NLP can be summarized quite neatly:

1. Where language needs to be considered only on the syntactic level—for example, for grammar-checking—the task of building a parser seems straightforward. If the context is restricted sufficiently to allow conveyance of semantic relations by refined syntactic formula (for instance, database interfacing), the requisite system can be created. However, that system will include much that is domain dependent.
2. If the context is less restricted than this, the domain may be mapped by semantic primitives. Yet again, the semantic primitives selected will contain several that are domain dependent (Schank & Abelson, 1977).
3. When the text understanding requires speech-act sensitivity (that is, a knowledge of the speaker's intent), a less-than-graceful degradation of performance occurs (Winograd, 1990). It is proving very difficult to handle context change.

In summary, then, NLP systems work well if the domain can be mapped syntactically, and second-generation systems work with semantic representations within specific domains. As yet, no principled methodology exists for moving between domains, nor for handling speech acts.

Expert Systems

Expert systems remain AI's major success story and thus require little introduction. Again, it is appropriate to distinguish between:

1. Systems that map the domain at a syntactic level. This is quite sufficient for rule-book applications (Feigenbaum & McCorduck, 1983).
2. Systems that attempt representation by structured object representations—for example, the graph theory application in Internist and Prospector's inference networks (Duda & Reboh, 1984).
3. The intractable problem of context-independent systems that map all possible domains at a fundamental level.

The more successful expert systems use a combination of structured objects and probabilistic reasoning with, as in robotics, a recent focus on fuzzy logic (I'm 40% sure of that).

Vision

The situation for vision is neatly summarized by Tanimoto (1990): "A computer system has not yet been created which can look at an image and describe the scene depicted" (p. 410). That goes even for static images. Movement has proven even more difficult to handle (Thompson & Peng, 1990). Again, we can distinguish between:

1. A description, like Marr's "primal sketch" notion of the syntax of the scene, which has proven to be a tractable problem.
2. The much more difficult task of scene description (Tanimoto, 1990).
3. The currently intractable problem of movement. Indeed, the focus of computer vision was until recently the reconstruction of a presumed static external world. Where it has been informed by Gibson, it has progressed quite quickly.

The Frame Problem

We have frequently met the frame problem in the course of this book. Let's encounter it now at home in AI.

Pylyshyn (1987) identifies the frame problem with the problem of relevance: "This, the problem of relevance, is what many believe lies at the heart of the frame problem" (p. x). Hayes (1987) in the same volume, indicates its aetiology: "The frame problem arises when the reasoner is thinking about a changing, dynamic world, one with actions and events in it" (p. 124). Essentially, it relates to the processing of change by a system based on updating of representations for handling change. No principled methods exist of determining what is relevant or otherwise in any change that occurs.

In essence, the frame problem is inescapable for any representationalist system, and it is as well to stress this point now. In fact, if we broaden the concept of change to include on the one hand change of domain for expert systems and NLP, and on the other movement for vision systems and change of speaker for speech-recognition systems, then the frame problem acquires a new, disturbing life. It then seems to reflect a much more fundamental difference between human cognition and AI than hitherto suspected. In fact, it threatens the representationalist paradigm as a good model for the one, and as a technical apparatus for the other.

Some within the connectionist community have argued that theirs is a new paradigm for AI: "The upshot of this is that connectionism provides a kind of Copernican revolution in cognitive explanation. Instead of having the running system revolve around an antecedent analysis of the task, we may make the analysis of the task revolve around an up and running system" (Clark & Lutz, 1990, p. 12). The domain will map itself onto the system by a "continued process of analysis" (p. 12). Gardner (1985) commented on the closeness to Gibson's system of PDP, but wisely refrained from taking sides on the issue of whether connectionism can provide a new framework for AI. It is only the more unconventional, non-back-propagation learning algorithms that might have anything to say on this score.

PDP As AI

The initial auguries are unpropitious: "Although the current generation of networks appears to be very good at performing/learning to do what are essentially static/spatial tasks, there has been relatively little progress on networks that can cope adequately with tasks which have an important temporal/sequential component to them" (Clark & Lutz, 1990, p. 11). Perhaps in the future PDP can evade the frame problem; at present, such is not the case for the standard models.

In all, the successes of PDP in pattern recognition and cognitive veracity must be set against their current failures as software, as manifest for example in the domain dependence of these systems.

Summary

We are left with the following picture of AI:

1. Many ingenious methods have been developed to treat various domains at a syntactic level for the modalities of speech and vision, and for reasoning.

2. Where a real-world application for a specific domain is required, the mapping always involves considerations relevant only to that domain.

3. No principled way has yet been found to handle domain change.

The Recent History of AI

We have rarely stained our hands with commerce in this book, but we may as well look briefly at market trends for AI as software. We've also mainly been concerned with how AI software works in terms of the categorization above; let's broaden things a little. Many 1980s startup companies folded, and the projected market for Lisp machines evaporated when it proved more cost-effective simply to use Lisp on the by now much faster PCs. To complicate matters further, much AI technology remains hidden in conventional software products; word processors may include grammar checkers, and even Cobol now has an object-oriented version. It is thus really difficult to gauge the size of the AI market. Automation of knowledge in its various forms may become a commercially hot issue soon, and AI may explicitly be in demand again. At the moment, we are in the paradoxical situation that many non-AI techniques (like statistical reasoning in case-based reasoning products, which attempt to derive conclusions on previous elaborated cases) are used in explicitly "AI" products, and conventional software uses AI techniques.

As people for some reason seem to want to spend more and more of their leisure time in passivity, being "stimulated" by bright colors and nice sounds, and (more concretely) as the amount of "information" available to oneself and one's competitors grows exponentially (witness, for example, the growth of traffic on the internet), automated personal assistants are coming to the fore. Soon, perhaps, we may not need to talk to each other at all but me, I'm going to the bar. Interest is growing in "agents" that can be set to perform particular tasks; for example finding a movie, or searching your e-mail for relevant items (an unenviable task, to be sure, but someone's gotta do it). The most interesting problems in agent technology relate to choice of actions; one has to be sure that one agent's action does not interfere with another's.

AI has been held partly to blame in this chapter for some of the functionalist excesses of CS. It should also be said that recently some AI researchers have produced brilliant implementations of situated, embodied themes. We already noted some such in active NLP and vision and the work of Rod Brooks. The culture of AI includes an implementation orientation, a sense of fun and adventure, and self-confidence that is often not even wholly misplaced, leading to the possibility of breakthrough. Virtual reality may progress to the point that Piaget's notion about à genetically constrained set of possible worlds may be tested; some recent less celebrated work by Patti Maes and her colleagues at MIT will reach the market in some form, probably as a computer game, soon. One looks into a body-length mirror screen and sees oneself accompanied by various creatures in an environment superimposed on the room one is in. One may interact with these creatures (for example, a cuddly dog) sometimes, as I witnessed, in rather morally abandoned and appalling ways by directing them to move, sit, and . . . I'd rather not say. The range of reference of this work is impressive, including using ethological methods to determine the salience of gesture (see Chapter 6). For me, this kind of work is AI at its best.

THE CURRENT METHODOLOGICAL DEBATE

Before entering the arena of this worthwhile and fascinating debate, one more fruitless option must be eschewed—cognitive psychology as AI. Human reasoning can only in a limited way emulate the kind of content independence that we've noted in AI production systems. The PDP situation, where the KL, algorithmic, and implementational levels are all bundled together, seems much more psychologically plausible. We have also looked in Chapter 4 at the evidence against GOFAI as any type of realistic psychological model; PDP has better claims. Interestingly, the systems like SOAR, which claimed some such plausibility, tend to be syntactic level, with all the technical shortcomings we have seen that involves; for example SOAR, like PDP systems, has to be rewritten to a fair degree in order to acquire a new problem space.

The issues current in AI as a theory of mind include the following:

1. Where do we attribute the KL description? The current answer is: the observer's perception of the organism in interaction with the environment. We're going to find that this is precisely analogous to Bateson's view of mind in nature.

2. What is reflection? Currently, one hypothesis (due to William J. Clancey, 1992, whose views we'll refer to as the Willie Clancey School) is behaviorist; reflection is revision in behavior.

3. We noted chunking in Chapter 2 with respect to a Morse code operator. Clancey reformulates it as regularization.

4. Conceptualization can be thought of as recomposing perceiving and behaving.
5. Understanding is viewed as a primary high-level function.

We are going to find ourselves agreeing with Point 1 as a general view of mind and with Points 2 through 5 as a GOFAI view of the processes involved. However, the view of AI emerging from Brooks and his confréres may define each of those terms quite differently, with respect to an organism's or robot's ongoing interaction with the environment rather than its conceptualization of it.

The debate about situated cognition recently occupied an entire special issue of the journal *Cognitive Science* (Vol 17, Jan-Mar 1993). We can learn much from it in that as a consequence of its main theme, it provided an excellent forum for discussion of (*inter alia*) the role of implementing computer systems in CS. I do not intend to try and resolve all the issues in this debate, but wish to flag certain points and consensuses relevant to us:

1. Symbolic cognition may also be situated, as we have continued to maintain.
2. The existence of specialized neural hardware for egocentric cognition is accepted even by the symbolic camp.
3. That camp feel that all that matters in CS is implemented computer systems.
4. Their notion of a symbol is that it is something that can designate or denote. The issues Searle raises (basically, designate or denote for whom?) are not confronted.
5. Anthropology's analysis of structures and relations in the human world may reveal much of significance about this world that the "symbolic" or "situated" paradigms cannot show.
6. The framework here, which contrasts egocentric and intersubjective on one criterion, and posits the dimensions of symbolic, operational and ontological on another, holds up well in the light of this debate.
7. To a certain extent, we are revisiting the empiricism-rationalism debate of Chapter 1.

Bateson's Cybernetic Approach To Mind

Clancey pointedly invokes Gregory Bateson. It is apposite to look at his work. Bateson (1979) has concentrated a great deal of effort on precisely those aspects of the relationship between organism and environment that are most in question here. Moreover, he gives an account of mind that defines it in terms of general interaction between interrelated components. For Bateson, mind is immanent rather than transcendent.

It must be remarked that Bateson is concerned first and foremost with restructuring those current concepts of mind and self he considers contributory to environmental destruction. "What must now be said is difficult . . . I believe it to be important to the survival of the whole biosphere, which as you know is threatened" (Bateson, 1979). On a personal level, holding on too firmly to those concepts may lead to cataclysm in, for example, alcoholism. Indeed, Bateson goes on to identify these concepts with the same Cartesian error to which Thines (1977) objects: "The sobriety of the alcoholic is characterized by an unusually disastrous variant of the Cartesian dualism, the division between mind and matter, or, in this case, between conscious will or 'self' and the remainder of the personality" (Bateson, 1972).

He suggests that there are specific errors in the Western view of self. These errors manifest themselves on the individual level in personal dysfunctions like alcoholism and on the level of social pathology in environmental destruction.

For Bateson, conscious purpose is a mixed blessing. It can act as a time-saving device but tears one away from one's environment. The consequent rootlessness is at the base of certain of our current environmental and specifically medical ills. "Purposive consciousness is now empowered to upset the balances of the body of society, and of the biological world around us" (Bateson, 1972). Consciousness is treated of as the time-saving device noted already. "Consciousness . . . is organized in terms of purpose. It is a short-cut device to enable you to get quickly at what you want: not to act with maximum wisdom in order to live." Indeed, there are certain ends—particularly creative ones—for which the necessarily purposive structure of consciousness is inappropriate. "We might say that in creative art man must experience himself-his total self—as a cybernetic model . . . in the making he must relax that arrogance in favor of a creative experience in which his conscious experience plays only a small part" (Bateson, 1972).

What alternative does Bateson offer to the apparently inappropriate view of consciousness rooted in Western society? Essentially, "The problem is systemic and the solution depends upon realizing this fact . . . man is only a part of larger systems and a part can never control the whole" (Bateson, 1972). The onset of systemic wisdom must have associated with it an entirely new view of self.

Bateson contrasts the systemic view, which takes interaction between people and environment as its focus for study, with the traditional tenet of a transcendent self. "The total self-corrective unit which processes information . . . is a system whose boundaries do not at all coincide either with the boundaries of the body or what is called the self." This information-processing entity is immanent as opposed to transcendent in character: "The system is not a transcendent entity as the self is supposed to be" (Bateson, 1972). Bateson considers the unsystemic viewpoint a characteristically Western error: "The average Occidental . . . even believes there is a delimited agent the "self" which performed a delimited purposive action" (Bateson, 1972). Perhaps the word *delimited* is more appropriate than *transcendent*.

What then is mind? In short, an aggregate of interacting parts of components. Bateson hopes to come to an understanding of mind by making a list of criteria "such that if any system satisfies the criteria listed, it is a mind. I should unhesitatingly say that the aggregate is a mind." Moreover: "I propose that the mind-body problem is soluble along lines here outlined" (Bateson, 1979).

A summary of Bateson's view is now called for, along with a process for relating them to certain themes of the present work. In essence, Bateson must be interpreted as proposing a revision of certain current conceptions of the relationship between what we term *self* and what we term *world*.

It should be obvious that Bateson's argument has marked similarities with Gibson's. What both Gibson and Bateson are saying amounts to a new account of the relationship between the internal and external worlds.

The view of mind emerging from AI (Point 1, in this section) is essentially Bateson's view. Points 1 through 5 are essentially engineering prescription. AI has landed us unexpectedly right back where we started in the world of Gibson, Piaget, and Merleau-Ponty. The champions of Bateson's position find arrayed against them a rearguard symbolic action; the framework of this book is proposed as a hospitable neutral forum.

CONTEXT, SYNTAX, AND SEMANTICS

To introduce this section, let's do a retake on several themes we introduced in Chapter 3. Sublanguage is a phenomenon in language where the context is sufficiently restricted to allow semantic relations to be given by syntactic formulae. At this level of restriction, the syntactic-level systems we discussed earlier can elicit the relations necessary. In short, if we look at the combination of system and environment, the latter aspect is well structured enough to afford the necessary relations after a syntactic analysis. The systems at the deeper level—that is, the semantic systems—work in less well-structured environments and so must have "semantics" built into them.

This leads us to the issue of what semantics in fact is. As a term, it is a late-19th-century innovation due to Bréal (Tamba, 1988). Its meaning is still unclear: Passmore (1966) cites several different meanings, including the study of how we can be confused by language. Moreover, the issue of what semanticians should actually be doing still awaits an answer. If they are merely characterizing the semantic content of various expressions, they lose connection with the world. If they insist, with Jackendoff (1987, 129-32) and against David Lewis, that semantics first requires characterization of a language of thought before proceeding, they run the risk of psychologism.

The viewpoint of this book is that many of these arguments can be resolved with a clearer model of context. Moreover, semantics, however understood, is not the sole vehicle for the communication of meaning. There is much truth in Edelman's and Polanyi's contention that meaning in an intersubjective domain requires consciousness and a self. The vehicle used can be syntax, pragmatics, semantics (either understood as "mentalese" or as model theoretic if a neat model of the domain exists), or, as is the case most often, a combination of all of these. What precisely is used depends on the degree of restriction of context.

Context is normally used in AI systems with respect to constraints on the moment-to-moment relevance of knowledge. Let's note that the systems given earlier work because no pragmatics or other issues are relevant. All knowledge and behavior are contextual. Much work remains to be done in the proper characterization of context. The starting point must be to shift the focus of analysis to system and environment.

MIND IN AI

Little remains to be added to the previous discussion, but let us first of all review the path taken in this chapter. We began by stressing the importance of AI for CS. This led us to discuss what exactly AI is, and to give a more veridical account of its history than normally appears. Science proceeds by paradigm shifts, and the most important audience for ideas is the next generation of talented researchers. For a variety of reasons, AI failed to grab these researchers for some time between the late 1960s and mid-1970s. AI is important for CS, but its influence has sometimes been subtly malign. We discussed the extent to which an overemphasis on mental operations as computational to the exclusion of everything else has damaged CS. This led us to a wide-ranging discussion on the nature of CS.

We then discussed skeptics and their techniques. Wittgenstein and Husserl were assigned knowledge representation. In Chapter 2, we allotted logic to Piaget. KR problems were pointed out by Winograd, and in our discussion of the frame problem as well as the methodological issues in PDP in Chapter 4. The notion of computation itself was assigned to Turing, Gödel, and Penrose, all of whom emphasize the fact that there exists a set of problems for which it cannot be proven that they have a solution in finite time. Chomsky introduced the idea of parsing in Chapter 3. Here, his work was put into a broader context. The recognition of languages by an automaton was seen as equivalent to assessing whether problems had solutions in finite time. We briefly mentioned Marr, a syntactician of vision, and had some fun with Myles. The probabilistic approaches increasingly being used in NLP were introduced in the words of the venerable Bayes himself.

A theme that continues to present itself in this book is the relation between syntactic and semantic. We use this distinction, coupled with subsymbolic, to describe the achievements of AI. The discussion of Bateson, at least some of whose work is relevant, explored the consequences of positing the knowledge-level description, or the attribution of mind, to the interaction of system plus environment. The framework of this book is enriched by this consideration, and holds up well in the current symbolic/situated debate (as it's often unfortunately put).

TEXTS ON AI

A plethora of texts exists. You could do much worse than use a combination of Tanimoto (1990) with its introduction to Lisp and working programs; and Partridge (1991), with its comprehensive account of the field.

• *six* •

ETHOLOGY AND ETHNOSCIENCE

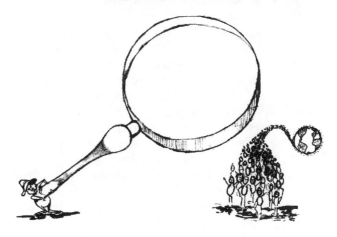

Can Ethology Explain Everything?

Animals often seem very stupid when put in continued experimental set-ups. Pigeons peck at lights in Skinner boxes when the reinforcement arrives according to a time, rather than a pecking schedule; rats continue to try and travel by a previously chosen path which is now electrically live. An adage that is used for these situations is that there are no stupid animals, but plenty of badly designed experiments. It seems appropriate to try and study the behavior of animals in their natural environment (ethology).

When we do so, we find many astonishing manifestations of mind in nature. In fact, here more than anywhere else we see that mind is best viewed as the adaptation of an organism to an environment over time, or better still of a species. This holds true regardless of whatever theory of evolution we choose, a choice that merits some comment.

First of all, when speaking of ethology, we are normally implicitly speaking of knowledge that is relatively directly genetically encoded. High school science worldwide describes how genetic information is encoded in deoxyribonucleic acid (DNA) and that a chain of chemical events leads through RNA and amino acid expression of this information until we end with specific instructions for protein formation. In particular, DNA consists of a long chain of four molecular compounds. Sequences of three of these bases are read at a time by a cell, at a speed and time also specified on the DNA strand. Each base instructs the cell on which amino acid to include in a protein, the structure of which also determines its (the protein's) function. However, several issues must already be raised. Does one's individual experience have any influence on the structure of one's DNA? (Do the sons of toil really have horny hands?) If we accept so, we find the epithet "Lamarckian" being hurled at us: Otherwise, we are politically correct neo-Darwinians. Secondly, how much of human behavior can be explained in terms of the unfolding of one's genetic inheritance (the genome)? Sociobiologists believe a great deal of it is.

Let's consider the first question now. Neo-Darwinism states that there are only two ways by which a mutation can occur. One may be through an event like radiation exposure affecting a change on the DNA. This is obviously inheritable and, if the offspring reproduces, it will be passed on. However, only a tiny fraction of these mutations are adaptive. An alternative route is a hitch in the transmission chain from nucleic through amino acids. Again, this is more than likely to be maladaptive and is probably not inheritable.

Lamarckianism, by contrast, insists that one's DNA reflects experiential data as well as experiences one undergoes passively, like Chernobyl or Sellafield. By historical irony, Darwin himself held a Lamarckian view of inheritance. This particular controversy has raged over the last century, causing the suicide of at least one brilliant evolutionary biologist (Paul Kammerer's story can be read in Arthur Koestler's *The Case of the Midwife Toad*) and the evidence is ambiguous, although analysis of bacterial immunology has been interpreted to indicate Lamarckian inheritance does occur, leading neo-Darwinians like Dawkins to shout fraud.

Let's start to put this debate in the wider context it deserves. We noted in Chapter 3 that language, considered as a static monolith, afforded only a puzzlingly layered system with paradoxical types of interactions between layers. Considered in use, the paradoxes disappeared. Similarly, when considered as theories of the progressive adaptation of a species to an environment—that is, mind in nature—there is no significant difference between neo-Darwinism and Lamarckianism. This progressive adaptation often involves the appropriation, over time, of a response to the environment that was originally purely experiential. An example is the ostrich's developing calluses on its behind, which is too specific a response (to pain!) to admit of a straight neo-Darwinian explanation. However, if viewed in the terms of the species, long-term engagement with its environment (what Waddington terms the *epigenetic landscape*), it is perfectly feasible that this response can be genetically assimilated.

Consequently, we need to look at the nexus of species and environment together over time in order to understand anything essential about evolution. A byproduct has been a resolution of the central abiding controversy in evolutionary biology. With that in mind, let's now examine that secular religion usually called sociobiology.

Like most secular religions, there is a creation myth. Self-replicating molecules emerge from the primeval soup at a time of darkness over the earth. These molecules attract the detritus of the depth and manage to find ways to breathe form into this detritus. And then there was life, because it helps ensure the future happy replication of these molecules. Not only that, the replicators instruct the detritus to form legs, fins, eyes, fur, and brains, depending on what the environment requires, until we end up with humans in a world curiously resembling Planet Earth, 2000 A.D. And yes, said the high priests of sociobiology, "Ye are that detritus. Only we are in contact with the Replicators." One now has precisely that sense of estrangement from one's own essence that the more nasty forms of religion can feed on, be they Freudianism or rampant Fundamentalism of any sort.

It is interesting that the Pontiflex Maximus of this particular superstition, Richard Dawkins, admits that the notion of these replicators consciously intending purposes, or using anything, is at best metaphorical (and at worst, perhaps, destructive nonsense). However, what we may term the *strong* sociobiology argument, taken to extremes as it often is, suggests that all the facts of human culture are gene expressions. Even if, as is sometimes granted, the quirks characteristic of any given culture are not genetically predetermined, the existence of a culture is.

We're again speaking eschatology (the religious sense of coming to an end), rather than science. Not one detailed aspect of higher level cognition has had a specific neurophysiological, let alone a genetic, correlate identified. Were the more ambitious claims of sociobiology valid, ethology would be the basis for all cognitive science. At present, these claims have about as much scientific evidence going for them as scientology. Let's press ahead in learning what *has* actually been established in ethology.

Ethology and Learning Mechanisms

Ethology can tell us about certain types of egocentric knowledge. Much like myth as we discussed it in Chapters 1 and 3, ethological knowledge tends to be unconscious and has a pervasive structuring effect on perception and action. It is not so much a building block as an architect's sketch for an entire part of the building.

The vocabulary of ethology must first be mastered before we pay attention to its specific findings. One issue that has already arisen with respect to child development is whether a species is precocial (is early-developing) or altricial (late-developing, with the attendant consequences for flexibility of later learning mechanisms). We must also introduce the notion of *set* as predisposing influence affecting the probability of an event. These events are normally types of behavior in response to environmental stimuli. Phylogenetic sets are due to one's species, ontogenetic sets to one's particular nature. We can also distinguish experiential and individual sets. An archetype of phylogenetic set is the digger wasp's egg-laying pattern. She builds a nest and kills a caterpillar that will feed the newborn. The nest is then marked by a marker like a pine cone.

Inherited learning patterns include items of various degrees of specificity. Kineses, which are stereotyped types of movement and reflexes, that also require certain stimuli, are very specific. Fixed action patterns, including, for example, smiling, are less so. It would obviously be a pointless exercise to try to base a worthwhile science of cognition on these impoverished foundations.

Let us note just one more critical concept. *Critical periods* refer to times during development when the learning of certain items is optimized for a species. If kittens don't get experience of vertical stripes early on, they remain blind to them. Close to birth, ducks can be imprinted on Konrad Lorenz as on their mother. A celebrated series of photographs shows the ducks dutifully following the famous ethologist. This type of knowledge, then, is hard-coded and may be hard-coded incorrectly. That fact certainly give pause.

Mind in Ethology

We've stressed that in biological systems, *a fortiori*, evolution can sensibly be viewed only over time and as species adaptation. In this, we see *Nous* at its most evident. The spider constructs a web as though it knows the principles of tensile engineering; the honeybee's dance shows a superb sense of how symbols can represent reality. Moreover, above all, we see the occasional necessity of distinguishing mind per se from conscious mental life.

ETHNOSCIENCE

Ethnoscience focuses on discovering how individuals in different cultures organize and use their cultures. In particular, it looks at how this knowledge manifests itself in language. As such, it is related to the following disciplines:

1. Ethnography, which focuses on the modes of life of various groups.
2. Anthropology, which exposes the basis structural relations underlying human social life and organization.
3. Lately, a lot of experimental research on cross-cultural cognition has been done, which attempts to perform a comparative analysis of the act of categorization in particular.

Ethnography and Anthropology

These disciplines were profoundly influenced by the work of Levi-Strauss, who was an admirer of Merleau-Ponty. His intellectual debt was more to structuralism than to phenomenology—the former discipline attempts to elicit the invariant laws of relation of the phenomena under examination. In linguistics, for example, the use of a word would be viewed only in the context of the other words with which it formed a structural whole. We are back to Wittgenstein: We know what *dog* means (almost), but for *the* we must look at how this word is used in the whole language itself.

Indeed, anthropology is seen as profoundly connected with linguistics, and Levi-Strauss would have been very sympathetic to Chomsky's search for a universal grammar. Linguistics is seen in this light as a social science: Sociology itself is viewed as an anthropology of a single society, a plotting out of the structural relations underpinning human life and organization for a single case.

It has to be said that neither subject can truly be said to belong to CS, which works best as a forum for studying the activity of an individual mind insofar as that activity can be informationally characterized. In the broader context of its role in a federation of sciences of mind, CS often finds itself being greatly informed by the conclusions of anthropologists and sociologists, but their activity in attempting to intuit structural relations is not essentially a CS one.

Anthropological fieldwork has varied greatly in quality. In Ireland, we are more used than most to intrusive researchers asking terribly stupid questions before writing up the extraordinary and deliberate fabrications they receive in reply as Ph.D. theses. The Samoan islanders found themselves in the 1930s presciently portrayed as 1960s flower children in Margaret Mead's *Coming of Age in Samoa.* To understand a culture seems to involve an immersion therein, a com-passionate desire to experience its depths as well as its heights, and much creative insight.

Sermon over, let's return to Levi-Strauss. His conclusions are interesting:

1. Consciousness arises neither from culture, nor language.

2. Language and thought are separate: The former is not necessary for the latter (this viewpoint is one that we expounded in Chapter 3).

3. Myths are all-pervasive in mental life, for which they supply the formal structures or patterns, even if their influence remains unconscious.

For Levi-Strauss, one of the crucial points about myths is that they reveal mind in its pure form, free from objects. He undertook an atomistic analysis of myths, noting elements like the undervaluing of blood ties exemplified by the content of the Oedipus myth and the foot deformity (swollen foot) mentioned in Oedipus' name. These concrete details, he argues, were used to approach more abstract struggles like that between nature and culture. They need have no precise content *a priori* in themselves: The architect's plan is not the brickwork (the map is not the territory). Again, as was the case in ethology, we find ourselves meeting powerful, structural forces just beyond the point at which we can articulate our experience.

Given ethnoscience's attempt to analyze the thought structures of ours and other cultures, we could perhaps usefully set it the task of comparing the analytic philosophy tribe with the Continentals. With this ice broken, the possibilities become endless. Eliminative materialists as cargo cultists . . . the milleniar teachings of sociobiology. In fact, the social sciences in general can yield rich pickings for researchers hungry to find ethnic groups working in closed cognitive systems safely remote from reality.

Cross-Cultural Cognition

Much research effort has gone into explicating the systems of categorizations different cultures use to deal with their environments. It is found, for example, that a Wall Street trader evaluating blue chips might use precisely the same formal structure as a south sea islander choosing a tree from which to build a boat. To spoil the story, the conclusion fits in very much with the principle of rationality: The cognitive system will work opportunistically to maximize its adaptation, using whatever formal structure fits. Indeed, the entire cultural system involving religion, tribal bonding, a language in which women, fire and dangerous things might have the same symbol (in Lakoff's famous example), can be seen as a program that optimally chunks experience.

A fundamental finding has been that certain (base) levels of conceptual analysis have privileged possibilities. The class *tool* admits of the base level of hammer, saw, and other levels like mallet, and hacksaw. Base level categories seem to have a psychological priority. Moreover, conceptual abstraction seems to be universally done by prototypes (for example, one visualizes an archetypal hammer), in contrast to which examples are seen as having a stronger or weaker family resemblance. (Two members A and B of a family may have the same color eyes, but a different nose; vice versa for members B and C, yet all are identifiable as siblings).

In conjunction with this research, Eleanor Rosch (1973) found a cross-cultural tendency for categorization of colors with respect to three foci on the spectrum that are roughly analogous to the primary colors. All this evidence together suggest that nominalism (cf. Chapter 1) is inferior to conceptualism in some ways: concepts seem to emerge naturally from experience, rather than impositions of one's vocabulary.

In fact, yet another alternative proposed foundation for CS focuses on cross-cultural cognition. The central notion is that cognition is strongly dependent on the nature of the brain–body unity and that many aspects of the conceptualization that structures our cognition derive from the kind of universal experience captured in image schemas and their like. Lakoff, we note below, rightly suggests that we extend the structures of physical experience by metaphor to other domains. This is very much compatible with the Nolanian framework but we shall note some caveats.

In this context, Terry Regier's work has received a loud fanfare. Its range of reference is impressively wide: Cognitive linguistics (whose aficionados have received him with open arms), linking of natural language and vision, cross-cultural studies of both perception and cognition, and some ingenious ad-hoc PDP solutions. The input his system receives is videos of simple block and blob shapes implementing actions that will be described by spatial prepositions from various languages. English is actually very weak in such constructs; for example, the notion "up from underneath" is handled by a single term in both Gaelic (*anios*) and Russian (*izpod*). Regier himself makes far fewer claims for his system than does George Lakoff, who sees predictions from his cognitive models notions of language fulfilled in detail. In fact, Lakoff is inclined to use Regier's work as proof positive that, yes, spatial language does in fact involve projection of the body and kinesthesis onto external space. For example, "on" = force + support. Lakoff continues to emphasize the point above that whole cognitive domains derive their structure from the metaphorical extension of others. Love is a journey, and a relationship is a vehicle that may be upended, stalled, or run off the road. One problem with this notion is that counterexamples tend simply to be ignored; it is difficult to see what Lakoff would accept as a counterexample. Love is a rose with thorns? . . . A many-splendored thing?

Another really consequential issue emerges in this context. The emphasis on the individual mind in CS is counterbalanced, as we saw in Chapter 1, by work like Hutchins', which looks at the cognitive artifacts in societies and (as we saw, fallaciously) proposes the internalization of one's dealings with these explained cognition. I feel the real question here is what is an object, that we should know it? For you and I to have dialogue, we must refer to a set of intersubjectively validated tokens, some of which can be identified with the "container" schema and its like. (It is argued in Chapter 8 that the experience of oneself as object is similarly compelling in the manner we sought for the foundations of psychology in Chapter 2). These schemas can be extended metaphorically, as noted above; it is my belief, however, that the intersubjective domain holds more than this as the operational knowledge interacts with the symbol systems.

Let's again look at the mathematical diversion that originally was Riemann geometry. Einstein found that, used in a four-dimensional space, it afforded precisely the kinds of effects (for example, the curving of space-time by gravity) that he needed for general relativity. In other words, the formal game turned out to be the best model of the universe. The relation of mind and world here is of quite a different nature to the necessarily psychologistic ethos of cross-cultural cognition. Something mysterious is afoot, some manner in which we indeed are microcosms.

It may be appropriate also to remind ourselves of culture specificity, and of pygmies' inability to interpret photos. Their native language of vision doesn't include this, nor the ability to determine that a buffalo one mile away looks small, but is really rather large. They are, in turn, unquestionably attuned to their environment in ways that we in the West cannot understand, and from which we have much to learn.

MIND IN ETHOLOGY AND ETHNOSCIENCE

In both these cases, mind is manifest and best appreciated *in situ* and as the process of adaptation. Moreover, the animal's being wrenched from its environment into the laboratory, or the non-Western human being asked questions from a Western academic's viewpoint, tears the fabric of the organism–environment continuum to the point where we completely lose what we set out to observe in the first place. We must also, from this chapter, yet again note the informing role of myth, archetypes, and ethological learning mechanisms. The role of anthropology in CS concerned us briefly, as did the nature of the intersubjective domain, leading to surprising conclusions about aspects of the mind–world relation.

FURTHER READING

Flanagan (1991) provides a worthwhile account of sociobiology in a CS setting. Gardner (1985) provides a good account of ethnoscience.

· II ·

A New Foundation for Cognitive Science

The general outlines for the new foundation for cognitive science will be reviewed at this stage. These following themes, the central principles of the theory of cognition herein, are consistent with and afford a perspective that allows insight into the main findings from the principal constituent disciplines of cognitive science.

1. Mind is best viewed in terms of the co-adaptation over time of organism and environment.
2. Human cognition admits of distinct egocentric and inter-subjective modes. The latter mode, in turn, consists of a contrastive autistic realm.
3. Symbols can usefully be viewed with respect to the onto-logical, symbolic, and operational knowledge dimensions.
4. It is useful to distinguish cognition from perception in the following terms (rather than those of a symbol–nonsymbol dichotomy): Cognition refers to any mental process by the organism that attempts to transcend its environment. Perception, by contrast, is a process that involves the maintenance of a stable relationship with the environment.
5. Cognition cannot be fully discussed except with respect to its development as progressive adaptation to and mastery of an environment.
6. The Nolanian framework has been elaborating itself. After we progress through the next two chapters, all will be revealed in Chapter 9.

These two chapters (7 and 8) broaden the context of the discussion. We need, first of all, to look at human symbolic behavior in as many of its manifestations as possible. Second, we must carefully scrutinize the topic that many people identify as mind—conscious experience. So much has been written about this recently that we must explicitly confront and criticize other viewpoints. More than any other, this topic will define what the sciences of mind, including cognitive science, have to contribute to our view of ourselves. Chapter 5 included a long discussion of what exactly CS's domain is vis à vis other sciences of mind.

The forthcoming account deliberately refers to real human experience in the real world a great deal. It must do so to have ecological validity. For its methodological justification, we journeyed down many nooks and crannies in Chapter 1. Its justification in terms of the other disciplines was spelled out at length in the appropriate chapters.

Cognitive science should tell us something new about our experience other than the pious and probably misguided hope that it will be eventually treated with the same concepts as the hard sciences. It should say that something with passion, rather than complacency accompanying the "certainty" that no life-enhancing notions will ever emerge from the grinding of its dark mills. In fact, eliminative materialists are probably correct in castigating a great deal of our folk psychology concepts: However, our notions of *self, intent, feeling,* and *belief* might just as easily be transcended through their correct analysis, as eliminated.

seven

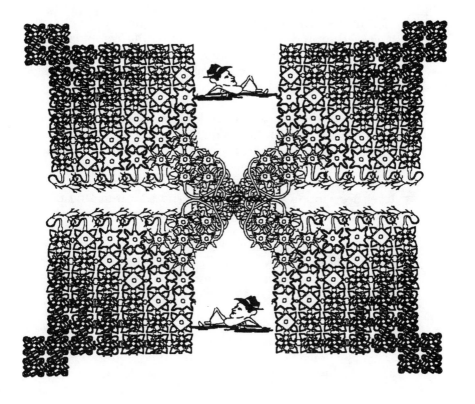

SYMBOL SYSTEMS

CHARACTERISTICS OF SYMBOL SYSTEMS

This chapter explores the nature and use of symbol systems like those of language, music, and mathematics. Many of these findings are also appropriate for vision—visual perception involves the use of symbols often unconsciously picked up from one's culture or, as in the case of Western society, produced by the conscious effort at realism in painting and photography. Gombrich's *Art and Illusion* (1959) is a superb history of pictorial representation that views the effort after realism in the arts before photography as a scientific enterprise, with one generation's hypotheses being refined and surpassed by the next. Moreover, just as we found in Chapter 3 that a generative grammar was a theory of the perception as it is of the production of language, so do we extend that bidirectionality to other symbol systems like music and mathematics. Finally, we find that the following properties hold for those systems as they did for language:

1. *A hierarchical organization.* In language, we found that a top-level description like *sentence* fragmented itself into further description like NP and VP with the possibility also that (there would be a recursive addition of a sentence within a sentence). Similarly, in music the top-level description of leitmotif governs the unfolding of a whole section of a sonata; a tennis player's game plan (I bring her to the net on a backhand approach, and lob her) will set down the rules of the grammar to which every shot must cohere; and a cubist painter's top-level theme regulates the structure of every fragment of a painting like Picasso's *Man with a Clarinet.*

2. *The symbol systems must be of a certain complexity, neither too great nor too small.* We noted that natural language falls between Chomsky Type 1 and Type 2. Remarkably, this structure holds also for music. For example, attempts to describe Irish folk music with pentatonic theory have come to grief. Conversely, whenever art music has exceeded a certain level of formal complexity, as in the cases of Schoenberg and Palestrina, a reaction has set in to simplify matters. For example, Monteverdi reinstated the use of monody (single note melodies) as a riposte to Palestrina's polyphonic excesses.

3. *A recursive structure.* I promise that I'm not going to give this natural language example again. This structure holds true for music to much the same extent: A phrase in music can be of the classic NL recursive form

$$S \rightarrow \overset{=}{x}\ \overset{=}{S}$$

that is, the "tail" of a musical phrase can become the theme of a quite separate development. Irrespective of the precise depth of recursion that humans can handle—and it undoubtedly can be increased greatly with expertise in the domain (shades of PDP)—its existence is not in doubt, or otherwise finite state grammars would be sufficient.

4. *Idiosyncratic combination with operational knowledge.* We noted that this is precisely the difficulty with NLP. Moreover, this combination is part of the definition of context.

5. *Metaphor.* The moon may be a ghostly galleon, and likewise Piet Mondrian will draw a busy jumble of little boxes and call it *Broadway Honky-Tonk* (Gombrich, 1959). In both cases, we need some initiation into the forms available to Noyes and Mondrian in order fully to appreciate the metaphor. Metaphor in art, like play, is *inter alia* the exploitation of the emotive qualities of acontextual material. We saw in Chapter 6 how it can be used as a general cognitive mechanism.

6. *Emotional impact.* One of the most appalling errors in cognitive science has been the notion that one can say anything coherent about cognition and its development without taking into account emotional and motivational factors. Moreover, as we saw in Chapter 2, "emotion" can have a "cognitive" content: the scare quotes are there to indicate how artificial this distinction often is. For a great artist, moreover, so certain is she of emotional impact that emotions are a vehicle rather than a destination—the final experience is as certain to be achieved by a careful experiencing of the artwork as the conclusion of proof of a theorem.

7. *The possibility of self-reference.* Gödel's work, which we outlined in Chapter 5, essentially establishes the following: Any formal system of power greater than or equal to

standard arithmetic will contain within itself propositions that can neither be proven nor disproved within
the system. One such proposition is "This system is
consistent." Another such is "This system is inconsis-
tent." (We shall call these respectively G(F) and (not
G(F)) in Chapter 8.) This state of affairs is best
described in philosophy by the paradox of Epimenides
the Cretan, who declares that "All Cretans are Liars." If
he's right, he's wrong (and vice versa).

Self-reference is a momentary realization as we eval-
uate systems, not a continual state of any type. We
noted in our discussion of post modernism in Chapter 5
that reading such a novel requires one at times to
undergo a jolting transition from one narrator's structure to another. In essence, the identifications and concerns one had at level 1 must be withdrawn from and
seen as objects at level 2 of the narrative. One must in
some sense become an object to oneself. That process
Penrose identifies as consciousness in its pristine nonalgorithmic form. It certainly is one type of cognitive
transition that is crucial to consciousness. Once fooled
that way once, we will never be fooled again, unless for
some reason (perhaps we are TV soap opera watchers)
we wish to be.

René Magritte famously produced a set of paintings
that referred to themselves at level 2 to isolate the
expectancies lined up at level 1—a picture of a dog might
be captioned *Ceci n'est pas un chien.* Hofstadter (1979)
has hundreds of such examples drawn from mathematics, logic, music, and art. Likewise, Bach's "eternally rising fugue" (a kind of musical barber pole) can be seen at
level 1, from the inside, as the exposition of a theme
within each separate key with frequent shocks as one
enters a new key and from level 2 as a prescription for
modulation between keys. Once seen from level 2, like
all the other examples in this section, we can enter level
1 only through a deliberate act of self-deception.

8. *A stack.* In order to implement recursion (as in 3), we
   need a stack. The weakest grammar that can support
   recursion necessarily uses the computational device of
   the stack. Burnod (1990) shows how stacks might be
   neurophysiologically implemented. The fact that recursion is such a dominant structure both in symbolic

behavior and in action (in order to do X, I might first have to do Y, which involves doing Z) not only testifies to the paramount importance of the stack structure, but also indicates that all these formal systems may be implemented at a neural level by a general-purpose symbol system. Thus, we are faced with two conclusions:

a. The semantics of all symbol systems are based in a common bank of conceptual structure, including operational knowledge.

b. Even at the syntactic level, these systems admit of a common neural architecture.

9. *Ambiguity.* Language we have explored; visual ambiguity is best illustrated with illusions such as the Müller-Lyer; musical ambiguity is a more subtle matter. Listen to the opening bar of "Autumn Leaves" (Figure 7.1). Is this major or minor? Obviously minor, you who have listened to it before will say. Yet that is an *a posteriori* decision: There is absolutely nothing in that bar to give away its harmonic nature. As is the case with language, disambiguation requires a context that is supplied only over time. Indeed, skilled musicians would regard the question as trite; to establish the key, one listens to a goodly section of the piece.

10. *Systematicity.* The effort to use this particularly buzz-word as a rod with which to beat PDP is a topic we've discussed in Chapter 4. The conclusion has to be that just as the nature of "variables" is a deeper and darker mystery than we might have thought, so also is human reasoning often quite content dependent precisely in the manner of PDP systems. Indeed, it seems necessary even in (Pythagorean, cf. Chapter 1) GOFAI systems to introduce content dependencies at the semantic level, as distinct from pure syntactic regularity, in order to increase the power of these systems. Finally, we saw

FIGURE 7.1.

that neural nets can be trained to perform the type of tasks that the wielders of systematicity like to focus on.

11. *A multilayered organization, with hypotheses being lined up in parallel.* We have emphasized in Chapter 3 that language can be understood only in this light and that nature has gifted us with the kind of blackboard architecture we need to implement it.

   The PDP model of reading text, where we've seen that words, collocations, and phrases can affect and be affected by phonemes as well as each other, can be extended to musical score reading. Familiar chords may be viewed as words in this light, familiar chord sequences as sentences. For example, we expect the notes GBD to occur in various permutations frequently for a piece in G major, because they form the tonic chord thereof. Likewise (to simplify) we expect the note sequence (in the same key) of CF♯ eventually to end with G natural as the piece resolves.

12. *Comprehensibility only with respect to a task.* We observed that language as a system seems an incomprehensible set of conundra until we observe it in practice (Ó Nualláin, 1993). The same holds for music: The latitude allowed for key modulations and rare intervals is going to vary greatly as the piece changes in length from a symphonic movement (with its great latitude) to a pop song (extremely slight).

13. *Various types of objectivity.* In language, we noted a huge range of the symbol–world relation from Wittgenstein's laborer's "Slab!" to extended discourse. Likewise, the visual arts might be directly representationalist like Constable, or allusive like Mondrian. Mathematics extends its objectivity from counting "four is the number of elements here" to Riemannian geometry, a theoretical formalist game that we saw turned out to be the best objective model of time-space. In music, we might usefully contrast the objectivity of the storm section in Beethoven's pastorale with his evocation of eternity in the opening section of Opus 131.

14. *Situatedness.* This we treat in our 3D notion of symbolic behavior. One does not truly perform any authentic symbolic act except in a social and cultural context. As you speak, you are tacitly aware of the expectations of those to whom you are speaking; you are an object to

them in the real sense. A pathological state of self-alien-
ation can arise if you become also a stranger to yourself
(cf. Psychogenic Fugue in Chapter 2; the topic of self-
alienation is handled brilliantly by the existentialist
psychiatrist R. D. Laing in *The Divided Self*). Similarly,
the meaning of a musical phrase is going to change
greatly depending on whether the musician is playing a
sonata, a concerto, or a pop song (where a long phrase
is normally acontextual, and may be there for humor-
ous effect, as in the opera section in "Bohemian
Rhapsody").

15. *Closely related to this is the notion that symbolic behavior of all sorts needs a* **native language.** It is a commonplace that nonnative speakers never fully master a
spoken language. Of equal interest are the native languages of vision and music. We have noted several
times that pygmies, lacking our Western exposure to
sharp angles in the course of their early development,
cannot interpret photographs as we do and that doubt-
less they are sensitive to many visual distinctions that
we miss. Our stock of visual distinctions we can regard
as our language of vision (at the syntactic level). We are
not stretching matters if we carry the analogy further to
the point where we insist that all languages of vision fall
within certain tightly circumscribed limits of formal
complexity. This is certainly the case for folk musics:
The native human language of music tends to be surprisingly complex. For example, the rhythmic patterns
of Balkan music exceed Western art music in complexity. Let us therefore jettison any Western chauvinism,
or—given the brilliance of much nonverbal symbolic
behavior—any intellectual chauvinism for verbal as distinct for other types of intelligence.

16. *Certain universals with respect to the learning of these
systems.* That this is the case for language we demonstrated in Chapter 3. Autistic *idiots savants* in other
modalities can perhaps best be viewed as the exceptions
that prove the rule. In general, musical or visual development will follow certain definite patterns. For example, a logarithmic law seems to relate number of trials
with the increase achieved in skill.

17. *Creativity.* It's appropriate here to make explicit a distinction that has so far in this chapter been implicit.

Symbol systems as formally treated demonstrate syntactic regularity captured by grammars and feature properties like 1, 2, 3, 4 (and so on) above. "Creativity" in this sense merely refers to the astounding fact that the number of possible English sentences within the compass of a native speaker exceeds the number of protons in the universe (or some such quantity). Symbol systems as used in cognition, normally in interaction with other cognitive abilities, feature properties like 4, 5, and so on, and it's these that bear a more interesting relation to creativity.

Computer creativity, including in music, has again been receiving a lot of attention. It is fair to say that a consensus is emerging that because we can view the talented composer (or author, or scientist) strictly in terms of the (musical) schemas (Bartlett, 1932) she has at her disposal, we can soon expect Mozart's 42nd, Beethoven's 10th (sometimes identified as Brahms' 1st) and so on. Much as I would enjoy these offerings, I doubt it very much. I believe that there are several good reasons why not.

One such is that creativity involves identifying problems as well as solving them. It can start just from that ill-defined feeling of dissatisfaction with established forms with which creative people terrorize the rest of us. Some evolutionary impulse drives them out to explore the space opened up by the symbol system. Interestingly, composers like Beethoven saw themselves as discoverers in such a space, not inventors. Reason 1, then, is that problem definition often emerges from visceral intuitions of mismatch that are totally unformalizable. In retrospect, we can of course formalize them; my hunch is that their true origin in the genius' relation to the world around him is currently totally beyond us.

Secondly, creativity often involves paradigm shifts. I don't wish to refer to anything as complex as the symphonic and sonata-form innovations of Beethoven here, or to general relativity. Let's take "Autumn Leaves" as an example again: Figure 7.1 is the first bar of a polite version of the tune. However, Miles Davis on "Somethin' Else" introduces it with this bass-line (Figure 7.2), written on the treble staff for the guitarists among you. It's written with two flats, and actually defines the old

FIGURE 7.2.

Church Dorian mode (Figure 7.3 is musically a clearer definition) so F major is the most appropriate scale. What has happened? Essentially, jazz has now left diatonic music behind; though Miles goes on to play the tune straight after the intro, a redefinition has been achieved.

Finally, in a way which cognitive linguists would approve, the moment of creation often seems inextricably tied in with aspects of our messy, imperfect, incarnated humanity. An example is Kékulé's discovery of the benzene ring. Stumped by the question of how six hydrogen and carbon atoms could link together, he was startled by a dream of a snake swallowing its own tail. This archetypal symbol has often been interpreted (by von Neumann, inter alia) as depicting the original state of consciousness in the child (see Chapter 8). Thus was the benzene ring discovered. One can hardly shy away from the conclusion that external reality seems to impress itself on us through visceral feelings, through dreams and in unpredictable ways inaccessible to algorithmic definition. And yes, this is relevant to cognitive science.

CONTEXT AND THE LAYERS OF SYMBOL SYSTEMS

Consider again the conventional layered model of language in Figure 3.15. A fuller, more accurate description is supplied in

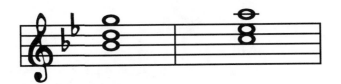

FIGURE 7.3.

Figure 3.16. Whatever the layers, the point to be made here is precisely the same. These layers are an artificial abstraction and need to be considerably revised. With restriction of context, the previously apparently well-defined stratification becomes deformed to the point where a single deflection of the orientation of one part of a letter (for example, K as R) can change the intent of a whole book.

The degree of restriction of context seems as counterintuitive *a priori* as a focus for study of CS as Gibson's perceptual affordances. Yet we have seen in the case of language that previously intractable problems fall readily from its analysis. A similar situation exists for music, where meaning is even more difficult.

MIND AND SYMBOL SYSTEMS

In this chapter, we've mainly been concerned with extending the analysis of language in use in Chapter 3 to symbol systems in general. A general architecture for these systems distinct from the specific of their use was proposed. We predicated a list of their attributes and yet again found the mind–world relation crucial in understanding their use.

FURTHER READING

Hofstadter's *Gödel, Escher, Bach* (1979) is a brilliant study of isomorphisms between music, logic, and art. Gombrich (1959) gave an analysis of the science of pictorial representation. Jackendoff (1987) is a scholarly analysis of parallels between music, language, and vision.

eight

CONSCIOUSNESS AND SELFHOOD

INTRODUCTION

With the advent of the scientific (which, ignoring matters of etymology, I shall identify with "empirical" for the purposes of this account) study of consciousness, we have reached a crisis in the sciences of the mind. It can justifiably be argued that this crisis, more than anything else, has caused the current turbulence in cognitive science. In fact, it can be argued that consciousness study will determine one limit of the empirical in the sciences of mind. The stakes are high indeed. We should consequently approach the subject with a degree of fear and trembling. It is not enough simply to investigate psychological processes, of whatever degree of interest (commisurectomy, subliminal "perception," and so on) and add the noun "Consciousness" to the title of what is essentially a paper about an information-processing (classical CS) phenomenon. One way out, of course, is to predicate a phenomenal aspect of information. The difficulty with this approach is that it requires that any information-processing device should by definition be considered conscious. We shall avoid any magic bullet solutions here; the path taken is to be quite different.

****

To complicate matters, all genuine spiritual traditions have a discipline involving the transformation of consciousness (as they conceive it) guided by an inner empiricism whose rules of inference and criteria of evidence may be quite different to what we call science. They state their methodology in a quaint language whose lexicon includes virgin births, *samsara*, and *karma;* the compilation of this into anything resembling normal Western discourse is complicated beyond belief (Needleman, 1982b). Yet this source of evidence cannot be ruled out. The traditions don't claim to talk directly to you or me; we must in some way be ready. The critical transitions of consciousness are intersubjectively validated (Polanyi, 1958, argues that Western science's criterion is precisely the same) despite their not being objective in the sense Western science allows, to which they answer "so much the worse for Western science." In short, this is empiricism of a different nature, and to spurn it is to throw away a huge part of humanity's search for self-understanding. As it stands, CS cannot take this inner empiricism on board; nor, in fairness, can they take on CS. The study of consciousness in CS must inevitably be essentially a projection into phenomenological space of the methods of objective science. However—and here comes the big disclaimer—we will have to concede that consciousness is a much larger topic than the subset of its manifestations that we study in cognitive science.

The notion of consciousness current in CS is something very close to Flanagan's (1992) idea (about qualia) that a conscious state has something "it is like" to be in it. We've had difficulty with yogis; we're now going to have difficulty with bats. If they are conscious, at first glance it seems there must be "something it is like" to be one. At one extreme, we can't include Ramana Maharshi; at the other, we can't yet handle rodents. All we can do is look at the functioning of conscious states and try to deduce general rules and constraints. I wish to argue that the problem is with the notion of consciousness as in some sense experiential in the everyday sense of the word (mine and your experience, right now). Consciousness may be less than this for a bat, and more for the self-realized. I for one am neither so I can't say for sure; all of us are in the same position. Consciousness is *not* a single entity that has to be the same for humans as for bats. In fact, the conception of it I find most useful allows it to manifest itself in different ways in different beings. This gets rid of the classic Nagel objection (Flanagan, 1992) that because we don't know "what it is like to be" a bat, we can't say anything coherent about consciousness.

Consciousness seems, experientially, in some way less an object than a medium in which events happen. Those who work in the spiritual traditions see it as an occasional achievement, and the science of consciousness essentially as the increasing of the frequency and duration of these achievements. The self-realized, we are told, are continually conscious. In fact, we end up with that notion of consciousness at the end of this chapter. I believe that its main cognitive function lies in these occasional achievements, if we subtract the information-processing function of attention. Moreover, the work of Baars brings us to the verge of this notion.

But what of the bat? It is here that we must look for some phylogenetic evidence. Edelman (1992), as we shall see, distinguishes clearly the consciousness of lower animals, a precursor of attention, which consists essentially in the necessarily information-processing capacity to detect the salience of time-varying signals entering through different sensory modalities, from that of humans, which consists also in the experience of a (mainly) linguistically-created self (Ó Nualláin, forthcoming). In other words, consciousness manifests itself in different ways. As we review the theorists in this chapter, we shall note bewilderingly diverse notions of it.

I believe that the insight that consciousness is not monolithic is the first step to constructing a valid theory thereof. Moreover, and here I am forced to be much more controversial, the essential grasp of what this thing consciousness *is* which manifests itself in such multifarious ways can only be arrived at experientially. There need not be anything it is like to be a bat, or even a dog; its manifestation at that level is other. (There is also a strong line of tradition that argues that consciousness is the basic stuff of the universe and matter but a fold in it. The universe is essentially a vehicle for *Geist* to become aware of itself, as evolution proceeds, through matter. Churchland [1988] reviews this and other such notions.)

More theology coming, I'm afraid. Mystics identify two paths toward the Godhead (interestingly identified as pure consciousness in some Indian mystical traditions), called the *via* (way) *positiva* and the *via negativa*. The former would emphasize that God is in the world and can be experienced by dwelling on positive qualities like truth and beauty. The latter emphasizes that God must be a truth and beauty beyond anything in the world with the appropriate call to indwelling. Scientists who study consciousness fit into similar negative and positive camps: those, like Penrose, who reserve it for cognition of a Platonic form and those like (surprisingly, Penrose's current colleague) Hameroff who argue that any creature with a cytoskeleton can be conscious. I will seem like a *via negativa* theorist by the end of this chapter, but this derives from the paucity of words in English to describe inner states; both paths are valid. I need to stake out an area of experience in which we authentically reach out to the external world, as distinct from the jumble of dulled sensation, daydream, stupid mistakes, and half-baked sexual fantasy that occupies us so much of the time, and I find myself compelled to use the word *consciousness* for this area. What we do the rest of the time, with respect to the cognitive achievements therein, will probably eventually prove largely simulable by computer.

How then should consciousness be scientifically studied? We are about to note theories of quantum physicists, neuroscientists, cognitive scientists, and philosophers (with rare reference to therapists and mystics). The first point is all these theorists need each other very badly. As a cognitive scientist, it helps me greatly to know the avenues opened by any demonstrations of quantum coherence in the cytoskeleton; yet it worries me that the scientists involved are inspired by the analogy with the "constant sense of self" at a time when the fragmentary notion of self is being emphasized in many contemporary studies. The notion of self, we shall see, is complex indeed. In other words, these theorists should become much more familiar with each others' work; that also holds for those who claim to speak about consciousness on behalf of the religious traditions. As we shall see, Baars' work is a psychologist's contribution; Jackendoff (1987) describes consciousness in CS terms as the projection of informationally characterized distinctions. We should also focus on the flip side, Con-scio-usness; that is, consciousness as integrative (con = with, scio = I know). An opportunity to unify the sciences of mind in some kind of loose federation on this topic may then be afforded.

****

We need first of all to discuss a spectrum of current views on consciousness and its connection with selfhood. Some, like Johnson-Laird's mental models view, are found inadequate for formal reasons. The others are investigated in the context of the historically conditioned nature of the related concept of selfhood. It is found that they involve prescriptions for the construal of selfhood that are invalid and perhaps destructive. We then move on to discuss a more adequate view, which interrelates the trio of selfhood, consciousness, and will. The theory and its minimal set of assumed constructs are first outlined. We then proceed to interrelate it to the considerations of the rest of this book. The conclusion is a new notion of what the real nature of consensually validated experience is.

COGNITIVE VIEWS

Dennett's (1992) recent book, *Consciousness Explained*, is a good starting point for this discussion. Apart from offering a readable review of the relevant findings on consciousness, it received massive publicity including, in Britain, a profile of the author in the London *Independent on Sunday*. (It is argued later that the publicity is more consequential than may immediately seem the case.) Let us examine Dennett's explanation of consciousness.

Two crucial computational concepts must again be introduced: That of process and parallelism. The activities of a computer can be described in terms of processes that can requisition the use of processors for their duration. In the human case, these processes may parse a sentence, construct a 2.5 D representation of a scene, or whatever. It is generally recognized that the great majority of fast processes must be unconscious. Moreover, given the relatively slow rate of neural transmission, the basic architecture must be parallel.

Consequently, Dennett (1992) summarizes his viewpoint thus:

> There is no single, definitive stream of Consciousness: Instead, there are multiple channels in which specialist circuits try, in parallel pandemonium to do their various things, creating multiple drafts as they go . . . some get promoted to further functional roles by the activity of a Virtual Machine in the brain. (pp. 253-254)

Dennett has several opposing positions in mind as his argument unfolds (p. 97ff). The most reviled of these is the notion of consciousness as a Cartesian theater, where scenes change in the presence of an audience that Déscartes assumed was a unified self.

However, it is appropriate to inquire whether Dennett's concept of a virtual machine has any more explanatory value than Déscarte's soul, interacting through the pineal gland. A virtual machine (VM) can be something as mundane as the user interface offered by an operating system (Lister & Eager, 1988). Dennett would have to be much clearer than he is about exactly what type of VM he's speaking about for his theory to have any real content. Perhaps the most damning comment is Edelman's statement that Dennett's theory doesn't address the issue. Or, to put it in other terms, it's not specific enough even to be wrong.

Dennett is even more scathing on Déscartes' view of selfhood. Self, he argues, is essentially fragmented (p. 426) and at best a center of narrative gravity (p. 410ff). In fact, in the case of multiple personalities, several such centers can exist. The consequences for moral responsibility are not spelled out in this popular book (p. 430). We must also ask whether experiencing one's self as narrative gravity is not perhaps an artefact of being a college professor. In other activities like dance and music, the contents of consciousness and self are nonverbal.

A great deal of the book concerns itself with phenomena like visual illusions, thought experiments (e.g., p. 124), neurophysiological evidence (e.g., p.144ff) (it goes without saying that Dennett, like the other theorists in this section, is a monist), psychotic events, and so on. In using this range of evidence and in his conclusions (and as he himself acknowledges—p. 257), Dennett owed much to Baars (1988). Let us now attend to Baars' viewpoint.

That phenomenological as well as scientific evidence is relevant in any account of consciousness and selfhood is obvious. Baars (1988) catalogues the relevant *explicanda* for any such account, detailing for example, self-attributed versus self-alienated experiences and eidetic imagery. He claims that the following should hold true for conscious experiences (pp. 362–363):

1. Conscious experience involves generally broadcast information. Thus, this information is available to all effectors and action schemata.
2. Conscious events are internally consistent. This distinguishes them from dreams, even when the content of dreams is generally broadcast.
3. Conscious events are informative; that is, they place a demand for adaptation on other parts of the system.
4. Conscious events require access by the self-system.
5. Conscious events may require perceptual/imaginal events of some duration.

Baars' method is above all contrastive (p. 26). Conscious events are, in turn, contrasted with similar events in sleep/coma, habituated events, unconscious problem solving, involuntary action, and direction of attention. Finally, the characteristics of self-attributed and self-alien experiences are contrasted.

Baars' schema is economical in the extreme. There are only three significant entities: A global workspace, specialized unconscious processes, and contexts (p. 359). We may define the myriad phenomena of conscious mental life in these terms. Self is identified with deeper levels within the context hierarchy (pp. 361–363). Goal contexts can explicate will as a phenomenon.

We end with three conceptions of self: "The enduring higher levels of the Dominant context hierarchy" (Baars, 1988, p. 327), or "That system whose change or violation as spontaneously interpreted as a loss of the sense of self" (p. 327), or "Self is that which has access to Consciousness" (p. 337).

The question arises as to whether these conceptions are formally identical. Baars does not answer it.

The range of evidence that Baars surveys is impressive. His attack on the Cartesian theater is less pointed than Dennett's and he finds room for some aspects of it in his overall theory (p. 28ff). He suggests certain consequences of his theory. For example, he proposes an exercise to assist social self-control (p. 364). We shall find much to use in Baars' findings; however, we shall also find much to disagree with in his basic schema.

Computational Theories of Consciousness

CONSCIOUSNESS AS AN OPERATING SYSTEM. Perhaps the best introduction to this area is the work of Johnson-Laird (1983, 1988). For him, the operating system metaphor is to be extended well beyond mere mention of processes: We are to view consciousness, voluntarism, and selfhood in its terms.

According to Johnson-Laird (1988): "Simple consciousness—the bare awareness of events such as pain—may owe its origin to the emergence of a high-level monitor from the web of parallel processes. This 'operating system' at the top of the hierarchy sets goals for lower level processes and monitors their performance" (p. 356).

This is an extraordinary statement. Such operating systems have been used for years, both on parallel and serial computers, without any imminent danger of consciousness emerging, even in the most far-fetched speculations of their creators.

Lister and Eager (1988) provide a concise outline of the architecture of a typical operating system. At the top level, the high-level scheduler assigns relative priorities to the processes in the process queue. On receiving these assigned priorities, the dispatcher selects a process to be run. The operating system is allowed to generate "interrupts" independently of the central processing unit, and thus may commence, abandon, and recommence a process as is appropriate. Finally, a great deal of thought goes into semaphore systems and algorithms (such as, the banker's algorithm) that maximize processor usage by processes. When abandoning one process in favor of another, the operating system must store the "volatile environment" of the abandoned process, if it is to be completed later. None of these complex operation require consciousness.

Despite this shaky ground, Johnson-Laird (1988) takes his argument several stages further:

The conscious mind is the result of a special mode of processing that creates the subjective experience of awareness. Once an operating system had evolved, it could take on such a function, and this mode of processing, I believe, is our capacity for self-awareness. (p. 360)

Whence this special mode of processing? We have seen that it is unnecessary for an operating system to be conscious. However, Johnson-Laird (1993) is willing to go even further still:

One of the operating system's options is to use its model of itself in tackling a problem, and this option in turn must be in the model, too. The circle is not vicious, but leads to the special mode of processing that is crucial of self-reflection and self-awareness. (p. 361)

However, the circle is vicious. No information-processing system can embody within itself an up-to-date representation of itself, including that representation. We have seen that Johnson-Laird is incorrect in his notion of the operating system origin of consciousness. His notion of a "special mode of processing" is also fallacious.

****

Let $A1 \ldots An$ represent the state of a system at time T. The system must also, according to Johnson-Laird, represent itself. Let us call this representation, for argument's sake, $An + 1$. At time $T + t$, the proposition Ao is added to the system. There must be time lags (a) before the proposition Ao is added to the system to produce $Ao \ldots An$ and (b) in particular, before $An + 1$ is altered to allow for the advent of Ao. Therefore, it will be some time after $T + t$ that the representation will be updated. We refer to a Gödelian argument again later in the discussion of Penrose.

****

Indeed, Johnson-Laird seems to notice this anomaly, and later refers to *partial models*. Yet the criticism advanced above still stands as a caveat. The more important point is that an operating system need not by any means be conscious.

So far, Johnson-Laird (1988) has outlined a mistaken theory of the origin of awareness and a fallacious idea of the nature of self-awareness. Unlike many other uses of the computational metaphor, he does not commit himself to determinism: "We are free, not because we are ignorant of the roots of many of our decisions, which we certainly are, but because our models of ourselves enable us to choose how to choose" (p. 365).

This is simply a statement of the inexhaustible nature of self, and has no explanatory value because of the flaws in the rest of Johnson-Laird's system. The major thrust of this system is a thoroughgoing computational metaphor for mind, and its ultimate significance may be sociological. Lasch (1985), like Cushman (1990), comments on the malleability of one's self-concept. Johnson-Laird (1988) may be the first person to see himself so completely as a complex version of Unix. The ethical implications need not be spelled out.

THE SOCIETY OF MIND.   For Minsky (1987) "Consciousness does not concern the present, but the past: It has to do with how we think about the records of our previous thoughts" (p. 150). As for selfhood, we construct the myth of ourselves. We must think of mind in terms of a system of agents with no central locus beyond a center of narrative gravity.

However, it can be argued that Minsky's statement on consciousness is quite simply wrong in that it cannot explain how consciousness can constitute objectivity and relate to the external world. On selfhood, he may be nearer the mark than Baars, but for the wrong reasons.

CONSCIOUS INESSENTIALISM: JACKENDOFF'S INTERMEDIATE LEVEL THEORY. Jackendoff (1987) continues to quote approvingly Lashley's dictum that mental events are unconscious: "Lashley's Observation points to the necessary unawareness of the nature of information processing, no matter whether in perception, action, thought, or learning" (p. 319).

Conscious experience, then, is noncausal. In particular, Jackendoff inveighs strongly against Johnson-Laird for suggesting that consciousness has the higher level contents he claims (pp. 285–287).

For Jackendoff, consciousness contents are intermediate-level entities like surface musical structure and phonological form (p. 289). Selfhood may exist in some sense, but if so it is grossly underrepresented in consciousness (pp. 299–300). Voluntarism may be discarded as an illusion if conscious events are in fact nonessential.

There is no questioning the excellence of Jackendoff's analysis of language and musical cognition. However, his enlistment of Lashley, whose work was done long before a lot of essential neurophysiological techniques were available, may be a tactical error. Perhaps the best way to note the dangers of quoting Lashley in support of a monist, inessentialist position is by two quotes from Penfield: "Memory . . . is not in the cortex" (Wolf, 1984, p. 175); and "In a sense, it is the mind . . . with its mechanisms which programs the brain" (Penfield, 1969, p. 904).

These quotes from another distinguished neuroscientist could be interpreted to support dualism: It is better, perhaps, to bracket both these and Lashley's statements pending appropriate deconstruction. It would be interesting to know what Lashley would have to say about findings such as those of Libet (1985). Certainly, it is not good policy, as noted above, to rest one's case in these matters on the authority of any single thinker, however eminent. Jackendoff gives no justification for his inessentialist position beyond Lashley's dictum. Were he to found his case on a variety of phenomenological, psychological, and neurophysiological data, it would be a great deal stronger.

The inessentialist position, even in its mildest formulation, is counterintuitive to the point of absurdity. It requires much more evidence than that supplied by Jackendoff. However, his contentions about the normal content of consciousness can be accepted. More recently, he has been willing to allow consciousness some degree of causal power in that attention, the bright spot at its center, increases information-processing space.

NEURAL DARWINISM. Neural Darwinism as neuroscience we looked at in Chapter 4. It is discussed as a theory of consciousness by Flanagan (1991, 1992) which we examine later.

The brain is essentially a Darwin machine, with the great majority of processes occurring unconsciously and all processes competing for resources. Evolution may have favored systems that allowed a subset of conscious processes along with these.

Edelman's own theory is adequate as far as it goes. He argues that consciousness in its pristine form is 300 million years old, thus, one can attribute it to snakes. He identifies it as "the ability to determine by internal criteria the salience of patterns among multiple parallel signals arising in complex environments" (1992, p. 133). This form of consciousness he describes with a striking metaphor: It is a beam of light illuminating a section of a dark room. However, higher level consciousness is interlinked with selfhood; that is, it "adds socially constructed selfhood" (p. 133). Edelman's neurobiological argument is as usual superb; the latter part of this chapter works out the cognitive consequences, on which Edelman is not so strong. The same holds for Crick's work.

A Mathematical View of Consciousness

Penrose's (1989) work is, as we've seen, an attack on his perception of the hard AI position. En route, he makes several far-reaching claims that we shall review later.

For the moment, let's consider his variations on Gödel. We can lexicographically or otherwise order the set of propositions $Pn(x)$ in any particular system. Let the nth such proposition applied to W be $Pn(W)$. Let $P_k(k)$ be the Gödelian sentence (G(F)) for this system F.

Penrose argues that we can "see" that $P_k(K)$ is true although formally/algorithmically, the evidence is otherwise.

Sloman (1992) argues against our seeing this, both on mathematical and intuitive grounds. He claims that the math is incorrect, and the substitution often of large numbers in this way is counterintuitive. Penrose would certainly argue against the latter point; in the former, the evidence is inconclusive. Sloman argues that there are models of F for which not (G(F)) is true; however, these models define nonstandard arithmetic. Penrose (1989) seems aware of the unprovability of the falsity of not G (F). His demonstration is more concerned with establishing the truth of Gödel's theorem using a particular formalism than anything else. Yet Sloman's point about the nonstandard systems is a palpable hit.

Penrose goes on to argue that the type of nonalgorithmic decision making that decides on G(F) is *a fortiori* a function of consciousness. In this, remarkably, he finds himself at one with Baars (1988, p. 75). For Penrose, mathematics is above all about meaning. Any attempts to justify the inference in terms of the development of increasingly encompassing formal systems is mathematically dubious (p. 143; cf. Johnson-Laird's work) and above all, misdirected. The truth of this and other such mathematical propositions can be established only by means of a "reflection procedure" (p. 145).

It is now that Penrose waxes mystical. Critics have tended to identify his position as Lucasian, a charge he rebuts with some ease. Consciousness, Penrose argues, is in fact direct contact with a Platonic form (p. 554)! (Perhaps his many hostile reviewers might have been better advised to take him on in philosophy, rather than his home ground of mathematics.)

There is something inherently attractive about this idea, yet one can refute it quite easily. Is one's consciousness of this book actually of an ideal such book, which it poorly reflects? The attractive point is that consciousness must eventually be of objects in the external world that it re-creates in intentional form. All that the cognitive and computational schematizations have given us is the result of internal processes constituting consciousness.

Penrose's main concerns relate more to describing consciousness in the physical terms of "wave-function breakdown" and spelling out the algorithmic consequences. His work is extremely worthwhile for its range of reference, if not its correctness.

Summary

Let us take stock. We may conclude that the following constructs are useful for any description of consciousness:

1. The notion of process.
2. Baars' five requirements.
3. The notion of consciousness as an entity that can be at least slightly causal.
4. Consciousness as a nonalgorithmic, relatively slow decision process.
5. The fact that consciousness is, inter alia, intentional; that is, directed at objects in a world at least conceived of as external.
6. Selfhood, consciousness, and perhaps also will are inter-related.
7. One may have grounds for positing different types of consciousness for logico–mathematical objects to normal consciousness.
8. Consciousness often is of the past, rather than the present.
9. Selfhood is in some sense created.

What is at Stake?

It may be as well to remind the reader of precisely what is at stake in this discussion. At first glance, the following issues seem to have emerged:

1. The existence of a "soul" or dualist "self-conscious mind" (Eccles, 1987).
2. Moral responsibility.
3. Consciousness and its relation to the world.

Yet the situation is even more fraught. The theories we have reviewed have found it essential to include will and selfhood in their discussion of consciousness. There is even more at stake than we might immediately discern.

Cushman (1990) is concerned with the notion of selfhood as it has historically unfolded. For Cushman, the concept of self is historically conditioned: "By the self I mean the concept of the individual as articulated by the indigenous psychology of a particular cultural group" (Cushman, 1990, p. 599). Moreover: "The self, as an artifact, has different configurations and different functions depending on the culture, the historical era, and the socioeconomic class in which it exists" (p. 601).

We may note in passing that for Karl Jaspers this chameleon quality is the most perplexing feature of self. For Jaspers, *Existenz* is "that capacity of our self for free decisions in virtue of which the self is inexhaustible by scientific knowledge, not because it is too complex to be fully described, but because there are no limits to what it can make of itself" (Passmore, 1966, p. 473). Let us return to Cushman.

The major argument in Cushman's article is that the present configuration of self is the "empty self" as distinct from, for example, the Victorian "sexually restricted self." The "empty self" is prone to abuse by "exploitative therapists, cult leaders and politicians." Psychology is to be castigated for playing a role in "constructing the empty self and thus reproducing the current hierarchy of power and privilege" (all quotations from Cushman, 1990, p. 599).

It is regrettable that cognitive science may also be to blame in this regard. The viewpoint criticized by Cushman can be seen also in Baars (1988) and reaches its nadir in Minsky (1987). For Baars, self is merely a level in the context hierarchy. For Minsky, the concept is more fugitive: "We construct the myth of ourselves" (Minsky, 1987, Section 4.2). Yet the constructor of the myth must also be in some sense identical with the myth! The only framework in which a notion like Minsky's works is the one like Jaspers' and it makes the self, as we have seen, inexhaustible by scientific knowledge. Of even more significance are the cultural consequences of such an empty self theory, which are negative in the extreme. The final point that must be made is that in the light of Cushman's view of self, Minsky has chosen one from a possible multitude of configurations of self and proposed it as the only valid one. His theory of self, as stated, is not just ethically questionable but scientifically incorrect. The hand-waving we have noted in Dennett's (1992) popular book is another such example. Indeed, in its conclusion he admits that he has not explained consciousness, despite the book's title (pp. 454–455), but has supplied a new set of metaphors.

We've seen in Chapter 5, in another popular book based on a TV series, the neurophysiologist Blakemore insists that we consider our notions of consciousness, selfhood, and free will simply as convenient fictions, genetically engendered (1968, p. 272). This is not a scientific hypothesis of any description; it is simply an assent to the prevailing "empty self" culture dressed in evolutionary clothes. Dennett (1990) similarly attempts to deprive us of intrinsic intentionality, while offering as little cogent argument as Blakemore and Minsky.

When it comes to discussing notions like self, cognitive science must begin to examine its own culturally conditioned origins. The alternative is that it merely assents to the *Zeitgeist,* while erroneously claiming objectivity and scientific corroboration. The consequence is not just incorrect scientifically but destructive ethically. We shall later look at features of selfhood that give it the labile qualities that Jaspers notes. This analysis is a enterprise in that it considers social factors as entities to be processed, rather than *sui generis* (Gardner, 1985). It is argued that selfhood, considered in the abstract, does not have this or any other fixed type of architecture. In keeping with the trend of this area, the argument is extended to treatments of consciousness and will. (This argument is reiterated in a sociological context in Ó Nualláin, forthcoming.)

CONSCIOUSNESS AS TREATED IN PHILOSOPHY

Analytic Philosophers Discuss Consciousness!

Yes, it does merit an exclamation mark: consciousness spent a lot of time in limbo, along with angels, God, and other topics that were sheer bad manners to discuss. Dennett we have looked at: His intriguing comment that no one is conscious may be nearer the truth than much of the rest of his book. Let's examine the work of Flanagan and Searle.

On Libet's (1985) findings, Owen Flanagan has much to say. In fact, he interprets them as indicating that "Conscious processes play variable but significant causal roles at various points in different cognitive domains" (1991, p. 348).

For Flanagan, consciousness is a "heterogenous set of events and processes that share the property of being experienced" (p. 364). It is essential to human nature (p. 365). It above all involves awareness (1992, p. 31); it comprises, *inter alia*, "qualia" that are experiences with "feel" (1992, p. 61). He is at pains to argue for the real existence of qualia. Again, self is a center of narrative gravity. One may decide to present one or another of one's possible such centers.

The arguments against Baars' position on consciousness below apply also to Flanagan: Likewise Flanagan's view of self needs to be reviewed. There is a tension in his later work between a notion of self as fragmented and Polonian advice on being true to oneself: "Your life will go best when this is so" (Flanagan, 1992, p. 211). He uncontroversially suggests that the methodology used for consciousness research should combine first person reports, psychological models, cognitive science (which he has astutely always been very careful to characterize in informational terms), and neuroscience. His major contribution is his inveighing against those obscurantists who insist that we can't study consciousness in a naturalistic way. When the name-calling and invective has subsided, it is hard to be convinced of Flanagan's argument. Consciousness research will certainly extend our conception of valid scientific method; in fact, Flanagan's "method" is such an extension, as is Dennett's. What is lacking in Flanagan is what is lacking in Dennett—a satisfactory theory of consciousness. Both are homuncular theories: In one, the homunculus is computational, and in the other evolutionary.

The same lack of a satisfactory theory of consciousness is true of John Searle, despite his brilliance as a destructive critic. He proposes a new science to supplant cognitive science: "The study of mind is the study of Consciousness" (1992, p. 228).

It has been argued throughout this book that CS must be extended to include consciousness; however, it is hard to see Searle's minimalist proposals (pp. 247-248) as a sufficient foundation. He is honest enough to admit that consciousness does not fit into the current scientific worldview; he compares it to electromagnetism before Maxwell (pp. 102–104). I believe this to be an understatement.

Searle wonderfully describes the process whereby standard texts on the mind bully the reader into accepting a form of materialism by offering dualism (and, presumably, the Spanish Inquisition) as the only alternative. He goes on to argue that materialism is philosophically incoherent (p. 53). Consciousness, he argues, is ontologically irreducible, with the consequence that it is something that must be explained in terms other than those that currently obtain. He posits a set of features of consciousness—its unity, mood content, aspect of familiarity, and so on (p. 127 ff). At this point the analytic Searle has become a hobbyist phenomenologist. We shall review the work of Merleau-Ponty, a full-time phenomenologist, presently.

. . . As Does Everyone Else

Above, we reviewed some computational, mathematical, and cognitive views on consciousness. Dennett's has been criticized for its substituting for the Cartesian homunculus the *deus ex machina* of a virtual machine. Johnson-Laird, in a similarly inappropriate fashion, appeals to the notion of an operating system. Jackendoff's formulation of conscious inessentialism lacks any strong evidence to back it up. Flanagan's schema is an exercise in evolutionary speculation, interesting in itself but unproven and perhaps unprovable. Penrose's Platonism requires a great deal of philosophical argument to support it and this Penrose does not supply! Cushman has alerted us to the urgent nature of these issues. To introduce an alternative view, we will look at just one issue: How can we say that consciousness constitutes the world, and yet avoid solipsism?

The answer is that we cannot say so at all if we reduce consciousness to mere qualia (Ayer, 1982, p. 219). Consciousness assumes, *a priori*, the existence of one's own and other bodies: "It is through my body that I understand other people and things" (Ayer, 1982, p. 220).

In his account of Merleau-Ponty, Ayer (1982, pp. 216–221) agrees with the French philosopher that a child must start from a concept of being itself, which includes

1. the embodiment of self and others,
2. the consciousness of others, and
3. the existence, *a priori*, of objects set apart in space,

in order for any cognitive development to occur.

Nor is it by any means a solecism in philosophy to insist on this primordial intent toward being: It can be found *inter alia* in Brentano, the originator of the term "intentionality" (Passmore, 1966). Baars' formulation, for all its rich range of evidence, limits itself to consciousness as a process and lacks this connection with being itself.

An enormous literature has grown up about the historicity of the notion of selfhood (Cushman, 1990; Taylor, 1989). The major current difficulty with the concept is the poverty of the current philosophical vocabulary used to discuss it. The task of the remainder of this chapter is chiefly to continue to argue ones grounds alone that this discipline is making the same mistake, and to argue—again using only the type of evidence that cognitive science allows—that as a cognitive construct, selfhood is altogether too fugitive a construct to lay on any Procrustean bed of computational theory. It is with selfhood that Baars' framework collapses.

In castigating the dearth of philosophical vocabulary as noted above, Taylor (1989) points to three characteristics of selfhood that yet endure:

1. The notion of depths within the self,
2. The affirmation of ordinary life that emerges, and
3. The notion of selfhood as somehow still embedded in nature.

The argument here is that Taylor's critique and positive recommendations are correct, but that the importation of such considerations into the AI framework first requires a perceived inadequacy of this framework *in its own terms.* By now, this perception comes easily to us.

THE DEVELOPMENT OF SELFHOOD

The Paradoxical Nature of Selfhood

One way to find the self is by dividing ourselves into subject and object in the manner we saw in Chapter 1 that Hume recommends. Here, the regress is infinite. We came to a crucial paradox—we cannot find self as an object. This does not call its existence into question; rather, it calls into question the applicability of normal objective observation in this field of study.

Our second path was to attempt to find self in terms of its contents. We noted that Baars (1988) considered that self could be found in terms of its context hierarchy. Self-ideals and self-image, as well as notions like the physical self, might constitute it in these terms.

Yet here, once again, the regress is infinite. As we attempt to abstract self and grasp it by separating it from its contents, we realize that nothing seems to remain. Jaspers' notion of *Existenz* now seems a profound one.

Self is, then, an extremely fugitive entity. It can be the unity of the person, and extremely severe brain ablation cannot infringe this unity, even when combined with an extremely contrived experimental set-up (MacKay, 1987; cf. Chapter 4). It can also be the "band of monkeys" we see when we introspect. Obviously, a new vocabulary is necessary; Ó Nualláin (forthcoming) provides it in detail, and it's outlined here presently.

It cannot be an object, or discovered through ordinary introspection, as Hume found; nor does any attempt to identify it with any mental content succeed. Part of its essence is its own tendency to identify, as described by Jaspers (Passmore, 1966). Its tendency to identify can transform mental life, and in this sense the notions of will and consciousness are causally dependent on the self-concept (Cushman, 1990).

It is time to make a few crucial distinctions. If you have attempted the Nolanian Meditations and tried to find self as an object, your target was the *punctual* self. That which Cushman focused on was the *individual*, a cultural and linguistic artefact. We shall upper-case the "unity of the individual" and call this the *Self*. That which maintains subject/object distinctions, as noted later, we term the *cognitive* self. The Self, that which has moral responsibility, is unitary. Only in the case of multiple personality psychoses is the individual multiple. The cognitive and punctual selves, intricately interrelated as they are, are both legion; we have myriad such. The problem with CS research is that it confuses the individual and the self. Each of our cognitive selves may have its own memory, in phenomenological terms. As you read these outlandish words, here is a thought experiment; try and remain the same self as you retrace, step by step, how you got to work this morning, including the thoughts that went through your head, the associations evoked by the familiar locations, and so on! For the remainder of this chapter, unless explicitly otherwise noted, we use self in its cognitive sense. As a hint about the overall theory of cognition and its development to be outlined in Chapter 9, it is appropriate to say that the cognitive self is context-dependent; its state of development is an index of the distinctions present in consciousness. As cognitive scientists, it is the only phenomenon of selfhood we should be concerned with. (Orthogonal to this is the degree of development of the individual, best thought of as a function of the quality of intercommunication of these selves [rather like an AI agent architecture!], and perhaps best labeled as that person's "level of consciousness.")

The Origins of Selfhood

Minsky, in one of his frequent visionary moments, ventures into the area of ontogeny: "We start as little embryos, which then build great and glorious selves" (1987, Section 4.3).

Let us first review one argument in this book: The nature of self is in essence paradoxical. Yet this fact may appear paradoxical only because our objectivist approach is incorrect.

Certain characteristics of self that render it inexhaustible and unobservable by and in the current cognitive science paradigm are pointed out above. Lasch (1985) and Cushman (1990) both comment on the cultural boundedness of any such paradigm. More importantly, Cushman goes on to argue that there is considerable danger involved in falsely pretending to have a coherent view of notions like selfhood.

I believe that will, consciousness and self are interlinked conceptually as well as in their ineffability. I consider this interlinkage to be best demonstrated by looking at the ontogenesis of self. The forthcoming account is prescription as well as description. It is an invitation to see one's own mental life in a certain manner as well as an objective description thereof. It has already been argued (Cushman, 1990) that this is inevitable in any description of selfhood. The theory will be outlined, followed by its relation to the known facts.

An Alternative Perspective: The Self and its World

We start life with a global notion of self, a self that does not acknowledge any differentiation between the physical body and the world. Nor has consciousness begun to be filled with the later categories that make intellectual life possible. What is the normal adult state?

For Brown (1977) "consciousness corresponds to stages in the development of the object world" (p. 150). Adult consciousness makes fine distinctions between perceptions and concepts, but only in the areas in which the person has expertise. We all have expertise in the physical environment (Piaget, 1960); however, attunement to, for example, legal objects requires the requisite training in law.

The notion of *process* (but not of operating system) is a useful one here. The normal adult state is that there should be a multitude of processes, with the great majority of these automatic. Consciousness resides at the process with the greatest number of degrees of freedom, or else is dulled by daydreams. (William James' caveat about the different types of consciousness being separated only by the "filmiest of screens" is being ignored on an "as if" basis. We are concerned here only with normal waking consciousness, as outlined by Baars.)

And self? Brown (1977): "The separation of the world leads only to a consciousness of the world and of self *qua* object in that world. Self awareness requires a further differentiation within self" (p. 151). Brown, though accurate, does not have the vocabulary to express this properly; see above. By self-awareness he means the "punctual" self.

Self is normally a fugitive tacit rather than an explicit experience (Polanyi, 1958). Only when will is in operation does the experience of self become less blurred: "Will is a prominence of self in the context of an action (or an inaction)" (Brown, 1977, p. 152).

In the phenomenological notion of authentic existence, according to Thinès (1977), the true nature of one's subjectivity is corevealed with the object to which the will is directed. Thus, Brown's interlinking of will, self and the consciousness of an action has a phenomenological counterpart. Johnson-Laird (1988) we have seen attempt a similar linkage through the notion of model in cognitive science.

Selfhood, then, is revealed as we leave the shelter of past experienc2. Johnson-Laird (1988), who often has a strong line in common sense, comments on the differences that can exist in strengths of will. In the schema here, that strength is related to one's striving to objectivity, and thus to authentication of selfhood.

We also have a contradiction of Minsky: "Consciousness does not concern the present, but the past: It has to do with how we think about the records of our previous thoughts" (1987, p. 150). This needs expansion: What Minsky talks about is only one of the modes of consciousness. As objectivity, consciousness is qualitatively different.

This theory is obviously also a new perspective on individuation. A pre-articulate striving to objectivity, and with it authentication of Selfhood, is the dynamo of mental life. Moreover, one's identity seems to consist in the accumulation of these moments of its cocreation with the subject's particular world of objects. The consequent conceptualization of the world is embedded in, and largely constitutes, the individual's consciousness. "Consciousness is a manifestation of both the achieved cognitive level and the full series of cognitive levels at a given moment in psychological time (Brown, 1977, p. 150).

Consciousness, will, and selfhood are not epiphenomena of mental life: They are its core. Together, they define the computational processes that take place, and constrain the operations of the machine. Human life is *a fortiori* a process of self-authentication. Even in the cases of severe brain ablation the Self and its will are unitary (MacKay, 1987). Moreover, there is no commitment to either a materialist or a dualist ethos in this theory. On a technical level, the urge toward Self-authentication means that formally equivalent human and machine systems will differ in that the former must by its very nature, in a way mediated by affect, consciousness, and selfhood, seek to extend its range of competence. On a metaphysical level, the central paradox is that the human subject continually attempts to realize its nature as an object in the world. The classic discovery of Archimedes (Lonergan, 1958) came from one such realization. Again on a metaphysical level, the stable relationship of subject and object that GOFAI requires becomes much more fraught, and cannot be considered in full apart from the unfolding of the person in his or her full individuality.

THE MINIMAL REQUIREMENTS FOR THIS THEORY

The Essential Constructs

It is fair to say that Baars takes some pride in the economy of his theory: There are only three entities required: specialized unconscious processors, a global workspace, and contexts (p. 359: also see above). For the moment, there is a pressing need for some explanations.

In fact, there are fewer assumptions than might immediately seem to be the case. Here they are:

1. An external world.
2. The "self" quite simply as a process of identification, which may identify with anything (or nothing).

3. A unified will that can direct consciousness outward (or unify a fragmented system of selves) when so directed.
4. Consciousness as, *inter alia*, intentional re-creation of the external world.

The first might seem an extremely controversial assumption. However, it is impossible even to start thinking about consciousness without relating it to an external world. If the theories described in the first section have taught us anything, it is surely the inadequacy of investing, for example, mathematical and logical certainty in the operations of a virtual machine that receives necessarily incomplete input only from processors. Moreover, how can one square this "pandemonium" notion of consciousness with its role in intentionality? We have throughout this book referred continually to the different types of objectivity possible; that is, the different theories of the external that are necessary for a coherent linguistics or neuroscience or whatever. Popper's (1974) theory of World 3, the world of our cultural artifacts, is relevant here (see Nolan, 1990).

The individual may be fragmented, unitary, or nonexistent according to the prescriptions it receives. In a healthy culture, its identifications are indeed at lower, more constant levels in the context hierarchy. However, it is thus directed by the functioning of will, the parameters of which are also set by the society. Thus, it is doubtful that the techniques Baars proposes for self-control (see above) can actually work due to their own culturally conditioned genesis.

It is frequently pointed out (e.g., Flanagan, 1991) that the origins of selfhood lie in immunology. It is necessary even for bacteria to recognize foreign bodies. This argument may be extended to the cognitive level. Once a misidentification with the external is corrected, the function of self in this context is to preserve the subject-object distinction thus uncovered (see Figure 8.1). For example, it is impossible for Archimedes ever again to fail to notice the water rising. Moreover, the Eureka moment is the epitome of consciousness; it is the task of will to direct attention toward the external world to maximize the number of such moments.

Perhaps the confession by Dennett at the end of *Consciousness Explained* (1992, pp. 454–455) that he has not explained consciousness is the best note on which to introduce the final point. Consciousness cannot be explained in purely internal processing terms. It is necessarily embodied and situated.

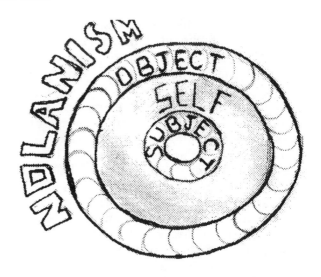

FIGURE 8.1.

Toward a New Vocabulary

It may help matters a great deal if we note the following:

1. Consciousness is quite different from mere "awareness" or "sentience" (English fails us here). It is possible to point to it as another level above sleep/coma and mere waking. Baars' set of requirements for consciousness are stringent enough to ensure that it is an occasional achievement, not a continual process. This I think is correct.

2. Selfhood as subjectivity, as socially conditioned (thus producing the individual), and as a process of identifica-

tion all need to be clearly distinguished. We may speak about the development of the individual *qua*, for example, historical incidents like the Russian serfs' right to stay on the land. However, the underlying processes of identification and correction of misidentification remain intact.

3. Will is the dynamo of mental life. It involves often paradoxical events (for example, realizing oneself as an object in the world).

Summary

The argument of this chapter to date can be summarized as follows:

1. There is an external world of objects.
2. Consciousness is consciousness of this external world, and develops throughout one's life.
3. It develops most of all through moments of authentic existence, which differentiate subject from object.
4. These moments are remembered because they correct any misidentifications of self/not self.
5. Cognitive development is therefore also a process of self-authentication.
6. Inauthentic identifications can lead to notions of oneself as empty, fragmented, or multiple.
7. Cognitive scientists (including workers in AI) have moral as well as scientific responsibilities in this area. So far it can be argued that we have failed to live up to them, surrendering instead to our necessarily ephemeral cultural context.

SELF AS A FILTER

We're gradually converging on a notion of self as a cognitive apparatus. On an experiential level, it is a process of identification, and in a processing sense of the correction of misidentification. In that, it recreates at a cognitive level what the bacterial immunological response performs at the biological level. It can sift through sensations, labeling the ego-alien material as "nonsense" and the rest as sensible. Authentic existence, where subject and object are co-revealed, reveals self as a tacit experience. In Figure 8.2, the

FIGURE 8.2.

machinery of the "self-service" in authentic existence is the Kantian categories and other structures and mechanisms that mediate between us and the world (that is, between subject and object): Self is a result, not a Cartesian homunculus. We must not confuse self and the epistemological subject.

We have noted time and again, in analysis of work like Sperling's, that a huge amount of information is neurally processed to some degree. We become aware of only a small fraction of it—the rest is jettisoned as ego-alien. People suffering from clinical autism and thus lacking this filter tend to be unable to cope properly with their environment, despite their vast other skills. Moreover, consciousness and selfhood are also interrelated in that conscious experiences are those that self identifies as nonalien. They are thus learnable, and can be consciously experience.

The phenomenon called blindsight also shows that nonconscious experiences are not learnable to anything *like* the same extent as conscious ones. We can, if we like, regard the processing requirements involved in existing socially as people in the world as a RAM disk, a drain on computational resources. Finally, all of this refers to focal awareness. Polanyi's notion of subsidiary awareness is indeed a powerful concept, but any virtual machine explanation for consciousness is a little too facile.

SELF AND MOTIVATION

We have, in Chapter 2, looked at Maslow's hierarchy of needs, culminating in Self-realization. This final notion can be considered also as a theory of cognition. Remember again Archimedes in his bath in Chapter 1. Some computational process must have been monitoring his physical impact, in much the same sense as Alexander's WIZARD system (cf. Chapter 4) could become attuned to the patterns of its own firing. This transition between egocentric and intersubjective, once achieved by a process like Archimedes', cannot except willfully be forgotten. In the terms of generative grammar, it becomes part of the individual's *competence.*

In fact, this type of process may be the crucial core of a new, ecologically valid theory of cognition. Remarkably, it is this most apparently private process of finding oneself as an object in the world that is the most consensually valid of all. A good education process encourages and indeed tries to provoke this transition from egocentric to intersubjective. The previously somatomotor experience acquires a symbolic context and an experiential context. It is that kind of experience in which we can have coherent discourse, at whatever level of human experience is in question (from learning to dance to a United Nations Security Council meeting). The roots of consciousness, will, and self may be seen in this perception of oneself as an object. Think about it: One is a successful agent in the domain, and truly conscious of the domain, to the extent to which one is aware of one's actions as an object in the domain.

Moreover, one may be considered as having free will to the extent that one can actually, having become aware of the consequences of one's actions, halt them. The desire to realize oneself as an object can thus be seen as a generic substratum, underlying self, consciousness, and will.

That notion I claim as ecologically valid. The notion of the world of coherent objects as those that can be without fear of contradiction intersubjectively defined allows us to take into account also the transcendent consciousness that was the goal of Husserl's later work. Moreover, once we leave Cartesianism behind in our analysis of selfhood, we may feel comfortable with a Husserlian notion of a transcendent self, not as a possession, but as an occasional visitor in the field of consciousness.

Then again, we may not. The scheme I have outlined allows different levels of free will in different people, different levels of consciousness between different people and different domains, and more or less unified overall notions of Self between people, depending on the extent to which they unify their social experiences. At one extreme, we might have multiple personalities and psychogenic fugue (which involves people literally forgetting who they are), at the other the (presumably) fully realized Selves of hermits who allow themselves little or no social contact.

CONCLUSIONS

This chapter began with a review of the theories of consciousness (and, where applicable, of selfhood) offered by Baars, Jackendoff, Minsky, Johnson-Laird, Flanagan, and Penrose. Some, like the mental models view, were found inadequate for formal reasons. The others were investigated on philosophical grounds, and in the context of the historically conditioned nature of the related concept of selfhood. It was found that in several cases they involved prescriptions for the description of selfhood that are unproved and perhaps destructive.

The chapter then switched to the task of giving an integrated account of consciousness with respect to cognitive development. The premise is that a theory of consciousness requires one of cognition, which in turn demands one of cognitive development. The distinctions available to consciousness are primarily cognitive achievements. One important such distinction is that between the subject and his world, as he conceives it. It is argues that the cognitive function of self, as distinct from the felt experience of self, lies in the preservation of this distinction.

The major points that emerge are the following:

1. Consciousness is another level above sleep/coma and mere waking.
2. Consciousness is of objects in an external world.

3. Consciousness develops, and does so most of all through moments of Heideggerian authentic existence, which differentiate subject from object.

4. The cognitive achievements of these moments lodge in the habitual structure of the mind, due to the cognitive activity of self noted earlier.

5. The development of both consciousness and cognition is thus primarily a process of self-authentication. Inauthenticity can lead to concepts of oneself as empty, fragmented or, in the extreme case, multiple.

FURTHER READING

Of the references given in the course of the chapter, Taylor's (1989) *Sources of the Self* is the most instructive.

nine

Cognitive Science
and the Search for Mind

INTRODUCTION

This final chapter resolves the themes introduced in the separate discussions to date. First of all, we review the strands introduced in the separate chapters and show where they relate to current controversies within cognitive science. Second, we explicitly discuss the views of mind (of various thinkers) that have often remained implicit to date. Third, we discuss what substantial conclusions emerge from the discussion of mind and CS in this book. Fourth, the future of CS is discussed, and (in the manner of much of the subject matter in this book) recommendations for this future that are both prediction and prescription are made. Finally, we comment on what consequences CS might have for that most urgent of issues—how human beings view themselves.

REVIEW

I am the proud possessor of an award conferred on me by the graduating Computer Science class of 1992 in Dublin City University, entitled simply the "Just to reiterate that one more time" award. The honor, I believe, was well deserved. My uncle, a pedant of the first degree, had informed me at the start of my career that teaching was all about "Repetition. Repetition. Repetition." (Some of this is lost in the translation from Gaelic!) Perhaps the review to follow is a little more than repetition. A collection of the main themes from the various chapters in one place will form a whole greater than the sum of its parts. That, to my mind, is the major justification for the study of cognitive science.

After the introduction, with its brief history of the area and outline of its current bones of contention, we began to concern ourselves with philosophical epistemology. Having discerned surprising affinities with the thrust of CS in the musings of philosophers, we gradually then began to uncover some of the basic methodological issues in CS. The first was the issue of acceptable data. We took this as comprising the computational and phenomenological realms. Unlike philosophers of yore, we can add the neurophysiological also. Associated with this was the criterion for the real in conscious human experience. To this we brought the analytic tool of consensual validation.

The mind–body (ontological) problem entertained us for a while before we began to proceed to the main business of the chapter, which was to set the general parameters for the studies of the various disciplines about to be undertaken. The ontological problem was approached most subtly by Aquinas. It was put into the context of cognition, which is where we want it, by modern existentialists. For them, cognition is being-in-the-world, not a Cartesian, disincarnate process. Therefore, we start with the notion of cognition as being an inevitable result of immersion in a life world. We found this idea was best formulated by Merleau-Ponty. However, his work is mainly an account of perceptual experience, if a brilliant one. A problem arises that stubbornly refuses to go away: How can we encompass this type of perceptual experience together with the kind of apparently insulated (from the world) processes that comprise much symbolic behavior in one framework? Merleau-Ponty, Piaget, Edelman, Gibson, Brooks . . . we find this problem continualy recurring in discipline after discipline. On the other side, we find that those who stress the symbolic side of cognition (Chomsky, practitioners of GOFAI) have precisely the complementary difficulty to Merleau-Ponty: How to ground these symbols? We have stumbled on one of the major tensions resolved in this book.

Philosophical schools neatly align themselves along each side of the fault line supplied by the problem of objectivity; that is, the relationship between mind and world or, in more technical terms, the degree to which we can have absolute as distinct from relative knowledge of the world. The intellectual operation of decoupling oneself from the world leads to many patent absurdities if the resulting standpoint is taken as the epitome of *all* perception and cognition. I hope the reader is convinced at this point that it is in fact just one of many possible mind–world relations. A sample absurdity: Berkeley's exposition of the perceptual frame problem allowed him to conclude from our inability to continually update representations, in the manner of early AI robotics systems, that a *deus* (not necessarily *ex machina*) was necessary to explain our intuitions of a stable world of objects. It has been argued throughout this book that this mind–world relation is part of the egocentric domain, handled by mechanisms supplied, inter alia, by neurons in the hippocampus.

One standard theory of CS supplies another model: Mental representations parsed by syntactic mechanisms and then semantically interpreted (Pylyshyn, 1984). Yet the range of phenomena this can usefully handle is similarly limited. Indeed, there are instances when semantic relations can be elicited from the syntax itself. Moreover, there are instances, at the other extreme, when a theory like Riemann's geometry, although developed solely as a mathematical diversion, turns out to be the most nearly correct model of reality. In natural language, our eliciting of meaning tends to be an often messy mixture of pragmatics, semantics, syntax, and lexical knowledge.

We are spending so much time on this point because it is vitally important. Let's spell it out once again: Semantics, whether understood as the activity of characterizing the semantic content of propositions in a formalism like set theory or the mapping onto "mentalese," is not the autocrat of meaning. That role is reserved for a real, conscious human being.

Our historical analysis of philosophy ended with the work of two genii, Kant and Merleau-Ponty, whose views of mind we took as indispensable. (Wittgenstein may have been after bigger game than immediately may appear to be the case, and this is discussed in the final section of this chapter.) With Merleau-Ponty, we found ourselves in a framework where consciousness was causal, paradoxical in nature, and characterized from birth by certain distinctions in being itself. The lack of a worked-out theory of cognition that is both symbolic and situated is perhaps the major lacuna in the combined efforts of these two great thinkers, and the greatest contribution CS can make to them.

Cognitive science should start by insisting that a theory of cognition also requires a theory of the development of cognition, and that the distinctions in the world that fall out naturally for one at a certain level of cognitive development, especially those crucial distinctions between oneself and the world, are the architectural features of the conscious mind. To extend this metaphor, as cognitive scientists we can either focus on characterizing issues like the semantic content of the walls and pillars or, like phenomenologists, we can make the architectural advance of the Greeks and consider the discipline as the organization of space, rather than building materials. The most encompassing theory of cognitive development still is Piaget's. It is, above all, a genetic epistemology, and cannot be understood as other than this. Moreover, it is a biologically based approach quite as much as Edelman's is. In both cases, the leap from biology to symbol occurs: In Piaget, it occurs earlier and with less neurobiological evidence, but it is less precipitous for its wealth of psychological detail. Piaget places the child in the Lebenswelt of Merleau-Ponty and invites us to witness the development of mind in all its human aspects.

We found time also to consider the role of factors often wrongly considered noncausal in cognition: the psychoanalytic unconscious, affect, and the related notion of the role of myth looms large in other chapters. Perception and cognition have a more dynamic relationship than often is conjectured. Just as a task that initially requires one's full conscious attention can become part of the habitual structure of one's mind, so also in this framework is a process now best considered as cognitive, now as perceptual. Edelman's work describes this habituation in the terms of re-entry.

Two other matters, both areas of empirical research, concerned us before time came for a concluding framework to be established. One was the matter of the echoic or iconic image, as manifest in the work of Sperling and Sternberg. This was to lead us to the notion of self as filter discussed in Chapter 8. The other was problem solving. The notion of *fine* solutions, the gift of a rho relation that encompasses subject and object, was epitomized by the perception of symmetry and contrasted with a representationalist view of the same matter. The notion of subject–object differentiation, in the sense of an awareness of one's own cognitive processes as object (and possibly in error; Flavell et al., 1986) we proposed as an alternative to the Piagetian notion of conservation. Children oscillate between two different perceptions (there's more water in this jug because it's fuller; more in this because it's wider) before becoming aware of this oscillation also as part of the phenomenon to be explained.

Moreover, Flavell's description of this breakthrough also is a paradigm case of a leap in consciousness. At this point, it is necessary to provide the promised relation of these issues to CS. It's an old joke, but a good one: Psychology began by losing its soul (with Hume), continued by losing the mind (behaviorism), and ultimately lost consciousness. Phenomenological psychology with its focus on consciousness (as recommended, *inter alia*, in Searle, 1992) offers a new framework for psychology. The leaps in being culminating in advances in consciousness afford a new opportunity for defining the intersubjective domain. They should be grist to our mills. I offer the examples of Archimedes and Flavell.

Years of practice as a computational linguist ensure that I approach the subject in fear and trembling. With the intention, uncharacteristic of this book, of displeasing as few people as possible, a review of the major linguistic theories first was given. A separate strand in this chapter invited the reader also to consider the ten thousand creatures that mediate between linguistics and computation, while also offering a review of computational linguistics. Several substantial issues, relevant to the major thrust of the book as a whole, emerged from both streams. The first, which featured also to some extent in Chapter 2, related to the grounding of symbols. This, I suggested, is their interaction with operational knowledge, as exemplified in Cullingford's scripts. The second is the reaction of syntax and semantics, and we mentioned a phenomenon called sublanguage where the burdens of tasks usually handled by semantics are transferred to syntax. A final issue, that of the nature of context, situated symbolic cognition, and the levels of language, broadened the domain of discussion reached in the journey to the last conclusion. A context, it was argued, is the interaction of the symbolic system with other knowledge. As context becomes further and further restricted, the stratification of language becomes less clear, rather like the way gravity increasingly distorts space time nearer to a massive body (we did mention Riemann!). *Contra* Edelman, that does not indicate that there is no autonomous formal system involved in the syntax of language or any other symbol system. Pro Edelman, it is agreed that meaning is a conscious intention, not a byproduct of any kind of formal analysis. In its account of the grounding of its symbols, the chapter steers a middle course between formal linguistics and cognitive grammatical theory.

Lakoff's cognitive semantics is, as Edelman acknowledges, compatible with his own particular neuroscientific thrust. In neural Darwinism we found a correlate to the dynamic principle called equilibration by Piaget, the principle of rationality by other cognitive psychologists, autopoeisis by cognitive theorists in biology, and selectionism in evolutionary theory. This manifestation of mind we can isolate as a major theme also. The brain we envisaged as promiscuous in its embracing of codes of interneural communication. Along with the propositional binary code, we find superimposed (much like the DNA molecule) signals as to the importance, interpretation, and role of a particular message. The result is the possibility of signals at numerous levels of abstraction. Pribram's work gives us the evidence for mild realism, already flagged by Edelman as important, which we need for the maintenance of our belief in systems such as Gibson's. It seems likely, moreover, that the brain works in a "systematic" way that distinguishes form from content when the occasion demands it. If such an exigency does not obtain, it is as unsystematic as is adaptive. Again, we experience a tension between the symbolic and the subsymbolic.

AI afforded us an opportunity, which we did not spurn, of identifying the attribution of the knowledge-level description with mind, and projecting this, in line with some current AI practice, solely to the interaction of system and environment. We discussed the current dominant paradigm within CS; that of computation as cognition. AI systems, we found, fell into the natural kinds of subsymbolic, syntactic, and semantic. Put another way, given a certain degree of restriction of context and a neat theory of the domain, merely syntactic operations could map directly to the world. In less ethereal worlds, a messy and domain-dependent model had to be constructed. Finally, sometimes egocentric cognition was the best way forward.

The next two chapters stated their cases briefly. Ethology reveals countless examples of mind in nature. Ethnoscience led us down the path of attempting to isolate, *in situ,* a particular type of act of mind before reminding us that any given activity is part of a whole culture and reflects it in a microcosmic way. On the positive side, we discovered that humans are serendipitous in their organization of their experience and will adopt whatever schema works. Chapter 7 was a brief interlude. After a quick outline of the main principles that remained intact through the rigors of Part I, we proceeded to discuss what symbol systems had in common. The distinction between the symbolic, intersubjective, and ontological components also has to hold for a cognitive act in any of these symbol systems.

Finally, we proceeded to the discussion of consciousness, and had to clear the ground first by examining current rival theories thereof. A great part of the task of this chapter was to outline a theory of consciousness and its development in a cognitive context.

A Theory Of Mind, Anyone?

A myriad views of mind has bubbled under the surface in this book. One's view of mind structures one's view of CS as well as, and much more importantly, one's view of oneself in relation to the world. Let's review the major theories from the time of Déscartes onward. The great Frenchman's view is deeply enmeshed in our Western self-concept. We reviewed it in Chapter 1. A minimalist view of mind is provided by David Hume, and we'll let the Scot himself speak: "Mind is a bundle of different perceptions which succeed each other with inconceivable rapidity and are in perpetual flux and movement" (Hume, 1777, p. 252).

Kant's accent on mind was that of categories mediated by schemas in their relation to the world. As a result, he is sometimes said to risk subjectivism, (the reduction of knowing to purely psychological processes). This is in contrast to scholastic views, which saw mind and object somehow being mediated by a "fantasm" of the object. Phenomenology, on the other hand, grounded its description of mind at the point at which there was no differentiation between subject and object. Consciousness was primary: We arrived at a theory of mind through its analysis. Merleau-Ponty is perhaps the finest thinker along these lines. His concern with the greater issues of being itself surpasses attempts to consider consciousness as merely intentional—that is, only as directed toward a specific object.

At around the same time as the beginnings of phenomenology, James was producing another theory of mind whose computational expression dominates current thinking. Mind is a set of functions. The CS view of mind as programs running on computers, the details of the architecture of which are irrelevant, is a direct descendant of James' views. So too, Fodor's modular mind is a Cartesian offspring that has sloughed off the dualism of its parent.

Finally to two recent views. Edelman insists that by ignoring the hardware, CS has assured its rebirth in one of the hellish worlds of ignorance. The current AI position is that mind is the observer's attributions of knowledge in her observation of system and environment together. And so on, and so on . . . there are literally thousands of variations on each of these themes. Our theory of mind will necessarily also be a theory of cognition (and vice versa), and we shall try to found a cognitive science on this. Yes, we are approaching my overall perspective: Much conceptual confusion vanishes if we view CS simply as the science that deals with cognition and refuse to stake its future on any single paradigm, computational, neuroscientific, or grammatical in inspiration.

More details later. Let's just say right now that the following is certainly true:

1. Mind is manifest in the adaptation of a species to an ecosystem over time.
2. Yet this is not in itself sufficient. We need a new set of categories in conjunction with the first point to explain human symbolic behavior.

Foundational Considerations

In Chapter 7, we glanced briefly at the themes that survived the analysis of the separate disciplines in Part I. The task of this section is to give further details of the surviving framework, and then discuss the nature of cognitive science in this context. Here, therefore, are the pillars:

1. Mind (and cognition) is manifest in the coadaptation of a species and an environment over time.
2. At the individual level, we can usefully discuss cognition only in terms of the organism's being enmeshed in a life world. The adaptation at an individual level is best treated in cognitive psychology via a principle of rationality and in neuroscience through a competitive principle of some sort. The paradoxical dynamic that compels the organism to seek stability in and yet increased mastery over the environment can be termed *equilibration.*
3. The focus of study of cognitive science is the combination of organism plus environment over time.
4. In the case of human cognition, a separate set of categories must be introduced to allow for symbolic behavior. In particular, we need our framework to have the capacity to ground symbols. Moreover, a theory of situated cognition requires that the causal role of context must be both defined and explained.
5. Two sets of distinctions emerge in the analysis of human cognition. In the first place, we can distinguish between egocentric and intersubjective cognition, the latter of which also admits of an autistic mode. (It might be conjectured that the autistic mode is nonconscious egocentric mentation in an intersubjective domain.) Second, we can distinguish between symbolic, operational, and ontological dimensions in human use of any symbol system.
6. Context now can be explicated. In the first place, all cognition is contextual. In symbolic, intersubjective behavior, context relates to the interaction of the symbol system with other types of knowledge. (Context is handled by specialized neural hardware in egocentric mentation.) With restriction of context, the interactions between the layers of the symbol system become altered; in effect, the layers compress.

7. Consciousness is best treated in terms of its development and as comprising critical moments of subject–object differentiation. Through these moments of authentic existence, the relationship of subject and object is enriched. The dynamic impelling one out to the world to enrich the distinctions in one's consciousness is the experiential correlate of equilibration.

8. A crucial such distinction is that between the epistemic subject and the world. The cognitive function of self in maintaining subject–object differentiation must be distinguished from the felt experience of self that is most valid in authentic existence. There may also be a form of authentic existence in quiescence. It is at this point that CS must hand over to consciousness studies.

9. Affect has a causal role in cognition. It must therefore be included in cognitive science.

CS ultimately focuses on the cognition of the individual. In order to characterize this, we need some way of distinguishing Cognitive Act 1 from Cognitive Act 2 and find we can use the resources of information theory to do this. *Pace* Searle, this does not commit us to buying into a notion that the information-processing level is a privileged one, nor to bracketing the neurophysiological level. Cognitive science is one of a federation of sciences of mind and seeks to be informed by the others, while maintaining its focus on the cognizing individual. For example, it accepts that sociology (Aron 1965) identifies trends in the society using its own methodology, but CS considers only how these present themselves to the individual. It accepts that depth psychology and consciousness studies reveal much about the mind, but waits until an informational characterization of their results obtains before incorporating these results. To do CS properly, one needs to know the basics of those sciences of mind that are peripheral to it as well as the main findings of those that are central. This pluridisciplinary approach, forbidding in scope though it is, is the only one that will pay dividends in the long run. The history of twentieth century thought is strewn with the corpses of previous inadequate approaches.

Along with the central and peripheral disciplines come the antagonistic. The central include cognitive psychology, epistemology (CS can claim to be the experimental wing), cognitive linguistics, cognitive neuroscience, AI, ethnoscience, and ethology. I regard the material in this book as the minimum one should know about these disciplines. The peripheral, at which we also had to glance, include sociology, phenomenology, neuroscience *per se*, and so on. The antagonistic will always include messianic figures, often coming from distinguished careers in other disciplines, who seek to impose their own Weltanschauung on the study of mind, and are less consequential than, for example, the philosophy of mind, which often attempts to do from a priori grounds what CS is doing also using experimental tools. So-called evolutionary psychology is often touted as a similar alternative.

But cognitive science is about computation! All cognitive and perceptual processes can be phrased in the vocabulary of computation, given the emptiness of the original concept. The problems arise when, however ingeniously, an attempt is made to construct a more elaborate language with this vocabulary and to express the whole domain of cognition in this (Pylyshyn, 1984).

But a theory of cognition must have solid biological foundations, and the standard CS theory makes erroneous assumptions both about the reaction of mind and world, and the hardware independence of mental processes! True, it must have biological foundations, and Edelman (1992) may win that particular argument. However, we lack sufficient neuroscientific data for explanation of higher order cognition and certainly don't know anything substantial about how massively complicated symbol systems are implemented.

Therefore, for language, that most essential of human faculties, the formal linguistic description (in some version or other) must take precedence! Or, the activity of CS itself is embedded in a specific culture and we need a well worked out anthropological theory to understand it. Alternatively, the personal motivations of researchers must be thoroughly researched in terms of their early experience to understand the form of their theories! There is a great deal of truth in every one of these positions.

In a sense, CS has always existed. In the last century, we can trace a science of mind (and experimental epistemology) defined by psychology before the domination by information theory, broadly defined, computationalism and now, possibly, neurobiology. In other words, the subject was, is, and always will be: A change in the dominant paradigm of the area is *not* its death knell. So let us continue, with open minds and a willingness to admit at any stage that our pet area must take a back seat for a while, to study this bewilderingly complicated and fascinating super discipline, which, as is argued here, is but one of a loose confederation of sciences that together may tease its secrets from mind.

CODA: THE NOLANIAN FRAMEWORK

Let's start by just recapping the view implicit in the book so far. The child is born with much innate equipment into a world in which the distinction between subject and object is much more primitive than the adult state will be. The first interactions of the child with the world are generalized from and so image schemas are generated. Later on, the symbol systems will interact with these schemas and other operational knowledge, creating contexts. None of these processes need be conscious; this realizes itself in explicit distinctions of self from world.

The function of self is to maintain subject–object distinctions. It also filters out noncontextual material to facilitate cognition and may have a role in memory in that to remember an event is to index the I who was there at the time. Integration of these Is is achieved by different people to different degrees.

Symbol systems allow construction of propositions that go well beyond our immediate sensorimotor experience. Some of these extensions are indeed metaphorical transfers but some are not. Incredibly, we find that reality can impress itself on our most complicated symbolic expression as on our egocentric behavior. As it does, its distinctions impose themselves on consciousness in an immediate way and for a reason that biological evolutionary theory may have to struggle to find. Why should we be able to know anything about the subject matter of general relativity? What possible biologically adaptive role can this have?

In a sense, this does not belong in this chapter, or perhaps in this book. Yet I regard it as intellectually dishonest not to outline what change might arise in our self-image from the study of CS as proposed here.

In the first place, it immerses the body–subject in a life world with other people right from the beginning. The environmentalist overtones in this phenomenological starting point are obvious. What must be dwelt on are the social implications. As a person among persons, one is committed to moral decision at the very least as manifested in authentic existence. Second, it posits a causal role for affect and its education. With this, we find ourselves in the realm that is dealt with in a good arts formation.

CS is, *inter alia*, the science of knowing, and ultimately should tell us the distinction between what we know and what we think we know. One interpretation of Wittgenstein (Needleman, 1982) distinguishes between his two phases in terms that will serve to introduce this new theme. The early Wittgenstein is attempting the semantic interpretation program of CS; the later is studying the ways in which, through language, we refer to ourselves inauthentically and fail to real-ize ourselves. We might find a lot of our experience to be unauthentic. Conversely, we might find the doors opening for new and beautiful ways of experiencing ourselves, others, and the world.

Finally, a re-emphasis on the primacy of consciousness and the experience of selfhood will be salutary. As we search deeper and deeper for the roots of each, we might find ourselves being pleasantly surprised by sources we denigrated as "woolly" or even (God help us!) "religious." In particular, the study of cognitive development with respect to consciousness might open the way toward experiences that relate us to the cosmos as intimately as to the immediately available world.

REFERENCES

Aleksander, I., & Burnett, P. (1984). *Reinventing man.* Middlesex, UK: Penguin.

Allen, J. (1987). *Natural language understanding.* Menlo Park, CA: Benjamin Cummings.

Allerhand, M. (1987). *Knowledge-based speech pattern recognition.* London: Kogan Page.

Anderson, J. R. (1989). *Cognitive psychology.* San Francisco: Freeman.

Arbib, M. (1987). *Brains, machines and mathematics* (2nd ed.). New York: Springer-Verlag.

Aron, R. (1965). *Main currents in sociological thought: Vol. I.* Middlesex, UK: Penguin.

Austin, J. L. (1962). *How to do things with words.* Oxford, UK: Oxford University Press.

Ayer, A. J. (1982). *Philosophy in the twentieth century.* New York: Bantam.

Baars, B. (1988). *A cognitive theory of consciousness.* Cambridge, UK: Cambridge University Press.

Bartlett, F. (1932). *Remembering: A study in experimental and social psychology.* Cambridge, UK: Cambridge University Press.

Bates, M., & Bobrow, R. J. (1984). *Natural language interfaces.* In W. Reitman (Ed.), *Artificial intelligence applications for business* (pp. 179–194). Norwood, NJ: Ablex.

Bateson, G. (1972). *Steps to an ecology of mind.* New York: Ballantine.

Bateson, G. (1979). *Mind and nature.* London: Fontana.

Baudonniere, P.-M., Lepecq, J.-C., & Jouen, F. (1992). *La reconnaissance de soi.* In A. Halley (Ed.), *Science Cognitives. Le Courier du CNRS, 79.* Paris: CNRS-Editions.

Beardon, C., Lumsden, D., & Holmes, G. (1991). *Natural language and computational linguistics: An introduction.* Chichester, UK: Ellis Horwood.

Berthoz, A., Israël, I., & Wiener, S. (1992). Motion perception and spatial representation. *Sciences cognitives: Le courrier du CNRS, 79* (50), 48.

Birnbaum, L., & Selfridge, M. (1979). *Problems in conceptual analysis of NL* (Tech. Rep. 168). New Haven, CT: Yale University, Computer Science Department.

Blakemore, C. (1988). *The mind machine.* London: BBC Books.

Bobrow, D. G., & Winograd, T. (1977). An overview of KRL, a knowledge representation language. *Artificial Intelligence, 8,* 155–173.

Boden, M. (1978a). *Artificial intelligence and natural man.* New York: Basic Books.

Boden, M. (1978b). *Piaget.* London: Fontana.

Boguraev, B. (1983). Recognizing conjunctions within the ATN framework. In K. Sparck Jones & Y. Wilks (Eds.), *Automatic natural language parsing* (pp. 39–45). Chichester, UK: Ellis Horwood.

Bolton, N. (1979). Phenomenology and psychology. In N. Bolton (Ed.), *Philosophical problems in psychology* (pp. 158–175). New York: Methuen.

Bower, T. R. G. (1979). Scripts in memory for text. *Cognitive Psychology, 11,* 177–220.

Brachman, R., & Levesque, H. (Eds.). (1985). *Readings in knowledge representation.* Los Altos, CA: Morgan Kaufman.

Brachman, R., & Schmolze, J. G. (1985). An overview of the KL-One knowledge representation system. *Cognitive Science, 9,* 171–216.

Breal, M. (1897). *Essai de semantique.* Paris: Hachette.

Brooks, R. (1991). Intelligence without reason. Computers and thought lecture, *IJCAI Proceedings,* pp. 569–595. Sydney: IJCAI.

Brooks, R. (1992). *Intelligence without reason.* In M. P. Papazoglou & J. Zeleznikow (Eds.), *The next generation of information systems.* New York: Springer-Verlag.

Brown, J. (1977). *Mind, brain, and consciousness.* New York: Academic Press.

Bruce, B. C. (1982). *Natural communication between person and computer.* In W. Lehnert & M. H. C. Ringle (Eds.), *Strategies for natural language processing.* Hillsdale, NJ: Erlbaum.

Burnod, Y. (1990). *An adaptive neural network: The cerebral cortex.* London: Prentice-Hall.

Burton, R., & Baum, J. S. (1977). *Semantic grammar: A technique for constructing natural language interfaces to instructional systems* (BBN Rep. No. 3587). Cambridge, MA: Bolt Beranek Newman.

Campbell, Jeremy. (1982). *Grammatical man.* Middlesex, UK: Penguin.

Campbell, Joseph. (1968). *Creative mythology.* Middlesex, UK: Penguin.

Carbonell, J., & Brown, R. (1988). Anaphora resolution: A multi-strategy approach. *COLING-88,* 96–102.

Carnap, R. (1932/1991). Uber Prokolsatze. *Erkenntis 3,* 215–28.

Carson, J. (1988). Unification and transduction in computational phonology. *COLING-88,* 106–111.

Charniak, E. (1981). *Passing markers: A theory of contextual influence in language comprehension* (Rep. TR-80). Providence, RI: Brown University, Department of Computer Science.

Charniak, E., & McDermott, D. (1985). *Introduction to artificial intelligence.* Workingham, UK: Addison-Wesley.

Charniak, E., Riesbeck, C. K., McDermott, D., & Meehan, J. (1987). *Artificial intelligence programming* (2nd ed.). Hillsdale, NJ: Erlbaum.

Charniak, E., & Wilks, Y. (Eds.). (1976). *Computational semantics.* Amsterdam: North-Holland.

Chomsky, N. (1957). *Syntactic structures.* The Hague: Mouton.

Chomsky, N. (1965). *Aspects of the theory of syntax.* Cambridge, MA: MIT Press.

Churchland, P. M. (1980). *Matter and consciousness.* Cambridge, MA: MIT Press.

Churchland, P. (1990). Representation and high-speed computation in neural networks. In D. Partridge & Y. Wilks (Ed.), *The foundations of artificial intelligence* (pp. 337–359). Cambridge, UK: Cambridge University Press.

Clancey, W. J. (1991). The frame of reference problem in the design of intelligent machines. In K. VanLehn (Ed.), *Architectures for intelligence* (pp. 357–424). Hillsdale, NJ: Erlbaum.

Clark, A., & Lutz, R. (1990). *Guest editorial. AI and Society, 4*(1), 3–17.

Conway, M. F. (1963). Design of a separable transition-diagram compiler. *Communications of the ACM, 6,* 396–408.

Copleston, F. (1962). A history of philosophy (in 9 volumes). New York: Doubleday.

Cottrell, G., & Small, S. (1983). A connectionist scheme for modeling word sense disambiguation. *Cognition and Brain Theory, 6*(1), 89–120.

Cowan, J., & Sharp, D. (1988). Neural nets and AI. In S. R. Graubard (Ed.), *The artificial intelligence debate* (pp. 85–122). Cambridge, MA: MIT Press.

Cullingford, R. (1981). SAM. In R. C. Schank & C. K. Riesbeck (Eds.), *Inside computer understanding: Five programs plus miniatures* (pp. 75–119). Hillsdale, NJ: Erlbaum.

Cullingford, R. (1986). *Natural language processing: A knowledge-engineering approach.* Tolswa, NJ: Rowman and Littlefield.

Cushman, P. (1990). Why the self is empty: Toward a historically situated psychology. *American Psychologist, 45*(5), 599–611.

Dale, P. (1972). *Language development.* New York: Dryden Press.

Damasio, A. R., & Damasio, H. (1992). Brain and language. *Scientific American, 267*(3), pp. 88–110.

De Jong, G. F., II (1979). *Skimming stories in real time.* Doctoral dissertation, Yale University, New Haven, CT.

De Jong, G. F., II (1982). An overview of the FRUMP system. In W. Lehnert & C. Ringle (Eds.), *Strategies for natural language processing.* Hillsdale, NJ: Erlbaum.

Dennett, D. (1990). Evolution, error and intentionality. In D. Partridge & Y. Wilks (Eds.), *The foundations of artificial intelligence* (pp. 190–212). Cambridge, UK: Cambridge University Press.

Dennett, D. (1992). *Consciousness explained.* London: Allen Lane.

Dennett, D. (1993). [Review of the book *The rediscovery of the mind*]. *The Journal of Philosophy,* pp. 193–205.

de Schonen, S., Burnod, Y., & Deruelle, C. (1992). Infant face recognition. In A. Halley (Ed.), *Sciences Cognitives. Le Courier du CNRS, 79.* Paris: CNRS-Editions.

de Sousa, R. (1987). *The rationality of emotion.* Cambridge, MA: MIT Press.

Doi, T. (1986). *The anatomy of self.* New York: Kondansha International.

Donaldson, M. (1978). *Children's minds.* Glasgow: Collins.

Donoghue, D. (1986). *We Irish.* New York: Knopf.

Dowty, D., Karttunen, L., & Zwicky, A. (Eds.). (1985). *Natural language parsing.* Cambridge, UK: Cambridge University Press.

Dreyfus, H. L., & Dreyfus, S. E. (1986). *Mind over machine.* New York: Free Press.

Dreyfus, H. L., & Dreyfus, S. E. (1988). Making a mind versus modeling the brain. In S. Graubard (Ed.), *The AI debate* (pp. 15–44). Cambridge, MA: MIT Press.

Duda, R., & Reboh, R. (1984a). AI and decision making: The PROSPECTOR experience. In W. Reitman (Ed.), *Artificial intelligence applications for business* (p. 111–147). Norwood, NJ: Ablex.

Dyer, M. G. (1991). Symbolic neurengineering for NLP. In J. A. Barnden & J. B. Pollack (Eds.), *High-level connectionist models* (pp. 32–86). Norwood, NJ: Ablex.

Earley, J. (1970). An efficient content-free parsing algorithm. *Communications of the ACM, 14,* 453–460.

Eccles, J. (1987). Brain and mind, two or one? In C. Blakemore & S. Greenfield (Eds.), *Mindwaves: Thoughts on intelligence, identity and consciousness* (pp. 293–306). Oxford, UK: Basil Blackwell.

Edelman, G. (1992). *Bright air, brilliant fire.* New York: Basic Books.

Eurotra. (1988). *Technical manual, version 5.0.* Luxembourg: CEC Publications.

Feigenbaum, E., & McCorduck, P. (1983). *The fifth generation.* Reading, MA: Addison-Wesley.

Fillmore, C. J. (1968). The case for case. In E. Bach & R. T. Harms (Eds.), *Universals in linguistic theory* (pp. 1–88). New York: Holt, Rinehart & Winston.

Fischbach, G. D. (1992). Mind and brain. *Scientific American, 267*(3), 48–60.

Flanagan, O. (1991). *The science of the mind* (2nd ed.). Cambridge, MA: MIT Press.

Flavell, J. H., Green, F. L., & Flavell, E. R. (1986). *Development of knowledge about the appearance-reality distinction.* Chicago: Society for Research in Child Development.

Fodor, J. A. (1975). *The language of thought.* New York: Crowell.

Fodor, J. A. (1983). *The modularity of mind: An essay on faculty psychology.* Cambridge, MA: Bradford Books, MIT Press.

Fodor, J., Bever, T., & Garret, M. (1974). *The psychology of language.* New York: McGraw-Hill.

Fodor, J. A., & Pylyshyn, Z. W. (1981). How direct is visual perception? *Cognition, 9*(2), 139–196.

Fujimoto, J., Yasuda, S., Kuriki, S., Kaneucki, K., Kawamoto, T., Muroi, T., & Nakatami, T. (1987). *Speaker-independent word recognition using fuzzy theory* (Tech. Rep.). Yokohama, Japan: Ricoh Research and Development Center.

Furth, H. G. (1981). *Piaget and knowledge: Theoretical foundations* (2nd ed.). Chicago: University of Chicago Press.

Gardner, H. (1985). *The mind's new science: A history of the cognitive revolution.* New York: Basic Books.

Gazdar, G., Klein, F., Pullum, G., & Sag, I. (1985). *Generalised phrase structure grammar.* Oxford, UK: Blackwell.

Gazdar, G., & Mellish, C. (1989). *Natural language processing in LISP: An introduction to computational linguistics.* Reading, MA: Addison-Wesley.

Gershman, A. (1982). *Knowledge-based parsing.* Doctoral dissertation (Research Rep. 156). Yale University, New Haven, CT.

Gibson, J. J. (1979). *An ecological approach to visual perception.* Boston: Houghton Mifflin.

Gold, E. M. (1967). Language identification in the limit. *Information and Control, 16,* 447–74.

Gombrich, E. (1959). *Art & illusion.* London: Phaidon.

Graubard, S. (Ed.). (1988). *The artificial intelligence debate.* Cambridge, MA: MIT Press.

Gray, J. (1987). The mind-body identity theory. In C. Blakemore & S. Greenfield (Eds.), *Mindwaves: Thoughts on intelligence, identity and consciousness* (pp. 461–484). Oxford, UK: Basil Blackwell.

Grishman, R. (1986). *Computational linguistics: An introduction.* Cambridge, UK: Cambridge University Press.

Grishman, R., & Kittredge, R. (Eds.). (1986). *Analyzing language in restricted domains: Sublanguage description and processing.* Hillsdale, NJ: Erlbaum.

Grosz, B., Sparck Jones, K., & Webber, B. (Eds.). (1986). *Readings in natural language processing.* Los Altos, CA: Morgan Kaufmann.

Grover, C., Carroll, J., & Briscoe, E. (1993). *The AI way natural tools of grammar 4th release* [technical report]. Cambridge University Computer Laboratory, Cambridge, UK.

Halley, A. (Ed.), (1992). *Sciences Cognitives. Le Courier du CNRS, 79.* Paris: CNRS-Editions.

Halliday, M.A.K. (1975). *Learning how to mean.* London: Arnold.

Handelman, D. A., Lane, S. H., & Gelfand, J. J. (1989). Integrating knowledge-based system and neural network techniques for robotic skill acquisition. In *Proceedings of IJCAI-89* (pp. 193–198). IJCAI: Detroit, Michigan.

Harris, L. R. (1984). Intelligent advisory systems. In P. H. Winston & K. A. Prendergast (Eds.), *The AI business* (pp. 149–162). Reading, MA: Addison-Wesley.

Haugeland, J. (Ed.). (1981). *Mind design.* Cambridge, MA: MIT Press.

Hawking, S. (1988). *A brief history of time.* London: Bantam.

Hayes, P. (1987). What the frame problem is and isn't. In Z. Pylyshyn (Ed.), *The robot's dilemma* (pp. 123–138). Norwood, NJ: Ablex.

Heidegger, M. (1967). *Sein und Zeit* [Being and time]. Oxford, UK: Basil Blackwell. (Original work published 1927).

Hendrix, G., et al. (1978). Developing a natural language on database systems to complete data. *ACM Transactions on Database Systems, 3*(2), 105–147.

Hendrix, G., Sacerdoti, E., Sagalavicz, D., & Slocum, J. (1986). Developing a natural language interface to complex data. In B. J. Grosz, K. Sparck Jones, & B. L. Webber (Eds.), *Readings in natural language processing* (pp. 563–584). Los Altos, CA: Morgan Kaufmann.

Hendrix, G., & Walter, B. (1987). The intelligent assistant. *Byte, 12*(14), 251–258.

Hillis, D. (1985). *The connection machine.* Cambridge, MA: MIT Press.

Hofstadter, D. (1979). *Gödel, Escher, Bach.* New York: Basic Books.

Hubel, D. H., & Wiesel, T. N. (1962). Receptive fields, binocular interaction and functional architecture in the cat's visual cortex. *Journal of Psychology, 160,* 106–154.

Hudson, L. (1972). *The cult of the fact.* London: Jonathan Cape.

Hume, D. (1888). *A treatise on human nature.* London: Oxford University Press. (Original work published 1777.)

Inhelder, B., & Piaget, J. (1958). *The growth of logical thinking from childhood to adolescence* (A. Parsons & S. Milgram, Eds.). New York: Basic Books.

Jackendoff, R. (1987). *Consciousness and the computational mind.* Cambridge, MA: MIT Press.

Johnson, M. (1987). *The body in the mind.* Chicago: University of Chicago Press.

Johnson-Laird, P. N. (1983). *Mental models.* Cambridge, UK: Cambridge University Press.

Johnson-Laird, P. N. (1988). *The computer and the mind: An introduction to cognitive science.* London: Fontana.

Johnson-Laird, P. N., & Wason, P. C. (Eds.). (1977). *Thinking: Readings in cognitive science.* Cambridge, UK: Cambridge University Press.

Joyce, J. (1922). *Ulysses.* Paris: Shakespeare.

Kamins, S. (1985). *Instructional manual for Q and A.* Cupertino, CA: Symantec.

Kaplan, R. (1971). The prelinguistic child. In J. Elliot (Ed.), *Human development and cognitive processes* (pp. 359–381). New York: Rinehart.

Karmiloff-Smith, A., & Inhelder, B. (1977). If you want to get ahead, get a theory. In P. N. Johnson-Laird & P. C. Wason (Eds.), *Thinking: Readings in cognitive science* (pp. 293–306). Cambridge, UK: Cambridge University Press.

Karttunen, L., & Kay, M. (1985). Parsing in a free word order language. In D. Dowty, L. Karttunen, & A. Zwicky (Eds.), *Natural language parsing.* Cambridge, UK: Cambridge University Press.

Kay, M. (1985). Parsing in functional unification grammar. In D. Dowty, L. Karttunen, & A. Zwicky (Eds.), *Natural language parsing.* Cambridge, UK: Cambridge University Press.

Kelly, G. A. (1955). *The psychology of personal constructs.* New York: Norton.

Kenny, A. (1973). *Wittgenstein.* Middlesex, UK: Penguin.

King, M. (1976). Generative semantics. In E. Charniak & Y. Wilks (Eds.), *Computational semantics* (pp. 73–88). Amsterdam: North-Holland.

King, M. (Ed.). (1983). *Parsing natural language.* London: Academic Press.

Kirsh, D. (1991). Foundations of AI: The big issues. *Artificial Intelligence, 47*(1–3), 3–30.

Koestler, A. (1971). *The case of the midwife toad.* London: Hutchinson.

Kosslyn, S. (1994). *Image and brain.* Cambridge, MA: MIT Press.

La Mettrie, J. O. de (1912). *L'homme machine* [*Man and machine*] (G. C. Bussey, Trans.). Chicago: University of Chicago Press.

Laing, R. D. (1969). *Self and others.* Middlesex, UK: Penguin.

Lakoff, G. (1987). *Women, fire and dangerous things.* Chicago: University of Chicago Press.

Lasch, C. (1985). *The minimal self: Psychic survival in troubled times.* London: Picador.

Lashley, K. S. (1942). The problem of cerebral organization in vision. In *Biological symposia: Vol. VII: Visual mechanisms* (pp. 301–322). Lancaster, UK: Jacques Cattell Press.

Lebowitz, M. (1980). Generalization and memory in an integrated understanding system. Doctoral dissertation, Yale University 1978. *Dissertation Abstracts International,* 41/11-B, 4185.

Lehnert, W. G., & Ringle, M. H. (Eds.). (1982). *Strategies for natural language processing.* Hillsdale, NJ: Erlbaum.

Lesmo, L., & Torasso, P. (1985). Weighted interaction of syntax and semantics in Natural language analysis. In *Proceedings of IJCAI* (pp. 772–778). Los Angeles, CA: IJCAI.

Libet, B. (1985). Unconscious cerebral initiative and the role of conscious will in voluntary action. *Behavioral and Brain Sciences,* 8(4), 529–566.

Lighthill, J. (1972). *AI: A general survey.* London: Science Research Council.

Lister, A. M., & Eager, R. D. (1988). *Fundamentals of operating systems* (4th ed.). London: Macmillan.

Lonergan, B. J. F. (1958). *Insight.* New York: Philosophical Library.

Lucey, J. (1987). *MIS.* Eastleigh, UK: DP Publications.

Luria, A. L. (1969). *The mind of a mnemonist.* London: Jonathan Cape.

Lyons, J. (1977). *Chomsky.* London: Fontana Modern Masters.

Lytinen, S. (1984). *The organization of knowledge in a multi-lingual, integrated parser.* Unpublished doctoral dissertation, Yale University, New Haven, CT.

Lytinen, S. L. (1986). Dynamically combining syntax and semantics in NLP. In *Proceedings of AAAI* (pp. 574–578). Philadelphia, PA: AAAI Press.

MacKay, D. (1987). Divided brains—divided minds. In C. Blakemore & S. Greenfield (Eds.), *Mindwaves: Thoughts on intelligence, identity, and conscience* (pp. 5–18). Oxford, UK: Basil Blackwell.

MacQuarrie, J. (1972). *Existentialism.* New York: World.

Marcus, M. P. (1980). *A theory of syntactic recognition for natural language.* Cambridge, MA: MIT Press.

Margenau, H. (1984). *The miracle of existence.* Woodbridge, CT: Ox Bow Press.

Martin, J. H., Appelt, D., & Pereira, F. (1984). Transportability and generability in a natural language interface system. In B. Grosz, K. Sparck Jones, & B. Webber (Eds.), *Readings in natural language processing* (pp. 585–594). Los Altos, CA: Morgan Kaufmann.

McCloskey, M. (1983). *Fragment of a grammar for modern Irish.* Unpublished doctoral dissertation, University of Austin, Texas.

McCulloch, W. S. (1988). *Embodiments of mind.* Cambridge, MA: MIT Press.

McTear, M. (1987). *The articulate computer.* Oxford, UK: Basil Blackwell.

Mellish, C. S. (1985). *Computer interpretation of natural language descriptions.* Chichester, UK: Ellis-Horwood.

Merleau-Ponty, M. (1962). *The phenomenology of perception* (C. Smith, Trans.). London: Routledge and Kegan Paul.

Meyer, M. (1982). *Logique Langage et Argumentation.* Paris: Hachette.

Miller, G. A. (1968). *The psychology of communication.* Middlesex, UK: Penguin.

Minsky, M. (1987). *The society of mind.* Guildford, UK: Heinemann.

Minsky, M., & Papert, S. (1969). *Perceptions: An introduction to computational geometry.* Cambridge, MA: MIT Press.

Monk, R. (1990). *Ludwig Wittgenstein: The duty of genius.* London: Jonathan Cape.

Montague, R. (1974). *Formal philosophy* (R. H. Thomason, Ed.). New Haven, CT: Yale University Press.

Moynihan, A. (1974). *The manager as intuitive statistician.* Unpublished doctoral dissertation, Trinity College, Dublin.

Murphy, G., & Kovach, J. K. (1972). *A historical introduction to modern psychology* (3rd ed.). New York: Harcourt Brace Jovanovich.

Nagao, M. (1983). Summary report on machine translation. *Prague Bulletin of Mathematical Linguistics, 39,* 7–9.

National Research Council—Automatic Language Processing Advisory Committee. (1966). *Language and machines: Computers in translation and linguistics* (Publication 1416). Washington, DC: National Academy of Sciences/National Research Council.

Needleman, J. (1982a). *The heart of philosophy.* New York: Harper Collins.

Needleman, J. (1982b). *Consciousness and tradition.* New York: Crossroads.

Neisser, U. (1976). *Cognition and reality: Principles and implications of cognitive psychology.* San Francisco: Freeman.

Newell, A., & Simon, H. (1972). *Human problem-solving.* Englewood Cliffs, NJ: Prentice-Hall.

Nirenberg, S. (Ed.). (1987). *Machine translation: Theoretical and methodological issues.* Cambridge, UK: Cambridge University Press.

Nirenburg, S., & Goodman, K. (Eds.). (1991). *The KBMT project.* San Mateo, CA: Morgan Kaufmann.

Nolan, J. (1983). *Problem-solving considered as creation of novelty.* Unpublished masters thesis, University College, Dublin.

Nolan, J. (1990). *The growth of consciousness* [technical report 2390]. Computer Applications Department, Dublin City University.

Nolan, J. (1992). The computational metaphor and environmentalism. *AI and Society, 6*(1), 50–61.

Oaksford, M., Chater, N., & Stenning, K. (1990). Connectionism, classical cognitive science and experimental psychology. *AI and Society* 4(1), 73–90.

Obermeier, K. K. (1987). Natural language processing. *Byte* 12(14), 225–232.

O'Brien, F. (1939). *At swim-two-birds.* London: Longman.

Ó Nualláin, S. (1992). On the problem of objectivity in cognitive science. *Proceedings of the fifth annual conference of the French cognitive science society.* Nancy: CNRS Editions.

Ó Nualláin, S. (1993a). Toward a new foundation for cognitive science. In Sorensen (Ed.), *AI/CS '91.* (pp. 3–26). London: Springer.

Ó Nualláin, S. (1993b). *Language-games and language-engineering: Theory and practice in computational linguistics.* Paper presented at the 2nd workshop on the cognitive science of NLP, July, 1993, Dublin City University.

Ó Nualláin, S. (1994). The search for mind. *Proceedings of philosophy and cognitive science workshop,* FISI, Buffalo, NY.

Ó Nualláin, S. (forthcoming). Some consequences of current scientific treatments of consciousness and selfhood. *AI and Society.*

Ó Nualláin, S., Farley, B., & Smith, A. (1994). *The spoken image system* [technical report]. Paper presented at the AAAI workshop on integration of natural language and vision, Seattle, WA.

Ó Nualláin, S., & Smith, A. (1994). *An investigation into the common semantics of language and vision.* Paper presented at the AAAI spring symposium, March 1993, Stanford, CA.

O'Rourke, P., & Ortony, A. (1994). Explaining emotions. *Cognitive Science,* 18, 283–323.

Papert, S. (1988). One artificial intelligence or many? In S. Graubard (Ed.), *The artificial intelligence debate* (pp. 1–14). Cambridge, MA: MIT Press.

Partridge, D. (1991). *A new guide to artificial intelligence.* Norwood, NJ: Ablex.

Partridge, D., & Wilks, Y. (1990). Does artificial intelligence have a methodology different from software engineering? In D. Partridge & Y. Wilks (Eds.), *The foundations of artificial intelligence* (pp. 363–372). Cambridge, UK: Cambridge University Press.

Passmore, J. (1966). *A hundred years of philosophy* (2nd ed.). London: Duckworth.

Penfield, W. (1969). Epilepsy, neurophysiology, and brain mechanisms related to consciousness. In H. H. Jasper, A. A. Ward, Jr., & A. Pope (Eds.), *Basic mechanisms of epilepsies* (pp. 791–805). Boston, MA: Little, Brown.

Penrose, R. (1989). *The emperor's new mind.* Oxford, UK: Oxford University Press.

Peschl, M. (1990). Cognition and neural computing—An interdisciplinary approach. *IJCNN,* 110–114.

Piaget, J. (1926a). *The child's conception of the world.* London: Routledge.

Piaget, J. (1926b). *The language and thought of the child.* London: Routledge.

Piaget, J. (1950). *The psychology of intelligence.* London: Routledge.

Piaget, J. (1960). *The child's conception of physical causality.* London: Routledge.

Piaget, J. (1970). *Genetic epistemology.* New York: Columbia University Press.

Piaget, J. (1971a). *Biology and knowledge.* Edinburgh: Edinburgh University Press.

Piaget, J. (1971b). *Insights and illusions of philosophy.* London: Routledge & Kegan Paul.

Piaget, J. (1972). *Principles of genetic epistemology.* London: Routledge & Kegan Paul.

Piaget, J. (1986). *Six psychological studies.* Sussex, UK: Harvester.

Piaget, J., & Inhelder, B. (1956). *The child's conception of space.* London: Routledge and Kegan Paul.

Pierce, J. (1966). *Language and machines: Computers in translation and linguistics* (Publication 1416). Washington, DC: National Academy of Sciences/National Research Council.

Pitrat, J. (1988). *An artificial intelligence approach to understanding natural language* (E. F. Harding, Trans.). London: North Oxford Academic Publications.

Polanyi, M. (1958). *Personal knowledge.* London: Routledge and Kegan Paul.

Polanyi, M. (1969). *Knowing and being.* London: Butler and Tanner.

Pylyshyn, Z. (1984). *Computation and cognition: Toward a foundation for cognitive science.* Cambridge, MA: Bradford Books, MIT Press.

Pylyshyn, Z. (Ed.). (1987). *The robot's dilemma: The frame problem in artificial intelligence.* Norwood, NJ: Ablex.

Reitman, W. (Ed.). (1984). *Artificial intelligence applications for business.* Norwood, NJ: Ablex.

Riesbeck, C. K. (1975). Conceptual analysis. In R. C. Schank (Ed.), *Conceptual information processing.* Amsterdam: North-Holland.

Riesbeck, C. K. (1980). You can't miss it: Judging the clarity of directions. *Cognitive Psychology, 4*(3), 285–303.

Riesbeck, C. K., & Kolodner, J. (Eds.). (1986). *Experience, memory and reasoning.* Hillsdale, NJ: Erlbaum.

Rips, L. J. (1990). Reasoning. *Annual Review of Psychology, 41,* 321–353.

Roesner, D. (1988). Why implementors of practical NLP systems cannot wait for linguistic theories. In panel discussion in language-engineering (M. Nagao, moderator), *COLING-88.*

Rosch, E. H. (1973). On the internal structure of perceptual and semantic categories. In T. E. Moore (Ed.), *Cognitive development and the acquisition of language* (pp. 112–144). New York: Academic Press.

Rosenblatt, F. (1962). *Principles of neurodynamics.* Washington, DC: Spartan Books.

Rumelhart, D., & McClelland, J. L. (1986). *Parallel distributed processing.* Cambridge, MA: MIT Press.

Ruwet, N. (1972). *Theorie syntaxique et syntaxe du francais.* Paris: Editions du Seuil.

Ryan, B. (1991, January). AI's identity crisis. *Byte,* pp. 239–248.

Schank, R. (Ed.). (1975). *Conceptual information processing.* Amsterdam: North-Holland.

Schank, R. (1982). *Dynamic memory.* London: Cambridge University Press.

Schank, R. (1986). *Explanation patterns.* Hillsdale, NJ: Erlbaum.

Schank, R., & Abelson, R. (1977). *Scripts, plans, goals and understanding.* Hillsdale, NJ: Erlbaum.

Schank, R., & Leake, D. B. (1986). *Computer understanding and creativity.* In H. J. Kugler (Ed.), IFIP Proceedings (pp. 335–341). Amsterdam: North-Holland.

Schwartz, J. (1988). The new connectionism. In S. Graubard (Ed.), *The AI debate* (pp. 123–142). Cambridge, MA: MIT Press. (Reprint of Daedalos, Fall 1988.)

Searle, J. R. (1969). *Speech acts: An essay in the philosophy of language.* London: Cambridge University Press.

Searle, J. R. (1980). Minds, brains and programs. *The Behavioral and Brain Sciences, 3.*

Searle, J. R. (1992). *The rediscovery of the mind.* Cambridge, MA: MIT Press.

Segundo, J. P., & Kohn, A. F. (1981). A model of excitatory synaptic interactions between pacemakers. *Biological Cybernetics, 40*(2), 113–126.

Sejnowski, T. J., & Rosenberg, R. (1987). Parallel networks that learn to pronounce English text. *Complex Systems, 1*(11), 145–168.

Shieber, S. M. (1984). *Evidence against the context-freeness of natural language* (TW-330). Menlo Park, CA: SRI International.

Shortliffe, E. (1976). *Computer-based medical consultations: MYCIN.* New York: Elsevier.

Shotter, J. (1975). *Images of man in psychological research.* London: Methuen.

Simmons, R., & Slocum, J. (1972). Generating English discourse from semantic networks. *Communications of the ACM, 15*(10), 891–905).

Simon, H. (1994). Literary criticism. A cognitive approach: *Stanford Humanities Review, 4*(1), 1–28.

Slezak, P. (1993). *Situated cognition.* IJCAI workshop on using knowledge in its context.

Sloman, A. (1992). [Review of book *The emperor's new mind.*] *Artificial Intelligence, 56*(2–3), 355–396.

Small, S., & Rieger, C. (1982). Parsing and comprehending with word experts. In W. Lehnert & C. Ringle (Eds.), *Strategies in NLP.* Hillsdale, NJ: Erlbaum.

Smith, N., & Wilson, D. (1979). *Modern linguistics: The results of Chomsky's revolution.* London: Middlesex.

Smolensky, P. (1986). Information processing in dynamical systems. In D. Rumelhart & J. L. McClelland (Eds.), *Parallel distributed processing*. Cambridge, MA: MIT Press.

Smolensky, P. (1990). Connectionism and the foundations of artificial intelligence. In D. Partridge & Y. Wilks (Eds.), *The foundations of artificial intelligence* (pp. 306–326). Cambridge, UK: Cambridge University Press.

Steiner, G. (1978). *Heidegger.* London: Fontana.

Stillings, N., Feinstein, M., Garfield, J., Russland, E., Rosenbaum, E., Weisler, S., & Baker-Ward, L. (1987). *Cognitive science: An introduction.* Cambridge, MA: Bradford Books, MIT Press.

Streri, A., & Lécuyer, R. (1992). The beginning of knowledge. In A. Halley (Ed.), *Sciences Cognitives. Le Courier du CNRS, 79.* Paris: CNRS-Editions.

Sugarman, S. (1987). *Piaget's construction of the child's reality.* Cambridge, UK: Cambridge University Press.

Tamba, I. (1988). *Semantique Que Sais-je Series.* Paris: Presses Universitaires.

Tanimoto, S. (1990). *The elements of artificial intelligence.* Oxford, UK: Freeman.

Taylor, C. (1989). *Sources of the self: The making of the modern identity.* Cambridge, UK: Cambridge University Press.

Thinès, G. (1977). *Phenomenology and the science of behaviour: An historical and epistemological approach.* London: Allen & Unwin.

Thinès, G., Costall, A., & Butterworth, G. (Ed.). (1990). *Michotte's experimental phenomenology of perception.* Hillsdale, NJ: Erlbaum.

Thompson, C. (1984). *Using menu-based NL understanding* (Tech. Rep. 84-12). Texas Instruments.

Thompson, H. (1981). *Chart parsing and rule schemata in GPSG.* Stanford, Department of Computer Science, University of Toronto.

Thompson, H. (1983). Natural language processing: a critical analysis of the structure of the field, with some implications for parsing. In Y. Wilks & K. Sparck Jones (Eds.), *Automatic natural language parsing* (pp. 22–31). Chichester, UK: Ellis-Harwood.

Thompson, W., & Peng, T. (1990). Detecting moving objects. *International Journal of Computer Vision, 4,* 39–57.

Toma, K. (1977). Systran. *Sprache und Datenverarbeitung, 1*(1).

Tomita, M. (1985). *Efficient parsing for natural language.* Boston: Kluwer.

Tourtezky, D. S., & Hinton, G. (1985). Symbols among the neurons. In *Ninth IJCAI* (pp. 228–243). Palo Alto, CA: Morgan Kaufmann.

Trotter, Y., & Burnod, Y. (1992). Cortical spatial representation. In A. Halley (Ed.), *Sciences Cognitives. Le Courier du CNRS, 79.* Paris: CNRS-Editions.

Tucker, A. B. (1987). Current strategies in machine translation R & D. In S. Nirenburg (Ed.), *Machine translation.* Cambridge, UK: Cambridge University Press.

Varela, F. J. (1988). *Connaitre.* Paris: Editions du Seuil.

Vaux, J. (Ed.). (1990). *AI and Society,* 4(1).

Von Eckardt, B. (1993). *What is cognitive science?* Cambridge, MA: MIT Press.

Vygotsky, L. S. (1962). *Thought and language* (E. Haufmann & G. Vakar, Eds. & Trans.). Cambridge, MA: MIT Press.

Wahlster, W. (1986). The role of natural language in advanced knowledge-based systems. In H. Winter (Ed.), *AI and man-machine systems* (pp. 62–83). Berlin: Springer-Verlag.

Walker, D., & Amsler, R. (1986). The use of machine-readable dictionaries in sublanguage analysis. In R. Grishman & R. Kittredge (Eds.), *Analyzing language in restricted domains.* Hillsdale, NJ: Erlbaum.

Wason, P. C., & Johnson-Laird, P. N. (1972). *Psychology of reasoning: Structure and content.* London: Routledge.

Weaver, (1955). Translation. In W. N. Locke & D. A. Booth (Eds.), *Machine translation of languages.* Cambridge, MA: MIT Press.

Weizenbaum, J. (1976). *Computer power and human reason.* Reading, MA: Addison-Wesley.

Wertheimer, M. (1959). *Productive thinking.* New York: Harper & Brothers.

Wilensky, R. (1987). *Some problems and proposals for knowledge representation* (Tech. Rep.). University of California at Berkeley.

Wilks, Y. (1975). An intelligent analyzer and understander. *Communications of the ACM, 8.*

Wilks, Y. (1976a). Parsing English I & II. In E. Charniak & Y. Wilks (Eds.), *Computational semantics* (pp. 89–100, 155–184). Amsterdam: North-Holland.

Wilks, Y. (1976b). Philosophy of language. In E. Charniak & Y. Wilks (Eds.), *Computational semantics* (pp. 205–233). Amsterdam: North-Holland.

Wilks, Y. (1977). Language boundaries and knowledge structures. *Communication and Cognition, 10*(2), 53–61.

Wilks, Y. (1990). Some comments on Smolensky and Fodor. In D. Partridge & Y. Wilks (Eds.), *The foundations of artificial intelligence* (pp. 327–336). Cambridge, UK: Cambridge University Press.

Wilks, Y., & Sparck Jones, K. (Eds.). (1983). *Automatic natural language parsing.* Chichester, UK: Ellis Horwood.

Williams, D. (1992). *Nobody nowhere.* London: Doubleday.

Williams, D. (1993). *Somebody somewhere.* London: Doubleday.

Winograd, T. (1972). *Understanding natural language.* New York: Academic Press.

Winograd, T. (1983). *Language as a cognitive process: Vol. 1: Syntax.* Reading, MA: Addison-Wesley.

Winograd, T. (1990). Thinking machines: Can there be? Are we? In D. Partridge & Y. Wilks (Eds.), *The foundations of artificial intelligence* (pp. 167–189). Cambridge, UK: Cambridge University Press.

Winograd, T., & Flores, C. F. (1986). *Understanding computers and cognition.* Norwood, NJ: Ablex.

Winston, P. H. (Ed.). (1986). *Artificial intelligence and man-machine systems.* New York: Springer.

Winston, P. H., & Horn, B. K. P. (1989). *Lisp* (3rd ed.). Reading, MA: Addison-Wesley.

Winston, P. H., & Prendergast, K. (Eds.). (1984). *The artificial intelligence business.* Reading, MA: Addison-Wesley.

Wittgenstein, L. (1922). *Tractatus Logico-Philosophicus.* Oxford, UK: Basil Blackwell.

Wittgenstein, L. (1967). *Philosophical investigations.* Oxford, UK: Basil Blackwell.

Wittgenstein, L. (1969). *Uber gewissheit* [On certainty]. Oxford, UK: Basil Blackwell.

Wolf, F. A. (1984). *Star waves.* New York: Macmillan.

Woods, W. A. (1969). *ATNS for natural language analysis.* Report CS-1, Harvard University.

Woods, W. A. (1970). Transition network grammars. *CACM 3*(10).

Woods, W. A. (1973). An experimental systems of TNGs. In R. Rustin (Ed.), *Natural language processing.* New York: Algorithmics.

Woods, W. A. (1980). Cascaded ATN grammars. *American Journal of Computational Linguistics, 1,* 1–12.

Woods, W. A. (1984). Natural language communication with machines. In W. Reitman (Ed.), *Artificial intelligence applications for business.* Norwood, NJ: Ablex.

Woods, W. A., Kaplan, R. M., & Nash-Webber, B. L. (1972). *The lunar sciences natural language information system: Final report* (BBN Report 2378). Cambridge, MA: Bolt Beranek and Newman.

Zarechnak. (1979). History of machine translation. In Hemisz-Dozent et al. (Eds.), *Machine translation.* The Hague: Mouton.

Zeidenberg, A. (1987). Modelling the brain. *Byte special issue.*

Zeki, S. (1992). The visual image in mind and brain. *Scientific American, 267*(3), pp. 68–78.

Readers should note that authors' names are mentioned in this index only when specific works are cited.